ABORTION
AND SOCIAL JUSTICE

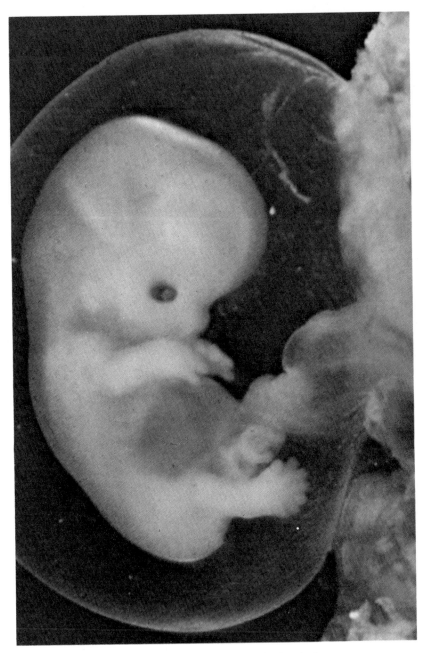

FIG. 1.   The unborn child at 6 weeks (est.) of age.

It seems to me as clear as daylight that abortion would be a crime.

—Mahatma Gandhi*

*From *All Men Are Brothers: Life and Thoughts of Mahatma Gandhi,* compiled and edited by Krishna Kripalani (Mystic, Conn.: Lawrence Verry, Inc.).

ABORTION
and
SOCIAL JUSTICE

EDITED BY

Thomas W. Hilgers, M.D.

*Fellow, Obstetrics and Gynecology, Mayo Graduate School of Medicine
Rochester, Minnesota*

AND

Dennis J. Horan, Esq., J.D.

*Member of Chicago, Illinois, and American Bars; Lecturer in Law at the
University of Chicago Law School.*

SHEED & WARD · NEW YORK

This book is supported by a grant from Americans United for Life. It represents the views of the contributors and not necessarily those of the institutions with which they are associated.

PHOTO CREDITS

Fig. 1 With permission, Joseph R. Stanton, M.D., Boston, Massachusetts.
Figs. 2-9 Spontaneously aborted babies photographed by
Charles O. Garrison, M.D., Rochester, Minnesota.
Figs. 10-12 Artificially aborted babies, with permission,
Russell Sacco, M.D., Portland, Oregon.
Plates One-Three With permission, William F. Colliton, Jr.,
M.D., Bethesda, Maryland.
Plate Four With permission, Russell Sacco, M.D., Portland, Oregon.

Contents

LEGAL

SOCIAL

Contents

Contents

COLOR PLATES
EPILOGUE

FOREWORD

The Democratization
of a Near Constant in History

As Chairman of Americans United for Life, I have been asked to write a Foreword to the rich and variegated essays by men and women of various walks of life and divergent competencies. It is the purpose of the Co-Editors, Thomas Hilgers, M.D., and Dennis J. Horan, J.D., to present to the still open-minded, and concerned, the full range of argumentation against abortion: biological, medical, psychological, sociological, legal, demographic, and ethical. Not a single essay or paper among the nineteen is theological or programmatically religious, although undoubtedly a religious conviction informs many of the writers thereof. The arguments against abortion as public policy can be cogently stated without resort to religious, ecclesiastical, or theological sanctions. And in a secular society, where state and church are constitutionally separated, it is entirely proper that we argue in the public domain against abortion in terms acceptable to humanists and theists alike.

However, religion itself can never be construed as irrelevant to current social and moral issues, and in the Foreword to our book I should like, as a professional church historian, to place some of our collective argumentation in historical and religious perspective—religious primarily in terms of the principal traditions in our country, Jewish, Catholic, and Protestant. I should, accordingly, like to quote from a famous Epistle by an unnamed Christian to a pagan Roman lawyer named Diognetus, dating from the second century, when Christians were still in danger of martyrdom at the hands of the pagan Roman Emperor and Imperial magistrates. The Epistle reads in part thus:

Christians cannot be distinguished from the rest of the human race by country or language or customs. They do not live in cities of their own; they do not use a peculiar form of speech; they do not follow an eccentric manner of life. Yet, although they live in Greek and barbarian cities alike, as each man's lot has been cast, and follow the customs of the country in clothing and food and other matters of daily living, at the same time they give proof of the remarkable and admittedly extraordinary constitution of their own commonwealth. They live in their own countries, but only as sojourners. They have a share in everything as citizens, and endure everything as aliens. Every foreign land is their fatherland, and yet for them every fatherland is a foreign land. They marry, like everyone else, and they beget children, but *they do not cast out their offspring.* They share their board with each other, but not their marriage bed. It is true that they are "in the flesh," but they do not live "according to the flesh." They busy themselves on earth, but their citizenship is in heaven. They obey the established laws, but in their own lives they go far beyond what the laws require. To put it simply: What the soul is in the body, that Christians are in the world. The soul is dispersed through all the members of the body, and Christians are scattered through all the cities of the world. The soul dwells in the body, but does not belong to the body, and Christians dwell in the world, but do not belong to the world. The soul loves the flesh that hates it, and its members; in the same way, Christians love those who hate them. The soul is shut up in the body, and yet itself holds the body together; while Christians are restrained in the world as in a prison, and yet themselves hold the world together.

You will observe that among the marks of the Christians within Roman imperial society was their abhorrence of the then common practice of casting out offspring by abortion, by exposure, or by selling them into slavery. We have come a long way since that ancient Christian wrote to the pagan Diognetus. What he said that Christians held about the sacredness of human life has long since become part of the canon law, the common law, the statutory law of all the states emerging from Christendom. Only in recent times have the laws against abortion, or their equivalent, been challenged.

Many high-minded people, leaders in good causes, have come to think that far from representing a relapse into callousness about human life, the espousal of abortion as a right of the woman in consultation with her physician represents somehow a more humane stage in the evolution of society. Many other persons of good will and sensitivity in other areas of life, on this issue have come to think of themselves as progressive, enlightened, and humane in following these leaders in law, medicine, and even religion in expressing concern for the rights of the woman over her own body and the wrongs of bringing unwanted or supernumerary or variously handicapped children into the world. But on the great issue which has summoned the contributors to this volume together from all walks of life and from diverse religious and cultural backgrounds, the espousal of abortion as a "right," is perceived by us as in fact a grave retrogression. Happily, the tide seems to have begun to turn again in our favor.

Some of our essays rehearse aspects of this shift. The fact is that the deep-seated moral recoil from abortion, embedded in our very being, is finding in many quarters fresh articulation, and we dare now to express some confidence that the worst that we feared may not come to pass and that some of the worst developments—for example, in New York—can be rectified. But the metaphor of the turning tide implies a moon and a periodical gravitational tug on the oceans of mankind. And we know that ebbing is as regular in its rhythm as the flow. Since I am reasonably confident that we are, in fact, going to be able successfully to resist the widespread demand for abortion, I should like to drop the metaphor of the tide and place our endeavors in a broad historical perspective, pointing to the process in which I see us engaged under the heading: "The Democratization of a Near Constant in History."

The phrase "Near Constant in History" comes from Professor John Noonan, Jr., in the introduction to a Harvard University book, *The Morality of Abortion* (1970). What Noonan referred to as a "near constant in history" was opposition to abortion, implied as something writ large in the natural law, as something repugnant to human nature. As a Catholic, he attached great importance to perceiving some universal pattern, which, apart from the direct revelation of God in the Scriptures, is accessible to all. On so decisive a moral issue as abortion Noonan expected and found a rough consensus cutting across many centuries. He limited himself to New Testament, patristic, and scholastic sources, in other words to the Roman Catholic tradition during its formative periods. In a larger essay of my own, published in *Theological Studies* (1970), I have been able to confirm this, giving attention to some pre-Christian Greek philosophy, to Hellenistic and rabbinical Jewish sources, and especially to classical Protestantism. Professor Noonan's generalization is valid in the scope he intended, namely, in Western Civilization as influenced by Scripture and Greek philosophy. Opposition to abortion has been truly a near constant in this development up to quite recent times.

But there are two further qualifications. On one of these I have no intention of expanding, important though it is, namely, that there has been some fluctuation in the definition of abortion and, to my surprise, some shifting in respect to what constitutes the graver of three kinds of intervention into the natural life process: contraception, abortion, and infanticide. Our present sense of the increasing gravity of these three actions has not been a constant. To this day, for example, in certain classes of the population in Latin America contraception seems to be regarded with more revulsion, for a variety of reasons, than abortion.

I said there were two qualifications of Noonan's dictum about opposition to abortion as a near constant in (Western) history almost to the present. That other qualification is the theme of my Foreword. The near constant was the conviction of philosophers, physicians with their Hippocratic oath, moral theologians, canonists, lawyers, divines; in other words, the professionals, groping amid biological, fetological, and philosophical uncertainties about the origins of individual human life. I will not here rehearse the three main theories of the origin and infusion of the human soul into the fetus, one of which was adopted fairly late in history by the Roman Catholic Church, while classical Protestantism divided on the theories, the Calvinists-Puritans continuing in the papal line, the Lutherans reappropriating for awhile, at least, another of the three theories of the origin of the soul inherited from patristic times. Nor is this the place to go into the theory of three kinds of souls within each person regardless of the origin of the highest, the rational soul. But clearly the theory of three souls infused in succession to each other, vegetal, animal, and rational, derived from Greek philosophy and notably from Aristotle and perpetuated by St. Thomas Aquinas, would long bear closely on the degree of gravity of abortion, depending upon whether the infusion of the highest and the distinctively human, rational soul was at conception or at the stage in fetal development when it could inform the emergent fetal brain.

Since today we talk less about the soul than about the genes and chromosomes, less about infusion than about the zygote, and less about quickening than about the fetal right to life as human, I shall not further refer to these immemorial issues, not because they have ceased to be important, but rather because they cannot easily be argued in the public domain of legislature and civil court in a land largely secular in its orientation and in any case where church and state are separated. And I concentrate instead on the process of democratization, amid and despite present-day challenges, of the *ideal* constant of the professional elites in Western history.

This near constant, the opposition to abortion however defined, has been largely articulated by professional people. Today we are involved in the laicization of this insight of the religious community and in the democratization of this conviction in society at large and its principal institutions: its legislative chambers, courts, hospitals, and schools. What has been within the competence and concern of the professional elites as indeed a near constant in Western history is becoming in our time the concern of the laity in general, speaking from the point of the Church, with Catholic doctors and lawyers, for example, carrying the charge formerly in the custody of the episcopal magisterium; and, the concern of the people at large, banded together in voluntary associations, to exert influence upon legislatures, hospitals, and the media.

If we can see the pro-life actions in this larger context, we will never be profoundly discouraged; and our strategies of the moment will be ever informed by an awareness of what *was* and by an assurance of what *can be.* Instead of being pessimistic, we should be optimistic and sustained by a solemn joy, for we who know that abortion is a wrong and not a right have been summoned to no less a role in the evolution of the conscience of society than to make the doctrine of the professional elites the interiorized code of all.

That the near constant in Western history was preeminently in the minds of the moral and professional elites rather than in the practice of the laity and the populace at large is something that is not generally recognized or acknowledged in conservative circles. What prelates, moral theologians, canonists, divines, physicians, and lawyers insisted was right was not in the past so clearly understood or practiced by ordinary people.

When two years ago I was commissioned to write an essay on the two-hundredth anniversary of an American denomination, I came across a resolution in their annual assembly, which occurred in Akron in 1886: "[W]e deplore the vastly multiplied crime of Christian mothers of Europe and America, taking the form of infanticide, whose records in the medical literature of Europe and America appall the lingering sense of humanity in our midst." Since the denomination into which that body is merged is today the most outspoken advocate of abortion on demand, and since I have always been opposed to abortion, I took the occasion of this resolution to draw attention to the fact that back in 1886 the same body had deplored abortion and even called it "infanticide," to underscore the enormity of the crime. But I have since found that the resolution meant what it said. Infanticide, direct or indirect, was in fact widely practiced well into the nineteenth century in both Catholic and Protestant lands, as my Harvard colleague in History, Professor William L. Langer, has vividly set forth in *Scientific American* (February, 1972), dealing expressly with data from England, France, and Germany particularly from 1750 to 1850. He includes pictures by William Hogarth and others and graphs to make vivid the appalling inhumanity of Protestant England and Catholic France in the thousands of infants each year that were abandoned or actually suffocated or otherwise done away with.

Now some demographers, sociologists, and even ethicists, using this kind of historical data, would argue that we cannot counter an inhuman or even vicious streak in the human race; for although the direct and indirect infanticide documented for 1750 to 1850 has virtually disappeared from society, the phenomenon of the battered child persists and may be on the increase, while the whispered quest for the eugenic equivalent is getting louder (chapter 8). But we in this volume with many others argue, to the contrary, that what has been the near constant in the moral teachings and practice of the professionals is destined in our time to become the deepening conviction and practice of an ever-growing segment of the population. To this end, we recognize that both law and education must complement each other, hence the stress in the collected essays of this volume.

As for law, we know that the heinous crime of murder is not wholly inhibited by law and police enforcement thereof. Moreover, murder is not, in any case, primarily prevented by law. It is rather by reason of the deep recoil in civilized persons from such an act. And so we whose essays are here gathered wonder how it is that *we* can feel in our very being that abortion is a degree of homicide even on the microscopic level, while other fellow citizens and even some friends and fellow-workers in other causes have no compunction about abortion and even advocate it for themselves, or at least for others, as the right of a woman "over her own body," or as the right of society to control itself demographically.

Opponents of abortion must face the fact that elan from a sense of righteousness prevails in both camps, ours and theirs. We do well to regard our foes on this issue not as fiends but as misguided friends.

The historical perspective which I have invited you to take into consideration in reading the following essays will help us in getting our bearings and in emboldening us to work all the more zealously for the cause, while proceeding charitably in dealing with our opponents.

When the Founding Fathers worked hard over the great state papers that led to the Declaration of Independence and the Constitution, and avowed to all the world that all men are created free and equal, some of them, perhaps most of them, were insensitive to the fact that a slave or two in their chambers ministering to their needs during the deliberations, and thousands more toiling on plantations back home, were not so much being excluded from the provision of their great document of the Republic as ignored; or not quite ignored: The very first paragraph of the Constitution still bears the horrible blemish, now happily enclosed in the square brackets of repeal, that people of a certain race, who now constitute perhaps twelve percent of the American population, count as but three-fifths of a person each—and even then only for purposes of southern representation by their white masters in the Congress. I mention this as we approach the two-hundredth anniversary of our Republic to underscore the fact that truly great and farseeing men can be fundamentally blind on a given point (chapter 7). As our forefathers were color-blind in the sense that they did not see the personhood of people of color, so our opponents today, otherwise earnest and no doubt good people, are night-blind, as it were, for they simply do not yet perceive the personhood of the diminutive denizens of the mysterious darkness of the maternal womb whence we all emerge. They do not yet perceive the civil rights of the fetus, so much taken up are they by their understandable concern for the rights of women.

Yet genetics and fetology make so clear to us what for our forebears could only be gropingly surmised; for they, until 1827, still worked with the then prevailing theory, going back to Aristotle, that the female contributed only the nurturing matrix and none of the attributes of the progeny. This sire-centered theory made of the mother but the fertile soil for the male seed. Today we all know that the haploid generation of the sperm or of the ovum gives way to the diploid generation of the zygote with its doubled panoply of chromosomes. Quite apart, then, from any theory of ensoulment, the biological fact is that something of an entirely different order comes into being at conception (chapter 1).

No doubt our opponents are able to get around the moral and civil libertarian implications of this biological fact because of their legitimate concern with the threat of overpopulation in some parts of our world, environmental pollution and the despoliation of the earth's reserves (chapter 8), and a heightened sensitivity to the rights of women in recognition of the historical fact that the rights of the fetus were in part won at the expense of the mother. Moreover, the whole debate over abortion now unfolds in the atmosphere of a profound sexual revolution (but see chapter 12), in which, among many other things, abortion seems to many but the normal extension of contraception and the prerogative of the "liberated" woman on her own.

In this climate of opinion much of the Protestant theological, ethical, ministerial, and organizational leadership has, alas, temporarily I judge, joined the other side. But opposition to abortion has been historically as intense on the Protestant and Jewish as on the Catholic side—indeed, certain principles connected with Martin Luther particularly may well have been a factor in the shaping and sharpening of the present papal moral teaching, which is so perfectly in accord with the fetological facts.

I do not believe that among faithful Protestant Christians as distinguished from some of the more articulate clerical leadership there is any substantial shift in the inherited repugnance to abortion, although we must learn to oppose abortion in such a way as to show we do take into consideration the concerns that have prompted so many Protestant and Jewish leaders to move to the other side.

I said near the outset, we are deep into the laicization of the opposition to abortion. This "near constant in Western history" is now in the process of being expounded and extended in the lay apostolate and through the priesthood of all believers. Many Christian and Jewish laymen and also many others whose stance is humanely humanistic are assuming responsibility for the clarification and implementation of the moral teachings formerly articulated and enforced by bishops, priests, canonists, rabbis, ministers, and philosophers. I said also that we are deep into the democratization of that same opposition in the public domain, contending for the inviolability of all human life—from conception to natural death.

Since many on the other side, too, claim that they are involved in the process of democratization and are insisting that, at long last, the woman should be as sexually free as the man and that the woman as an individual citizen has full rights over her own body, we should ourselves become very clear at exactly what point we join issue with them. Without having to take a stand on the sexual revolution as a whole and no doubt being ourselves broadly in sympathy with every appropriate equalization of the life opportunities for women, we solemnly sound a warning:

It is often argued today that the law against abortion is a statutory relic of male moral chauvinism, originally imposed by celibate moral theologians and canonists upon women, and perpetuated unthinkingly by men in the various professions of medicine, law, and divinity. It is true that the whole fabric of law is largely the product of men and that the full recognition of the equal rights of women is still to be worked through alike in law and in culture and custom. But the simple unalterable biological fact that every person comes into the world as a result of the genetic conjunction of two other persons does not make of that generating couple or of the mother alone an absolute sovereign over the new human being up to the moment of its birth. To be sure, in ancient Rome by both law and custom the man as sire could abort the fetus in his wife or servant without her consent and even sell his own offspring into slavery. Alas, the last traces of this sire-centered sovereignty over seed and offspring did not disappear from even our own country until after the Civil War. But society will surely have evolved no further in its moral sensitivity to life within the womb it if merely accords now to the woman a prerogative that in the evolution of civilization was gradually taken away from the omnipotent male.

The truth defended by us in this book is surely destined to become the conviction and practice of ordinary people in society at large, in the public domain, not only because of the sanctions of law and religion. It will also presently appear as evident to all who take the time to inspect the marvelous color photography of the stages of fetological development (chapter 1) and see that the fetus is human, that it has the inalienable right to life and the pursuit of happiness as a *civil liberty* (see chapter 10). Just as we now take for granted nearly two centuries after the founding of this Republic that indeed all men, all men and women, black and white, are created free and equal, so we will see emerge in our time the legal constitutional principle of plenary humane rights accorded the fetus.

If we sometimes feel, amid the often shrill clamor for relaxing the laws that still protect the unborn, that we are somehow coercive and intrusive, imposing our moral standards upon others, let us be again reminded that it is those who would lift society's protection from its most helpless wards who may be incipient totalitarians. If we sometimes wonder whether our instinctive repugnance to abortion is being phased out in the cause of progress, let us remember that we are more likely to be in league with a cosmic power greater than ourselves. We are part of a gradual revolution, made possible in part by the marvels of scientific scrutiny, in part by the growing moral sensitivity of our youth, in society's reverent perception of the mystery of human life. A reverence for life within the womb is ultimately one with a reverent sense of responsibility and accountability for our global environment in the ecological concern of our time. But surely we will never be able to marshal the moral energy and self-discipline on an international scale to save some of the wilderness areas and to protect the myriad species of other forms of life now threatened with extinction if we do not have the ethical discernment and moral courage to oppose every facile acquiescence in individual and institutional violence against the mysterious sanctuaries of human life itself.

In the accelerated democratization and personal interiorization of the historic near moral constant about unborn life (formerly upheld most articulately by the professional elites), we admittedly face today the countervailing hazard of the onrushing devolution of individualist sovereignty to the point where the individual may claim even an absolute right of life or death over himself in suicide as well as a right over the fetus within. Thus in the process of state referendums on abortion and in changes going on in legislatures and hospitals in response to *momentary* popular pressures of the more articulate, we must reckon realistically with the ever-present threat of a possibly coercive *temporary* majority, ethically and biologically uninformed or partisan, all in the name of individualism, personal rights, and social welfare. Accordingly, the purpose of the following chapters is both to inform further all those readers who are still open-minded about entertaining new points on the abortion issue and also to confirm in their convictions all those, like the authors of our book, who already perceive that, however much we are all concerned to secure individual liberties and women's rights, we dare not extend them at the expense of the unborn, who need only time to become one with us!

George H. Williams
Hollis Professor of Divinity
Harvard University
Chairman of Americans United for Life

LIST OF CONTRIBUTORS

CARROLL, CHARLES: Priest of the Episcopal Diocese of California. Former Executive Director of the Center for Human Values in the Health Sciences at the University of California, San Francisco. A former student of international law at Harvard, Yale and, during the Hitler period, the University of Berlin. An officer of the United States Military Government in Germany from 1947 to 1949. A personal observer at the doctors' war-crime trials in Nuremburg. Married and the father of four children. Currently a fellow at the Institute of Ecumenical and Cultural Research, Collegeville, Minnesota.

CRAVEN, ERMA CLARDY: Chairman of the Minneapolis Commission of Human Rights. Member of the Women's Advisory Committee of the Minnesota State Commission of Human Rights. Formerly probation officer with magistrate courts, New York City, girls' term and women's division; psychiatric social worker with the Manhattan After-Care Center; and community organization secretary with the Milwaukee Urban League. Currently a social worker for the Hennepin County Social Welfare Department in the Family Counseling Division.

CRISHAM, THOMAS M., J.D.: Member of the Bar of the State of Illinois and the United States Supreme Court. Member of the American, Illinois and Chicago Bar Associations and of the Defense Research Institute; officer of the Trial Lawyers Club of Chicago. A graduate, cum laude, of the Loyola University School of Law.

DYCK, ARTHUR J.: Mary Saltonstall Professor of Population Ethics, Center for Population Studies, Harvard University. Member of the faculty, Harvard School of Public Health. Author of "Population Policies and Ethical Acceptability," in *Rapid Population Growth:*

Some Consequences and Some Public Policy Implications (Johns Hopkins Press, 1971).

FRAZEL, JEROME A., JR., J.D.: Member of the Bar of the states of Illinois, Indiana and Florida. An attorney in *Doe v. Scott,* a three-judge federal court case involving the abortion statute in the state of Illinois. A 1950 graduate of the College of Law, University of Notre Dame.

GARRISON, CHARLES O., M.D.: Chief Resident Associate in Pathology, Mayo Graduate School of Medicine, Rochester, Minnesota.

GORBY, JOHN D., J.D.: A 1968 graduate of the University of Michigan School of Law. Completed doctoral studies in law at the University of Heidelberg in Germany. Fellow at the Max Planck Institute, 1968–70, where he co-authored a book on the civil right to demonstrate as it exists in ten different nations. Contributor to a three-volume work about the forms of judicial protection against the executive in thirty-one different nations. Co-author of several briefs on abortion before the United States Supreme Court.

HEFFERNAN, BART T., M.D.: Director, Galvin Heart Center, St. Francis Hospital, and Chief of the Department of Medicine, St. Francis Hospital, Evanston, Illinois. Member of American Medical Association, Chicago Medical Society, Illinois State Medical Society and the American Society of Internal Medicine. Assistant Clinical Professor of Medicine, Stritch School of Medicine. Guardiem ad Litem for the class of unborn children in the state of Illinois.

HORAN, DOLORES B., J.D.: Graduate of Northwestern University School of Law. Specializes in the defense of indigent criminals. Member of the Chicago Bar Association, Illinois Bar Association and American Bar Association. Co-author of several briefs on abortion and participant in a number of abortion cases. Attorney for an abortion case presently pending before the United States Supreme Court.

JOYCE, MARY R.: Philosopher, author, teacher and housewife. Together with her husband, Robert Joyce, she is the author of *New Dynamics in Sexual Love* (St. John's University Press, Collegeville, Minnesota, 1970) and *Let Us Be Born: The Inhumanity of Abortion* (Franciscan Herald Press, Chicago). Also the author of *Love Re-*

sponds to Life (PROW Books, Kenosha, Wisconsin, 1971) and *The Meaning of Contraception* (Alba House, New York, 1970).

KNIGHT, JILL, M.P.: Member of the British Parliament. World traveler and lecturer, wife and mother of two children. Currently Chairman of the Parliamentary Group for Responsible Family Planning at Westminster.

LAMPE, JOSEPH A.: State Coordinator for MINNESOTA CITIZENS CONCERNED FOR LIFE, INC.

LILEY, ALBERT W., PH.D., F.R.C.O.G. Research Professor in Perinatal Physiology at the Postgraduate School of Obstetrics and Gynaecology, National Women's Hospital, Auckland, New Zealand. Often referred to as the "Father of Fetology" for his development of the intra-uterine transfusion to treat unborn children afflicted with Rh disease.

LOUISELL, DAVID WILLIAM: Elizabeth Josselyn Boalt Professor of Law, University of California; J.D., University of Minnesota. Author: *Modern California Discovery,* 1963; Co-author: *Trial of Malpractice Cases,* 1960 (rev. ed., *Medical Malpractice,* 1969); *The Parenchyma of Law,* 1960; *Pleading and Procedure, State and Federal,* 2d ed., 1968; *Jurisdiction in a Nutshell,* 2d ed., 1968; *Cases and Materials on Evidence,* 1968; *Principles of Evidence and Proof,* 1968; *Organ Transplantation,* 1970.

MALL, DAVID J.: Former Director of the Intercollegiate Discussion Program at Purdue University and the Intercollegiate Debate Program at Fordham University. Currently completing his doctoral work in Speech and Communications at the University of Minnesota, where he is specializing in the Rhetoric of Social Movements.

MCLUHAN, H. MARSHALL: Communications specialist, educator and writer. Presently the Director of the Centre for Culture and Technology, University of Toronto. Author: *The Mechanical Bride,* 1951; (with E. S. Carpenter) *Studies in Communications,* 1960; *The Gutenberg Galaxy* (Gov. Gen.'s literary award for critical prose, 1963), 1962; *Understanding Media, The Extensions of Man,* 1964; (with Quentin Fiore) *The Medium Is the Message: An Inventory of Effects,* 1967.

MECKLENBURG, FRED. E., M.D.: Assistant Clinical Professor of Obstetrics and Gynecology, University of Minnesota Medical School.

Director of Family Planning Program, University of Minnesota. Member of American Association of Planned Parenthood Physicians. Department Chairman, Obstetrics and Gynecology, the St. Louis Park Medical Center.

MECKLENBURG, MARJORY: Chairman of the Problem Pregnancy Research and Advisory Committee of Minnesota. Founding member of Minneapolis BIRTHRIGHT. Mother of four children. Currently President of MINNESOTA CITIZENS CONCERNED FOR LIFE, INC.

NOONAN, JOHN T., JR.: Professor of Law, University of California Law School (Boalt Hall); LL.B., Harvard University; M.A. and Ph.D., Catholic University of America; grad. Theological Union, University of San Francisco. Author: *The Scholastic Analysis of Usury*, 1957; *Contraception: A History of Its Treatment by the Catholic Theologians and Canonists*, 1965. Editor: *Natural Law Forum*, 1961-1970; *American Journal of Jurisprudence*, 1970-; *The Morality of Abortion*, 1970.

RIORDAN, GAYLE, R.N., B.S.N.: Former head nurse in obstetrics at St. Mary's Hospital in Rochester, Minnesota. Nurse Advisor in South Viet Nam 1967-68. Presently Director of the L.P.N. Nursing Program, St. Mary's School of Nursing.

ROSENBLUM, VICTOR G.: Educator; A.B., LL.B., Columbia University; Ph.D., University of California, Berkeley; D.H.L., Hebrew Union College. Admitted to Illinois and New York Bars, also United States Supreme Court; formerly Professor in Political Science at University of California, Berkeley, President of Reed College and Visiting Fulbright Lecturer at the University of Louvain. Presently Professor of Political Science and Law at Northwestern University. Author: *Law as a Political Instrument.* Editor: *Law and Society Journal.*

STEVENS, AUDRA: Currently a freshman in college and a member of S.O.U.L. (Save Our Unwanted Life).

WILLIAMS, GEORGE H.: Educator. A.B. St. Lawrence University; Th.D. Union Theological Seminary. Ordained to ministry of Unitarian and Congregational Churches. Formerly the head, Department of Church History, Harvard Divinity School; now Hollis Professor of Divinity. Chairman of the Committee on Church and State, Massachusetts Council of Churches; Chairman of the Governor's Committee on Birth Control. Protestant observer at Vatican II. Chairman of AMERICANS UNITED FOR LIFE. Author of a variety of works in church history and, in 1970, of "The Sacred Condominium," in *The Morality of Abortion* (Harvard University Press, 1970).

THE EDITORS

HILGERS, THOMAS W., M.D.: A 1969 graduate of the University of Minnesota School of Medicine. Author of a number of papers on the subject of abortion, including contributions to the *DePaul Law Review,* Amicus Curiae Brief to the United States Supreme Court; co-author of *Induced Abortion: A Documented Report,* written for presentation to the Minnesota State Legislature. A co-founder and member of the Advisory Committee of the National Youth Pro-Life Coalition. Currently a Fellow in Obstetrics and Gynecology at the Mayo Graduate School of Medicine.

HORAN, DENNIS J., J.D.: Instructor in Law, University of Chicago Law School; Member of the American, Chicago and Illinois Bar Associations as well as the Chicago Trial Lawyers Club. Author of several articles on Trial Techniques. Co-author of six briefs on abortion; co-author of article on abortion appearing in the Fall 1972 *DePaul Law Review.* Attorney in *Doe* v. *Scott,* a three-judge abortion case involving the Illinois statute now on appeal to the United States Supreme Court.

The editors would like to thank Mrs. Marcy Sneed for her editorial assistance in the preparation of chapters 3, 4 and 9.

MEDICAL

▪ 1 ▪

THE EARLY BIOGRAPHY
OF EVERYMAN

Bart T. Heffernan, M.D.

We have seen in recent years a strange, but sad to say not a new, phenomenon in the affairs of men. The data of science have been manipulated, denied or distorted to fit a political or sociologic posture. The abortionists have propagandized our citizens with pseudoscience in order to protect the theories and humanitarian claims of their cause. The blob theory, the main tenet of the tissue-of-the-mother school of embryology, has been advanced for public scrutiny without so much as a note of public criticism from the scientific community or the medical profession.

Our society, because of these failures, stares at the wall of the abortorium and fails to see that it is no different from the barbed inclosures of another recent time. It is clean, aseptic and run by well-dressed, efficient men in white. The victims are anonymous and unseen. Pseudoscience has redefined them in order to rob them of their rights.

It is in response to this tragedy that the following data have been assembled. We should read this account with interest and some fascination, for it represents a biography of everyman during those moments of his greatest potential and most rapid development.

The unborn offspring of human parents is an autonomous human being.

Even before implantation in the wall of the uterus the unborn child may be responsible for the maintenance of the pregnant state in the maternal metabolism (1). The child whose tissue is antigenically

3

different from the mother sets up protective mechanisms to prevent
maternal immunologic responses from causing fetal distress (2). The
newly formed child has a remarkable degree of metabolic autonomy
(3). For example, the fetal endocrine system functions autonomously
(4).

The recent recognition of this autonomy has led to the development of new medical specialties concerning the unborn child from the
earliest stages of the pregnancy, i.e., fetology and perinatology (56).

Modern obstetrics has discarded as unscientific the concept that
the child in the womb is but tissue of the mother. As Dr. H. M. I.
Liley, the New Zealand pediatrician (and research assistant to her
famous husband, Dr. Albert Liley, who perfected the intra-uterine
transfusion), has said:

Another medical fallacy that modern obstetrics discards is the idea that the
pregnant woman can be treated as a patient alone. No problem in fetal health
or disease can any longer be considered in isolation. At the very least two
people are involved, the mother and her child. (5 at p. 207)

From conception the child is a complex, dynamic, rapidly growing
individual. By a natural and continuous process the single fertilized
ovum will, over approximately nine months, develop into the trillions
of cells of the newborn. The natural end of the sperm and ovum is
death unless fertilization occurs. At fertilization a new and unique
individual is created which, although receiving one-half of its chromosomes from each parent, is really unlike either (8, 6, 9; 10 at p. 18).

The events that follow fertilization are self-generated by the new
individual under the guidance of his new and absolutely unique
hereditary plan. The new combination of chromosomes sets in motion the individual's life, controlled by his own individual code
(genes) with its fantastic library of information projected from the
past on the helix of Desoxyribonucleic acid or DNA. A single thread
of DNA from a human cell contains information equivalent to six
hundred thousand printed pages with five hundred words on a page,
or a library of one thousand volumes. The stored knowledge at
conception in the new individual's library of instructions is fifty times
more than that contained in the *Encyclopedia Britannica* (7). These
unique and individual instructions are operative over the whole of the
individual's life and form a continuum of human existence even into
succeeding generations. Dr. Hymie Gordon, Chief Geneticist at the
Mayo Clinic, states it thus:

... from the moment of fertilization, when the deoxyribose nucleic acids from the spermatozoon and the ovum come together to form the zygote, the pattern of the individual's constitutional development is irrevocably determined; his future health, his future intellectual potential, even his future criminal proclivities are all dependent on the sequence of the purine and pyrimidine bases in the original set of DNA molecules of the unicellular individual. True, environmental influences both during the intra-uterine period and after birth modify the individual's constitution and continue to do so right until his death, but it is at the moment of conception that the individual's capacity to respond to these exogenous influences is established. Even at that early stage, the complexity of the living cell is so great that it is beyond our comprehension. It is a privilege to be allowed to protect and nurture it. (71)

About seven to nine days after conception, when there are already several hundred cells of the new individual formed, contact with the uterus is made and implantation begins. Blood cells are formed by seventeen days and a heart as early as eighteen days. This embryonic heart, which begins as a simple tube, starts irregular pulsations at twenty-four days which, in about one week, smooth into a rhythmic contraction and expansion (8, 9, 10, 6).

Straus et al. have shown that the Electrocardiogram (ECG) on a 23 mm embryo (7.5 weeks) presents the existence of a functionally complete cardiac system and the possible existence of a myoneural or humoral regulatory mechanism. All the classic elements of the adult ECG were seen (11). Marcel and Exchaquet observed occasional contractions of the heart in a 6 mm (2 week) embryo. They also obtained tracings exhibiting the classical elements of the ECG tracing of an adult in a 15 mm embryo (5 weeks) (12).

One commentator has indicated that about four days post-conception under a special microscope the prospective sex can already be determined (10 at p. 23).

Commencing at eighteen days the developmental emphasis is on the nervous system, even though other vital organs, such as the heart, are commencing development at the same time. Such early development is necessary since the nervous system integrates the action of all other systems. By the end of the twentieth day the foundation of the child's brain, spinal cord and entire nervous system will have been established. By the sixth week after conception this system will have developed so well that it is controlling movements of the baby's muscles, even though the woman may not be aware that she is pregnant. By the thirty-third day the cerebral cortex, that part of the central nervous system which governs motor activity as well as intellect, may be seen (8, 13, 10).

The baby's eyes begin to form at nineteen days. By the end of the first month the foundation of the brain, spinal cord, nerves and sense organs is completely formed. By twenty-eight days the embryo has the building blocks for forty pair of muscles situated from the base of its skull to the lower end of its spinal column. By the end of the first month the child has completed the period of relatively greatest size increase and the greatest physical change of a lifetime. He or she is ten thousand times larger than the fertilized egg and will increase its weight six billion times by birth, having in only the first month gone from the one-cell state to millions of cells (8, 9, 10, 6, 13).

Shettles and Rugh describe this first month of development as follows:

This, then, is the great planning period, when out of apparently nothing comes evidence of a well-integrated individual, who will form along certain well-tried patterns, but who will, in the end, be distinguishable from every other human being by virtue of ultra microscopic chromosomal differences. (10 at p. 35)

By the beginning of the second month the unborn child, small as it is, looks distinctly human. Yet, at this time the child's mother may still not be aware that she is pregnant (6).

As Shettles and Rugh state:

And as for the question, "when does the embryo become human?" the answer is that it *always* had human potential, and *no other,* from the instant the sperm and the egg come together because of its chromosomes. (Emphasis in original) (10 at p. 40)

At the end of the first month the child is about one-fourth of an inch in length. At thirty days the primary brain is present and the eyes, ears and nasal organs have started to form. Although the heart is still incomplete, it is beating regularly and pumping blood cells through a closed vascular system (8). The child and mother do not exchange blood, the child having from a very early point in its development its own and complete vascular system (8, 9, 10, 12, 13). Even at five and a half weeks the fetal heartbeat is essentially similar to that of an adult in general configuration (12, 13). The energy output is about 20% that of the adult, but the fetal heart is functionally complete and normal by seven weeks (12, 13).

By the end of the seventh week we see a well-proportioned small-scale baby. In its seventh week, it bears the familiar external features and all the internal organs of the adult, even though it is less than an inch long and weighs only 1/30th of an ounce. The body has become nicely rounded, padded with muscles and covered by a thin skin. The arms, only as long as printed exclamation marks, have hands with fingers and thumbs. The slower-growing legs have recognizable knees, ankles and toes (8, 9, 10, 6). Shettles and Rugh describe the child at this point of its development as a one-inch miniature doll with a large head, but gracefully formed arms and legs and an unmistakably human face (10 at p. 54).

The new body not only exists, it also functions. The brain in configuration is already like the adult brain and sends out impulses that coordinate the function of the other organs. Reflex responses are present as early as forty-two days. The brain waves have been noted at forty-three days (14). The heart beats sturdily. The stomach produces digestive juices. The liver manufactures blood cells and the kidneys begin to function by extracting uric acid from the child's blood (13, 49). The muscles of the arms and body can already be set in motion (15).

After the eighth week no further primordia will form; *everything* is already present that will be found in the full-term baby (10 at p. 71). As one author describes this period:

A human face with eyelids half closed as they are in someone who is about to fall asleep. Hands that soon will begin to grip, feet trying their first gentle kicks. (10 at p. 71)

From this point until adulthood, when full growth is achieved somewhere between twenty-five and twenty-seven years, the changes in the body will be mainly in dimension and in gradual refinement of the working parts (8, 46).

The development of the child, while very rapid, is also very specific. The genetic pattern set down in the first day of life instructs the development of a specific anatomy. The ears are formed by seven weeks and are specific, and may resemble a family pattern (16). The lines in the hands and fingerprints start to be engraved by eight weeks and remain a distinctive feature of the individual (45, 49).

The primitive skeletal system has completely developed by the end of six weeks (8, 9). This marks the end of the child's embryonic (from the Greek, "to swell or teem within") period. From this point, the child will be called a fetus (Latin, "young one or offspring") (9).

In the third month, the child becomes very active. By the end of

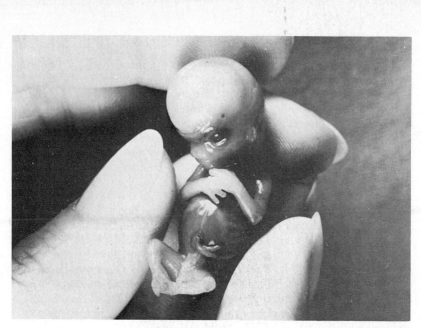

FIG. 2.   8 weeks of age.

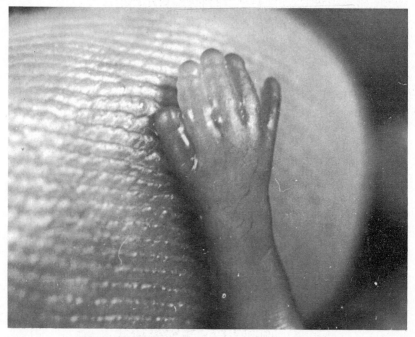

FIG. 3.   Right hand on adult index finger—8 weeks.

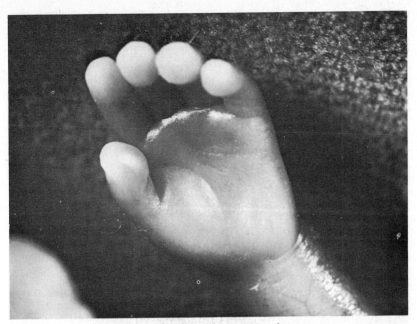

FIG. 4. Left hand at 14 weeks of age.

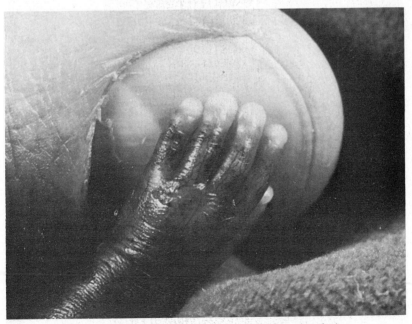

FIG. 5. Left hand on adult thumb nail—14 weeks of age.

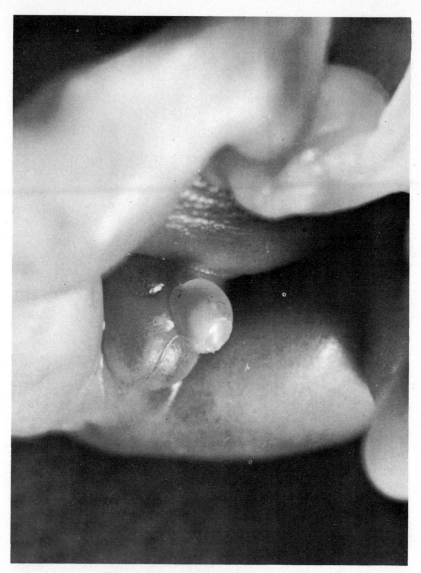

FIG. 6. Male genitalia—14 weeks of age.

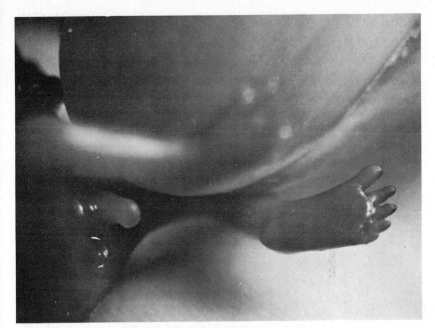

FIG. 7. Left foot—8 weeks of age.

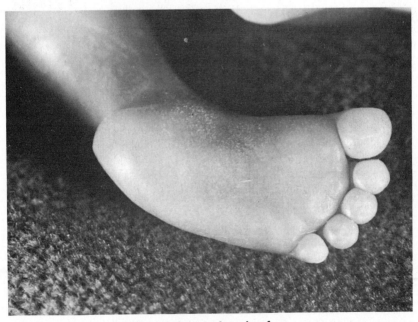

FIG. 8. Left foot—14 weeks of age.

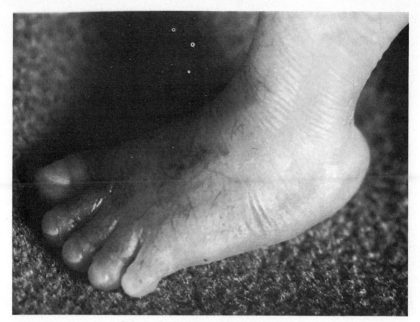

FIG. 9. Left foot—14 weeks of age.

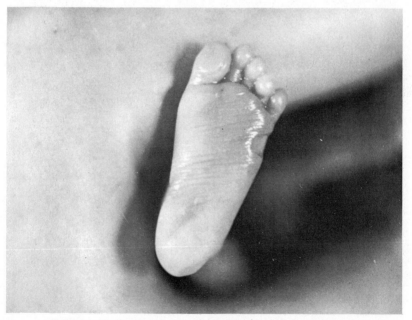

FIG. 10. Right foot grasped in adult hand—22 weeks of age.

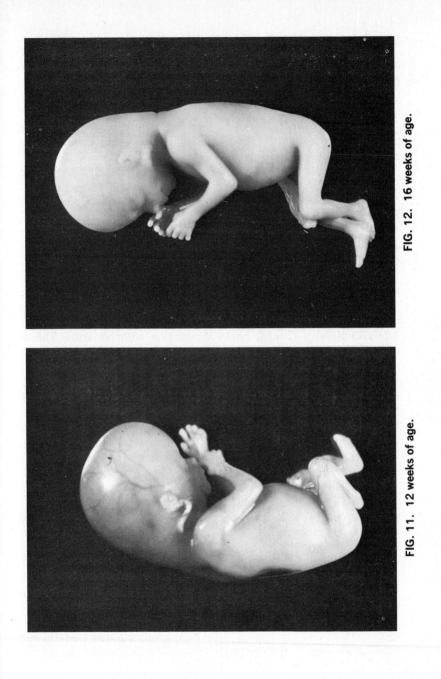

FIG. 12. 16 weeks of age.

FIG. 11. 12 weeks of age.

the month he can kick his legs, turn his feet, curl and fan his toes, make a fist, move his thumb, bend his wrist, turn his head, squint, frown, open his mouth, press his lips tightly together (15). He can swallow and drinks the amniotic fluid that surrounds him. Thumb sucking is first noted at this age. The first respiratory motions move fluid in and out of his lungs with inhaling and exhaling respiratory movements (13, 15).

The movement of the child has been recorded at this early stage by placing delicate shock-recording devices on the mother's abdomen, and direct observations have been made by the famous embryologist Davenport Hooker, M.D. Over the last thirty years, Dr. Hooker has recorded the movement of the child on film—some as early as six weeks of age. His films show that prenatal behavior develops in an orderly progression (15, 17, 18).

The prerequisites for motion are muscles and nerves. In the sixth to seventh week, nerves and muscles work together for the first time (8). If the area of the lips, the first to become sensitive to touch, is gently stroked, the child responds by bending the upper body to one side and making a quick backward motion with his arms. This is called a total pattern response because it involves most of the body, rather than a local part. Localized and more appropriate reactions, such as swallowing, follow in the third month. By the beginning of the ninth week, the baby moves spontaneously without being touched. Sometimes his whole body swings back and forth for a few moments. By eight and a half weeks the eyelids and the palms of the hands become sensitive to touch. If the eyelid is stroked, the child squints. On the stroking of the palm, the fingers close into a small fist (17, 15, 13, 64).

In the ninth and tenth weeks, the child's activity leaps ahead. Now, if the forehead is touched, he may turn his head away and pucker up his brow and frown. He now has full use of his arms and can bend the elbow and wrist independently. In the same week, the entire body becomes sensitive to touch (15).

The twelfth week brings a whole new range of responses. The baby can now move his thumb in opposition to his fingers. He now swallows regularly. He can pull up his upper lip—the initial step in the development of the sucking reflex (5). By the end of the twelfth week, the quality of muscular response is altered. It is no longer marionette-like or mechanical—the movements are now graceful and fluid, as they are in the newborn. The child is active and the reflexes are becoming more vigorous. *All this is before the mother feels any movement* (5, 64).

The phenomenon of "quickening" reflects maternal sensitivity and not fetal competence. Dr. Hooker states that fetal activity occurs at a very early age, normally *in utero,* and some women may feel it as early as thirteen weeks. Others feel very little as late as twenty weeks, and some are always anxious because they do not perceive movement (17).

Dr. Liley states:

Historically, "quickening" was supposed to delineate the time when the fetus became an independent human being possessed of a soul. Now, however, we know that while he may have been too small to make his motions felt, the unborn baby is active and independent long before his mother feels him. Quickening is a maternal sensitivity and depends on the mother's own fat, the position of the placenta and the size and strength of the unborn child. (5 at pp. 37, 38)

Every child shows a distinct individuality in his behavior by the end of the third month. This is because the actual structure of the muscles of the face, for example, follows an inherited pattern. The facial expressions of the baby in his third month are already similar to the facial expression of his parents (13, 14, 49).

Dr. Arnold Gesell states: "By the end of the first trimester (12th week) the fetus is a sentient moving being. We need not pause to speculate as to the nature of his psychic attributes, but we may assert that the organization of his psychosomatic self is now well under way." (49 at p. 65)

Further refinements are noted in the third month. The fingernails appear. The child's face becomes much prettier. His eyes, previously far apart, now move closer together. The eyelids close over the eyes. Sexual differentiation is apparent in both internal and external sex organs, and primitive eggs and sperm are formed. The vocal cords are completed. In the absence of air, they cannot produce sound; the child cannot cry aloud until birth, although he is capable of crying long before (8, 13, 9, 5).

Dr. Liley relates the experience of a doctor who injected an air bubble into an unborn (eight months) baby's amniotic sac in an attempt to locate the placenta on x-ray. It so happened that the air bubble covered the unborn baby's face. The moment the unborn child had air to inhale, his vocal cords became operative and his crying became audible to all present, including the physician and technical help. The mother telephoned the doctor later to report that whenever she lay down to sleep, the air bubble got over the unborn baby's face and he was crying so loudly he was keeping both her and her husband awake (5 at p. 50; 15 at p. 75).

The taste buds and salivary glands develop in this month, as do the digestive glands in the stomach. When the baby swallows amniotic fluid, its contents are utilized by the child. The child starts to urinate (8, 13, 19).

From the twelfth to the sixteenth week, the child grows very rapidly (50). His weight increases six times, and he grows to eight, to ten inches in height. For this incredible growth spurt the child needs oxygen and food. This he receives from his mother through the placental attachment—much as he receives food from her after he is born. His dependence does not end with expulsion into the external environment (8, 9,13,6,10). We now know that the placenta belongs to the baby, not the mother, as was long thought (5).

In the fifth month, the baby gains two inches in height and ten ounces in weight. By the end of the month he will be about one foot tall and will weigh one pound. Fine baby hair begins to grow on his eyebrows and on his head and a fringe of eyelashes appear. Most of the skeleton hardens. The baby's muscles become much stronger, and as the child becomes larger his mother finally perceives his many activities (8). The child's mother comes to recognize the movement and can feel the baby's head, arms and legs. She may even perceive a rhythmic jolting movement—fifteen to thirty per minute. This is due to the child hiccoughing (13, 5, 6). Dr. Keith Russell of the University of California at Los Angeles reports that clicking sounds from the pregnant woman's uterus are fetal hiccoughs stimulated by swallowing amniotic fluid. The doctor can already hear the heartbeat with his stethoscope (8, 13, 6).

The baby sleeps and wakes just as it will after birth (63, 5). When he sleeps he invariably settles into his favorite position, called his "lie." Each baby has a characteristic lie (5). Dr. Liley states that fetal comfort determines fetal position. When he awakens he moves about freely in the buoyant fluid, turning from side to side and frequently head over heels. Sometimes his head will be up and sometimes it will be down. He may sometimes be aroused from sleep by external vibrations. He may wake up from the turning on of a loud tap on the tub when his mother is taking a bath. A loud concert,or the vibrations of a washing machine, may also stir him into activity (13). The child hears and recognizes his mother's voice before birth (19, 20). Movements of the mother, whether locomotive, cardiac or respiratory, are communicated to the child (19). Emotional distress in the mother is communicated to the child and is manifest by a marked increase in activity (68).

In the sixth month, the baby will grow about two more inches, to become fourteen inches tall. He will also begin to accumulate a little fat under his skin and will increase his weight to a pound and three-quarters. This month the permanent-teeth buds come in, high in the gums behind the milk teeth. Now his closed eyelids will open and close, and his eyes look up, down and sideways. Dr. Liley feels that the child may perceive light through the abdominal wall (20). *Dr. Still has noted that electroencephalographic waves have been obtained in 43- to 45-day-old fetuses, and so conscious experience is possible after this date* (14).

The electrophysiologic rhythm develops early. Detailed EEG tracings have been taken directly from the head end of the 16mm (crown rump) human embryo at 40-odd days of gestation in Japan (66).

As one writer said: "Thus at an early prenatal stage of life the EEG reflects a distinctly individual pattern that soon becomes truly personalized." (67)

In the sixth month, the child develops a strong muscular grip with his hands. He also starts to breathe regularly and can maintain respiratory response for twenty-four hours if born prematurely. He may even have a slim chance of surviving in an incubator. The youngest children known to survive were from twenty to twenty-five weeks old (13). The concept of *viability* is not a static one. Dr. Andre Hellegers of Georgetown University states that 10% of children born between twenty weeks and twenty-four weeks gestation will survive (44A and 44B). Modern medical intensive therapy has salvaged many children that would have been considered non-viable only a few years ago. The concept of an artificial placenta may be a reality in the near future and will push the date of viability back even further, and perhaps to the earliest stages of gestation (43, 48). After twenty-four to twenty-eight weeks the child's chances of survival are much greater.

This review has covered the first six months of life. The individuality of the unborn human being is clear to all unbiased observers. Dr. Arnold Gesell has said:

Our own repeated observation of a large group of fetal infants (an individual born and living at any time prior to forty weeks gestation) left us with no doubt that psychologically they were individuals. Just as no two looked alike, so no two behaved precisely alike. One was impassive when another was alert. Even among the youngest there were discernible differences in vividness, reactivity and responsiveness. These were genuine individual differences, already prophetic of the diversity which distinguishes the human family. (49 at p. 172)

When we view the present state of medical science, we find that the artificial distinction between born and unborn has vanished. As Dr. Liley says:

In assessing fetal health, the doctor now watches changes in maternal function very carefully, for he has learned that it is actually the mother who is a passive carrier, while the fetus is very largely in charge of the pregnancy. (5 at p. 202) (65)

The new specialty of fetology is being replaced by a newer specialty called perinatology which cares for its patients from conception to about one year of extra-uterine existence (56). The *Cumulative Index Medicus* for 1969 contains over fourteen hundred separate articles in fetology. For the physician, the life process is a continuous one, and observation of the patient must start at the earliest period of life. (See 42 U.S.C. 289[d].)

A large number of sophisticated tools have been developed that now allow the physician to observe and measure the child's reactions from as early as ten weeks. This has been termed *fetal interrogation* by Dr. C. Norman Smith of the University of London (70). At ten weeks it is possible to obtain the electrocardiogram of the unborn child (22, 11, 12). At this stage also the heart sounds can be detected with new ultrasonic techniques (45). The heart has already been pumping large volumes of blood to the fast-growing child for six weeks. With present-day technology, the heart of the child is now monitored during critical periods of the pregnancy by special electronic devices, including radiotelemetry (23, 60). Computer analysis of the child's ECG has been devised and promises more accurate monitoring and evaluation of fetal distress (14). A number of abnormal electrocardiographic patterns have been found before birth. These patterns forewarn the physician of trouble after delivery (57, 58, 62). Analysis of heart sounds through phonocardiography is also being done (25, 53). A further check on intra-uterine conditions is afforded by a telemetering system based on the MRC radio pill. This is a miniature transistor-transmitter sealed Perspex which is introduced into the uterus through the cervix to lie outside the membranes above the presenting part of the child. The signal is picked up by a receiver and allows continuous observation of maternal and fetal heartbeat and uterine contraction (70).

With the new optical equipment, a physician can now look at the amniotic fluid through the cervical canal and predict life-threatening problems that are reflected by a change in the fluid's color and turbidity (26, 27). In the future, the physician will undoubtedly be able to look directly at the growing child, using new fiber optic devices (through a small puncture in the uterus), and thereby diagnose and prescribe specific treatment to heal or prevent illness or deformity (21, 55).

For the child with severe anemia, the physician now gives blood, using an unusual technique developed by Dr. A. Liley of New Zealand. This life-saving measure is carried out by using new image-intensifier x-ray equipment. A needle is placed through the abdominal wall of the mother and into the abdominal cavity of the child. A special catheter has been developed for simultaneous intra-uterine transfusion and fetal electrocardiography (69). For this procedure the child must be sedated (via maternal circulation) and given pain-relieving medication, since it experiences pain from the puncture and would move away from the needle if not premedicated. As Dr. H. M. I. Liley states:

When doctors first began invading the sanctuary of the womb, they did not know that the unborn baby would react to pain in the same fashion as a child would. But they soon learned that he would. By no means a "vegetable," as he has so often been pictured, the unborn knows perfectly well when he has been hurt, and he will protest it just as violently as would a baby lying in a crib. (5 at p. 50)

The gastro-intestinal tract of the child is outlined by contrast media previously placed in the amniotic fluid and then swallowed by the child (52). We know that the child starts to swallow as early as fourteen weeks (5); estimates about one liter a day. The child drinks more if the fluid is artificially sweetened and less if it is given an unpleasant taste. When the gastro-intestinal tract is outlined by contrast media, pathologic conditions can be diagnosed just as they are in the adult patient, i.e., diaphragmatic hernia.

Some children fail to get adequate nutrition when *in utero*. This problem can be predicted by measuring the amount of estradiol in the urine of the mother and the amount of PSP excreted after it is injected into the child (29). Recent work indicates that these nutritional problems may be solved by feeding the child more directly by introducing nutrients into the amniotic fluid which the child normally swallows (250 to 700 cc a day). In a sense, we may well be able to offer the child that is starving because of a placental defect a nipple to use before birth (30).

The amniotic fluid surrounding the unborn child offers the physician a convenient and assessable fluid that he can now test in order to diagnose a long list of diseases, just as he tests the urine and blood of his adult patients. The doctor observes the color and volume of amniotic fluid and tests it for cellular element, enzymes and other chemicals. He can tell the sex of his patient and gets a more precise idea of the exact age of the child from this fluid. He can diagnose conditions such as the adrenogenital syndrome, hemolytic anemia, adrenal insufficiency, congenital hyperuracemia and glycogen-storage disease. Intra-uterine convulsive disorders have been diagnosed *in utero.* Some of these, and hopefully in the future all of these, can be treated before birth (31, 32,33, 34, 35, 36, 37).

At the time of labor, the child's blood can be obtained from scalp veins and the exact chemical balance determined before birth. These determinations have saved many children who would not have been considered in need of therapy had these tests not been done (38, 39). The fetal EEG has also been monitored during delivery (61).

A great deal of work has been done to elucidate the endocrinology of the unborn child. Growth hormone is elaborated by the child at seventy-one days, and ACTH has been isolated at eleven weeks gestation (40). The thyroid gland has been shown to function at ten and a half weeks (51), and the adrenal glands also at about this age (40). The sex hormones—estrogen and androgen—are also found as early as nine weeks (40).

Surgical procedures performed on the unborn child are few. However, surgical cannulation of the blood vessels in an extremity of the child has been carried out in order to administer blood. Techniques are now being developed on animals that will be applicable to human problems involving the unborn child. Fetal surgery is now a reality in the animal laboratory, and will soon offer help to unborn patients (28, 41, 42).

Dr. Ronald E. Meyers, Chief of the National Institutes of Health Laboratory of Perinatal Physiology in San Juan, states that with more experience the human fetologist will be able to look forward to a surgical survival rate of at least 60%. Fetologists at Columbia and

Yale Universities hope to operate on certain heart and blood vessel defects, diaphragmatic hernia, fetal tumors, hearing defects and hydrocephalus.

The whole thrust of medicine is in support of the notion that the child in its mother is a distinct individual in need of the most diligent study and care, and that he is also a patient whom science and medicine treats just as it does any other person (21, 5).

BIBLIOGRAPHY

1. Short, R. V.: Implantation and the Maternal Recognition of Pregnancy. *Foetal Autonomy: A Ciba Foundation Symposium,* ed. G. E. W. Wolstenholme and Maeve O'Connor. London, J. A. Churchill Ltd. (104 Gloucester Place), 1969.
2. Currie, G. A.: The Foetus as an Allograft: The Role of Maternal "Unresponsiveness" to Paternally Derived Foetal Antigens. Op. cit. supra, note 1.
3. Rutter, W. J.: Independently Regulated Synthetic Transitions in Foetal Tissues. Op. cit. supra, note 1.
4. Jost, A.: The Extent of Foetal Endocrine Autonomy. Op. cit. supra, note 1.
5. Liley, H. M. I.: *Modern Motherhood,* rev. ed. New York, Random House, 1969.
6. Ingelman-Sundberg, Axel; and Wirsen, Cloes: *A Child Is Born: The Drama of Life Before Birth,* photos by Lennart Nilsson. New York, Dell Publishing Co., 1965.
7. Houwink, R.: *Data: Mirrors of Science,* pp. 104-190. New York, American Elsevier Publishing Co., Inc., 1970.
8. Arey, Leslie B.: *Developmental Anatomy,* 6th ed., chs. 2, 6. Philadelphia, W. B. Saunders Co., 1954.
9. Patten, Bradley M.: *Human Embryology,* 3rd ed., ch. 7. New York, McGraw-Hill Book Co., 1968.
10. Rugh, Robert; and Shettles, Landrum B.; with Richard N. Einhorn: *From Conception to Birth: The Drama of Life's Beginnings.* New York, Harper and Row, 1971.
11. Straus, Reuben, et al.: Direct Electrocardiographic Recording of a Twenty-Three-Millimeter Human Embryo. *The American Journal of Cardiology,* September 1961, pp. 443-447.
12. Marcel, M. P.; and Exchaquet, J. P.: L'Electrocardiogramme du Foetus Human avec un Cas de Double Rythme Auriculaire Verifie. *Arch. Mal. Couer* (Paris), 31:504, 1938.
13. Flannagan, G. L.: *The First Nine Months of Life.* New York, Simon and Schuster, 1962.
14. Still, J. W.: *J. Washington Acad. Sci.,* 59:46, 1969.

15. Hooker, Davenport: *The Prenatal Origin of Behavior*. Lawrence, Kansas; University Press of Kansas, 1952.
16. Streeter, Geo. L.: Development of the Auricle in the Human Embryo. *Contributions to Embryology,* Vol. XIV, No. 69 (1922).
17. Hooker, Davenport: Early Human Fetal Behavior with a Preliminary Note on Double Simultaneous Fetal Stimulation. *Proceedings of the Association for Research in Nervous and Mental Disease*. Baltimore, The Williams & Wilkins Co., 1954.
18. Gesell, Arnold, M.D.; Amatruda, C. S., M.D.: *Developmental Diagnosis*. P. S. Hoeber, 1958, pp. 8-9.
19. Wood, Carl: Weightlessness: Its Implications for the Human Fetus. *J. Obstetrics & Gynecology of the British Commonwealth,* 77: 333-336, 1970.
20. Liley, Albert W.: Auckland M.D. to Measure Light and Sound Inside Uterus. *Medical Tribune Report,* May 26, 1969.
21. Fetology: The Smallest Patients. *The Sciences,* published by The New York Academy of Sciences, Vol. 8, No. 10, Oct. 1968, pp. 11-15.
22. de Smoler, Dr. Paulina Eisenberg: Fetal Heart Activity Is Recorded Routinely by 10th Week of Life. *Medical Tribune,* Feb. 2, 1970.
23. Neuman, M. R.: An Intravaginal Fetal Egg Telemetry System. *Obstetrics and Gynecology,* Vol. 35, No. 1, Jan. 1970, pp. 96-103.
24. Curran, J. T.: A Practical System of Fetal Egg Analysis by Computer. *J. Physiology,* 303, July 1969.
25. Massorrio, M.: Phonocardiography in the Diagnosis of Fetal Distress. *Archivio per le Scienze Mediche.* U 125, Dec. 1968, pp. 860-865.
26. Henry, G. R.: The Role of Amnioscopy in the Prevention of Ante-Partum Hypoxia of the Fetus. *J. Obstet. Gynec. British Commonwealth,* 76:790-794, Sept. 1969.
27. Rieppi, G.; Cargnello, U.: Amnioscopy in the Diagnosis of Fetal Distress. *Friuli Medico (Udine),* V. 23, Nov.-Dec. 1968.
28. Intrauterine Transfusion and Erythro Blastosis Fetalis. Report of 53rd Ross Conference on Pediatric Research, Sept. 1966.
29. Kimura, C.; Yamaguchi, R.: Clinical Significance of the Fetal DSP Test. *Tohoku J. Exp. Med.,* 99:165-170, 1969.
30. Sevilla, Rafael M.: Oral Feeding of Human Fetus: A Possibility. *JAMA,* May 4, 1970, pp. 713-717.
31. Horger, E. Q. III; Hutchinson, D. L., M.D.: Diagnostic Use of Amniotic Fluid. *J. of Pediatrics,* Vol. 75, No. 3, pp. 503-508, Sept. 1969.
32. Floyd, Wm. S., M.D.; Goodman, Paul A.; Wilson, A., CT: Amniotic Fluid Filtration and Cytology. *Obstetrics and Gynecology,* Vol. 34, No. 4, Oct. 1969.
33. Szijarto, di Antonino: Modern Diagnostic Criteria of Fetal Suffering. *Fracestoro,* Vol. 61, pp. 914-930, Nov.-Dec. 1968.
34. Parmley, Tim; Miller, Eugenia: Fetal Maturity and Amniotic Fluid Analysis. *Am. J. Obstet. and Gynec.,* Vol. 105, No. 3, pp. 354-362.

35. Berman, Peter, M.D.; Balis, M. E., Ph.D.; Dancis, J., M.D.: A Method for the Prenatal Diagnosis of Congenital Hyperuracemia. *J. of Pediatrics,* Vol. 75, No. 3, Sept. 1969.

36. O'Doherty, N.: The Prenatal Treatment of Adrenal Insufficiency. *Lancet,* No. 29, 1969, 2:1194–1195.

37. Nadler, H. L., M.D.: Prenatal Detection of Genetic Defects. *J. of Pediatrics,* Vol. 74, No. 1, Jan. 1969, pp. 132–143.

38. Wood, Carl; Newman, Warwick; Lumley, Judith; Hammond, Judith: Classification of Fetal Heart Rate in Relation to the Fetal Scalp Blood Measurements and Apgar Score. *Am. J. Obstet. and Gynec.,* Vol. 105, No. 6, Nov. 1969, pp. 942–948.

39. Kibli, F. W., et al.: Observations on Heart Rate and PH in the Human Fetus During Labor. *Am. J. Obstet. and Gynec.,* Vol. 104, No. 8, Aug. 15, 1969, pp. 1190–1206.

40. Abramovich, D. R.: The Importance of Fetal Physiology and Endocrinology in Obstetrics. *The Med. Journal of Australia,* 2:408–411, 23 Aug. 1969.

41. Jackson, Ben J.: Approach to Fetal Research—Present and Future. *Am. J. Diseases of Children,* Vol. 118, Dec. 1969, pp. 812–816.

42. Hodari, A. A.; Thomas, Lorna: Experimental Surgical Procedures Upon the Fetus in Obstetric Research. *Obstet. and Gynec.,* Vol. 34, No. 2, Aug. 1969, pp. 204–211.

43. Zapol, Warren; and Kolobow, Theodore: *Medical World News,* May 30, 1969.

44. (a) Monroe, *Canadian Medical Association's Journal,* 1939.
    (b) Hellegers, Andre, M.D.: National Symposium on Abortion, May 15, 1970, Prudential Plaza, Chicago, Illinois.

45. Miller, James R.: Dermal Ridge Patterns: Technique for Their Study in Human Fetuses. *J. Pediatrics,* Vol. 73, No. 4, Oct. 1969, pp. 614–616.

46. Potter, Edith: *Pathology of the Fetus and Infant.* Chicago, Year Book Publishers, Inc., 1961.

47. Ian, Donald: Sonar As a Method of Studying Prenatal Development. *J. of Pediatrics,* Vol. 75, No. 2, Aug. 1969. pp. 326–333.

48. Alexander, D. P.; Britton, H. G.; Nixon, D. A.: Maintenance of Sheep Fetuses by an Extra-Corporeal Circuit for Periods up to 24 Hours. *Am. J. Obstet. and Gynec.,* Vol. 102, No. 7, Dec. 1968, pp. 969–975.

49. Gesell, Arnold: *The Embryology of Behavior,* chs. 4, 5, 6, and 10. New York, Harper & Brothers, Publishers, 1945.

50. Hellman, L. M., et al.: Growth and Development of the Human Fetus Prior to the 20th Week of Gestation. *Am. J. Obstet. and Gynec.,* Vol. 103, No. 6, March 15, 1969, pp. 789–800.

51. Shepard, Thomas: Onset of Function in the Fetal Thyroid: Biochemical and Autoradiographic Studies from Organ Culture. *J. Clin. Endocrinology,* 27:945–958, July 1967.

52. Pritchard, Jack A.: Fetal Swallowing and Amniotic Fluid Volume. *Obstet. and Gynec.*, Vol. 28, No. 5, Nov. 1966.

53. Huntingford, P. J.; and Pendleton, H. J.: The Clinical Application of Cardiotocography. *J. Obstet. and Gynec. Brit. Commonwealth*, 76: 586–595, July 1969.

54. Barton, John J.: Evaluation of the Doppler Shift Principle as a Diagnostic Aid in Obstetrics. *Am. J. Obstet. and Gynec.*, Vol. 102, No. 4, Oct. 1968, pp. 563–570.

55. Mori, et al.: The Original Production of the Glass Fiber Hyteroscope and a Study of Intrauterine Observation of the Human Fetus and the Inner Things Attached to the Fetus and Inner Side of the Uterus Wall in Late Pregnancy and the Beginning of Delivery by Means of Hysteroscopy and Its Recording on Film. *J. Jap. Obstet. and Gynec. Society* (Eng.) 15:87–95, April 1968.

56. Gairdner, Douglas: Fetal Medicine: Who Is to Practice It. *J. Obstet. and Gynec. Brit. Commonwealth*, 75:1123–1124, Dec. 1968.

57. Silber, David L.; Durnin, Robert E.: Intrauterine Atrial Tachycardis. *Am. J. Diseases of Children*, Vol. 117, June 1969, pp. 722–726.

58. Blumenthal, S., et al.: Congenital Atrial Flutter: A Report of a Case Documented by Intrauterine Electrocardiogram. *Pediatrics*, 41:659–661, March 1968.

59. Nielsen, J. S., et al.: Foetal Electrocardiographic Studies of Cardiac Arrhythmias and the Heart Rate. *Acta. Obstet. and Gynec. Scand.*, 47:246–256, 1968.

60. Inserted Intrauterine Transmitter for Measurement of Fetal Heart Rate. *Med. Biol. Engr.*, 6:549–551, Sept. 1968.

61. Rosen, Mortimer B.: Fetal Electroencephalographic Studies of the Placental Transfer of Thiopental and Ether. *Obstet. and Gynec.*, Vol. 30, No. 4, Oct. 1967.

62. Cameron: Fetal Electrocardiography: A Study of the Literature. *Developmental Medicine and Child Neurology*, 9:329–337, June 1967 (61 references).

63. Petre-Quadens, O., et al.: Sleep in Pregnancy: Evidence of Fetal Sleep Characteristics. *J. Neurologic Science*, 4:600–605, May–June, 1967.

64. Hooker, Davenport: *The Origin of Overt Behavior.* Ann Arbor, Univ. of Michigan Press, 1944.

65. Turnbull, A. C.; Anderson, Anne B. *Postgraduate Medical Journal*, Jan. 1969, Vol. 45, pp. 65–67.

66. Okomoto, Y.; and Kirikae, T.: Electroencephalogic Studies on Brains of Foetus, of Children of Premature Births and Newborns Together with Notes on Foetal Brainwaves. *Folia Psychiatrica Neurol. Jap.*, 5:135 (1951).

67. Hamlin, Hannibal: Life or Death by EEG. *J. Am. Med. Assn.*, 190:112–114 (1964).

68. James, Wm. H.: The Effect of Maternal Psychological Stress on the Foetus. *Brit. J. Psychiatry,* 1969, 115, 811-825.
69. Crosby, Warren M.: A Catheter for Simultaneous Intrauterine Fetal Transfusion and Fetal Electrocardiography. *Am. J. Obst. and Gynec.,* Aug. 15, 1968, pp. 1136-1137.
70. Electronics in Perinatal Studies. *Biomedical Engineering,* March 1969.
71. Gordon, Hymie: Genetical, Social and Medical Aspects of Abortion. *South African Medical Journal,* July 20, 1968, pp. 721-730.

▪ 2 ▪

THE FOETUS IN CONTROL
OF HIS ENVIRONMENT

Albert W. Liley, F.R.C.O.G., PH.D.

My subject, the foetus in control of his environment, is concerned not primarily with the pronouncement of a few facts which are easily come by and soon forgotten but with the more difficult task of presenting a concept—that the foetus is not a passive, dependent, nerveless, fragile vegetable, as tradition has held, but a young human being, dynamic, plastic, resilient and in very large measure in charge of his environment and destiny. The traditional attitude is understandable because for many centuries the only serious students of the foetus were accouchers and embryologists. The accoucher was concerned primarily with mechanical problems in delivery, so that the only aspects of the foetus which mattered were the presenting part and its diameters in relation to the diameters of the birth canal. For proof of this contention we need only reflect that, apart from Semmelweis, the great and famous in obstetrics are those who worked out better ways of delivering breeches or posteriors, better ways to design and use forceps or how to do caesarean sections. No one can deny the tremendous benefits conferred on humanity by these men, but their work left untouched the whole of foetal life and development. The embryologist studied dead, static tissue and attempted to deduce function from structure—no easy task when we remember that there are physicians still practising today who recall being told as medical

This paper was first presented by Dr. Liley as the Montgomery Spencer Memorial Oration before the Royal Australasian College of Physicians in September 1967. It is presented here with only minor editorial revisions.

27

students that the pituitary gland was a vestigial structure with no known function. The embryologist's wildest surmises fell short of the dynamic realities of foetal life. But in the meantime, the attitude had become fixed; that apart from some aimless kicking which began in the fifth month, the foetus was a placid, dependent creature who developed quietly in preparation for a life that started at birth.

The legacies of this attitude are not hard to find. Birth is the crowning achievement of motherhood. Women speak of their waters breaking or their membranes rupturing, when they really belong to the foetus. The deep symbolism attached to cutting the cord, separating the baby from his mother, is entirely lost when it is realized that cutting the cord really means simply separating the baby from his own organ, the placenta, which he no longer needs. We could dismiss these misconceptions as harmless folklore but for some rather sinister infiltration of these ideas into the law. By legal definition the baby only acquires proper status as a member of the human race when, *inter alia*, the cord is severed and he has independent circulation, a requirement which sublimely ignores the fact that he has had an independent circulation for the whole pregnancy.

We may feel that we have outgrown these fallacies, but the terminology and the viewpoint stubbornly prevail. The sebaceous retention cysts and witch's milk of the neonate, the labial development and withdrawal bleeding of the baby girl are explained in a dozen textbooks as the effects on the foetus of exposure to high levels of maternal hormones, when really it is the mother who is exposed to high levels of foetal hormones. Because the medicine of adults preceded the medicine of the infant, neonate and foetus a tendency has grown up in fields from surgery to psychiatry to start with adult life and work backwards. And since the standard of all that is normal in medicine has been the fit young adult male, any function in the baby which differs from this standard has been considered as immaturity, and by inference inferiority. The net effect has been to consider the foetus and neonate as a poorly functioning adult rather than as a splendidly functioning baby. Neonatal kidney function provides a ready example; for, by adult standards, the baby lacks the ability to concentrate urine. He handles a water load well but cannot cope with a large solute load, or at least not unless he has plenty of water to handle it with. Both before and after birth the baby lives on a diet with a very high water content which he must convert to relatively anhydrous tissue. From an osmometric point of view he lives in constant danger of drowning, but his assymetric kidney function is precisely what he needs to cope with this situation. It is only misguided adults who embarrass this function by failing to give artificially fed babies additional fluid in situations of high water loss—for instance, heat waves. Left to himself, on demand feeding, the baby would not get into this plight. We do not regard the foetal cardiovascular system as one big heap of congenital defects, but rather as a system entirely appropriate to his circumstances, and there is little reason to regard his "immature" kidney function in any different light.

The foetus lives in a very warm and very wet environment. He is neither in stupor nor hypoxic coma. By electroencephalographic studies he shows cyclical activity, the lighter periods of which correspond in the neonate with a drowsy wakefulness from which he is readily aroused by external stimuli. He is disturbed by flashing lights on the abdominal wall and responds to sound, human voices included, from as early as twenty-five weeks. He is aware of pain and discomfort. The foetus responds with violent movement to needle puncture and the intramuscular or intraperitoneal injection of cold or hypertonic solutions. Although we would accept that these stimuli are painful for adults and children and, to judge from his behavior, painful for the neonate, we are not entitled to assert that the foetus feels pain. It would seem prudent to consider at least the possibility that birth is a painful experience for a baby. Radiological observation shows foetal limbs flailing during contractions, and if one attempts to reproduce in the neonate by manual compression a mere fraction of the cranial deformation that may occur in the course of a single contraction, the baby protests violently.

It is the purposeful search for comfort which determines foetal position *in utero*. Getting comfortable presents little problem in the first half of pregnancy when he is relatively small and in a globular cavity. He has no position of stability and moves freely and rapidly. Occasionally these conditions still prevail in late pregnancy, for instance in the presence of polyhydramnios or with the uterine cavity truncated by a placenta praevia or fundal placenta. Normally in the second half of pregnancy the uterus is no longer globular but ovoid, with the lower pole narrower, and the foetus elongates more rapidly than the uterus. However, amniotic fluid volume reaches a maximum at 28–32 weeks, and up to this time the foetus, although now normally restricted to a longitudinal lie, is by no means cramped or under any obligation to lie well-flexed. As amniotic fluid volume diminishes from 32 weeks to term, comfort becomes more difficult to achieve. If the foetus elects to flex his legs at the knees, he will fit in best as a cephalic presentation, since his head forms a smaller pole than his back, thighs, calves and feet. If, however, he elects to extend his legs at the knees, then he will usually be most comfortable as a breech, since his tapering lower trunk and thighs form a smaller pole than his head, calves and feet. Variations of uterine contour, abnormal size or location of the placenta, and the presence of another foetus may all present further challenges to comfort and ingenuity and result in stable malpresentations.

Foetal position, whether he lies with his back anterior, posterior or lateral, is determined by other influences, notably the tone of the mother's uterine and abdominal wall, the shape of the maternal lumbar lordosis and the inclination of the pelvic brim. Maternal movement and changes in maternal position, Braxton-Hicks' contractions and external palpation, all disturb the foetus and may provoke him to seek a new position of comfort. He purposefully seeks to evade the sustained pressure of a phonendoscope or knuckle on prominences.

Although the very early embryo develops in flexion, beyond this stage there is little evidence to justify the traditional assumption that flexion is fundamental in foetal musculoskeletal development. In midpregnancy, with plenty of room, the foetus can move as he pleases. Nearly buoyant and with intervertebral discs virtually synovial joints, he can assume postures difficult or impossible for the child or adult. In late pregnancy, when the foetus elongates more than the uterus, he must fold to fit in. Commonly the attitude is again one of flexion, but sometimes he elects to lie with neck, limbs or trunk extended, and sometimes grossly hyperextended, a preference he continues to express as his position of comfort after birth if nursed naked in a warm environment.

The realization that the foetus himself determines the way he will present in labor by making the best he can of the space and shape available to him puts the practice of version in new perspective, and nowadays fewer obstetricians assume that they know better than the foetus how he will be most comfortable. Of course, in selecting a position of comfort in late pregnancy, the foetus may have chosen a position which is hazardous or impossible for vaginal delivery. In this regard he may be said to lack foresight, but this is a trait not unknown in adults.

The foetus is responsible for the regulation of his own amniotic fluid volume. The foetus does not need his kidneys to regulate his body water and electrolytes, his placenta handling this task; but he does need his kidneys for maintenance of amniotic fluid volume. A patent and functional gastrointestinal tract is also required. That the foetus drinks his amniotic fluid is readily demonstrated, and the rate of drinking averages out at about 25ml per hour. Foetal swallowing is important because it appears to be the major, if not the only, significant route by which the osmotically active colloids of amniotic fluid can be removed.

That foetal swallowing regulates amniotic fluid volume raises the question of what regulates foetal swallowing. Whereas foetal micturition does not contribute to foetal hydration, foetal swallowing does appear to contribute to foetal nutrition, for babies who cannot swallow amniotic fluid (e.g. in oesophageal or duodenal atresia) are smaller, maturity for maturity, than normal babies. This evidence raises the possibility that foetal hunger in fact regulates foetal swallowing. Traditionally it has been considered that hunger is a powerful and brand-new experience for the baby after birth, and that before birth an obliging mother and faithful placenta have supplied all baby's needs. But does the foetus really live in a metabolic Nirvana? We know that fluctuations in maternal blood-sugar levels and many other substances are reflected transplacentally, and the sight of babies who have been malnourished *in utero* makes it difficult to believe that the foetus has been a stranger to hunger before birth. Have we perhaps a clue to the polyhydramnios of the pregnancy in the diabetic mother or the oligohydramnios of toxaemic pregnancy?

The foetus has much greater ambitions, however, than simply the control of his immediate confines. For the duration of pregnancy he rules his mother's body, for it is the foetus who induces all the changes which make his mother a suitable host for him. From soon after conception, neither maternal pituitary nor ovaries are necessary for successful pregnancy; the newly conceived supplies all the hormones necessary for maintenance of the decidua. The effects of foetal rule are seen most strikingly in changes of maternal excretory function. It is progesterone produced by the conceptus which induces the hyperventilation and mild respiratory alkalosis of pregnancy. Since the foetus lacks external surface of his own for heat dissipation, he must use his mother's skin as a radiator. The expansion of the mother's plasma volume necessary for vasodilation and a high skin circulation is induced by oestrogen made by the foetus. Changes in maternal kidney function are the least satisfactorily explained, although in part at least the dilution of plasma protein contributes to the increased glomerular filtration and the fall in haematrocrit to the increased renal plasma flow.

These changes, induced by the foetus, in maternal excretory function appear somewhat extravagant and overdone. They are well established before the conceptus is of any significant metabolic size, and even at peak foetal excretory demand greatly exceed his needs. On the other hand, from the mother's point of view the additional renal osmotic work required is quite modest, just as the 20-25% increase in cardiac output is quite modest in comparison with effects of even mild exercise. Traditionally, pregnancy has been considered a time of metabolic stress, of increased metabolic rate for the mother's body. In fact there is little evidence to justify this view. The measured increase in oxygen consumption in pregnancy is neatly accounted for by foetal oxygen consumption, a state of affairs mirrored by the increase in maternal haemoglobin mass, which both in time and magnitude matches foetal growth and oxygen consumption. Mother's personal oxygen consumption in pregnancy is virtually unaltered; and since certain structures, notably uterus and breasts, are metabolically more active, it follows then that other tissues must be less active. This quiescence is seen in the diminished muscle tonus, the diminished peripheral thyroid activity and the relative insulin resistance of pregnancy. In summary, the foetus organizes his mother so that she shows an increased acquisition of nutrients, some increase in storage, notably fat and possibly calcium, and a general metabolic quiescence so that nutrients are deflected for foetal needs.

Another type of foetal control, and perhaps his most dazzling achievement, is seen in his command of a parabiotic situation. In an outbred population, mother and foetus are inevitably immunological foreigners, and yet for successful pregnancy they must be made to accept each other as mutual homografts. (The baby is immunologically foreign to the mother as the frequently rejected heart transplant is immunologically foreign to the recipient.) The magnitude of this homograft problem and a measure of its successful solution is the fact that it is quite possible for a woman to bear more than her own body-weight of babies during her reproductive career. Early explanations of this mutual acceptance of a homograft attempted to give the mother credit for the performance. However, the uterus is certainly not an immunologically privileged site, and the conceptus can grow in sites other than the uterus—for instance, tube or peritoneum. There is no evidence of any but the feeblest weakening of immunological reactivity in the mother during pregnancy. On the other hand, we cannot plead the old parrot cry of immaturity in the foetus. It is now known that transplantation antigens appear very early in embryonic life and that the human foetus is immunologically competent by at least as early as 12-14 weeks, so that clearly the homograft problem is a two-way affair. Nevertheless it is a component of the foetus which ensures the immunological success of pregnancy. This component is the trophoblast, which not only forms a continuous barrier between the circulations of mother and foetus but also fails to express any transplantation antigens itself. The trophoblast acts as an immunological barrier or buffer between mother and foetus so that each is completely indifferent not only to the transplantation antigens of the other but even to a specific sensitivity of the other against its own antigens.

Throughout pregnancy it is the mother, not the foetus, who is passive and dependent. Therefore it might be fitting if we could ascribe to the mother a positive role in ending pregnancy, in initiating labor, just as she had a positive role originally in allowing conception. Older theories generously gave the mother this privilege, but one by one these theories have been found inadequate. The idea that labor is an eventual immunological rejection of the foetus fails to explain labor in isogenic strains. Theories invoking cervical distension cannot explain labor with transverse lies. Uterine distension appears plausible in view of the premature labors with polyhydramnios and multiple pregnancy but founders badly on advanced extra-uterine pregnancies where "false" labor is a common presenting symptom. Despite the fact that oxytocin infusion may produce an excellent clinical labor, theories involving maternal oxytocin and oxytocinase are becoming harder to accept with an increasing body of evidence that oxytocin has little if any part in spontaneous labor. The possibility that it was the foetus who determined when labor should start was inherent in theories of hormone, especially progesterone, withdrawal, for it is the foetus who makes the hormones. However, the role of the foetus has been made even more unequivocal by the studies in foetal surgery and endocrinology of my colleague, Dr. G. C. Liggins. His work may be summarized very briefly—no foetal pituitary, no labor! Since even a hydatidifrom mole has a labor of sorts, it is evident that the natural tendency of a uterus to expel any object distending it provides a backstop, but it appears inescapable that normally the onset of labor is a unilateral declaration of independence by the foetus. This conclusion puts concepts of term and postmaturity in new perspective and suggests that in deciding on induction of labor the obstetrician should have good reason to believe that he knows better than the baby when it should be born.

These five topics I have discussed—foetal position, amniotic fluid regulation, maternal body function, the homograft situation and the initiation of labor—demonstrate the physiological dominance of the foetus in pregnancy. The list of topics could be expanded, but always the conclusion is the same—it is the foetus who is in charge of the pregnancy. This of course is not news to any woman with an unplanned pregnancy, but it is a relatively new concept in obstetric physiology and the implications are far-reaching. No longer can we accept the foetus as a placid vegetable, growing structures and maturing in blind anticipation of a life to begin at birth. Instead, from as early as we can recognize, development of structure and development of function go hand in hand.

The foetal visual machinery is bombarded by and responds to photons; it has been shown that flashing lights applied to the maternal abdominal wall produce fluctuations in the foetal heart rate. The foetal auditory system is bombarded by and responds to sound; sudden noise in a quiet room startles the foetus lined up under an image intensifier. Although we do not know if the flavor and taste of amniotic fluid vary much, the great Dutch obstetrician de Snoo demonstrated that the foetus drinks more amniotic fluid if it is sweetened with saccharin. Conversely, the foetus swallows very little if the amniotic fluid is injected with the contrast medium, Lipiodol[R]—an iodinated poppy-seed oil which tastes foul to an adult or child and which causes a neonate to grimace and cry. Because the foetus often lies with his face in close proximity to his hands and feet, it is not uncommon in obstetric radiology to detect the foetus sucking thumbs, fingers or toes, and thumb-sucking has been photographed as early as nine weeks. The foetal larynx works at its primary phylogenetic task as a respiratory tract sphincter. All the foetal endocrine glands have their task *in utero*. The foetal gonads might appear exceptions, and certainly the foetal ovary awaits an assignment, but the foetal testis is necessary for male sex differentiation. It is true of course that the task some foetal structures perform is not the same and/or not for the same purpose as they will have after birth. Particular examples are the adrenal glands, which produce large quantities of oestrogen precursor for the placenta and the liver, which for much of pregnancy is a major haemopoietic organ.

These multifarious activities of the foetus challenge the obstetric physiologist because clearly we cannot understand the physiology of pregnancy if we remain in ignorance of the physiology of the dominant partner in this relationship, the foetus. Just as nowadays we would maintain that the responsibilities of the obstetrician may start before conception, so we would maintain that the responsibilities of the pediatrician may start before birth—that no longer should pediatricians accept with a resigned fatalism what time, intra-uterine life and the obstetrician present them with at birth—or, worse still, forty-eight hours after birth. The list of foetal maladies which can be diagnosed and managed in one way or another grows steadily. Indeed in some conditions we can accurately diagnose and hopefully treat the foetus as a patient as early as seventeen weeks, a time when the reformers of abortion law would cheerfully maintain that he is not yet human. Nowadays, apart from parents, it is only lawyers, administrators and astrologists who attach any significance to the date on which we were born. From a medical standpoint we are looking after the same person before and after birth, and it may be entirely fortuitous whether he be born under Capricorn or Pisces.

There is room for practitioners of adult medicine to show a little more respect for pregnancy and its master, the foetus. We should reserve the right to consider heart disease as a complication of pregnancy rather than take the medical textbook view that pregnancy is a complication of heart disease. Recently, a surgeon friend of mine remarked how fortunate we were at National Women's Hospital in that we dealt with expendable organs. But these expendable organs are the means of creating a new human being, the greatest responsibility and the only immortality most of us will ever know. Not only the obstetrician and immunologist have something to learn from the foetus. He heals fractures much more readily than adults, shows a much more prompt and efficient haematological response to haemorrhage than adults, and his ability to heal experimental burns would be the envy of a plastic surgeon. In many respects it would be more appropriate to consider the adult as a poorly functioning foetus than the foetus as a poorly functioning adult.

In antenatal education the effect of animating the foetus is most dramatic. Fascination with foetal development and life not only takes a mother's mind off all the minor miseries of pregnancy but, most important, leads parents to accept that the baby is not a by-product of pregnancy but the end-product; in fact, he is the pregnancy, and yet the one party who did not enter into the arrangement by choice.

Not all of us will live to be old, but we were each once a foetus. We had some engaging qualities which unfortunately we lost as we grew older. We were supple and physically active. We were not prone to disc lesions and were not obese. Our most depraved vice was thumbsucking, and the worst consequence of drinking liquor was hiccups. We ruled our mothers with a serene efficiency which our fathers could not hope to emulate. Our main handicap in a world of adults was that we were small, naked, nameless and voiceless. But surely if any of us count for anything now, we counted for something before we were born.

∎3∎

THE INDICATIONS FOR INDUCED ABORTION:
A Physician's Perspective

Fred E. Mecklenburg, M.D.

Proponents of abortion-law change have put forward a variety of arguments or reasons for abortion. Some of them are supposedly based on medical facts and others espouse purely social tenets. Although few hard-core pro-abortionists really will accept anything less than wide-open abortion, or abortion-on-demand, many persist in presenting the "medical hardship" arguments. These are calculated to win over a sympathetic, concerned public to the acceptance of abortion as a simple expedient solution to grave "medical" problems. From there, the indications can be readily loosened or expanded.

Most state laws permit abortion only when necessary to save the life of the mother. Adherence to these laws has never limited a physician, acting in good faith, from delivering good medical care.

Twelve states have adopted laws based on section 230.3 of the Model Penal Code of the American Law Institute. This code would permit a physician to abort an unborn child if he felt there was a "substantial risk that continuation of the pregnancy would gravely impair the physical or mental health of the mother or that the child would be born with grave physical or mental defects, or that the pregnancy resulted from rape, incest or other felonious intercourse." (1)

The grim spectre of deaths and grave medical complications re-

Medical

sulting from poorly done "back alley abortions" is often added to the list of medical indications put forth for relaxing the laws.

To the average man in the street, each of these "medical problems" may well present what appears to be a valid reason to relax the law; but the confusing evidence supporting each of these so-called indications must be closely examined. Furthermore, the record of abuses and distortions of the law in some of the states that adopted such legislation needs to be exposed. It is of interest that many of those who worked so hard to get these laws passed only a short time ago are now the same ones who are expending energy to further relax, revise or repeal these already relaxed laws.

Only after examining the evidence can you gain a true perspective of the significance of the supposed medical indications for abortion.

PREGNANCY AS A HAZARD TO THE PHYSICAL HEALTH OF THE MOTHER

Medical science has made truly amazing advances over the last thirty years. As a result, it is now extremely rare for any pregnancy to be so hazardous to the life of the mother as to necessitate abortion. In fact, there are very few, if any, medical conditions which, in the present state of medical knowledge, comprise automatic indications for abortions (2, 3). There certainly was a time when toxemia of pregnancy, diabetes, high blood pressure, pulmonary tuberculosis, acute rheumatic fever and congenital heart defects were all considered good indications for abortion. Now, with modern methods of treatment, the risks are *rarely* so great that they require abortion (4).

In a recent review of this subject presented to the 1971 meeting of the American Medical Association, Kenneth R. Niswander, M.D., Chairman of the Department of Obstetrics and Gynecology at the University of California, Davis, and an avid pro-abortionist, stated:

... few abortions need to be performed for organic disease in a well-conducted contemporary medical practice if the traditional demand of hazard to life is followed. Cardiovascular disease, for example, has long been known to increase the risk of maternal death during pregnancy. Yet "recent research" has shown that nearly every pregnancy of a cardiac patient can be completed successfully with little risk of maternal death. ... A small number of pregnant patients with severe renal disease and decompensating renal function seem truly threatened by pregnancy. Even in this instance, however, heroic measures such as the use of a dialysis unit may see these women through severe life-threatening episodes. ... Neurologic disease is an occasional indication for abortion. The patient with multiple sclerosis, for example, sometimes is, indeed, made worse by pregnancy. The effect of pregnancy in this instance is unpredictable, however, and the condition of some patients actually improves. The effect of pregnancy on epilepsy is equally uncertain and pregnancy itself does not increase the risk of death for the pregnant women. . . . Tuberculosis accounts for nearly all of the pulmonary conditions thought to indicate therapeutic abortion. But with the advance of drug therapy, abortion rarely seems necessary for this disease. . . . Malignancy is occasionally an indication for legal abortion. There is little convincing evidence, however, that pregnancy in any way adversely affects the outcome of neoplastic disease. Even with cancers known to be endocrine dependent, such as cancer of the breast, the survival seems unaffected by pregnancy interruption. (5)

Let it be said that there are very rare and very individual circumstances which may require therapeutic abortion in order to save the life of the mother. However, when this situation arises, it poses one of the most difficult decisions in medicine and *always* represents an unpleasant endeavor. When the death of one of your patients is the *only* alternative available, then the decision truly weighs heavily. The doctor never really has to decide, however, whether to save the life of the mother or that of the baby. The choice is whether to do *everything* possible to save the life of the mother, or to risk the death of *both* your patients. Fortunately, these situations arise very infrequently.

THREAT TO THE MENTAL HEALTH OF THE MOTHER

There are no known psychiatric diseases which can be cured by abortion. In addition, there are none which can be predictably improved by abortion. Noyes and Kolbe's standard textbook of psychiatry, used in most medical schools in the United States, states that "experience does not show that pregnancy and the birth of the child influence adversely the course of schizophrenia, manic depressive illness or the majority of psychoneuroses" (6). On the other hand, those psychoses which are *initiated* by pregnancy rarely persist. Patients tend to recover after a comparatively short period of time and in some cases may recover spontaneously before full term is reached. Women who show permanent impairment of mentality following childbirth belong to the class of the potentially psychotic for whom pregnancy is merely an ancillary factor in the pathogenesis of the psychosis (7). In such women, an induced abortion cannot be curative and it may leave unresolved conflicts coupled with guilt and added depression, which may be more harmful than the continuation of the pregnancy (8). (See below, chapter 4, pp. 57-85, section on complications—psychiatric sequelae, p. 75.)

Furthermore, there is good evidence to suggest that serious mental disorders arise following abortion more often in women with real psychiatric problems. Paradoxically, the very women for whom legal abortion may seem most justifiable are also the ones for whom the risk is highest for post-abortion psychic insufficiency (9, 10).

It should be pointed out that suicide in the pregnant woman is *extremely* rare. In fact, it is about 1/6 the rate seen in nonpregnant women of the same age (11). Furthermore, as Asch pointed out, it is virtually impossible to ascertain whether or not a woman is suicidal (12). In the State of Minnesota, the Minnesota Maternal Mortality Committee reported only 14 suicides associated with pregnancy in well over 1.5 million live births between 1950 and 1966 (13). (The Minnesota Maternal Mortality Committee studies *in detail* all deaths in women which occur during pregnancy or within a period of 90 days *following* delivery.) Ten of these 14 *had delivered* before the suicide, and all 14 were married (14). In retrospect, these deaths probably could have been prevented if adequate psychiatric care had been obtained and utilized (15). Lindberg, in Sweden, while studying 304 patients whose request for therapeutic abortion had been refused, observed that not one actually committed suicide; although 62 indicated they would if their request was refused (16).

The explanation of why so few pregnant women commit suicide is not readily apparant. It may be related to the fact that women—including the unwed—receive a good deal more attention from society when pregnant than when not pregnant. Also, there may be certain physiologic and instinctive factors which manifest themselves in greater maternal protectiveness (17, 18).

Eminent psychiatrists from throughout the world agree that if *all* the evidence is taken into careful consideration, few neurotic or psychotic women are *ever* benefited by abortion and that the few that would be are extremely difficult to select (19, 20, 21, 22, 23, 24, 25).

When abortion is substituted for adequate psychiatric care—and there is ample evidence to suggest that this is already happening (26, 27)—then there is a distinct danger of minimizing established psychotherapeutic principles (28). Unfortunately, it is the distressed woman who ultimately faces the dulling impact of this minimization. She is the one who cries for help and she is also the one who is turned away.

This abuse is clearly seen in many states where the mental health clause of the American Law Institute has been adopted. In Colorado, 71.5% of all abortions are performed on psychiatric grounds (29), in Oregon, 97% (30), and in California, 90% (31). If we are to believe these figures (and there is little doubt as to their accuracy), then we must be willing to accept the fact that in these states serious mental illness is 15–20 times greater than serious physical illness in pregnant women (32), and that 25–50% of pregnant women are mentally ill. What in reality began as limited abortion in these states has now become (also in reality) abortion-on-demand, and this is primarily due to gross abuse of the mental health clause which obtains in each of these states. These abuses have led Denis Cavanaugh, M.D. (Professor of Obstetrics and Gynecology in Tasmania, Australia, and consultant to the Dean of Obstetrics and Gynecology, St. Louis University School of Medicine) to publicly reverse his position on abortion (33). These abuses, he says, have led to a decline in the quality of patient care and an increased dishonesty within the medical profession (34). Psychiatrists in these states and others have allowed themselves to be prostituted, misrepresenting social problems and personal inconvenience as "grave impairments to mental health."

POTENTIAL DEFORMITY OF THE UNBORN CHILD

Those who promote abortion have often argued that this procedure should be available to prevent the birth of malformed children. Were it allowed, it would mean the destruction of many more normal children than abnormal, as the following discussion points out. This, alone, should inhibit us from allowing "eugenic" abortion. But the failure of the abortion concept to produce certain expressed results should again be noted; countries that have had an extended experience with abortion to prevent the birth of malformed children have found that the number of children born each year with defects remains the same and that the use of abortion has failed to reduce, much less eliminate, the defective child (35, 36).

A child can be born deformed (mentally or physically) as the result of an anomaly in his genetic material (either inherited or occurring during the process of conception), an accident which occurs to the child during pregnancy and while still in the womb (e.g., German measles or drug ingestion), or because of some event which occurs during the birth process (e.g., premature delivery, anoxia or trauma). While the first two will be briefly discussed here because they directly relate to the abortion controversy, it should be noted that the leading cause of mental and motor retardation in the United States is prematurity (37). The only effect that legalizing abortion will have on this is to cause an increase in prematurity, and along with it, its inherent tragedy. (See below, chapter 4, pp. 57-85, section on complications—premature delivery, p. 72.)

Congenital Anomalies Which Are Present at the Time of Conception

There are several hundred disorders which occur as the result of a single "abnormal" gene inherited from one parent, or from a related pair of "abnormal" genes. The inheritance of such diseases follows the simple laws of genetics described by Gregor Mendel in 1866 (38). Examples of these problems include: Huntington's Chorea, osteogenesis imperfecta, Marfan's syndrome, achondroplasia, phenylketonurea, the Düchenne type of muscular dystrophy and the hemolytic anemia due to glucose-6-phosphate dehydrogenase (G6PD) deficiency.

For the most part, these diseases are *extremely rare. Never* is the risk in any one pregnancy greater than 50% for the child to be born abnormal (39). This also means that the chances are *at least* 50% for the child to be normal and that to advocate abortion when these factors arise would allow the destruction of many more normal children than abnormal. Additionally, an increasing number of these diseases can be adequately treated after the child is born (40).

There can also occur chromosomal abnormalities, which are present from the moment of conception. Down's anomaly (Mongolism) is an example. Down's anomaly occurs in 1 in 600-700 live births (41), but it is more common in the child born of women over 35 years of age. Ninety-four percent of Down's anomaly is of the "standard" type with a recurrence rate of less than 1%; only 2-3% of cases of Down's anomaly have a tendency to recur, and even in these cases the risk of recurrence is not greater than 20%. The standard type shows little tendency to recur because it is probably the result of an isolated accident in the development of a particular ovum and does not reflect a generalized chromosomal or other genetic defect in the parents.

Amniocentesis is a new diagnostic tool which is now being advocated by many to make intra-uterine diagnoses. In this way, the selective destruction of unborn children could be calculated. In speaking before a legislative subcommittee on abortion reform in the Minnesota State Legislature, March 1971, Hymie Gordon, M.D., chief geneticist at the Mayo Clinic, had this to say about amniocentesis:

There have recently been developed methods of antenatal diagnosis in which a more precise evaluation of a risk situation is possible. This is the method of amniocentesis. A needle is inserted into the pregnant uterus; some fluid is aspirated and the cells in that fluid are studied. A very small number of extremely rare conditions, and I can't emphasize how *extremely rare* these conditions are, can now be detected with greater or lesser degrees of precision by a chemical analysis of this fluid or some of these cells. But let me hasten to point out that such examination of the cells may take up to a month to complete; this means that by the time the diagnosis is available, the pregnancy is too far advanced to allow an abortion without a major operation. And even more so, let me emphasize to you that these are all experimental techniques of diagnosis.

No one anywhere in the world has had any consistent experience on which he can make any claim to reliability. And more and more, I am hearing both privately amongst geneticists and in published reports of false diagnoses. I think you have heard testimony given before this committee on a previous occasion about the diagnosis of this dreadful Tay-Sachs disease by amniocentesis. At the last meeting of the American Society of Human Genetics, researchers reported a case in which they suspected Tay-Sachs might be present. Amniocentesis was done. The fluid was examined and found to show that the baby had Tay-Sachs disease. That pregnancy was terminated, and the baby was examined and found to be perfectly normal. A little while ago in New York a woman was told as a result of amniocentesis that her baby had a mucopolysaccharidosis, a dreadful disease which has the unfortunate popular name of "Gargoylism," so you can imagine what it's like. Naturally, the woman was frightened almost to death. However, she vacillated and eventually it was too late to perform an abortion. But the story has a happy ending because she gave birth to a perfectly normal child.

Now there is another use of amniocentesis which involves examining the chromosomes. This is a procedure which is recommended for the antenatal diagnosis of Down's anomaly, which is popularly known as Mongolism. This seems very easy because all one has to do is count the number of chromosomes in the cell, and if there is one too many, the baby is likely to have Down's anomaly. But it is nothing nearly as easy as that, because again reports are now coming out in the medical literature (one recently appeared in the Oct. 10, 1970, *Lancet*) in which a pregnancy was terminated because of the finding of extra chromosomes in the cells; but in actual fact, the baby that was killed in this case turned out to be perfectly normally formed.

Mistakes of this sort have been reported, and are being spoken about, with increasing frequency. I would emphasize that this is an experimental method which may have great potential for antenatal treatment of genetic defects; but at the moment it is only experimental. Remember, too, that it involves inserting a needle into the uterus, and this is a uterus in the very early stage of pregnancy when it is just a delicate globule distended up like a balloon. Remember that most of the baby at this time consists of the brain. One wonders how often the so-called amniotic fluid is in fact being taken from the baby's cerebrospinal fluid. One wonders because one doesn't know just how often is a normal fetus damaged or destroyed by the procedure. One doesn't know. There is no information.

One wonders how often is that little uterus, a rather fragile structure in this state, torn and irretrievably harmed by this procedure. One doesn't know. There is no information. All I can say about this procedure is that it is at the moment highly suspicious and highly experimental and should by no means enter into any consideration at the moment of such fundamental decisions such as changing the abortion law. (42)

Following his testimony, Dr. Gordon was asked the following question by the chairman of the subcommittee: "Are there any fellow colleagues within your profession who disagree with you?" Dr. Gordon replied:

I should think that a great many do. A great many of my colleagues in genetics, of course, are engaged in investigating amniocentesis. Many of them, I think, have been far too easily persuaded of its efficacy and accuracy. I am sorry to say that they are going to be rudely shaken as their experience increases. This is not the first time that the geneticists have made very unfortunate decisions regarding the sanctity of human life. I need only remind you of the criminal use of genetic theory in Germany and other places during the 1930's. I hope that the geneticists are not going to make the same mistake in the 1970's. (43)

It has been, of course, frequently pointed out that mentally and physically retarded citizens will never enjoy the delights of intellectual or physical achievement known to the normal person. This is true. However, by the same token, the normal person can never enjoy the intellectual excellence of the genius or the physical prowess of the athlete. And yet, this is hardly sufficient cause for considering the elimination of all but the genius and the athlete.

Harmful Effects to the Child During Pregnancy

The child can be damaged in many ways during pregnancy. Various infections (German measles, syphilis, etc.), maternal illnesses (diabetes, high blood pressure, etc.), the ingestion of drugs (thalidomide), cigarette smoking and radiation, can all affect the child adversely. Even such things as overeating by the mother and selection of improper diet can be harmful to her unborn child. This discussion will limit itself to a review of the effects of drugs (especially LSD) and German measles (rubella) upon the unborn, since it is here that a vast amount of misinformation has been propagated.

1. THE INGESTION OF DRUGS DURING PREGNANCY.

The tragic "epidemic" incidence of children born with defective limbs because the tranquilizer thalidomide was used during pregnancy has received widespread attention. This experience has led to a more cautious attitude in the use of drugs during pregnancy and to a reappraisal of principles regulating the approval of new drugs by the Food and Drug Administration (44). Because of these new restrictions, it is unlikely that a drug with such a teratogenic capability as thalidomide could ever pass the new progeny requirements (45).

Pursuant to the disaster of the thalidomide tragedy, Dr. Gustav Hauberg of the Anna Stift Rehabilitation School in Hanover, Germany, put the noblest medical traditions to practice in his work with the thalidomide babies. Following his lead, a team of orthopedists, social workers, and teachers have been engaged in developing the capabilities of the thalidomide-damaged children so that, despite their heavy handicaps, they will still value life. Mental and psychological development has been normal, in most cases, and higher education potential is attributed to most (46).

Now, with the lonely denizens of the youth subculture using more and more LSD, this becomes a new consideration. It, too, has been shrouded in a less than distinct appraisal. Many have feared that LSD would cause birth defects in the offspring of users.

An excellent review of LSD's teratogenic effects was published in *Science,* April 30, 1971. The conclusions of this study were based upon the author's own work and an examination of the medical literature—68 studies and case reports published in the past 4-5 years. The investigation concluded that, while there is some increased risk of spontaneous abortion, there is no evidence that *pure* LSD is a cause of birth defects in man (47).

2. GERMAN MEASLES.

In 1941, Gregg reported that if a woman contracted German measles in the first four months of pregnancy, there was a 75% incidence of fetal defect (48). This marked the beginning of the discussion on the "congenital rubella syndrome." Much new knowledge about this syndrome has since been accumulated. A vaccine has been developed to prevent the disease. Yet, Gregg's original 75% incidence, while totally false, continues to reach the lay public only to frighten thousands of women unnecessarily.

Gregg's original study was *retrospective*. This and other uncritical *retrospective* studies of selected cases have given the impression that maternal rubella, when contracted by the mother in early pregnancy, leads to deformity in the majority of infants (49). The true incidence of defects resulting from German measles can *only* be determined by the use of *prospective* studies.

A. Bradford Hill, world-renowned statistician, points out the basic difference between *retrospective* and *prospective* study as follows:

To determine the probability that an illness of the mother during pregnancy will give rise to a congenital malformation in the infant, essentially demands a prospective method of inquiry. In other words, the attack of illness in the pregnant woman must first be observed and medically diagnosed, and the condition of the child born to her must subsequently be noted. The retrospective approach, i.e., noting first the congenital deformity in the new-born child and then obtaining the history of the mother during pregnancy, inevitably omits the normal children whose mothers were affected, and is thus bound to give a highly exaggerated picture of the risks involved. The prospective inquiry is, however, extremely difficult to carry out on an adequate scale. The attack rates from infectious diseases are relatively low in adult life and very large numbers of women must be observed. It is specially important, too, that the occurrence of disease in the mother be recognized and recorded at a time when she may not even know that she is pregnant, i.e., during the first month of pregnancy. (50)

Several excellent prospective studies have been carried out to determine the correct incidence of fetal defect following German measles in the mother. Warkany and Kalter reviewed 15 such studies of 421 live-born children of women who contracted rubella during the first trimester of pregnancy. Of these, congenital malformations were found in 71, or 16.9%. The incidence and degree of malformation varied according to the time of maternal infection. Rubella contracted during the first four weeks of pregnancy resulted in 23.4% defective live-born children, in the second month, the incidence was 21.3% and in the third month, 10.4%. Rubella contracted after the twelfth week of pregnancy did not result in an incidence of congenital malformations greater than that experienced by a control group (51).

A prospective study of the effects of rubella was done by Dr. David Pitts, who found the incidence of first trimester congenital anomaly due to maternal rubella to be 21.4% (52).

Perhaps the most comprehensive survey available eventuated from the 1964 rubella epidemic. John L. Sever, M.D., Ph. D., and his associates, studied this epidemic under the auspices of the National

Institutes of Health. Of the 6,161 women in that study, 54 contracted rubella in the first trimester of pregnancy (serologic methods—by far the most accurate means of detecting rubella—were used to confirm diagnosis). Of this number, 8 had induced abortions and 46 continued to term and delivery. Of these 46, 5, or approximately 11%, gave birth to babies with congenital anomalies (53).

In order for a child to even be put at risk by rubella, the mother must be susceptible to the infection herself. Since 80-90% of women are immune to rubella because of infection in early childhood, and thus will never contract the disease (54), this eliminates the overwhelming majority of women from even being concerned with the problem. Now, with the advent of rubella susceptibility testing and the subsequent vaccination of young girls lacking immunity, the elimination of rubella as a factor in birth defects is just around the corner.

To make any discussion of rubella complete, one must focus upon what actually happens to the child who is damaged by the rubella virus. When this child is considered, along with the *80-90% normal children* of mothers who contract rubella in the first trimester, it becomes perfectly self-evident that abortion is not indicated in rubella infection.

Rendle-Short reported that of those children who are affected: (1) 50% have partial to complete hearing loss, but *most* of these defects can be corrected or improved by a hearing aid; (2) just under 50% have some form of congenital heart defect—most common of which is patent ductus arteriosis (P.D.A.)—and all are potentially curable by modern surgical techniques (especially P.D.A.); (3) 30% have cataracts, which are often unilateral and surgically correctable, with most affected children having fair vision; (4) mental retardation, while it is often severe when present, is only present in 1.5% (not much greater than the overall incidence of 1% within a given community) (55).

Spontaneous abortion and stillbirth incidence for the rubella-affected mother are increased, while many of the most severely affected children will die within the first months after birth. Rendle-Short states emphatically that "when presented with the true situation, most parents will not press for termination of pregnancy" (56).

Finally, we can go back and look at Gregg's original patients. In 1967, Gregg's students reported a 25-year follow-up study of 50 of these patients. Forty-eight were deaf, 26 had eye defects, 11 had congenital heart anomalies and 5 were mentally subnormal (one severely so). In spite of this dismal picture, 46 of the patients were gainfully employed and only the one with severe mental subnormality was regarded as unemployable. Several had received a higher education. Eleven had already married and 7 had become parents. The authors commented that "a striking feature was the good socio-economic adjustment made by most patients" (57).

If we are to consider abortion for any congenital malformation, we must recognize that it can in *no way* be called therapeutic for the unborn child. While it may be comforting to feel that abortion is being performed for the sake of the child, honesty requires us to admit that it is performed for the convenience of adults. Who is to judge what degree of disability makes life not worth living? Does the fact that physically handicapped people have a lower suicide rate than we supposedly normal people suggest an answer? Surely life with handicaps must be judged preferable to extermination!

RAPE

The question of rape always stirs the emotions whenever it is introduced into the abortion debate. Unfortunately, the emotional impact of rape often clouds the real issues and the real facts.

The proponents of abortion suggest that abortion is necessary because many women are criminally attacked. What is seldom pointed out is just how infrequently the victim of such an attack might conceive. Is pregnancy the only serious result with which we must concern ourselves?

Pregnancy resulting from rape *is* extremely rare. In Buffalo, New York, there hasn't been a pregnancy from confirmed rape in over 30 years (58), in Chicago, over 9 years (59), and in St. Paul, over 10 years (60). A report out of Washington, D.C., claims only one pregnancy in over 300 rape victims (61).

What of all those who haven't become pregnant? Are they, for some reason, without psychological trauma? In a study of 14 city and county health departments, only 4 of the departments reported an organized effort by the police department to take the victim to a hospital or physician for examination and emergency treatment. *None* of the respondents reported having a formal program for nursing follow-up, or indicated that any specific community efforts were being made to provide medical and psychiatric assistance beyond the emergency service for women and girls (62). Couldn't it just be possible that by crying abortion for the victims of rape, we might literally be ignoring the real problems of rape victims?

The probability of pregnancy resulting from rape is considerably lower than what would be expected from a single unprotected act of coitus (which is 2-4%, as determined by Tietze) (63). There are good reasons for this. First of all, a completed act of intercourse itself does not occur in 100% of forcible rape cases (89% in the Washington, D.C., series). Secondly, it is improbable with a normal 28-day menstrual cycle, that the attack will occur on the 1-2 days of the month in which the woman would be fertile. Third, medical research indicates that a woman exposed to emotional trauma (such as rape) will not ovulate even if she is "scheduled" to. In Germany, during World War II, the Nazis tested this hypothesis by selecting women who were about to ovulate and sending them to the gas chambers, only to bring them back after their realistic mock-killing, to see what effects this had on their ovulatory patterns. An extremely high percentage of these women did not ovulate (64). Finally, there is good evidence that men who commit this crime are frequently not fertile because of other aberrant sexual behavior, such as frequent masturbation, which makes the likelihood of impregnating significantly less.

A major problem is one of definition—just when does an act of intercourse become rape? How does one define or prove rape when the allegation is made many weeks or months later? In all too many cases, the rape victim is in fact not a victim at all, but very much a rational participant. Josephine Barnes, M.D., eminent British gynecologist, writing on this, says: "It is easy for a woman to allege that she has been raped, and frequently the story of the circumstance is fabricated by a 'victim' in order to account for facts which would otherwise be hard to explain" (65).

Let us finally look at what happens when rape is allowed to become an indication for abortion. In the State of Colorado, this provision was instituted on April 25, 1967. The table indicates the

YEAR	RAPE ABORTIONS	TOTAL ABORTIONS
1967 (April 25–December 31)	12	140
1968	60	497
1969	78	946
1970	71	2091
1971 (January-November)	69	3341
TOTALS	290 (4.1%)	7015

number of abortions for rape which were performed for each year since then (66).

During this period of time, *no rapist was even charged with his crime, much less convicted of such* (67). This casts some real doubt on the reality of the alleged rapes.

There are indeed some very real questions which need to be asked regarding abortion consequent of rape. Is any thought really ever given to the mother? Is the *real* harm not already done? Does abortion, in robbing the unborn child of life, heal or compound the mother's wounds (this in light of the lack of any evidence to suggest that psychological trauma would be prevented, unaffected or intensified by compounding the shame of rape with the possible guilt of abortion)? Is the principal purpose of the law to reduce the number of sex crimes or merely to eliminate the lives of the innocent victims?

INCEST

Incest, too, poses a difficult emotional problem, in debate. Actually, most cases go unrecognized because the victim or her mother will shrink from the social and/or financial ruin involved in accusing a father, brother or other male relative of such a heinous act. In 1966, there were only twelve indictments entered for incest in Chicago's Cook County. Only a fraction of these involved pregnancies to which therapeutic abortion might have related, under any law (68).

Furthermore, the incestuous relationship requires psychiatric care. With proper management, the outcome of incest may not always be as traumatic as was previously believed inevitable. Incest is basically a family pathology. Treating it as such, there is evidence that there may be gain for all concerned when the family cooperates in treatment (69). Aborting an innocent unborn child will neither correct the pathology nor mend the hurts. The problem exists with or without pregnancy, with or without abortion.

LEGAL ABORTION AS A DETERRENT TO CRIMINAL ABORTION

It is widely believed that legalizing abortion will eliminate the problems of criminal abortion. This, however, is verifiably untrue (70). (Accumulated data is worldwide, including references from The German Democratic Republic, Japan, Great Britain, Yugoslavia, Hungary, Czechoslovakia, Bulgaria, Poland, USSR and Colorado.)

Surprisingly, illegal abortions increased in East Germany between

1948 and 1950, a period in which the abortion laws were relaxed to allow abortion on social as well as medical grounds. At the end of 1950, however, the abortion laws were again severely restricted, whereupon the trend of illegal abortions declined (71).

In Japan, in 1955, when abortions were available on request and as many as 1,170,141 "legal" abortions were performed, the Japanese Minister of Health estimated that from 300,000 to 400,000 criminal abortions were performed as well (72).

Even Christopher Tietze, the excellent statistician of the Bio-Medical Division of The Population Council, and an outspoken pro-abortionist, admits that "criminal abortion and/or self-abortion have not disappeared, even in Hungary, where abortion has been available on request for more than a decade." (73)

The estimation of criminal abortion rates is, of course, very difficult because the abortionists do not publish their statistics and their victims seldom admit to the procedure. However, in 1951, Ingleman-Sundberg (74) (and later in a continuation of that study, in 1968, Huldt [75]) was able to secure reliable data from Stockholm, where all pregnancies are registered. Of those which end in abortion, a known number are legal abortions (the nonlegal abortions then will include spontaneous and criminal abortions combined). There is no reason to expect any significant changes in the annual spontaneous abortion rate. Therefore, any variation in the nonlegal abortion rate is due to changes in the criminal abortion rate. There is, in fact, no correlation between the legal abortion rate and the spontaneous and criminal abortion rate. Huldt concluded that "apparently the abortion law in its present form has not reduced criminal abortion" (76).

We should hopefully be able to learn from the experience of others who have traveled this path before us, fully aware that their attempts have resulted in unqualified failure. We should then approach the problem of criminal abortion from a realistic new perspective, one which is based in the education of the public on the hazards of abortion and the alternatives which are available within the community. This, alone, is the solution which does not jeopardize the children of this generation.

CONCLUSION

The American Law Institute proposal for the relaxation of abortion laws opened the door for abortion enthusiasts. The so-called medical hardship cases which were outlined in their Model Penal

Code were accepted as real needs by well-intentioned legislators in twelve states. Since then, experience has shown that the vast majority of abortions in these states are for indications other than those envisioned by the authors of the laws. No one is satisfied with them. Pro-abortionists clamor for repeal of these as well as other abortion laws, to allow for abortions of convenience without the necessity of trumped-up psychiatric indications. In every state where the law has been weakened by adoption of the American Law Institute proposal, there have been efforts to introduce further relaxation or outright repeal. But, there is no debate. We must either have respect for life on all levels or we open the way for disrespect of life on every level.

The abortion laws of a large majority of states in the union allow abortion only to save the life of the mother. This position upholds and fosters the deep respect for human life which has characterized our pluralistic society. It also permits the doctor to provide the best possible medical care for *both* his patients—mother *and* child.

When we allow loopholes to appear in the law which permit abortion for convenience under the guise of "medical indications" and "good medical care," we are simply allowing the abortion mentality to gain a foothold. The sanctity of human life is thereby threatened just as really, if somewhat more subtly, as by the total repeal of abortion laws.

BIBLIOGRAPHY

1. American Law Institute, *Model Penal Code,* Proposed Official Draft, Section 230. Philadelphia, American Law Institute, 1962. Pp. 187-193.
2. British Medical Association Committee on Therapeutic Abortion. Indications for Termination of Pregnancy. *Brit. Med. J.,* 1:171, 1968.
3. Decker, D. G. Medical Indications for Therapeutic Abortion: An Obstetrician's View. *Minn. Med.,* 50:29, 1967.
4. Ibid.
5. Niswander, K. R. Indications and Contraindications. Highlight from 1971 A.M.A. Meeting. In: Abortion—A Legal Fact. *Audio Digest: Obstetrics and Gynecology,* Vol. 18, Aug. 3, 1971.
6. Noyes, A., and Kolbe, L. *Modern Clinical Psychiatry,* 7th ed. Philadelphia, W. B. Saunders Co., 1968.
7. Anderson, E. W. The Psychiatric Indications for Termination of Pregnancy. *Proc. Roy. Soc. Med.,* 50:321, 1957.
8. See the following:
    ____Arbuse, D. I., et al. Neuropsychiatric Indications for Therapeutic Abortion. *Amer. Pract. Dig. Treatment,* 1:1069, 1950.

_____Bartemeier, L. H. In Aarons, Z. A. Therapeutic Abortion and the Psychiatrist. *Amer. J. Psychiatry*, 124:745, 1967.

_____Fultz, G. S. Therapeutic Abortions. *South. Med. J.*, 1954.

_____Harrington, J. A. Psychiatric Indications for the Termination of Pregnancy. *Practitioner*, 185:654, 1960.

_____Jannsen, B. Mental Disorders After Abortion. *Acta. Psychiat. Scand.*, 41:87, 1965.

9. Ekblad, M. Induced Abortion on Psychiatric Grounds. A Follow-Up Study of 479 Women. *Acta. Psychiat. Neurol. Scand.*, Suppl. 99:238, 1955.

10. Spontaneous and Induced Abortion, report of a scientific group. *World Health Organization Technical Report Series*, No. 461, p. 40, 1970.

11. Rosenberg, A. J., et al. Suicide, Psychiatrists and Therapeutic Abortion. *Calif. Med.*, 102:407, 1965.

12. Asch, S. S. "Mental and Emotional Problems," in *Medical, Surgical, and Gynecological Complications of Pregnancy*, A. F. Guttmacher and J. J. Rovinsky (eds.). Baltimore, The Williams and Wilkins Co., 1960, p. 375.

13. Barno, A. The Minnesota Mortality Study. *Am. J. Obstet. Gynec.*, Jan. 15, 1968.

14. Ibid.

15. Bernstein, I. C. Psychiatric Indications for Therapeutic Abortion. *Minn. Med.*, 50:51, 1967.

16. Lindberg, B. *Svenska Läk-Tidn*, 45:1381, 1948.

17. Rosenberg, op. cit.

18. Bernstein, op. cit.

19. Anderson, op. cit.

20. Arbuse, et al., op. cit.

21. Bartemeier, op. cit.

22. Fultz, op. cit.

23. Jannsen, op. cit.

24. Bernstein, op. cit.

25. See the following;

_____Curran, D. Psychiatric Indications for Termination of Pregnancy. *New Zealand Med. J.*, 60:467, 1961.

_____Deghwitz, R. The Influence of Pregnancy on Neurological and Psychiatric Diseases. *Fortsch. Neurol. Psych.*, 32:105, 1964.

_____Hauschild, T. B. The Role of the Psychiatrist in Therapeutic Abortion. *Med. Bull. U.S. Army Eur.*, 20:322, 1963.

_____Johnson, J. Termination of Pregnancy on Psychiatric Grounds. *Med. Gynaec. Sociol.*, 2:2, 1966.

_____Joyston-Bechal, M. P. The Problem of Pregnancy Termination on Psychiatric Grounds. *J. Coll. Gen. Pract.*, 12:304, 1966.

26. Droegemueller, W., et al. The First Year of Experience in Colorado with the New Abortion Law. *Am. J. Obstet. Gynec.*, 103:694-698, 1969.

27. Overstreet, E. W. Therapeutic Abortion: Current Problems and Trends. *Audio Digest: Ob.-Gyn.,* Vol. 16, No. 23, Dec. 2, 1969.
28. Hauschild, T. B., op. cit.
29. Droegemueller, op. cit.
30. Therapeutic Abortions in Oregon—January-December, 1970, a report issued by the Oregon State Board of Health.
31. Overstreet, op. cit.
32. Cavanagh, D. Legalized Abortion: The Conscience Clause and Coercion. *Hospital Progress,* 1971.
33. Ibid.
34. Cavanagh, D. Reforming the Abortion Laws: A Doctor Looks at the Case. *America,* pp. 406-411, Apr. 18, 1970.
35. The Swedish Register of Congenital Malformations 1964-1969. Series: Patient Statistics, No. 7. Published by the Swedish Board of Health and Welfare. S 105 30. Stockholm. Printed in Sweden by Göteborges Offset-tryckeri AB, Surte 1971. P. 6.
36. Källén, Bengt: Lunds Universitet Embryologiska Institutionen. Biskops-gatan 7, 223 62 Lund, Sweden: Personal Communication.
37. Schaeffer, A. J. *Diseases of the Newborn,* 2d ed., p. 29. Philadelphia, W. B. Saunders Co., 1966.
38. Gordon, H. Genetical, Social, and Medical Aspects of Abortion. *S. A. Med. J.,* p. 721, July 20, 1968.
39. Ibid.
40. Ibid.
41. Ibid.
42. Gordon, H. Genetic Aspects of Abortion. Testimony given before a House subcommittee hearing on abortion reform. Minnesota State Legislation, March 1971. Written copy available from MCCL, 4803 Nicollett Ave., Minneapolis, Minnesota 55409.
43. Ibid.
44. Moloshok, R. E. Fetal Considerations for Therapeutic Abortion and Sterilization. *Clinical Obstet. Gynec.,* 7:82-99, 1964.
45. Diamond, E. F. In ISMS Symposium on Medical Implications of the Current Abortion Law in Illinois. *Ill. Med. J.,* pp. 677-680, May 1967.
46. Ibid.
47. Dishotsky, N. I., Loughman, W. D., Mogar, R. E., and Lipscomb, W. R. LSD and Genetic Damage. *Science,* 172:431-440, April 30, 1971.
48. Gregg, N. M. (1941). *Trans. Ophthal. Soc. Aust.,* 3,35.
49. Gordon, op. cit.
50. Hill, A. Bradford, et al. Virus Diseases in Pregnancy and Congenital Defects. *British Journal Preventive Society of Medicine,* 1958, Vol. 12, p. 1.
51. Warkany, J., and Kalter, H. Congenital Malformations. *New England J. Med.,* 265:993-1046, 1961.

52. Pitt, D. Results of Rubella in Pregnancy. *The Medical Journal of Australia,* Vol. 2, No. 16, pp. 647-651, Oct. 16, 1965.
53. Sever, J. L. Rubella Epidemic, 1964: Effect on 6000 Pregnancies. *American J. Dis. Child.,* 110:395-407, Oct. 1965.
54. Banatrala, J. E. Laboratory Investigations in the Assessment of Rubella During Pregnancy. *Brit. Med. J.,* 1:561, 1968.
55. Rendle-Short, J. Maternal Rubella: The Practical Management of a Case. *Lancet,* 2:373, 1964.
56. Ibid.
57. Meuser, M. A., Dods, L., and Harley, J. D. A Twenty-Five-Year Follow-Up of Congenital Rubella. *Lancet,* 1347, Dec. 23, 1967.
58. Sims, B. M. A District Attorney Looks at Abortion. *Child and Family,* 8:176-180, Spring 1969.
59. Diamond, op. cit.
60. Bailey, C. Sex—Homicide Division of the St. Paul Police Department: Personal Communication.
61. Hayman, C. R., Stewart, W. F., Lewis, F. R., and Grant, M. Sexual Assault on Women and Children in the District of Columbia. *Public Health Reports,* pp. 1021-1028, Dec. 1968.
62. Hayman, C. R., Lewis, F. R., Stewart, W. F., and Grant M. A Public Health Program for Sexually Assaulted Females. *Public Health Reports,* 82:497-504, June 1967.
63. Tietze, C. Probability of Pregnancy Resulting from a Single Unprotected Coitus. *Fertility and Sterility,* 11:485-488, 1960.
64. Hellegers, A., U.S.C.C. Abortion Conference, Washington, D.C., October 1967.
65. Barnes, J. Rape and Other Sexual Offenses. *Brit. Med. J.,* 2:293-295, 1967.
66. Archibald, J. E., Counsellor and Attorney-at-law, Denver, Colorado: Personal Communication.
67. Ibid.
68. Diamond, op. cit.
69. Kennedy, M. Cormier, B. M. Father-Daughter Incest—Treatment of the Family. *Laval Medical,* 40:946-950, Nov. 1969.
70. See the following:
   _____Abortion Act (1967). The Findings of an Inquiry into the First Year's Working of the Act: Conducted by the Royal College of Obstetricians and Gynaecologists. *Brit. Med. J.,* 2:529-535, 1970.
   _____Droegemueller, W., et al., op. cit.
   _____Hirschler, I. The Situation of Abortion in Hungary. Mehlan, K.-H., editor. *Internationale Abortsituation, Abortkampfung, Autikonzeption.* Leipzig, George Thieme, 1961.
   _____Mehlan, K.-H. Abortion Statistics and Birth Frequency in the German Democratic Republic. *Deutsch. Gesendh.,* 10:1648, 1955.
   _____Mehlan, K.-H. The Effects of Legalization of Abortion on the

Health of Mothers in Eastern Europe. *Proceedings of the Seventh Conference of the IPPF,* Singapore, 1963. New York, Excerpta Medica Foundation, 1964.

_____Mehlan, K.-H. Reducing Abortion Rate and Increasing Fertility by Social Policy in the German Democratic Republic. *Proceedings of the World Population Conference,* 1965.

_____Muller-Dietz, H. Abortion in the Soviet Union and in the East German States. *Rev. Soviet. Med. Sci.,* 1964.

_____Novak, F. Effects of Legal Abortion on the Health of Mothers in Yugoslavia. *Proceedings of Seventh Conference of the IPPF.* Singapore, 1963. New York, Excerpta Medica Foundation, 1964.

_____Svendi, B., et al. Maternal Death in Relation to Obstetric Cases of 10 Years in Bekes County. *Nepegeszsegugy,* 45:24, 1964.

_____Tietze, C. Abortion Laws and Abortion Practices in Europe. From *Excerpta Medica International Congress Series, No. 207.* Advances in Planned Parenthood—V. *Proceedings of the Seventh Annual Meeting of the AAPPP,* San Francisco, 1969.

_____Vojta, M. Some Questions of Unwanted Pregnancy and Legal Abortion As a Solution at the Present Day. *Rev. Czech. Med.,* 5:207, 1959.

71. Frederiksen, H., and Brackett, J. W. Demographic Effects of Abortion. *Public Health Reports,* 83:999–1010, Dec. 1968.

72. *Times Weekly Review,* May 31, 1962.

73. Tietze, op. cit.

74. Ingleman-Sundberg, A. (1951). *Svenska Läk-Tidn,* 48, 1017.

75. Huldt, L. Outcome of Pregnancy When Legal Abortion Is Readily Available. *Lancet,* pp. 467–468, Mar. 2, 1968.

76. Ibid.

▪4▪

THE MEDICAL HAZARDS OF LEGALLY INDUCED ABORTION

Thomas W. Hilgers, M.D.

In the summer of 1971, the American College of Obstetricians and Gynecologists (ACOG), together with the American Medical Women's Association, the American Psychiatric Association, the New York Academy of Medicine and 181 medical school deans, professors and individual physicians—most of whom were men of position and power—filed their support for abortion-on-demand in an *amicus curiae* (friend of the court) brief which was presented to the United States Supreme Court as an intervention in the constitutionality hearing of the Georgia abortion statute (*Doe* v. *Bolton*) (1). For the American College of Obstetricians and Gynecologists, this action represented a decision without sanction of the members of the College or even of their Board of Directors.

The brief itself relied heavily in its argumentation on the safety of legally induced abortion. After focusing on Hungarian abortion mortality rates (reportedly 1.2/100,000) and comparing them to the maternal mortality rates in the United States (28.0/100,000), it claimed that "the medical procedure of induced abortion . . . is potentially 23.3 (28.0/1.2) times as safe as the process of going through ordinary childbirth" (2). There was no indication of various complications which can occur.

Similar statements of safety have been widely distributed in the newspapers and lay periodicals. However, this action by powerful groups of physicians marked the first time that the medical profession had attempted to influence the highest court in our land, while conspicuously suppressing any consideration of the overwhelming medical evidence against such a claim. Although the security-seeking majority fervently wish to believe in the ongoing integrity of the medical profession, the reality of this action was one which argues against such blind faith: the claim of safety was obviously fabricated in an attempt to sell abortion to the court and, consequently, to the American people.

In order to observe this fabrication from a vantaged perspective, the complications of legally induced abortion will be presented herein, utilizing the vast body of the world's medical literature on the subject, in an attempt to arrive at a comprehensive total analysis.

In beginning such a discussion, it must first be pointed out that narrowing one's focus to reflect upon merely the legal abortion mortality figures obtained from selected countries around the world, projects the risks of legal abortion through tunnel vision. The complete medical picture *cannot* be appreciated without a look at the early and the late physical and psychological complications of abortion. Indeed, these are the complications which affect the greater number of people and result in what a World Health Organization scientific group said was "a great amount of human suffering"(3).

PROFESSIONAL ORGANIZATIONS SPEAK ON MEDICAL HAZARDS

The Executive Board of the American College of Obstetricians and Gynecologists (ACOG) and a majority of its fellows approved the following official statement in May 1968. This statement, which is directly contrary to their 1971 action, gives sharp insight into the political-persuasive nature of their most recent court involvement:

It is emphasized that the inherent risk of such an abortion is not fully appreciated both by many in the profession and certainly not by the public. ... The public should realize that in countries or societies that permit abortion on demand, many, if not the majority, are performed in physicians' offices. Under these circumstances it is reasonable to conclude that *the mortality from this operation may exceed the maternal mortality of the United States* [emphasis supplied] and Canada while *the incidence of serious complications is substantial* [emphasis supplied].(4)

The minority report was prepared by Sprague H. Gardiner, M.D. (current President-elect of the ACOG), Bernard J. Pisani, M.D.

(Chairman), and Richard F. Mattingly, M.D., and was issued in May 1969. It stated:

The inherent risks of a therapeutic abortion are serious and may be life-threatening; this fact should be fully appreciated by both the medical profession and the public. In nations where abortion may be obtained on demand, *a considerable morbidity and mortality have been reported.* [emphasis supplied] (5)

On March 26, 1966, the Council of the Royal College of Obstetricians and Gynaecologists in Great Britain unanimously approved the following statement which supports the ACOG statement:

Those without specialists' knowledge, and these include members of the medical profession, are influenced in adopting what they regard as a humanitarian attitude to the induction of abortion by a failure to appreciate what is involved. They tend to regard induction of abortion as a trivial operation, free from risk. In fact, even to the expert working in the best conditions, the removal of an early pregnancy after dilating the cervix can be difficult, and is not infrequently accompanied by serious complications. This is particularly true in the case of the woman pregnant for the first time. For women who have a serious medical indication for termination of pregnancy, induction of abortion is extremely hazardous and its risks need to be weighed carefully against those involved in leaving the pregnancy undisturbed. *Even for the relatively healthy woman, however, the dangers are considerable.* [emphasis supplied] (6)

In 1970, the Royal College of Obstetricians and Gynaecologists re-emphasized:

The risks of any of the currently available methods of terminating pregnancy, which involve general anesthesia, have always been recognized by gynaecologists but have been dismissed by others as non-existent and imaginary [ed. note: and not all gynecologists]. The long-term hazards to physical well-being require follow-up studies which so far have not been undertaken in this country. Nevertheless, *reports from other countries where abortion on demand has been the rule for several years show that late physical ill-effects are not uncommon.* [emphasis supplied] (7).

On March 26, 1970, the Medical Society of the State of New York issued a set of "abortion guidelines" in which they wrote:

The Medical Society of the State of New York would like to caution all physicians that an abortion performed after the twelfth week of gestation is fraught with tremendous danger [emphasis theirs]. (8)

In the Consultants Report on Abortion from the survey done by the Royal College of Obstetricians and Gynaecologists in Great Britain, it was stated:

Eight maternal deaths occurred in relation to 27,331 terminations of pregnancy during the year 1968-69. This gives a mortality rate of 0.3 per thousand (30/100,000), which is higher than the maternal mortality rate (including abortions, criminal or otherwise) for all the pregnancies in England and Wales at the comparable time. A statement issued by the Secretary of State of Parliament on 4 February 1970, reveals a similar state of affairs in respect to about 54,000 induced abortions notified from all sources during 1969; among these there were 15 maternal deaths. (9)

NEW YORK CITY ABORTION DATA UNRELIABLE

On June 29, 1971, Mr. Gordon Chase, the administrator of the Health Services Administration for the City of New York (and a strong advocate of abortion), announced that "we have a remarkable record of safety" when New York's mortality rate is compared to those in countries like Great Britain and Scandinavia (10). He announced this rate to be 5.3 deaths/100,000 abortions (11). This mortality rate, quite honestly, cannot be taken seriously.

It should first be pointed out that 55.5% of all the 150,629 abortions legally performed in New York City between July 1, 1970, and May 31, 1971, were performed on *out-of-state residents,* and another 3.3% were done on residents of New York State who were not residents of New York City (12). Thus, 58.8% of the legal abortions were difficult, if not impossible, to follow up.* This is reflected in a report from the New York Hospital-Cornell Medical Center, which showed that indeed 53.5% of their patients were lost to follow-up (13). Many physicians are currently treating women who are suffering severe complications from New York abortions, and these cases will never appear in the New York statistics. In fact, hair-raising anecdotes of "fall-out" from New York City abortions are related everywhere (14, 15).

Robert E. Hall, M.D., a leading proponent of legal abortion, reported to the 27th Midwest Clinical Conference of the Chicago Medical Society that one abortion clinic in New York City has been performing 700 each week, with no after-care (16). He also said that

---

* This figure, as of March 1972, has increased to 68 percent (cf. *Bulletin on Abortion Program, March 1972,* Department of Health, Health Services Administration, City of New York).

because the caseload is five times greater than hospitals can handle, unaffiliated clinics have mushroomed. Facilities are being bought or built, one of them close to Kennedy Airport, to accommodate out-of-state women who fly in, have the abortion, and fly out the same day (17).

Joseph J. Rovinsky, M.D., reported that "it is noteworthy that the medical services of all three New York City area airports have since July 1, 1970, experienced a vast increase in the number of women requiring assistance for sequelae of induced abortion or actually aborting at the airport!" (18). This evidently has been disturbing to both the airlines and their passengers. Dr. Hall concludes that this situation leads to the neglect of complications when they arise, the rate of which has been high (19).

The 5.3 rate in New York City was arrived at by disregarding 7 abortion deaths in New York City on the unsubstantiated claim that these 7 were not performed ". . . under legal auspices" (20). At an earlier time, Rovinsky concluded that ". . . the estimated maternal mortality rate is 38 per 100,000!" (21). He also says that we cannot be certain that even these figures are complete (22):

There is at least one apocryphal story circulating about an abortion death in a physician's office from air embolisation when an aspiration pump acted as a pressure rather than a suction device; following which the woman's corpse was transported back to her home state and the true cause of death there was not recorded. (23)

Just how many women have died as the result of a New York City abortion will never be known. However, deaths resulting from legal abortion in New York City which do not appear in the Health Services Administration's statistics have definitely been reported in Indiana (24), Ohio (25) and Boston (26). How many others have followed a similar, but unregistered, course will forever be unknown.*

EASTERN EUROPEAN ABORTION MORTALITY RATES COMPLEX AND OFTEN INCOMPLETE

The proponents of abortion are, however, quick to point out the incredibly low abortion mortality rates from countries in Eastern Europe. While focusing *only* on data from Eastern Europe, they make the claim that "induced abortion is potentially X-times (23.3) as safe as the process of going through ordinary childbirth" (27).

In Table One, a number of countries with vast experience in

* As of March 1972, the number of women who have died as the result of legal abortion has exceeded the number dying from illegal abortion by almost two to one. (Cf. *Bulletin on Abortion, March 1972,* Department of Health, Health Services Administration, City of New York.)

Table One: Abortion Mortality vs Maternal Mortality

COUNTRY/STATE	YEAR	LEGAL ABORTIONS	DEATHS	ABORTION MORTALITY/ 100,000 ABORTIONS	MATERNAL MORTALITY/ 100,000 LIVE BIRTHS
Denmark (28)	1960–66	27,435	9	30	10–20
England and Wales (29)	1968–69	27,331	8	30	Abortion mortality higher than maternal mortality.
Sweden (30)	1960–66	30,600	12	39	14.0 (31)
Yugoslavia (Skopje Univ.) (32)	1965–68	18,758	2	10.6	96.5 (33)
Hungary (34)	1964–68	939,800	11	1.2	49.7 (35)
Oregon (36)	1970	7,196	1	13.9	8.4
Maryland (37)	1968–70	7,664	3	40.5	23.1 (38)

performing legal abortions are compared.

The first thing to note is that Denmark, England and Wales, Sweden, Oregon and Maryland all have abortion mortality rates which exceed their respective maternal mortality rates. Secondly, it seems that *only* Eastern European countries have legal abortion mortality rates which are less than the corresponding maternal mortality rates. To see this in perspective, one must recognize that Denmark and Sweden have been legally inducing abortion 10-15 years longer than any Eastern European country (39), and as such, have a much longer experience (40).

One should not, of course, ignore the extraordinarily large maternal mortality rates which exist in Yugoslavia and Hungary (Table One)—mortality rates which are 2-4 times higher than the maternal mortality in the United States (41). Maternal mortality rates are an excellent indication of the quality of medical care given to the whole population of women in each country. Indeed, in Eastern European countries that are considered "... not as sophisticated, medically developed or experienced" (42), one would expect the high maternal mortality rate, but hardly the declared expertise in performing legal abortions.

Some Eastern European investigators have now admitted that complications are almost certainly under-reported because patients treated outside of hospitals are seldom included in hospital statistics (43). It has been said, however, that the mortality rates in Eastern Europe are so incredibly low largely because 95-100% of their abortions are done in the first trimester of pregnancy (44). It is certainly recognized that abortion in the later stages of pregnancy will result in a higher abortion mortality rate (45), and that this may account for some of the increased abortion mortality in Western and Northern Europe. However, before one makes such claims, one must examine the data more carefully.

Table Two examines the legal abortion mortality rates of various countries in which the deaths resulted from legal abortions performed *only in the first trimester of pregnancy.*

Here it can again be adequately shown that while most countries find legal abortion safer in the first trimester, the mortality from abortion continues to exceed the mortality of childbirth; Eastern European countries continue to be noteworthy exceptions. The Hungarian data, however, are not in line with what is observed in Denmark, Oregon, or even its Eastern European ally, Yugoslavia.

Before leaving the Eastern European data, we should look at one

Table Two: Legal Abortion Mortality—First Trimester Only*

COUNTRY/STATE	YEAR	ABORTIONS 1st TRIMESTER	DEATHS	ABORTION MORTALITY/ 100,000 ABORTIONS	MATERNAL MORTALITY/ 100,000 LIVE BIRTHS
Denmark (46)	1961–66	8,684	2	23.0	10–20
Yugoslavia (Skopje Univ.) (47, 48)	1965–68	7,833	2	25.5	96.5 (49)
Hungary (50)	1964–68	939,800	11	1.2	49.7 (51)
Oregon (52)	1970	5,351	1	18.6	8.4

* Breakdown data for England and Wales and Sweden are not available. There were no early abortion deaths in Maryland 1968–70, but a relatively small number (3,900) were performed early (53).

Table Three: Abortion Deaths (All Causes) Per Unit Population*

COUNTRY	ABORTION DEATHS 1967 (ALL CAUSES)	EST. 1967 POPULATION	ABORTION DEATHS/ 1,000,000 POPULATION
Hungary	21 (55)	10,255,000	2.06
United States	160 (56)	197,576,952	0.80

* All population figures are from *Encyclopedia Americana.*

64

other method of examining abortion mortality data—a method which has not been overlooked by the proponents of abortion (54), but, nonetheless, a method which is seldom openly discussed. In Table Three, the total number of abortion deaths (from all causes—spontaneous, criminal and legally induced) are compared for Hungary and the United States.

While 1967 has been selected for comparison, there is little difference in whatever year one would like to consider. There were 21 abortion deaths in Hungary and 160 abortion deaths in the United States in 1967. The figure for the United States is larger; however, one must remember that the population of the United States is considerably larger, so that in order to compare the risks of abortion in the two countries, one must compare the abortion deaths per unit population (obviously, the United States with a larger population would be expected to have a larger number of deaths due to any cause, including abortions). When this comparison is made, one can see that for any *individual woman,* the risk of dying from abortion (all causes) is 2.6 times greater in Hungary than it is in the United States.

In summary, then, the Eastern European mortality statistics are noteworthy in the following ways:

1. Their abortion mortality rates are incredibly low even when compared with countries who have an equal or greater experience.

2. The maternal mortality in Eastern Europe is astoundingly high, and this is an excellent indication of the quality of medical care delivered to the total population of women.

3. Hungarian women are 2.6 times more likely to die from abortion than women in the United States.

Some very important observations must be made from this data:

1. Where the maternal mortality rate is so large (in Hungary) and where the loss from abortion of all causes is so great (also Hungary), one would not expect to see one area of such great perfection as the figures for their legal abortion mortality would claim. As a result, one can seriously question if all the induced abortion deaths are being reported, or if, perhaps, some of them are hidden in the maternal mortality and abortion (all causes) mortality rates.

2. If, on the other hand, we assume that the number of legal abortion deaths is correct, then one of the following must also be true:

    a) Hungarian physicians are not as capable at treating spontaneous abortions as physicians in the United States. However, with their claimed expertise at performing legal abortions, one would not expect this to be true.

b) The number of criminal abortions in Hungary is still amazingly high, and this accounts for the large number of "other" abortion deaths—all of this would be in spite of a phenomenal number of legal abortions (126 legal abortions/100 live births in 1967) (57).

3. The individual Hungarian woman is 2.6 times more likely to die from abortion, and 2.0 times more likely to die from childbirth than the individual woman in the United States. This difference is *very real* and not a supposition. It alone can speak for the Hungarian experience!

It can readily be seen from this analysis that the interpretation of abortion mortality statistics can be very complex. However, it can also be just as readily seen that to make exorbitant claims regarding the safety of legal abortion from these statistics is simply not justified. The claim that abortion is X-times as safe as childbirth is a fabrication invented to sell abortion. Certainly it is not justified on the basis of available information.

CHILD MORTALITY IN ABORTION

In a discussion of abortion mortality rates, the death of the child should not be disregarded (although this, unfortunately, is invariably absent from such discussions). The American conscience must be aroused to the reality of the countless thousands of unborn children whose lives are legally being snuffed out each year in the United States. [In New York, for example, at least 215,453 children were killed in the first year of legalized abortion (58).] This violent trend is changing the healing art of medicine into a source of efficient, swift and sure destruction of human life. Even our learned medical journals are now producing a setting for the work of the physician who reports an exact and scientific countdown of a human heart from 180 beats per minute to zero and ultimately death (see Fig. 1) (59).

It would be gravely remiss not to state emphatically that, of these deaths, many did not occur to *pre-born* children. The official statistics from the first year's experience in New York, with a weak abortion law, revealed sixty-two attempted abortions which resulted in "live births." Fifty-six of these died (indicating infanticide and not abortion), while there were no recorded death certificates for the remaining six (60). This, however, does not even begin to tell the infanticide

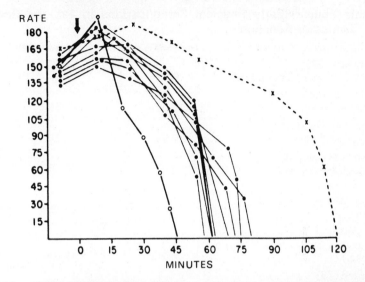

RATE

MINUTES

FIG. 1. FETAL HEART RATE.* Fifteen consecutive cases monitored for fetal heart rate are illustrated. The majority of the fetal hearts are undetectable one hour following the deposition of the hypertonic solution in the amniotic sac.

story in New York State. If you carefully examine the official New York abortion report, you will find that 1,802 "abortions" were performed by hysterotomy (61). If the child is alive before this operation is performed (and this is usually the case), then he will be born alive (by any legal definition of live-born birth) only to immediately face death from exposure in his infancy.

This discussion of mortality from abortion (both mother and child) should begin to shed some light on the "safety" of this procedure. However, one cannot limit this discussion (as so many have) merely to mortality rates. There are numerous other resultant complications which must be carefully analyzed in order to see the "safety" of abortion procedures in total perspective.

OTHER COMPLICATIONS OF LEGALLY INDUCED ABORTION

"Abortion may impair a woman's health through a variety of complications. These may occur at the time of or soon after the abortion, or be discovered much later, perhaps in connexion with

* Reproduced from Figure 1 on page 137 of Thomas D. Kerenyi's "Outpatient Intra-amniotic Injection of Hypertonic Saline," *Clinical Obstetrics and Gynecology,* Volume 14, No. 1, 1971. With the permission of the author and Harper & Row, Publishers.

Table Four: %Early Physical Complications in 1st and 2nd Trimester Abortion

COUNTRY/INVESTIGATOR	1st TRIMESTER	2nd TRIMESTER
Denmark (67) (Olsen, Nielsen, Ostergaard)	5.4%	2.5—9.1%
California (68) (Banner, et al.)	11.0%	17.0%
New York City (69) (Kaye—NY Lying-In)	2.5%	12.7%
New York City (70) (Douglas—Bellevue)	——	20.9%
Elmhurst, N.Y. (71) (Rovinsky—City Hospital Center)	5.0%	15.6%
Rochester, N.Y. (72) (Choate—Strong Memorial Hosp.)	8.2%	12.6%
Poland (73) (Midak)	4.4%	——
Czechoslovakia (74) (Kotasek)	5.0%	——
Sweden (75) (Bengtsson)	——	9.4—10.1%
Great Britain (76) (Menzies)	——	30.8%
Japan (77) (Wagatsuma)	——	14.0%

another pregnancy or with efforts to become pregnant again. The complications may result in the death of the woman" (62).

This discussion will first present those physical complications which occur within the first few days after the abortion (early physical complications). Following this, those physical complications which can occur several weeks to several years after an abortion (late physical complications) will be projected. Finally, the psychological complications will be analyzed.

THE EARLY PHYSICAL COMPLICATIONS OF LEGALLY INDUCED ABORTION

The most common early complications of legally induced abortion are infection, hemorrhage, perforation of the uterus and laceration of the cervix. Table Four lists a representative sample of studies which have been done around the world and in the United States to define the incidence of early physical complications.

Stallworthy, Moolgaoker, and Walsh reported, in the prestigious British medical journal *Lancet* (Dec. 4, 1971), the complications which they noted when performing 1,182 legal abortions (63). While there were no deaths, 9.5% of their patients required blood transfusion, 4.2% had cervical lacerations, and in 1.2% the uterus was perforated (64). All of the perforations were associated with suction curettage. Emergency exploratory abdominal surgery was required for the recovery of six patients and hysterectomy was necessary for two others to save their lives. Post-abortion infection occurred in 27% (65).

Commenting upon these complications, in the discussion which followed the presentation of their results, they said (66):

The incidence of the complications described and the severity of some of them are disquieting. Some may claim that termination of pregnancy is much safer in their hands. If so, they are to be congratulated. The present figures represent the combined experience of five consultants and a series of experienced lecturers, senior registrars, and registrars. It is perhaps significant that some of the more serious complications occurred with the most senior and experienced operators. This emphasizes that termination of pregnancy is neither as simple nor as safe as some advocates of abortion-on-demand would have the public believe. ... It is disquieting that post-abortal infection, which is one of the common causes of death after criminal abortion, should have occurred in 27% of this series. Septicemia, peritonitis, and paralytic ileus are potentially fatal complications, and the risk of death increases if they occur after the patient is discharged from hospital and there is delay in diagnosis.

They went on to further observe:

If termination of pregnancy were as safe as so many advocates of liberal abortion maintain, a patient suffering as a result of the operation could claim that professional negligence was responsible for her subsequent distress or disaster and plead *res ipsa loquitur*. Such claims would generally be grossly unfair. There would be great sympathy for a 16-year-old girl whose uterus was torn beyond repair; for the married woman with gut resection and peritonitis; for the mother in monthly distress following hysterotomy because of implantation endometriosis in her abdominal wall, vagina, or bladder; for the anxious infertile wife who knows that the tubal damage which now denies her the baby she desires is the delayed price she is paying for her teenage abortion. But the fact remains that none of these situations may be the result of negligence. They are complications which, though well known to, and well documented by, those with wide experience of an operation which is neither simple nor safe, are seldom mentioned by those who claim that abortion is safe and merely an extension of contraceptive techniques.

There is evidence to suggest that these complications are far more frequent in the young woman pregnant for the first time, presumably because the cervix is much more rigid in women who have not previously given birth (78, 79, 80). [Note that 57.3% of the abortions performed in New York City from July 1, 1970, to May 31, 1971, were performed on women pregnant for the first time (81).]

Infection may be localized as in endometritis, salpingitis or parametritis. It may be more regionally located resulting in pelvic thrombophlebitis, pelvic cellulitis or pelvic peritonitis. It may be distant as infection in pneumonia, endocarditis, or septic emboli to the lungs or brain. Or, the infection may be generalized as in septicemia (82). The infection is usually the direct result of the instrumentation involved in the abortive technique, and is the usual cause of any subsequent sterility because the infection scars the tubes to a point where they either obstruct or malfunction.

Hemorrhage is not uncommon following induced abortion even early in pregnancy. The uterus is a highly vascular organ during pregnancy because of its natural response to the life support of the child. Hemorrhage usually results when this vascular organ is lacerated, perforated, ruptured, fails to contract (uterine atony), or because of retained placental tissue (83). In the first year of the Colorado abortion law, 8.0% of women undergoing the operation needed at least one unit of blood (84). [For a discussion of the inherent dangers of blood transfusions—allergic reaction, serum hepatitis, etc., see J. A. Merritt, et al., "Management of Emergencies: Untoward Reactions to Blood Transfusion," *N.E.J.M.*, 274:1426, 1966.] In a series of 100 early suction abortions performed by Dr. Robert E. Hall, *at least* 5% had "excessive blood loss" (greater than 350cc) (85). Of course, not all women will require blood transfusion, but Carlton, et al., in one of the few series of its kind, noted that 30% of his overall group were anemic following abortion (hemoglobin less than 9.0 gms), and of those done in the first trimester 9% were anemic (86).

Perforation of the uterus occurs in 1.0-2.0% of legally induced abortions, and may occur with the traditional D&C or the newer method of suction curettage (87, 88, 89, 90). Perforation occurs primarily because the surgeon operates by "touch" alone, and not under direct vision. Secondarily, the pregnant uterus is much softer than the nonpregnant uterus, lending itself to easy perforation (91). If, in the process of perforation, the bowel or a blood vessel is torn, overwhelming infection and/or hemorrhage may occur, necessitating exploratory laparotomy. (It has been reported that 30-65% with perforation will eventually require exploration.) (92, 93)

Early physical complications which are very significant when they occur, but are less frequent, include the following:

1. Coma and/or convulsions because of the effects on the central nervous system and/or kidneys of hypertonic saline entering the bloodstream directly or via the peritoneal cavity (94).

2. Embolisation of air, most commonly, or by particulate matter (fat, placental products, amniotic fluid) in the heart, pulmonary artery, brain and other organs (95).

3. Anesthetic accidents resulting in cardiac arrest or aspiration pneumonia (96).

4. Disturbances in the coagulability of the maternal blood (97, 98, 99, 100). In fact, a mild form of consumption coagulopathy is very common with saline abortion (manifest by hypofibrinogenemia and thrombocytopenia) (101).

5. The abortion of only one twin while the other survives and delivers normally several months later (102, 103). The psychological effect on the mother and the surviving twin in such cases has not been investigated.

6. It is now becoming apparent that, contrary to wishful thinking, abortion can be a relatively uncomfortable procedure. For early abortion many patients can be managed adequately with mild sedation and paracervical local anesthesia, but for a "considerable" number this is not sufficient to provide satisfactory analgesia, nor to prevent agitated and abrupt pelvic movements which can only contribute to increasing the complication rate (104).

THE LATE PHYSICAL COMPLICATIONS OF LEGALLY INDUCED ABORTION

The late physical complications of legally induced abortion have as yet been incompletely evaluated, and there is literally nothing from the American literature which would be of help. Nonetheless, there is a copious amount of information available from the experience of other countries, and this is now presenting substantial evidence to suggest that it is in this category that the most significant medical and ultimate sociological sequelae exist.

Through increased knowledge and experience, we are now beginning to see and understand how our careless use of natural resources and destruction of, or interruption of, natural life-cycles in land, water, and air is having a disastrous impact on the environment. Nobody really knows for certain what results we might see in a few years in women and those dependent upon them if the natural life-cycle within them is radically interfered with. However, some insight into the ultimate ecological disaster may be gathered by a close look at the late physical complications (and psychological complications).

COMPLICATIONS IN SUBSEQUENT PREGNANCIES

Subsequent pregnancies are more often pathological following legal abortion, and this, it seems to me, represents some of the most significant complications of all. Any one of these could produce an individual disaster at least equivalent to any unwanted pregnancy and one which may be far more difficult to handle.

Premature Labor and Delivery

The prematurity rate in Hungary in 1954 (before legalized abortion) was 7%. However, in 1968 (14 years after legalization) it had increased to 12% (105). The incidence of prematurity developing in any one individual has been shown to be well correlated with the number of abortions a woman has. Hungarian studies reveal that the likelihood of premature labor and delivery following one previous abortion was increased to *14%;* after two abortions, to *18%;* and after three abortions, to *24%* (106). In Czechoslovakia a comparison of women who have never had a previous legal abortion with women who had such a history revealed the prematurity rate in the former group to be *5%,* while in the latter group it had increased to *14%* (107). Similar experience has also been seen in Japan (108). The increase in prematurity is thought to be a direct result of the instrumentation required in early abortion; dilating the cervix may leave the cervix incompetent to retain the child for the full nine months (109).

The significance of this trend lies in the fact that premature birth is the leading cause of infant death, and *one of the leading causes of mental and motor retardation* (110). This is reflected in the extraordinarily high infant mortality rate in Hungary due to birth injury, postnatal asphyxia and atalectasis (the leading causes of death in the premature infant)—1,278.2 per 100,000 live births (111) compared to a similar death rate in the United States of 549.4 per 100,000 live births (112). Indeed, there "has been a doubling of the perinatal mortality in Hungary following the introduction of 'abortion on request'" (113). Thus, Klinger, in commenting on the Hungarian situation, concludes:

Induced abortion plays an important role in the development of a subsequent child [and that] the impact of premature birth on infant mortality and on the mental and physical development of the child is connected with the frequency of abortions. (114)

Ectopic Pregnancies

A number of countries have reported a significant increase in the incidence of ectopic pregnancy (115, 116). One Japanese study revealed that *3.9%* of women with previous history of legal abortion had a subsequent ectopic pregnancy (117). This is eight times the incidence of ectopic pregnancy in the United States (the incidence of ectopic pregnancy in the United States in 1967 was about 0.5%) (118). An ectopic pregnancy, of course, is not infrequently life-threatening because of rupture and hemorrhage. This, therefore, subjects an individual woman to a very substantial future risk. The risk of death from ectopic pregnancy in the United States is approximately 300/100,000 (119). Again, tubal malfunction, usually secondary to post-abortal infection, seems to be the prime cause.

Other Complications in Subsequent Pregnancies

The incidence of spontaneous abortion in women with a history of previous legal abortion is reported to be *30-40%* higher than in those without such a history (120, 121), and the incidence of fetal death during pregnancy is twice as great (122). Also, complicated labors (prolonged labor, placenta previa, adherent placenta) (123, 124, 125, 126, 127) and excessive bleeding at the time of delivery (128) have all been noted to occur more commonly in subsequent pregnancies to women with a previous history of legal abortion. These, of course, all result in increased obstetrical intervention.

STERILITY

Several studies "prove that repeated abortions can cause secondary sterility" (129). One report from Poland showed that *6.9%* of women were sterile on a 4–5 year follow-up (130). And in Japan, *9.7%* were subsequently sterile on a 3 year follow-up (131). Other countries have had a similar experience (132, 133, 134). Sterility results primarily as an after-effect of post-abortal infection which results in either tubal obstruction or malfunction. Eminent British gynecologist T. N. A. Jeffcoate's comment is particularly pertinent here:

> If this happens when a first pregnancy is interrupted for a non-recurrent indication, such as rubella or a fleeting psychological upset, the situation is tragic. (135)

Transplacental Hemorrhage

It has long been known that a woman who is Rh negative is very susceptible to a very special kind of problem when her consort is Rh positive. Any given pregnancy may be a stimulus for the mother to develop antibodies against the baby's red blood cells (i.e., she becomes sensitized to the baby's red blood cells) so that in a subsequent pregnancy these antibodies may destroy the baby's red blood cells, resulting in an anemia which may be life-threatening to the baby *in utero,* or subject him to the threat of mental and motor retardation after he is born. This sensitization occurs through a leakage of the baby's red blood cells into the mother's circulation (transplacental hemorrhage), usually at the time of delivery. Therefore, first-born children are rarely affected. However, with *all* methods of legally induced abortion, sensitization has been reported to occur in 3–10% of Rh negative women (136, 137, 138, 139, 140, 141, 142). This can now be effectively treated with the recent development of anti-Rh-negative gammaglobulin (Rhogam), and its routine use in the abortion of Rh negative women has been frequently recommended (143, 144). However, because certain tests on the fetus cannot be performed, many women will be needlessly exposed to therapy. And, in spite of the existence of this highly effective treatment, there is good evidence to suggest that it is being grossly neglected. In a study conducted by the New York State Department of Health of women having abortions in *all* of New York State, *48.7%* of women known to be Rh negative were left untreated, and thus unprotected from the possibility of sensitization and its inherent risks in future pregnancies (145).

OTHER LATE PHYSICAL COMPLICATIONS

1. A woman's sexual libido is reported to decrease in *14-33%* of women with a previous legal abortion. This is theoretically due to the psychotraumatic experience of the interruption and the emotional weakness that follows (146, 147).
2. Endometriosis is an infrequent sequel to hysterotomy (148).
3. Many pregnancies which follow an abortion performed by hysterotomy will need delivery by caesarian section to eliminate the possibility of rupture of the hysterotomy scar (149).
4. Gross irregularity in the appearance of the menstrual period, heavy bleeding at the menses or complete absence of menstruation has been reported in *1-12%* of patients who have had legal abortions (150, 151, 152).

PSYCHIATRIC PROBLEMS FOLLOWING ABORTION

A World Health Organization scientific group concluded that "there is no doubt that the termination of pregnancy may precipitate a serious psychoneurotic or even psychotic reaction in a susceptible individual" (153). Some investigators have indeed noted lasting psychiatric reactions (154). However, there has been much variation in the medical literature regarding the incidence of psychological sequelae of induced abortion.

The Swedish experience with therapeutic abortion has been well documented with several well-planned studies. The best of these is Ekblad's. He studied 479 women at the time of the abortion and again 2-3 1/2 years later. At follow-up, he found that *10%* continued to feel the operation unpleasant; *14%* had mild self-reproach; *11%* had serious self-reproach and self-regret; and *1%* had gross psychiatric breakdowns (155).

Seigfried, in 1951, reported on 61 women followed up for two years after abortion, and found *13%* to have serious self-reproach (156). Niswander and Patterson, in 1967, studied 90 women aborted for psychogenic reasons, and found 21 had an immediate negative reaction, and 11 had a negative long-term effect (at least 8 months). Eleven of 17 aborted for rubella had an immediate negative reaction, and 8 of those 17 continued to have a long-term negative reaction (157).

Recent studies have shown "that serious mental disorders arise more often in women with previous emotional problems; thus the very women for whom legal abortion is considered to be justified on psychiatric grounds are the ones who have the highest risk of post-abortal psychiatric disorders" (158).

Jewish Freudian psychiatrist-obstetrician Julius Fogel, who admits to having executed hundreds of abortions, observed:

Abortion is an impassioned subject. . . . Psychologically and emotionally we are only beginning to learn something of its effects on the women involved. I think every woman—whatever her age, her background or sexuality—has a trauma at destroying a pregnancy. A level of humanness is touched. This is a part of her own life. She destroys a pregnancy; she is destroying herself. There is no way it can be innocuous. One is dealing with the life force. It is totally beside the point whether or not you think life is there. You cannot deny that something is being created and that this creation is physically happening. (159)

Fogel does not claim that mental illness automatically follows abortion. Says he:

Often the trauma may sink into the unconscious and never surface in the woman's lifetime. But it is not as harmless and casual an event as many in the pro-abortion crowd insist. A psychological price is paid. I can't say exactly what. It may be alienation, it may be a pushing away from human warmth, perhaps a hardening of the maternal instinct. Something happens on the deeper levels of a woman's consciousness when she destroys a pregnancy. I know that as a psychiatrist. (160)

The psychiatric problems following abortion are not limited to the mother. When Cain reported his observations of eighty-seven children whose mothers had abortions (type not specified), he found two categories of reactions: an immediate type, characterized by anxiety attacks, nightmares, increased aggressiveness, stuttering, running away, death phobias, increased separation anxiety, sudden outbursts of fear or hatred of the mother, and even suicide attempts; a late type included effects ranging from isolated fantasies to pervading, crucial and disabling illness (161).

Beyond all of this, still others are confronted with certain psychological reactions to abortion. The disquieting reactions of hospital staff to this procedure has been well documented (162, 163, 164, 165, 166). Some nurses find it difficult when legitimate surgery is pushed aside to make room on the operating schedule for abortions and when abortion equipment is purchased in priority over other needs involving patient care in the hospital (167). Others have developed an intense anxiety over which patient should be given care at a given moment—the woman threatening to spontaneously abort (for whom the nurse is involved in saving life), or the woman in the next bed about to abort because of the salt which has been previously instilled in the fluid surrounding her baby (168).

In Hawaii, McDermott and Char reported that "the nurses themselves felt that they had replaced the illicit underground abortionists in other cities, and, like them, they were personally involved in the slicing and chopping up of 'babies' (the word they used to describe expelled fetal parts and fetuses that were warm and sometimes breathing)" (169). Kibel reported nightmares in nurses who had participated in many abortions (170). He concluded that "regardless of one's religious or philosophic orientation, the unconscious view of abortion remains the same . . . that unconsciously the act of abortion was experienced as an act of murder" (171).

Physicians are no more immune. Many countries have reported increased depressive reactions and breakdowns among their guilt-ridden doctors (172, 173). Resident doctors in obstetrics and gynecology have expressed their dissent at having to spend "inordinate portions of their learning time carrying out too many distasteful abortions" (174). It seems that a robot-like constitution is needed when carrying out large numbers of abortions.

It should be pointed out that the interpretation of the results of psychiatric studies has always been made difficult by the lack of uniform standards for the assessment of psychological impairment and of suitable controls (175). Unfortunately, over the last several years, several unscientific papers have appeared in the medical literature, written by advocates of abortion, blindly stating that psychiatric sequelae of abortion are a myth. One should read a few of these papers to appreciate the bias (176, 177). At the same time, in order to comprehend what has been done in this area of psychiatry and what needs to be done, one should also read Simon and Senturia's excellent review and critical analysis of the available psychological literature (178), and Heath's praiseworthy treatise (179).

CONCLUSION

The medical hazards of legally induced abortion are very significant and should be conscientiously weighed to obtain a balanced and ethical viewpoint. Singling out only one set of "facts" or figures to serve as evidence of safety cannot occasion this end. Abortion must be recognized for what it is: a morbid invasion of a *healthy* woman's body with the purpose of destroying new life. One wonders what pressures in our modern society have brought about so radical a change in moral climate that powerful groups of physicians feel compelled to mislead the public regarding this danger-fraught reality.

BIBLIOGRAPHY

1. *Amicus Curiae* brief filed on behalf of the American College of Obstetricians and Gynecologists, the American Medical Women's Association, the American Psychiatric Association, the New York Academy of Medicine, medical school deans and professors, and certain individual physicians, in *Doe* v. *Bolton,* U. S. Supreme Court No. 70-40, 1971.
2. Ibid., p. 13.
3. *Spontaneous and Induced Abortion.* Report of a World Health Organization scientific group. World Health Organization Technical Report Series, No. 461, p. 40, 1970.
4. *College Statement and Minority Report on Therapeutic Abortion.* Issued by the American College of Obstetricians and Gynecologists, Chicago, Illinois, May 1, 1969.
5. Ibid.
6. *Legalized Abortion.* Report by the Council of the Royal College of Obstetricians and Gynaecologists. *British Medical Journal,* 1:850-854, April 12, 1966.
7. *The Abortion Act (1967).* Findings of an inquiry into the first year's working of the Act conducted by the Royal College of Obstetricians and Gynaecologists. *Brit. Med. J.,* 2:529-535, May 30, 1970.
8. Klemfuss, R.: *State M.D.'s Clarify Abortion Stand.* News release, Med. Soc. of the State of N.Y., March 26, 1970.
9. *The Abortion Act (1967),* op. cit., p. 533.
10. Chase, Gordon: *Gordon Chase Cites Success of First Year of New York's Abortion Law in Twelve-Month Report on 165,000 Abortions.* News release, Health Services Admin., The City of N.Y., June 29, 1971, p. 1.
11. Ibid.
12. Ibid., Appendix C—Place of Residence (%).
13. Seiner, C. H.; Mahoney, E.: Coordination of Outpatient Services From Patients Seeking Elective Abortion. *Clin. Obstet. and Gynec.,* 14:48-59, March 1971.
14. Rovinsky, J. J.: Abortion in New York City: Preliminary Experience with a Permissive Abortion Statute. *Obstet. and Gynec.,* 38:333-342, Sept. 1971.
15. Stone, M. L.; Gordon, M.; Rovinsky, J.: The Impact of a Liberalized Abortion Law on the Medical Schools. *Am. J. Obstet. Gynec.* 111:728-735, Nov. 1, 1971.

16. Gaps in N.Y. Law Blamed for "Gross" Abortion Abuses. *Ob. Gyn. News, Physicians International Press,* p. 1, April 1, 1971.
17. Ibid.
18. Rovinsky, "Abortion in New York City," op. cit., p. 337.
19. "Gaps in N.Y. Law," op. cit.
20. Chase, op. cit.
21. Rovinsky, "Abortion in New York City," op. cit., p. 336.
22. Ibid.
23. Rovinsky, J. J.: *Abortion in New York City.* A paper presented to the meeting of the Am. Assn. of Planned Parenthood Physicians, President Hotel, Kansas City, Mo., April 5-6, 1971.
24. *Morbidity and Mortality.* U.S. Dept. of H.E.W., Center for Disease Control. Weekly Report for week ending June 12, 1971, Abortion Mortality, N.Y.C., 20:208-209.
25. Death Linked Here to Abortion. *The Middletown Journal,* Middletown, Ohio. Friday, Oct. 18, 1971.
26. Boston Woman, 23, Dies After Abortion Performed in Office of Physician Here. *The New York Times,* Saturday, Oct. 17, 1970.
27. *Amicus Curiae,* op. cit.
28. Olsen, C. E.; Nielsen, H. B.; and Ostergaard, E.: Complications to Therapeutic Abortion. *Int. J. Gynec. Obstet.,* 8:823-829, Nov. 1970.
29. *The Abortion Act (1967),* op. cit.
30. Tietze, C.: *Abortion Laws and Abortion Practices in Europe.* From Excerpta Medica International Congress Series, No. 207. Advances in Planned Parenthood—V. *Proceedings of the Seventh Annual Meeting of the A.A.P.P.P., San Francisco, 1969,* p. 198.
31. *World Health Statistics Report,* Vol. 23, No. 7, pp. 546-549, published by WHO. The year 1967 is the latest for which world statistics on maternal mortality are available. Denmark's maternal mortality rate was 19.2 and 20.9/100,000 live births for 1966 and 1967 respectively. Sweden's maternal mortality in 1966 was 11.3/100,000. Yugoslavia's 1966 rate was 105.3/100,000, and Hungary's was 48.4/100,000. In comparison, the U.S. maternal mortality in 1966 was 21.9/100,000 and 28.0/100,000 in 1967.
32. Jurokovski, J.: Complications Following Legal Abortion. *Proc. Roy. Soc. Med.,* 62:830-831, Aug. 1969.
33. *World Health Statistics Report,* op. cit.
34. Klinger, A.: Demographic Consequences of the Legalization of Induced Abortion in Eastern Europe. *Int. J. Gynec. and Obstet.* 8:680-691, Sept. 1970.
35. *World Health Statistics Report,* op. cit.
36. *Therapeutic Abortions in Oregon—January-December, 1970.* Report issued by the Oregon State Board of Health. Oregon was selected because abortion is limited to state residents, a high volume of abortions are being performed (200.8/1,000 live births) and it is recognized that

their reporting system is "complete or nearly complete." (See *Abortion Surveillance Report—Hospital Abortions, Jan.-June, 1970.* Distributed by the U. S. Dept. of H.E.W., Center for Disease Control, Atlanta, Georgia 30333.)

37. Cushner, I. M.: Pregnancy Termination: The Impact of New Laws. An Invitational Symposium. *J. Reprod. Med.,* 6:62-63, June 1971.
38. *Vital Statistics of the United States;* Vol. I, "Natality," and Vol. II, Part B, "Mortality." U. S. Dept. of H.E.W., U. S. Public Health Service, 1967.
39. Tietze, op. cit.
40. Ibid.
41. *World Health Statistics Report,* op. cit.
42. Tovell, H.: Symposium on Legal Abortion. Panel discussion, Am. Col. Obstet. and Gynec. Annual Meeting Dist. II, Oct. 28-Nov. 1, 1970. Paradise Island, Nassau, Bahamas. In *Clin. Obstet. and Gynec.,* 14:303, March 1971.
43. Jurokovski, J.; Sukarov, L.: A Critical Review of Legal Abortion. *Int. J. Gynec. and Obstet.,* 9:111-117, May 1971.
44. Tietze, op. cit.
45. WHO Technical Report Series, op. cit., pp. 38-39.
46. Olsen, et al., op. cit.
47. Jurokovski, op. cit.
48. Jurokovski, et al., op. cit.
49. *World Health Statistics Report,* op. cit.
50. Klinger, op. cit.
51. *World Health Statistics Report,* op. cit.
52. *Therapeutic Abortions in Oregon,* op. cit.
53. Cushner, op. cit.
54. Tietze, op. cit., pp. 205-206.
55. Klinger, op. cit.
56. *Vital Statistics of the United States,* Vol. II, "Mortality," published by the U. S. Public Health Service of H.E.W. The Official Vital Statistics list 160 maternal deaths from abortions of all causes. This is a figure hotly disputed by pro-abortionists, who at times have placed the number of annual maternal deaths from illegal abortion at anywhere from 500 to 10,000, depending upon their audience. It is this kind of exaggeration that has helped the pro-abortionists create an hysteria for change in the abortion debate. However, it is interesting to note that one of the proponents of induced abortion, when discussing the same statistics at a recent pro-abortion conference, had this to say: "I might say we have a fairly high rate of discovery in New York City. The opportunity of obscuring an abortion death is very unlikely. We have a very effective Health Department, which screens all the death certificates, and anything unusual would be referred to us, particularly in a woman of

childbearing age." *Abortion in a Changing World,* Vol. II, Columbia University Press, at p. 52 (1970).

57. Klinger, op. cit.
58. Ingraham, H. S.: *Report of Selected Characteristics on Induced Abortion Recorded in New York State, July 1, 1970-June 30, 1971,* p. 1. New York State Department of Health. October 1971.
59. Kerenyi, T. D.: Outpatient Intra-Amniotic Injection of Hypertonic Saline. *Clin. Obstet. Gynec.,* 14:137, March 1971.
60. Ingraham, op. cit., p. 2.
61. Ibid., Tables 7 and 15.
62. WHO Technical Report Series, op. cit., p. 37.
63. Stallworthy, J. A.; Moolgaoker, A. S.; Walsh, J. J.: Legal Abortion: A Critical Assessment of its Risks. 2:1245-1249. *Lancet,* Dec. 4, 1971.
64. Ibid.
65. Ibid.
66. Ibid., pp. 1248-1249.
67. Olsen, et al., op. cit.
68. Banner, P. H.; Kirshen, E. J.; Didio, J. M.: Therapeutic Abortion: A Review of 567 Cases. *Calif. Med.,* 115:20-28, July 1971.
69. Kaye, R. E.: Procedures for Abortions at The N.Y. Lying-In Hospital. *Clin. Obstet. and Gynec.,* 14:153-165, March 1971.
70. Douglas, G. W.: Complications of Saline Induction of Abortion. A talk given at Cook County Hospital, Dec. 16, 1971.
71. Rovinsky, op. cit.
72. Choate, J. W.: Pregnancy Termination: The Impact of New Laws. An Invitational Symposium. *J. Reprod. Med.,* 6:45-72, at p. 62, June 1971.
73. Midak, E.: Early and Late Sequelae of Abortion. *Pol. Tyg. Lek.,* 21:1063, 1966.
74. Kotasek, A.: Artificial Termination of Pregnancy in Czechoslovakia. *Int. J. Gynaec. and Obstet.,* 9:118-119, May 1971.
75. Bengtsson, L. P.: Legal Abortion Induced by Intra-Amniotic Injection, (1): Technique, Effect, Risks and Mode of Action. *Lakartidninger,* 64:5037, 1967.
76. Menzies, D. N., et al.: Therapeutic Abortion Using Intra-Amniotic Hypertonic Solutions. *J. Obstet. and Gynaec. Brit. Comm.,* 75:215, 1968.
77. Wagatsuma, T.: Intra-Amniotic Injection of Saline for Therapeutic Abortion. *Am. J. Obstet. and Gynec.,* 93:743-745, 1965.
78. *Legalized Abortion,* op. cit.
79. Kotasek, op. cit.
80. Trca, S., et al.: Relationship Between Development of Inflammation After Induced Abortion and the Duration of Pregnancy. *Cesk. Gynaek.,* 29:613, 1964.
81. Chase, op. cit., Appendix D. Pregnancy Order (%).

82. Sandberg, E. C.: Surgical Complications of Therapeutic Abortion (Highlights from 1971 A.M.A. Meeting). *Audio-Digest Obstet. Gynec.,* Vol. 18, No. 15, Aug. 3, 1971.

83. Ibid.

84. Droegemueller, W., et al.: The First Year of Experience in Colorado with the New Abortion Law. *Am. J. Obstet. and Gynec.,* 103:694-698, 1969.

85. Hall, R. E.: Induced Abortion in New York City. Report of six separate studies. *Am. J. Obstet. and Gynec.,* 110:601-611, July 1, 1971.

86. Carlton, M. A.; Hegarty, R.: The Immediate Morbidity of Therapeutic Abortion. *Med. J. Aust.,* pp. 1071-1074, Dec. 5, 1970.

87. Olsen, et al., op. cit.

88. Banner, et al., op. cit.

89. Kaye, op. cit.

90. Stallworthy, et al., op. cit.

91. Ibid.

92. Poradorsky, K.: Lacerations of Cervix and Perforation of Uterus in Artificial Interruption of Pregnancy. *Cesk. Gynek.,* 25:682, 1960.

93. Vasiliad, M., et al.: On Uterine Perforation. *Obstet. and Gynec.,* 10:247, 1965.

94. WHO Technical Report Series, op. cit., p. 38.

95. Ibid.

96. Ibid.

97. Skipetrov, V. P.: Changes in the Blood Coagulation in Artificial Abortion. *Vop. Okhr. Materin. Det.,* 11:69, 1966.

98. Wroblewski, M., et al.: Evaluation of Blood Clotting and Fibrinolysis in Early Pregnancy and After Its Interruption. *Ginek. Pol.,* 36:141, 1965.

99. Zwarik, E.: Afibrinogenemia After Artificial Interruption of Pregnancy. *Zbl. Gynaek.,* 86:1097, 1964.

100. Zwarik, E.: Study of Blood Coagulation and Fibrinolysis in Connection with Artificial Interruption of Pregnancy. *Gynaecologia* (Basel), 162:197, 1966.

101. Douglas, op. cit.

102. Carlton, et al., op. cit.

103. Sood, S. V.: Complications of Hysterotomy, *Br. Med. J.,* 4:495-496, Nov. 21, 1970.

104. Rovinsky, op. cit., p. 338.

105. Klinger, op. cit., p. 691. The prematurity rate in the United States is about 7%.

106. Ibid.

107. Slumsky, R.: Course of Delivery of Women Following Interruption of Pregnancy, *Cesk. Gynek.,* 29:97, 1964.

108. Harmful Effects of Induced Abortion, N.P. Family Planning Federation of Japan, 1966.

109. Ibid.

110. Schaeffer, A. J.: *Diseases of the Newborn,* 2d ed., Philadelphia, W. B. Saunders Co., 1966.
111. *World Health Statistics Report,* op. cit.
112. Ibid.
113. Jurokovski, et al., op. cit.
114. Klinger, op. cit.
115. Ozsvath, I.; Rado, S.: Experience with Interruption of Pregnancy, *Nepegeszsegugy,* 42:121, 1961.
116. Sawazaki, C.; Tanaka, S.:*Harmful Effects of Induced Abortion* (Reports of Studies Conducted by the Subcommittee on the Study of Induced Abortion), p. 49, Family Planning Federation of Japan, Tokyo, 1966.
117. Hayasaka, Y., et al.: Japan's 22-Year Experience with a Liberal Abortion Law, Twelfth International Congress of FIAMC, Washington, D. C., October 11-14, 1970.
118. WHO Technical Report Series, op. cit., pp. 27-28.
119. Ibid.
120. Kotasek, op. cit.
121. Kuck, M.: Abortion in Czechoslovakia, *Proc. Roy. Soc. Med.,* 62:831-832, 1969.
122. Ibid.
123. Jurokovski, et al., op. cit.
124. Kotasek, op. cit.
125. Slumsky, op. cit.
126. Kuck, op. cit.
127. Hofman, D.: Statistical Studies on Some Obstetric Relations, Especially the Relation of Abortion to Late Post-Partum Complications, *Zbl. Gynaek.,* 87:1537, 1964.
128. Slumsky, op. cit.
129. Klinger, op. cit.
130. Midak, op. cit.
131. Hayasaka, et al., op. cit.
132. Kotasek, op. cit.
133. Mehlan, K.-H. The Effects of Legalization of Abortion on the Health of the Mothers in Eastern Europe, *Proceedings of the Seventh Conference of the IPPF, Singapore, 1963.* New York, Excerpta Medica Foundation, 1964.
134. Milosevic, B., et al.: Sterility with Special Reference to Induced Abortion, *Srpski. Arh. Celukupno. Ledarstvo,* 94:1, 1966.
135. Jeffecoate, T. N. A.: Indications for Therapeutic Abortion, *Brit. Med. J.,* 1:581, 1960.
136. Gellen, J., et al: Maternal-Fetal Microhemotransfusion as a Result of Induced Abortion, *Orr. Hetil.,* 107:732, 1966.
137. Gellen, J., et al: Surgical Termination of Pregnancy as a Cause of Rhesus Sensitization, *Brit. Med. J.,* 2:1471, 1965.

138. Jorgensen, J.: Rhesus Antibody Development After Abortion, *Lancet,* 2:1253-1254, 1969.

139. Mathews, C. D.; Mathews, A. E. B.: Transplacental Hemorrhage in Spontaneous and Induced Abortion, *Lancet,* 1:694-695, 1969.

140. Parmley, T. H., et al.: Transplacental Hemorrhage in Patients Subjected to Therapeutic Abortion, *Am J. Obstet. and Gynec.* 106:540-542, 1970.

141. Voight, J. C., et al.: Feto-Maternal Hemorrhage in Therapeutic Abortion, *Brit. Med. J.,* 4:395-396, 1969.

142. Lakoff, K. M.; Klein, J.; Bologuese, R. J.; and Corson, S. L.: Transplacental Hemorrhage During Voluntary Interruption of Pregnancy, *J. Reprod. Med.,* 6:19-20, June 1971.

143. Ibid.

144. Sprague, C.: The Role of Rhogam in Therapeutic and Spontaneous Abortion. *Hawaii Med. J.,* 29:450-451, July-August, 1970.

145. Ingraham, H. S.; Longwood, R. J.: Abortion in New York State Since July 1970, *Clin. Obstet. and Gynec.,* 14:5-24, March 1971.

146. Midak, op. cit.

147. Cepelak, J., et al.: Influence of Interruption of Pregnancy on the Sexual Life of the Woman, *Cesk. Gynek.,* 25:609, 1960.

148. Potts, D.: Termination of Pregnancy, *Brit. Med. Bull.,* 26:65-71, 1970.

149. Sood, op. cit.

150. Midak, op. cit.

151. Kuck, op. cit.

152. Osadchaia, O. V.: Immediate and Remote Results in Induced Abortion, *Zdravoorkhr Belorussii,* 9:59, 1963.

153. WHO Technical Report Series, op. cit., p. 41.

154. Ebaugh, F.; Heuser, K.: Psychiatric Aspects of Therapeutic Abortion, *Post-Graduate Medicine,* 2:325, 1947.

155. Ekblad, M.: Induced Abortion on Psychiatric Grounds, A Follow-Up Study of 479 Women, *Acta. Psychiat. Neurol. Scand. Suppl.,* 99:238, 1955.

156. Seigfried, S.: Psychiatric Investigation of the Sequelae of Interruption of Pregnancy, *Schweiz. Arch. Neurol. Psychiat.,* 67:365, 1951.

157. Niswander, K. R.; Patterson, R. J.: Psychologic Reaction to Therapeutic Abortion. *Obstet. Gynec.,* 29:702-706, May 1967.

158. WHO Technical Report Series, op. cit., p. 42.

159. *A Psychological View of Abortion.* A Commentary by Colmin McCarthy. St. Paul Sunday Pioneer Press. From the *Washington Post,* March 7, 1971.

160. Ibid.

161. Cain, A. C.; Erickson, M. E.; Fast, I.; and Vaughan, R. A.: Children's Disturbed Reactions to Their Mother's Miscarriages. *Psychosom. Med.,* 26:58-66, 1964.

162. Heller, A.; Whittington, H. G.: The Colorado Story: Denver General

Hospital Experience with the Change in the Law on Therapeutic Abortion. *Amer. J. Psychiat.,* 125:809-816, 1968.

163. Julienne, M.: Suddenly I'm a Legal Abortionist. *Medical Economics,* 93-95, 152-168. Nov. 23, 1970.

164. Thompson, H., Cowen, D. L., Berris, B.: Therapeutic Abortion: A Two-Year Experience in One Hospital. *JAMA,* 213:991-995, 1970.

165. Kibel, H. D.: Staff Reactions to Abortion, A Psychiatrist's View. *Obstet. Gynec.,* 39:128-133. Jan. 1972.

166. McDermott, J. F.; and Char, W. F.: Abortion Repeal in Hawaii: An Unexpected Crisis in Patient Care. *Amer. J. Orthopsychiat.,* 41:620-26, July 1971.

167. Ibid., p. 621.

168. Ibid., p. 622.

169. Ibid.

170. Kibel, op. cit., p. 132.

171. Ibid.

172. Connor, E. J.: Therapeutic Abortion. *Audio-Digest Ob. Gyn.,* Vol. 17, No. 16, Aug. 18, 1970.

173. Ratner, H.: A Public Health Physician Views Abortion. *Ill. Med. J.,* May 1967.

174. Marder, L.: Liberal Therapeutic Abortion: Cure or Cause of Mental Illness. *Audio-Digest Ob. Gyn.,* Vol. 16, No. 17, Sept. 2, 1969.

175. WHO Technical Report Series, op. cit.

176. Fleck, S.: Some Psychiatric Aspects of Abortion. *J. Nerve. Ment. Dis.,* 151:42-50, 1970.

177. Kummer, J. M.: Post-Abortion Psychiatric Illness—A Myth? *Am. J. Psychiat.,* 119:980-983, 1963.

178. Simon, N. M.; Senturia, A. G.: Psychiatric Sequelae of Abortion. *Arch. Gen. Psychiat.,* 15:378-389, Oct. 1966.

179. Heath, D. S.: Psychiatry and Abortion. *Canad. Psychiat. Ass. J.,* 16:55-63, Feb. 1971.

LEGAL

▪5▪

THE WORLD IN
PERSPECTIVE

Joseph A. Lampe

In nearly two-thirds of the world, abortion is prohibited except in cases in which the pregnant woman's life is in danger (1). Until quite recently, the remaining one-third, including the Soviet Union, most of Eastern Europe, Scandinavia, Japan, China, and a few jurisdictions in the United States, permitted abortion under certain other circumstances (2, 3, 4). In very recent years this latter group has been enlarged by the addition of Great Britain, South Australia, Denmark, Finland, Canada, India, Singapore, Turkey and seventeen states in the United States (5, 6).

The permissive laws range from New York's abortion-on-demand under twenty-four weeks and the Soviet Union's abortion-on-demand under twelve weeks, to Scandinavia's strictly controlled abortions for broadly defined indications (7, 8, 9).

A review of some aspects of representative permissive abortion laws is presented here in an attempt to understand and place in perspective this worldwide phenomenon which killed over 1,546,000 nascent human beings in only one year in but six of these countries (Bulgaria, Hungary, Czechoslovakia, Yugoslavia, Poland and Japan) (10, 11).

EASTERN EUROPE

In 1920, the Soviet Union instituted abortion-on-demand, but in

Appreciation is extended to Robert P. N. Shearin, M.D., Fellow in general surgery at the Mayo Graduate School of Medicine, for his assistance in the preparation of this paper.

Legal

1936, restricted the operation to strictly medical and eugenic grounds (12). In 1955, it once more relaxed its prohibitions (13). With this exception, and that of Poland, where abortion was permitted in the case of pregnancy resulting from rape, abortion was illegal in Eastern Europe during the pre-World War II period (14). The war years and the post-war period saw great disruptions of the social, economic and political fabric of society, a breakdown in law and order, and consequent increases in the incidence of rape and illegal abortion. During this time there also was essentially no effort being directed toward contraception (15, 16).

In 1947, East Germany relaxed its abortion law, permitting abortion for medical, ethical, eugenic and socio-medical indications (17). This, however, led to an increase in both legal and illegal abortions, and the law became restrictive again in 1950, with some relaxation occurring in 1965 (18). From 1951, the other communist-block countries of Eastern Europe began to relax, and in some instances subsequently to restrict, their laws regarding abortion (19).

Rather than enumerate the present laws of the Soviet Union, Poland, East Germany, Czechoslovakia, Hungary, Rumania, Bulgaria, and Yugoslavia regarding abortion, let us note certain similarities and dissimilarities.

All of the countries listed essentially restrict abortion to the first trimester, i.e., the first twelve weeks of pregnancy, exceptions being made only when there is grave danger to the woman's life or if serious eugenic reasons prevail (20). This fact should be kept in mind when attempting to compare abortion morbidity and mortality statistics from these communist countries with other countries which do not have such restrictions.

The most permissive laws—i.e., abortion-on-demand—were found in the Soviet Union, Bulgaria, Hungary, and, until 1966, Rumania. In that year, Rumania, where a great number of abortions were being performed, restricted the operation to socio-medical indications because of "great prejudice to the birth rate" (as well as) "severe consequences to the health of the woman" (21, 22). In 1968, Bulgaria slightly restricted its abortion law, denying abortion to childless women except on medical grounds (23).

The other countries of Eastern Europe are generally similar in their allowance of abortion on widely interpreted socio-medical grounds (24). Most of these countries require contraceptive counseling as a part of their abortion procedure (25).

Dr. Alfred Kotasek has recently reported that various undesirable consequences of Czechoslovakia's abortion law have led to official recognition that it must be amended, especially with regard to primigravidas, i.e., women pregnant for the first time. It is hoped that with the increased availability of contraceptives, sex education and a higher standard of living, the number of legal abortions will decrease (26).

It is interesting that in Yugoslavia the abortion commission is required to point out the dangers of abortion and the advantages of contraception. Also, "A health worker should regard abortion as biologically, medically, psychologically and socially harmful. Corresponding to the principles of socialist humanism and medical knowledge, human life must be respected from its beginning" (27). Similar dissuasive measures are taken in the USSR; moreover, the permissive regulations issued in 1955 include a list of contra-indications (28).

East German Professor K.-H. Mehlan has stated the reasons for which the communist countries of Eastern Europe weakened their abortion laws; first, there were no highly effective contraceptives available at that time and, second, there was a desire to wage an intensive campaign against illegal abortion. But he goes on to say:

Legalizing abortion does not mean a permanent solution to the problem; the People's Republics have noted this, too. Criminal abortion will be combated in the future in the following ways:
1. Promotion of the desire to have children by a generous family policy.
2. Establishment of counseling centers for contraception to enable each woman to prevent an unwanted pregnancy; this is meant as a measure of health protection.
3. Promotion of sex education aiming at appropriate attitudes between sexes. (29)

Bucic and Knezevic, speaking of abortion as a means of birth control in Yugoslavia state: "In comparison to other methods of birth control, interruption of pregnancy represents the most grave and dangerous method because of its expansiveness and its consequences" (30).

Budvari, speaking in regard to legal abortion in Hungary and its value as a birth control measure and its efficiency in combating illegal abortion, concludes: "It appears to us that the best solution is not the 'liberalization' of abortion, but the use of contraceptives, particularly oral contraceptives. This way appears to us to be more humane, more ethical and more 'medical' than 'authorized' abortion" (31).

WESTERN EUROPE

The abortion laws of non-communist Europe are generally of three types: those which restrict abortion except in life-saving circumstances, as in France, Austria and Germany; those which permit abortion for certain more or less broad medico-social reasons, as well as eugenic reasons and instances of pregnancy following sexual offenses (the types of laws existing in Scandinavia) (32, 33, 34, 35); and the third type, found in Great Britain, which has gone beyond the Scandinavian models to permit abortion for a unique quasi-social reason, although it seems clear that the legislators did not wish to approve, literally, of abortion-on-demand (36, 37).

The British Abortion Act of 1967 permits abortion on four grounds:

a. [if] the continuance of the pregnancy would involve risk to the life of the pregnant woman greater than if the pregnancy were terminated; or
b. that it would involve risk of injury to the physical or mental health of the pregnant woman greater than if the pregnancy were terminated; or
c. that it would involve risk or injury to the physical or mental health of any existing children of the pregnant woman's family greater than if the pregnancy were terminated; or
d. that there is substantial risk that if the child were born it would suffer from such physical or mental abnormalities as to be seriously handicapped. (38)

A provision for conscientious objection on the part of the physician is present, in that "no person shall be under any legal duty to participate in any treatment authorized by the Act to which he has a conscientious objection unless the treatment is necessary to save the life or prevent grave permanent injury to physical or mental health of a pregnant woman" (39).

Although fetal age is not specifically mentioned in the Act, it is commonly understood to restrict abortions to fetuses less than twenty-eight weeks of age, in accordance with the Infant Life Act of 1929.

It may be of interest to mention a few opinions of the British Medical Defense Union on the interpretations of the Act's provisions likely to protect the physician from civil or criminal proceedings. If, for example, a physician who conscientiously objects to abortion is confronted by a pregnant woman he should (to be "safe") ask himself the question: "Might this be a case where abortion could be lawful and in which my opinion to the contrary could be challenged on the ground that my good faith was impaired by my conscientious objection?" (40). If the answer is in the affirmative, the gynecologist should refer the woman to a colleague "untroubled by conscientious objection" (41).

Again, in the opinion of the Medical Defense Union, while the consent of the woman is always required prior to abortion, that of her husband, while it should be sought, is not essential even if he strongly objects to the abortion. Also, in the case of a girl between the ages of sixteen and twenty-one, the physician may, only with the girl's permission, seek the consent of her parents for the abortion, but such consent is not essential. If the girl is under age sixteen, the physician should in all cases inform her parents and ask their consent for the operation but, again, such consent is not deemed essential. In the last case the Union admits the possibility of the parents suing the abortionist for assault upon their daughter but feels that "it is very improbable that such a claim would be upheld" (42).

More than a year after the British law was enacted, the Royal College of Obstetricians and Gynaecologists reported on a questionnaire of members concerned with its functioning. In the same issue of the *British Medical Journal* an editorial concerning the report pointed out that a third of the abortions were being carried out by a tenth of the consultants. It is also noted that

it appears from the report, consultants are agreeing to terminate every pregnancy on request without serious question, not because they believe in that course, but because the brevity of their decision allows proper time for the treatment of other patients and the teaching of staff and students. If abortion on demand was made legal that would not make it ethical. (43)

The editorial continues:

It is fashionable nowadays to speak of a "failure in communication" if people do something that seems against all reason and their own interests when a better course is known. But the fact is that many people are unreasonable and lack any sort of foresight. They may well be the most likely to neglect contraception measures and to think abortion will brighten their day as harmlessly as a shampoo. (44)

ASIA

Of the three most populous nations of Asia—China, Japan and India— the former two appear to have *de facto* abortion-on-demand. India formerly permitted abortion only when there was risk to the life of the woman, but the "Medical Termination Act of 1971," passed by Parliament, allows abortion up to twenty weeks if a pregnancy threatens a woman's physical or mental health, taking into consideration her "actual or reasonably foreseeable environment" (45, 46). While little has been published concerning the Chinese statute on abortion, their practice is fairly well known (47). The Japanese Eugenic Protection Law of 1948, as amended in 1949, is, on the other hand, quite well known and similar to Scandinavian abortion laws in that it permits abortion when the woman's "health may be affected seriously by continuation of pregnancy or by delivery from the physical or economic viewpoint" (48).

Manabe has commented that the unsettled social conditions which were a feature of the post-war period in Japan, coupled with the infrequent use of the relatively crude contraceptives then available, were both factors, along with the high incidence of pulmonary tuberculosis as a complication of pregnancy, in enactment of the Japanese abortion law (49). It is conceded by several authors that broad interpretation of the "economic hazard" clause withholds abortion in Japan from essentially no one (50, 51, 52). Indeed, the total number of abortions in Japan each year is estimated to be at least double the reported number of 700,000 to 900,000 in view of tax cheating by the approximately 12,500 specially trained M.D.-abortionists (53).

Easy profits made from induced abortion by these specialists tend to perpetuate Japan's abortion epidemic. But despite the opposition of gynecologists who make a living from abortion, a major effort to impose restrictions on legal abortion is being made in the Diet by the Liberal Democratic party; there is more and more criticism of the practice in newspapers and on television (54). At its regular Cabinet meeting on May 23, 1972, Prime Minister Sato's government approved a bill intended to remove from the law the clause allowing abortion for economic reasons (55).

Singapore's 1969 abortion act specifies that the "environment," including the woman's family and financial circumstances, constitutes an indication *per se;* this is in contrast to the previously described position in Great Britain, where the environment is merely a factor that may be taken into account in assessing the risk to the woman's health (56).

United States

Prior to 1967, essentially all of the fifty states prohibited induced abortion except to protect the life of the pregnant woman (57). The twenty-nine states which at present have such laws, and the dates of enactment, are shown in the table on page 95.

The following two states are in basically the same grouping, but have laws with substantially different wording:

Massachusetts (1845): Statute prohibits "unlawful" abortion, or abortion which is "malicious" or performed "without lawful justification," Case law, *Commonwealth* vs. *Wheeler* (1944), allows abortion to preserve the pregnant woman's "life or health" which would otherwise be in great peril, providing that the physician's belief coincides "with the average judgment of the doctors in the community in which he practices."

Pennsylvania (1860): State law prohibits "unlawful" abortions; however, "unlawful" has not been defined either by the courts or by the legislature. Similar use of the word "lawful" is made in other Pennsylvania statutes, however, and it is commonly understood that "lawful" abortions are those performed to preserve the life of the mother.

The abortion laws of laws of Alabama (1951) and the District of Columbia (1901), permit abortion not only to preserve "life," but also for reasons of "health." Mississippi (1966) allows pregnancy resulting from felonious intercourse as a justifiable reason for abortion.

In 1959, the American Law Institute (A.L.I.) recommended in its Model Penal Code that abortion be *legally* justified on any of three grounds: (1) when continuance of the pregnancy would gravely impair the physical or mental health of the mother; (2) when the child would be born with a grave physical or mental defect; (3) when the pregnancy resulted from rape, incest or other felonious intercourse,

STATE	ENACTMENT DATE	STATE	ENACTMENT DATE
Arizona	1865	New Hampshire	1848
Connecticut	1972	New Jersey	1849
Idaho	1863	North Dakota	1943
Illinois	1874	Ohio	1841
Indiana	1838	Oklahoma	1910
Iowa	1843	Rhode Island	1913
Kentucky	1910	South Dakota	1896
Louisiana	1914	Tennessee	1833
Maine	1840	Texas	1859
Michigan	1846	Utah	1876
Minnesota	1851	Vermont	1867
Missouri	1835	West Virginia	1848
Montana	1864	Wisconsin	1960
Nebraska	1873	Wyoming	1869
Nevada	1861		

including illicit intercourse with a girl under the age of sixteen (59). The Model Penal Code also recommended that abortion on these grounds be performed only by a licensed physician, and only after consultation with one colleague (60). In the years prior to 1967 these recommendations were considered and rejected by the legislatures of Illinois, Minnesota, New York and New Hampshire (61). Since that time, thirteen states have adopted abortion laws similar to the American Law Institute's Model Penal Code (62).

Colorado, on April 25, 1967, was the first state to enact an abortion law modeled after the American Law Institute's proposal, but only after considerable "molding of public opinion" in that state by the bill's proponents (63). The thirteen states with these laws, and the dates of enactment and significant variations from the model are:

Arkansas (1969)
California (1967)—(does not have fetal indication in the law)
Colorado (1967)
Delaware (1969)
Florida (1972)—(specifies "health" rather than "mental health")
Georgia (1968)—(does not recognize incest as a reason)
Kansas (1969)
Maryland (1968)—(does not recognize incest as a reason)
New Mexico (1969)
North Carolina (1967)
Oregon (1969)—(see paragraph below)
South Carolina (1970)
Virginia (1970)

Oregon's law is similar to the A.L.I. model code, but it adopts the following language: "In determining whether or not there is substantial risk ... account may be taken of the mother's total environment, actual or reasonably foreseeable" (64).

The weakest abortion laws in the United States place no legal restrictions on reasons for which an abortion may be performed. The states with these laws, all enacted in 1970, are: Alaska, Hawaii, New York and Washington. They require that the abortion must be performed by a physician and, except for New York State, in a hospital or other approved facility (65). Because these latter state laws are more permissive than any other abortion laws in the world, the New York law is presented here in detail as representative:

The people of the State of New York represented in Senate and Assembly, do enact as follows:

Section 1. Subdivision three of section 125.05 of the penal law is hereby amended as follows.

3. "Justifiable abortional act." An abortional act is justifiable when committed upon a female with her consent by a duly licensed physician acting (a) under a reasonable belief that such is necessary to preserve her life, or (b) within twenty-four weeks from the commencement of her pregnancy. A pregnant female's commission of an abortional act upon herself is justifiable when she acts upon advice of a duly licensed physician (1) that such act is necessary to preserve her life, or, (2) within twenty-four weeks from the commencement of her pregnancy. The submission by a female to an abortional act is justifiable when she believes that it is being committed by a duly licensed physician acting under the reasonable belief that such act is necessary to preserve her life, or, within twenty-four weeks from the commencement of her pregnancy. (66)

Distinctive features of this law include: (1) attempts at self-abortion "upon the advice of a duly licensed physician" are permitted; (2) demand of the pregnant woman is a sufficient ground for abortion up to twenty-four weeks of pregnancy; (3) there are no provisions regarding the age of consent, place of abortion, common basis for determining the gestational age of the fetus, or any other legal problems likely to spring from its implementation, including the liability of the physician or hospital that conscientiously objects to the performance of abortion.

The Medical Society of the State of New York (MSSNY) opposed enactment of this bill (67). Subsequent to its enactment, the MSSNY felt it necessary to discuss certain points in its "Abortion Guidelines" (paraphrased, except where quoted):

A. The term abortion applies only to the end of the twentieth week of gestation (four weeks earlier than the legal deadline).
B. After twenty weeks, emptying the uterus "constitutes an actual birth process."
C. The phrase "within twenty-four weeks from commencement of her pregnancy" would be confusing because the "exact date when pregnancy begins cannot be determined accurately."
D. "Where *the infant is born alive,* a birth certificate is required. The *subsequent death of such an infant* necessitates the filing of the usual death certificate" (emphasis supplied).
E. "Because the chances of fetal survival increase each week, abortive acts should not be initiated after the twentieth week of gestation."
F. "The Medical Society of the State of New York would like to caution all physicians that an abortion performed after the twelfth week of gestation is fraught with tremendous danger" (emphasis theirs). (68).

TRENDS

From the preceding summary it can be seen that the first state to relax its abortion law in recent years did so in 1966, two did so in 1967, one in 1968, five more in 1969, and, finally, six in 1970. In 1971, when nearly all the state legislatures were in session, no permissive abortion bill passed; such legislation was positively set back or defeated in some thirty-four states which considered it (69).

Thus far in 1972, Florida and Connecticut have passed new abortion laws in response to court decisions declaring their previous statutes unconstitutional. The new Connecticut law is virtually identical to the old law, but attempts to overcome the objections of the court by adding language to clarify the legislative intent of the law and the grounds on which abortions may be performed (70).

The circumstances surrounding enactment of the new Florida abortion law are complex. On February 14, 1972, the Florida Supreme Court struck down both Florida abortion statutes, on the ground that they were unconstitutionally vague. In so doing the court held that the statutes violated the *state* constitution, and that regardless of what the United States Supreme Court might do, the *state* decision would supersede; that the common law became effective, and that this prohibited the abortion of a quick child; that the legislature was urged to pass a new law, and that it would be constitutional if it provided for abortion to preserve the life *or health* of the mother. The court stayed the effect of its decision sixty days to allow the legislature time to enact new legislation. The state Attorney General hailed the decision as a great step and did not appeal it.

In effect, the court gave the legislature sixty days in which to write a law with A.L.I. provisions, and such a law was subsequently passed on April 7, 1972. Many legislators who had opposed abortion in the past, and who would otherwise not have voted for a permissive abortion bill, voted for the bill only as preferable to the common law (71).

A far more significant development occurred in New York State in May 1972. By larger margins than those with which the 1970 abortion-on-demand bill had passed, the State Assembly and Senate successively voted to repeal the two-year-old abortion law. Only Governor Nelson Rockefeller's subsequent veto prevented New York from restoring its original "life of mother" abortion law. A massive, long-term, grass-roots lobbying effort was ultimately responsible for the vote. The campaign, directed by Catholic and Orthodox Jewish leaders and dozens of right-to-life organizations around the state, mobilized thousands of concerned citizens. One rally in New York City's Central Park turned out 34,000 people (72,73,74).

Attempts to secure passage of a uniform national abortion law and further relaxation of state abortion statutes will doubtless continue for years to come. However, 1971 clearly marked the beginning of effective efforts in nearly all states in the country to reverse the previous trend toward easy abortion.

Efforts at further relaxation of the law having thus been effectively stymied in the legislatures, there is a feeling among advocates of abortion that relief will be found through the courts and not through the legislatures (75,76). Because the courts are not as susceptible to the kind of public pressure that has prevented pro-abortion legislative successes since 1970, it is likely that the strategy of those groups and individuals favoring legalized abortion will increasingly shift toward attempts to influence the courts to declare abortion statutes unconstitutional. In the words of University of California demographer Judith Blake Davis, "A Supreme Court ruling concerning the constitutionality of existing state restrictions is the only road to rapid change in the grounds for abortion" (77).

An even more recent development is also worth noting. Perhaps spurred on by the successful passage of Referendum 20, legalizing abortion in the state of Washington, abortion advocates have attempted to place referenda on abortion on the ballots in at least two states in 1972: Michigan and North Dakota (78).

Whether this strategy will be successful remains to be seen,* but the 1970 experience of Washington State is perhaps instructive. The referendum for abortion-on-demand was placed on the ballot for the election of November 1970 by a special session of the legislature. In February of 1970, polls taken in Washington showed that only 20% of the people of the state were opposed to Referendum 20. Yet, with just over one million votes cast, nearly 46% opposed the referendum on November 3rd. The abortion issue is often portrayed as "Catholics versus the house," but only 13% of Washington is Catholic and 65% of the residents of the state have no formal religious affiliation. Obviously, the majority of the opposition to abortion had to come

---

* In the November 7, 1972, general election, voters in both North Dakota and Michigan overwhelmingly defeated proposals which would have brought abortion-on-demand to their states. This is in direct contradiction to recent misleading public opinion polls which would indicate contrary voter sentiment.

from outside the Catholic community, and certainly a substantial opposition from those who had no religious affiliation whatsoever (79).

It should be noted that the above result occurred despite great hostility and non-cooperation on the part of the press and the radio and television stations, which made it impossible for those opposed to the referendum to use the mass media to convey their message to the public. A large-scale public education program on abortion was nevertheless undertaken by thousands of volunteers of Voice For the Unborn and other right-to-life groups prior to the election and, given enough time, it would appear that such efforts have the potential to persuade a majority of voters to oppose legalized abortion (80).

SUMMARY AND CONCLUSIONS

At this point it should be apparent that frequent and substantial changes in abortion legislation have been made in recent years in many countries, generally in the direction of making abortions easier to obtain. Several countries, however, after adopting very permissive abortion legislation, have subsequently modified certain provisions and made their legislation more restrictive. Other countries are in the process of doing so.

One is tempted to observe that all of these changes are merely a continuing, fruitless search for the nonexistent "Ideal Abortion Law," and represent a failure to effectively treat the underlying social pathology. Neither allowing abortion nor prohibiting it has done anything to correct the underlying social and economic conditions which cause women to seek abortions. In the long run, only by confronting and solving these problems are we likely to find an exit from what has been termed "the abortion dilemma."

BIBLIOGRAPHY

1. Tietze, C., and Lewit, S.: Abortion. *Scientific American,* 220:21-27, 1969.
2. Ibid.
3. de Moerloose, J.: Abortion: A Survey of Current Legislation. *WHO Chronicle,* 25:328-333, 1971.
4. Duffy, E. A.: The Effect of Changes in the State Abortion Laws. *HEW Public Health Service Publication No. 2165,* Feb. 1971.
5. de Moerloose, op. cit.
6. Duffy, op. cit.
7. State of New York in Assembly. Chapter 127, Laws of 1970. March 23, 1970.

8. Tietze, C.: Abortion in Europe. *Am. J. Public Health,* 57:1923-1931, 1967.
9. Tietze and Lewit, op. cit.
10. Manabe, Y.: Artificial Abortion at Midpregnancy by Mechanical Stimulation of the Uterus. *Am. J. Obstet. Gynec.,* 105:132-146, 1969.
11. Mehlan, K.-H.: Combating Illegal Abortion in the Socialist Countries of Europe. *World Med. J.,* 13:84-87, 1966.
12. Potts, M.: Legal Abortion in Eastern Europe. *Eugenics Rev.,* 59:232-250, 1967.
13. de Moerloose, J.: Abortion Throughout the World. *Nursing Times,* 2:678-680, 1971.
14. Potts, op. cit.
15. Mehlan, op. cit.
16. Milosovec, B., et al.: Contraceptives Versus Abortion. *Proceedings of the Fourth Conference of the Region for Europe, Near East, and Africa of the IPPF.* New York, Excerpta Medica Foundation, 1965.
17. Breitenecker, L., and Breitenecker, R.: "Abortion in the German-Speaking Countries of Europe." *Abortion and the Law,* ed. David T. Smith. Cleveland, Ohio: The Press of Western Reserve University, 1967.
18. Ibid.
19. Roemer, R.: Abortion Law: The Approaches of Different Nations. *Am. J. Public Health,* 57:1906-1922, 1967.
20. Potts, op. cit.
21. Ibid.
22. Tietze, op. cit.
23. Tietze and Lewit, op. cit.
24. Potts, op. cit.
25. Mehlan, op. cit.
26. Kotasek, A.: Artificial Termination of Pregnancy in Czechoslovakia. *Int. J. Gynaec. Obstet.,* 9:118-119, May 1971.
27. Potts, op. cit.
28. de Moerloose, *Nursing Times,* op. cit.
29. Mehlan, op. cit.
30. Bucic, M., et al.: Le problème de l'avortement dans la regulatione des naissances en Yugoslavie. *Annales de Médecine Légale,* 47:513-518, 1967.
31. Budvari, R.: La lutte contre l'avortement criminel et la regulation des naissances en Hongrie. *Annales de Médecine Légale,* 47:519-520, 1967.
32. Borell, U., and Engstrom, L. Legal Abortions in Sweden. *World Med. J.,* 13:72-75, 1966.
33. Breitenecker and Breitenecker, op. cit.
34. Roemer, op. cit.
35. Tietze, op. cit.
36. Addison, P. H.: Abortion Act 1967. *Lancet,* 2:503-507, 1968.

37. Medical Defence Union: The Abortion Act 1967—Memorandum from Medical Defence Union. *Brit. Med. J.,* 1:759-762, 1968.
38. Ibid.
39. Ibid.
40. Ibid.
41. Ibid.
42. Addison, op. cit.
43. Consultant's Report on Abortion: An editorial. *Brit. Med. J.,* 2:491-492, 1970.
44. Ibid.
45. Population Reference Bureau: The Population Year in Review: 1971. *Population Profile,* January 1972.
46. India Abortion. *The Washington Post,* April 1, 1972.
47. Wu, P.: The Use of Vacuum Bottle in Therapeutic Abortion—A Collective Survey. *Chinese Med. J.,* 85:245-248, 1966.
48. Suzumura, M., and Kikuchi, S.: Induced Abortion in Japan—Review of the Literature. *J. of the Jap. Ob. Gyn. Soc.,* 13:179-197, 1966.
49. Manabe, op. cit.
50. Ibid.
51. Suzumura and Kikuchi, op. cit.
52. Tietze and Lewit, op. cit.
53. Hayasaka, Y., et al.: Japan's 22-Year Experience with a Liberal Abortion Law. *Twelfth International Congress of FIAMC.* Washington, D.C., Oct. 11-14, 1970.
54. Ibid.
55. Government Plans Stricter Abortion Law. *Mainichi Daily News,* May 24, 1972.
56. de Moerloose, *WHO Chronicle,* op. cit.
57. George, B. J., in *Abortion and the Law,* supra.
58. Granfield, D.: *The Abortion Decision.* New York, Doubleday and Co., 1971.
59. American Law Institute, *Model Penal Code,* Proposed Official Draft, Section 230. Philadelphia, American Law Institute, 1962. Pp. 187-193.
60. Ibid.
61. George, op. cit.
62. Duffy, op. cit.
63. Downing, S., et al.: Abortion Under the New Colorado Law. *Nebraska Med. J.,* 55:24-30, 1970.
64. Statement on Therapeutic Abortion. *American College of Obstetricians and Gynecologists Newsletter,* June 1968.
65. Duffy, op. cit.
66. State of New York in Assembly, op. cit.
67. Klemfuss, R.: *State M.D.s Clarify Abortion Stand.* News release, Medical Society of the State of New York, March 26, 1970.

68. Ibid.
69. Taylor, M.: Memorandum. National Right to Life Committee, Washington, D.C., Dec. 22, 1971.
70. Connecticut Ban on Abortions Gains. *The New York Times,* May 23, 1972.
71. Horkan, T.: Memorandum. Florida Catholic Conference, Tallahassee, Florida, April 10, 1972.
72. Backlash on Abortion. *Newsweek,* May 22, 1972.
73. Rally Protests Law on Abortion. *The New York Times,* April 17, 1972.
74. The Abortion Law Scored by Rabbis. *The New York Times,* April 24, 1972.
75. Duffy, op. cit.
76. George, op. cit.
77. Blake, J.: Abortion and Public Opinion: The 1960-1970 Decade. *Science,* 171:540-549, 1971.
78. Taylor, M.: Memorandum. National Right to Life Committee, Washington, D.C., Jan. 29, 1972.
79. Van Derhoef, K.: Anti-Abortion Forces Gained in Washington. *National Catholic Reporter,* Nov. 27, 1970.
80. Ibid.

▪ 6 ▪

THE LEGAL CASE FOR
THE UNBORN CHILD

Dennis J. Horan, Jerome A. Frazel, Jr.,
Thomas M. Crisham, Dolores B. Horan,
John D. Gorby, John T. Noonan, Jr.,
David W. Louisell

ABORTION AND CIVIL RIGHTS

Abortion is not a private matter. The destruction of human life, even "incipient" or developing human life in the womb, can never be considered a private matter under our law. The contention that it is a private matter would be too ludicrous and absurd to even argue were it not so often put forth under such intellectually impeccable auspices. Would those civil libertarians who argue that abortion is a private matter argue that the exercise of civil rights is purely a private matter between the Black man and the man that thwarts them? Certainly not. Just as the civil right to vote must be protected by law, so too the most fundamental and basic of all civil rights—the Right to Life—must be protected by law.

Nor is abortion a merely sectarian religious problem or one for the area of "private" morality. Abortion is nothing less than a question of *civil rights:* Does the unborn child have a civil right to life? If he or she does, is it not then the duty of *all* citizens in a pluralistic society, regardless of religious faith or private moral sensitivities, to protect the unborn child's civil rights?

In various sections of this paper we have developed the legal rights of the unborn child in torts, property and equity cases, as well as under the criminal law. We argue, in still another section, that the purpose of the abortion statutes in the criminal law was for the protection of the unborn child. Proponents of abortion on demand have very cleverly convinced a segment of the courts that the historical purpose of abortion laws was merely to protect the health of the mother against the onslaught of young and foolhardy surgeons. Nothing could be further from the truth. Although hundreds of types of surgery are performed, why has only abortion been prohibited by the criminal law? The answer is simple, yet ignored. Because only in abortion are we talking about the destruction of another human life.

The position that our law takes on abortion indicates the position it will take on euthanasia, genetic engineering, cloning, and all of the difficult human life problems facing our society in the years ahead. Those who argue for the unborn child's right to life are arguing not only for the unborn child, but for the civil right to life of every human being—the mentally ill, the aged, the genetically incompetent, the idle, the useless. If the law vacates the protection of the civil rights of the innocent child in the womb, it will one day vacate its protection of the civil right to life of the mentally incompetent, the senile and the hopelessly ill. It will vacate its protection of your civil rights.

The position that the authors take on the abortion issue is simple yet fundamental and was adequately stated by the Supreme Court of Pennsylvania in 1850:

By the well settled and established doctrine of the common law, the civil rights of an infant *en ventre sa mare* are fully protected at all periods after conception.[1]

That "civil rights" includes more than just property rights, and indeed, includes, as we argue, the civil right to life, was stated as recently as 1970 when a three-judge federal court held:

Once human life has commenced, the constitutional protection found in the Fifth and Fourteenth Amendments imposes upon the state the duty of safeguarding it.[2]

Not only is that duty imposed upon the state, but also on every good citizen concerned with the protection of those who cannot protect themselves.

ABORTION AND MARITAL RIGHTS

There is an interest of husband and wife to preserve their conjugal relations from state interference.[3] The usual criminal abortion statute[4] does not affect the sexual relations of husband and wife. Limitation on abortion does not entail state interference with the right of marital intercourse. Nor does enforcement of the statute require invasion of the conjugal bedroom.

Assume *arguendo* that a married couple has the right not to have, raise and educate a child they do not want. Although this right may be unlimited before conception, after a new human being has come into existence compelling state interests then enter the picture. The most fundamental of all state interests is the protection of the lives of its people. Although it may be socially desirable that every child be a "wanted child," the parents' attitude cannot under our Constitution be the single criterion which determines the right of a living unborn child to continue its existence.

In this area there has been a gradual evolution of civilized thought. In the Roman Republic the father, by virtue of the *patria potestas,* had the literal power of life or death over his children.[5] As one commentator pointed out: "Within the family the paterfamilias enjoyed a lifetime despotism."[6]

Over a period of about two thousand years the state has built up a defense in behalf of children, born and unborn, against the aggressive and proprietary instincts of their progenitors. The problem of the "battered" child today is evidence, if evidence is needed, that the state must still by law restrain the freedom of conduct of parents toward their children.[7]

Prior to the seventeenth century the prevailing doctrine had been that of the Aristotelian school. Aristotle taught that forty days after conception the fetus underwent a transformation which made it human. This notion was successfully attacked in 1621 as medical nonsense by Paolo Zacchia in his *Questiones Medico-Legales,* 9.1. Thereafter, the medical profession gradually accepted the view that there was no valid line to be drawn within the womb, and the law slowly but surely followed the medical lead.

Today there can scarcely be a return to the Roman law theory that a parent has absolute dominion over his offspring, or a return to the ancient notion that a fetus is "part" of his mother. The autonomy of the unborn child is established clearly by modern fetology. In the light of this evolution of legal thought and medical knowledge, it would indeed be to turn back the clock to hold that some vague legal notion of marital privacy can take precedence over a child's right to life.

A fortiori, the same considerations apply to the argument that a woman has a right to destroy any fetus of her own that she, in the most literal sense, finds "unbearable." This contention of a right to an abortion vested in a woman has, of course, no Constitutional precedent. Nevertheless this contention may be the emotional heart of the almost hysterical attacks being made upon the abortion statutes. No such right is referred to in any of the Amendments to the Constitution; therefore, it is necessary to determine whether any such right is implied in any provision of the Bill of Rights or can be found within the penumbra of any of the same.

The claimed right of marital privacy, to a woman's absolute control over her body, is not unconstitutionally restricted by a criminal abortion statute, which logically assigns greater value to the life of the child who will be killed by the abortion.

When one becomes a member of society, he necessarily parts with some privileges which, as an individual not affected by his relations to others, he might retain. It has been said that society based on the rule that each one is a law unto himself would soon be confronted with disorder and anarchy, and that the liberty of one individual must necessarily be subject to the same right in all others. Hence, liberty does not signify unrestrained license to follow the dictates of an unbridled will. Individuals may be deprived of life or liberty as punishment for crime. *And one who is prevented from injuring another cannot justly assert that he has himself been deprived of any right.* (emphasis added)[8]

If one recognizes in women the right to possession and control of their own person, then surely they must recognize the same right in their unborn children to possession and control of their own persons.

Constitutional liberty is always a relative term and, at most, means liberty regulated by just and impartial laws; . . . a statute does not deprive a citizen of his liberty in the constitutional sense simply because it imposes burdens, abridges freedom of action, regulates occupations, or subjects individuals to restraints in matters which affect public interests or the rights of others.[9]

The claim of freedom over one's body is, of course, a self-evident right, if it means that a woman should be free to refuse sexual intercourse or free to practice contraception. But as Judge Ainsworth said in speaking for the majority of a three-judge court:

We do not find that an equation of the generalized right of the woman to determine whether she shall bear children with the asserted right to abort an embryo or fetus is compelled by fact or logic.[10]

The criminal abortion statutes in our various states do not require a woman to subject her body to the burden of pregnancy. But the further claim that a woman is free to destroy the being once conceived, makes sense only if that being can be regarded as part of herself, a part which she may discard for her own good. If the child is mere "tissue," a part of the mother, then there cannot be any legal limitation upon what she may do with "it." If the unborn child is a legal person, then no arguments about privacy, eugenics, social problems, etc., can prevail over his or her right to life. He or she is entitled under our Constitution to the same protection as the mother—no more, no less.

PROPERTY RIGHTS OF THE UNBORN PERSON ARE PROTECTED BY LAW

For centuries the English common law of property has recognized the unborn child as an autonomous human being. It has thus reflected a basic psychological evaluation that in law, as in ordinary thought, "child" includes the conceived but as yet unborn. In 1795 an English court interpreted the ordinary meaning of "children" in a will to include a child in the womb: "An infant *en ventre sa mare,* who by the course and order of nature is then living, comes clearly within the description of 'children living at the time of his decease.' "[11] Thereafter another court rejected the contention that this was a mere rule of construction invoked for the benefit of the child: "Why should not children *en ventre sa mare* be considered generally as in existence? They are entitled to all the privileges of other persons."[12] To the argument that such a child was a non-entity that court replied:

Let us see what this non-entity can do. He may be vouched in a recovery, though it is for the purpose of making him answer over in value. He may be an executor. He may take under the statute of distributions. He may take by devise. He may be entitled under a charge for raising portions. He may have an injunction; and he may have a guardian.[13]

When the English property rules were adopted by American courts, the same approach was taken. In an early Massachusetts decision the issue before the court was whether a bequest to grandchildren "living at my decease" was valid and the court was asked to say that *"in esse"* was not the same as "living" and that for a child to be "living" the mother must be at least "quick."[14] It was there held that a conceived child fell within the meaning of the language and quoted with approval the English precedent: "The principal reason I go upon is that a child *en ventre sa mare* is a person in *rerum natura,* so that, both by the rules of the civil and common law, he is to all intents and purposes a child, as if born in the father's lifetime."[15]

The path of Anglo-American common law has been followed by the statutes. For example, most states provide that: "A posthumous child of a decedent shall receive the same share of his ancestor's intestate estate as if he had been born in his father's lifetime."[16] Numerous cases have interpreted the law, and recognized the rights of the unborn child pursuant to it if the child is born alive.[17] Many Conveyance Acts further provide that a posthumous child will take an interest in real estate "by any conveyance limited in remainder to the son or daughter, or to the use of the son or daughter of any person to be begotten."[18] Some Public Health Codes define a live birth as follows:

"Live birth" means the complete expulsion or extraction from its mother of a product of human conception, irrespective of the duration of pregnancy, which after such separation breathes, or shows any other evidence of life such as beating of the heart, pulsation of the umbilical cord, or definite movement of voluntary muscles, whether or not the umbilical cord has been cut or the placenta is attached.[19]

Other sections of the same statute require a registration of each live birth which occurs in the State,[20] and in the case of a fetal death which occurs after a gestation period of twenty completed weeks or more, it shall be also registered as a regular death is registered by the funeral director or person acting as such who first assumes custody of the fetus.[21]

The significance of these statutes, and of this body of law, is the recognition which they give to the legal existence of the unborn person. These concepts have been in our laws for many generations, and they must be examined, and considered in arriving at a decision on the legal status of the unborn person. It would indeed be a pernicious legal system which would, on the one hand, give to the unborn person the right to inherit property, to own property and recognize his status by requiring the public control over his life and death, as with all other persons, and yet abdicate the protection of his life to the whim of his mother. Consider the mischief which can arise if abortion-on-demand is made legal. The mother who is with child at the time of her husband's death would be free to decide whether she will destroy that child's rights of inheritance by killing the child, and perhaps thereby increase her own share of the inheritance.

These property cases established two propositions: First, the ordinary person when he uses "children" in a will means to designate by the term children those who are conceived but not yet out of the womb. It has been generally accepted as a fair interpretation of the ordinary use of language and of the ordinary person's notion of who are "children." Second, the child in the womb has property rights if there is a will, trust or intestate disposition leaving property to a class of living persons in which he is included.

From these propositions it is our position that the state legislatures may properly defend those whom ordinary language designates as "children," and they may properly prevent the unregulated extinction of such children who may own or inherit property. It would indeed be a strange inversion of values if it were the crime of embezzlement for a parent or guardian to steal an unborn child's property or income, but no crime at all to kill the child who is the owner of that property, or the recipient of that income.

TORT LAW RECOGNIZES AND PROTECTS THE RIGHTS OF THE UNBORN PERSON

In the area of tort law, a dramatic change has been occurring in the status of the unborn. Well into the twentieth century most American decisions denied recovery in tort to the human offspring injured while in the womb. The denial was based in part on the danger of fraudulent claims, in part on the difficulty of proving causation, but principally on the ground that "the defendant was not in existence at the time of his action."[22] The theory followed was that succinctly expressed in an early Massachusetts decision: "The unborn child was a part of the mother at the time of the injury."[23]

The California courts appear to have been the first to hold that a child might sue for an injury caused before birth:

The respondent asserts that the provisions of Section 29 of the Civil Code are based on a fiction of law to the effect that an unborn child is a human being separate and distinct from its mother. We think that assumption of our statute is not a fiction, but upon the contrary, that it is an established and recognized fact by science and by everyone of understanding.[24]

The District of Columbia did not lag far behind.[25] Since 1946 the California and District of Columbia approach has become general:

... (A) series of more than 30 cases, many of them expressly overruling prior holdings, have brought about the most spectacular abrupt reversal of a well settled rule on the whole history of the law of tort.[26]

As another commentator stated:

The battle in jurisprudence is almost over. The developments of the infant's right of action has illustrated the inherent capacity of legal systems to adjust to new situations.[27]

Until 1953, there existed no cause of action in Illinois, as in most states, for the wrongful death of a child injured in the womb. The issue of whether or not such child must be born alive and then die before there could be a cause of action was then presented to the Illinois Supreme Court. The law of Illinois was changed, and now allows tort recovery for a child injured *en ventre sa mare,* where the child is born alive:

Upon a reappraisal of the question, we conclude that the reasons which have been advanced in support of the doctrine of non-liability failed to carry conviction. We hold, therefore, in conformity with the recent decisions of the Courts of Last Resort of New York, Maryland, Georgia, Minnesota and Ohio and the District Court for the District of Columbia, that Plaintiff as adminis-tratrix of the estate of a viable child, who suffered prenatal injuries and was thereafter born alive, has a right of action against the defendant, whose alleged negligence caused the injury.[28]

In 1961 an Illinois Appellate Court held that a cause of action for prenatal injuries does not depend upon viability.[29] The court there quoted with approval a *Pennsylvania* decision:

As for the notion that the child must have been viable when the injuries were received, which has claimed the attention of several of the states, we regard it as having little to do with the basic right to recover, when the fetus is regarded as having existence as a separate creature from the moment of conception.[30]

The same court also quoted with approval the following language from a New Jersey decision:

Medical authorities have long recognized that a child is in existence from the moment of conception, and not merely a part of its mother's body.[31]

For a time there was hesitation as to whether recovery must be restricted to a child who was "viable" or "whether alternatively, that the mother at least be 'quick' at the time of the injury."[32] But the majority of courts have imposed no such limitation upon the right to recover.[33] There seems no reason to condition the rights of a fetus on such a shifting and uncertain standard, no reason to draw a line based upon age or size within the womb. As Professor Prosser observes: "Certainly, the infant may be no less injured, and all logic is in favor of ignoring the stage at which it occurs."[34]

As to action for wrongful death resulting from negligent injuries to the unborn, the situation on a national basis is complicated by the varying provisions of the states' wrongful death statutes. One question has been whether an unborn child is a "person" within the meaning of the controlling statute. A majority of courts passing on this question have said yes and held that an action for the wrongful death of an unborn child is maintainable even when he is stillborn.[35]

It is sometimes argued that a legislature may define "child" for some purposes and exclude it for others. This may be true, but certainly not in the unlimited sense implied. The United States Supreme Court considered this proposition and held:

To say that the test of equal protection should be the "legal" rather than the biological relationship is to avoid the issue. For the Equal Protection Clause necessarily limits the authority of the State to draw such "legal" lines as it chooses.[36]

On the authority of the above U.S. Supreme Court decision, it is readily apparent that a state may not define a person as "legally" beginning at birth, if, in fact, he biologically begins to exist at conception, so as to deny that unborn person equal protection of the laws.

The dean of authorities on tort law notes that all writers[37,38] on the subject have maintained "that the unborn child in the path of an automobile is as much a person in the street as the mother."[39] Does such a child become less a person when, instead of an automobile, a physician's forceps, curettage or suction machine is directed to his destruction?

The tort development summarized above is taken as a prime example of the effect of scientific development on law by one writer who concluded: "that the meaning and scope of even such a basic term as 'legal person' can be modified by reason of changes in scientific facts—the unborn child has been recognized as a legal person, even in the law of torts."[40]

If the unborn child qualitatively is as much a human being as an adult, as science indicates and modern law has recognized, then the state can no more exclude the unborn child from the law's protection than it could any other segment of humanity. Suppose a state's homicide laws applied only if the victims were between the ages of five and eighty, or only if the victims were white. No citation of law is necessary to observe the clear violation of the Equal Protection Clause of the Fourteenth Amendment by the state in failing to provide equal protection. It may be urged that if the fetus is a human being entitled to the Constitution's Equal Protection, then a state's general laws on homicide would be applicable to an abortion, and that the separate crime of abortion would be unnecessary or unequal in protection since the criminal penalties for the latter are less severe than for other forms of homicide.

The difference in degrees of punishment bespeaks not a difference, qualitatively, in the status of the victim, but rather a difference in the circumstances of killing. There is no general homicide statute; rather, different forms of homicide are recognized in the law with differing criminal sanctions, and this is no less true as regards the crime of abortion. As long as the right of an individual is protected, the legislature has the right to determine the nature and degree of punishment to be executed upon the offender.

The property and tort cases cited herein stand for the proposition that the law recognized the legal existence of the unborn child for those purposes. They are precedent for the recognition of "legal existence" for the purpose of determining whether a state has a Constitutional right to legislate their protection through the enactment and enforcement of laws prohibiting social abortion.

It is sometimes argued that recognition of property and tort rights requires that the child be born alive, therefore the cases prove nothing concerning the child's prior legal existence. We have shown that this is not true in wrongful death actions in many jurisdictions; but even aside from that, it is a fallacious argument. If "nothing" existed at the time prior to birth when the injury occurred or the property interest arose, how then could there be any rights which suddenly came into existence at birth? The fact that some of these rights, in some jurisdictions, have no remedies unless the child is born alive does not negate the child's legal existence when the rights arose. There can be no right to enforce at birth if the person was not in legal existence at the time of the injury or the time the property right first arose.

THE UNBORN PERSON'S RIGHT TO LIFE HAS BEEN PREFERRED BY LAW OVER CERTAIN CONSTITUTIONAL RIGHTS OF THE PARENTS

Notwithstanding the precedents of property and tort law recognizing the rights of the fetus, it might be argued that the law does not accord this recognition where the interests of the unborn child clash with those of his parents. Such modern law, however, as has developed in this unusual area is to the contrary. Where the life of the fetus has been balanced with some lesser interests of the parents, the fetus has been preferred.

One type of case has arisen through the advances of medicine in the science of fetology. Techniques have been developed since 1963 to make life-saving transfusions of blood to fetuses who have developed acute anemia in the womb because of the incompatibility of the fetus' blood with the mother's blood.[41]

A conflict of interests between fetus and parent has occurred where the parent by religious conviction has believed it sinful to permit a blood transfusion. In *Raleigh Fitkin-Paul Memorial Hospital* v. *Anderson*,[42] the mother refused, for religious reasons, to have blood transfusions which had been diagnosed as medically necessary to save her unborn child's life. The New Jersey Supreme Court stated:

We are satisfied that the unborn child is entitled to the law's protection and that an appropriate order should be made to insure such transfusions to the mother in the event that they are necessary in the opinion of the physician in charge at the time.[43]

The life of the unborn child was treated as a value outweighing even the sacred Constitutional right to the free exercise of one's religion.[44]

Elsewhere, the choice between the interests of the fetus and the civil rights of the parent has been presented in a different context. For example, in *Kyne* v. *Kyne*,[45] the issue was whether a man might be compelled to support a fetus for whose conception he was responsible. A suit seeking support was begun by the fetus' guardian ad litem when the fetus was less than six months old. The court there applied the California Civil Code, Section 196a, providing that: "the father as well as the mother of an illegitimate child must give him support and education suitable to his circumstances." The court held that Section 29 of the Civil Code "must be read together with Section 196a so as to confer the rights of an unborn child through a guardian ad litem to compel the right to support conferred by the Code."[46]

The State has a compelling interest in the welfare of its children whether born or unborn which supersedes even Constitutional rights of the parents.[47] Historically, the law has recognized the inviolability of the unborn child by providing for the suspension of execution of pregnant women under death sentence, at least when "quick."[48] This solicitude continues in modern statutes without regard to the state of pregnancy.[49]

If an unborn child has rights to support from his parents, rights enforceable by a guardian ad litem and sanctioned by the criminal law of neglect, and his right to life is paramount even to Constitutional rights of his parents, then certainly he has a right to be protected from social abortion. It would be incongruous that an unborn child should be protected by the state from wilful harm by a parent when the injury was inflicted indirectly but not when it was inflicted directly.

In these several ways, then, the law has found a well-defined cluster of human rights in the unborn child, from conception. This convergent development of property, tort, welfare, criminal and Constitutional law was not at the dictate of some hidden and impermissible theological impulse. The legislatures, the judges, the commentators, have responded to the reality of life they found within the womb. Such sturdy guardians of secular good sense as Justice Buller and Chief Justice Shaw did not invent some imaginary beings when they said that the unborn child could have rights of inheritance. Such a perspicacious molder of the best modern trends in tort as Dean Prosser did not indulge in metaphysical fancy when he found all commentators treating a fetus in the womb on a par with the mother in the path of an automobile.

That the American approach is not some national aberration is testified to by the action taken by the United Nations. In 1959 the United Nations adopted a "Declaration of the Rights of the Child" which supplemented the United Nations' statement entitled "The Universal Declaration of Human Rights." One reason for the supplementary Declaration was stated in its Preamble as being because "the child, by reason of his physical and mental immaturity, needs special safeguards and care, including appropriate legal protection, before as well as after birth."[50] Thus, the representatives of most of the nations of the world recognized that the unborn deserved recognition as children and were entitled to legal protection.

If the unborn child can inherit by will and by intestacy, be the beneficiary of a trust, be tortiously injured, be represented by a guardian seeking present support from the parents, be protected by the criminal statutes on parental neglect, *a fortiori,* the legislature may guard that unborn child from intentional extinction.

THE LAWS PROHIBITING ABORTION EXCEPT WHEN NECESSARY TO PRESERVE THE LIFE OR HEALTH OF THE MOTHER ARE NOT UNCONSTITUTIONALLY VAGUE

To be unconstitutionally vague, the language complained of must be so vague that it fails to give warning to the particular defendants who might be charged under the law. "Vagueness" is essentially objectionable because it is unfair. If a given defendant knows perfectly well that what he is doing under the statute is a crime, he may be convicted under it, even though some hypothetical case could be imagined where someone could genuinely be in doubt about the legality of his conduct. The legislature has, under our scheme of government, the right and responsibility of trying to draw the line between conduct which is socially acceptable and that which is not. Although this line is frequently difficult to define, the legislature's attempt to do so should not be upset by the courts unless there has been a clear failure by the legislature. This proposition was rather forcefully stated by Mr. Justice Frankfurter in his dissenting opinion in *Winters* v. *New York,* where he said:

What risks do the innocent run of being caught in a net not designed for them? How important is the policy of the legislation, so that those who really like to pursue innocent conduct are not likely to be caught unaware? How easy is it to be explicitly particular? How necessary is it to leave a somewhat penumbral margin but sufficiently revealed by what is condemned to those who do not want to sail close to the shore of questionable conduct? These and like questions confront legislative draftsmen. Answers to these questions are not to be found in any legislative manual nor in the work of great legislative draftsmen. They are not to be found in the opinions of this Court. These are questions of judgment, peculiarly within the responsibility and the competence of legislatures. The discharge of that responsibility should not be set at naught by abstract notions about "indefiniteness."[51]

THE VAGUENESS ISSUE SHOULD BE MOOT

The United States Supreme Court recently rejected an attack upon the abortion statute of the District of Columbia. In *United States* v. *Vuitch,*[52] the District Court dismissed an indictment against

Milan Vuitch on the grounds that the abortion statute was unconstitutionally vague in its prohibition of abortions except as "necessary to the preservation of the mother's life or health."[53]

Mr. Justice Black, writing for the court, upheld the constitutionality of the District of Columbia abortion statute, stating:

Indeed Webster's Dictionary, in accord with that common usage, properly defines health as "the state of being sound in body or mind." Viewed in this light, the term "health" presents no problem of vagueness. Indeed, whether a particular operation is necessary for a patient's physical or mental health is a judgment that physicians are obviously called upon to make routinely whenever surgery is considered.

We therefore hold that properly construed the District of Columbia abortion law is not unconstitutionally vague, and that the trial court erred in dismissing the indictments on that ground.

That decision should have put to rest the vagueness issue; however, it is being treated in this paper because since the *Vuitch* decision, other litigants as well as some lower courts have continued to raise the issue.

Notwithstanding the holding in the case of *People* v. *Belous*[54]— which was that the old California abortion statute granting an exception where the abortion was performed to save the life of the mother was void owing to vagueness—there were, at about the same time as the *Belous* decision, two other decisions which held similar statutes not to be vague. In a New Jersey case, it was held that the statutory exception of "lawful justification" was not vague.[55] The Supreme Court of Massachusetts held that the word "unlawfully" in the abortion statute was not vague in light of prior decisions of that court. The court held:

We are of the opinion that any uncertainty has been made sufficiently definite by decisions of this Court. In our cases it has been stated over the years that a physician may lawfully perform an abortion if he acts in good faith and in an honest belief that it is necessary for the preservation of the life or health of the woman.[56]

In both the *Belous* case and under the statute in Illinois, it is clearly spelled out that the exception is for the preservation of the life of the woman. How much clearer that is than the word "unlawfully"; yet the Massachusetts court found that doctors in that state could clearly understand that phrase. Although both the *Moretti* and *Kud-*

ish cases were decided about the same time as *Belous,* neither received the wide publicity that attended the *Belous* opinion.

The vagueness argument is so totally without merit that even the court in *Babbitz v. McCann,* which held the Wisconsin abortion statute unconstitutional on other grounds, saw the vagueness argument for what it was, and rejected it.[57]

In general, it may be said that the persons customarily charged with crimes of abortion—persons operating secretly in out-of-the-way, non-hospital locales—are fully aware that their behavior is proscribed by the usual statute.[58] Looking at the Massachusetts, New Jersey, Wisconsin and California cases, it is difficult to believe that what is comprehendible to physicians in Massachusetts, Wisconsin and New Jersey, is not comprehendible to those in California.

This vagueness argument has also been rejected in four recent decisions, two of which are by state supreme courts.[59]

Penal Codes contain many prohibitions of conduct depending upon ascertainment, through fallible judges and juries, of a man's intent or motive. Every one of us runs the risk of having a jury of his peers misjudge him if we practice such conduct. Mr. Justice Holmes gave the conclusive answer to the suggestion that the due process clause protects against such hazards when he said:

The law is full of instances where a man's fate depends on his estimating rightly, that is, as the jury subsequently debates it, some matter of degree. If his judgment is wrong, not only may he incur a fine or a short imprisonment, as here; he may incur the penalty of death.[60]

Justice Holmes later, speaking for a unanimous court in *United States v. Wurzbach,* said:

It is argued at some length that the statute, if extended beyond the political purposes under the control of Congress, is too vague to be valid. The objection to uncertainty concerning the persons embraced need not trouble us now. There is no doubt that the words include representatives, and if there is any difficulty, which we are far from intimating, *it will be time enough to consider it when raised by someone whom it concerns.* The other objection is to the meaning of "political purposes." This would be open even if we accepted the limitations that would make the law satisfactory to the respondent's counsel. But we imagine that no one not in search of trouble would feel any. Whenever the law draws a line there will be cases very near each other on opposite sides. The precise course of the line may be uncertain, but no one can come near it without knowing that he does so, if he thinks, and if he does so it is familiar to the criminal law to make him take the risk.[61]

THE STATUTES PROHIBITING ABORTION WERE INTENDED TO PROTECT THE UNBORN CHILD AS WELL AS THE MOTHER

By prohibiting abortions except when necessary to perserve the life or health of the woman, our legislatures were creating a standard to protect the rights of the unborn.[62] The requirement that the abortion be performed by a physician licensed to practice medicine, and in a licensed hospital or other licensed medical facility, was to safeguard the health of the woman. But note that the abortion cannot even be performed by a licensed physician in a licensed hospital unless it is necessary for the preservation of the woman's life or health, as the case may be under the specific statute. This was the balance struck by the legislatures in measuring life against life.

Some courts have held that the purpose of the abortion statutes is for the protection of both mother and child. A review of American abortion cases, beginning with *State* v. *Howard*,[63] reveals that in the opinion of the courts who commented on the point, the abortion laws under discussion in those cases were either for the protection of the unborn child only or for both the unborn child and the mother. "The statute defining abortion is designed to protect the life of the mother as well as that of the child";[64] "the intention of the lawmakers was to protect the health and lives of pregnant women and their unborn children from those who intentionally and not in good faith would thwart nature by performing or causing abortion and miscarriage";[65] "the abortion statute . . . was enacted to alter this rule and make abortion a crime even though performed before the fetus had 'quickened,' the object being . . . not only the protection of the unborn child, but to protect the life and health of the mother as well. . . . "[66] "This statute is designed to protect the life of a child *en ventre sa mare*."[67] This same theme recurs in tort cases which have arisen out of abortions: ". . . the abortion statute is not designed for the protection of women" (citation omitted), "only of the unborn child and through it society . . .";[68] ". . . we hold that the anti-abortion statutes in Oklahoma were enacted and designed for the protection of the unborn child, and, through it society."[69]

The Supreme Court of Virginia reversed a jury verdict for a plaintiff in a tort case and held that a consenting plaintiff had no cause of action against the abortionist who had injured her. This court defined the purpose of the abortion statute as follows:

This statute was passed, not for the protection of the woman, but for the protection of the unborn child and through it society.[70]

The New Jersey Supreme Court has stated:

The abortion statute ... was enacted to alter this rule and make abortion a crime even though performed before the fetus had "quickened," the object being, according to *State* v. *Murphy,* 27 N.J.L. 112, 114, not only the protection of the unborn child, but to protect the life and health of the mother as well. See also *State* v. *Loomis,* 89 N.J.L. 8, 9 (Sup. Ct. 1916) affirmed 90 N.J.L. 216 (E & A 1917).[71]

In effect, the legislatures in enacting statutes prohibiting abortion, adopted a minimal norm of due process and equal protection for the unborn by specifically forbidding taking their lives unless necessary for preservation of the mother's life.

There is nothing unusual, arbitrary, or vague in a legislature exercising its inherent legislative authority to protect the civil rights of the unborn. The progress of our law in recognition of the fetus as a person has been constant and roughly parallel to the growth of knowledge of biology, embryology, fetology, genetics and perinatology. Many urged that abortion statutes be considered only from the viewpoint of the mother, whereas, this paper is intended to show that a fair reading of the language of these acts, coupled with the common understanding of the purpose of abortion statutes as stated by a large number of courts, requires that the subject be considered from the standpoint of both the mother and the unborn child. If this law was designed only to protect women from a dangerous surgical procedure, why have the legislatures limited it to abortions? All surgery was dangerous in the nineteenth century, but there was no law making gall bladder operations or tonsilectomies a crime. The abortion statutes recognized what we all now know, that the unborn child is a separate person and the statutes exist to protect his Constitutional right to life. As a three-judge Federal Court said:

Once human life has commenced, the Constitutional protection found in the Fifth and Fourteenth Amendments imposes upon the state the duty of safeguarding it.[72]

Had the legislatures intended to protect only the mother, then no balancing of rights between those of the unborn and the mother would have been necessary. The legislature, from the mother's point of view only, would have simply limited the statute to the requirement of performance of the abortion by a licensed physician operating in a licensed hospital. By limiting even licensed physicians to those few situations where it was necessary for the preservation of the woman's life, the legislatures could only have intended to protect the life of the unborn in all other situations where the exception did not exist.

ABORTION AND THE CRIMINAL LAW

Prior to the present era there has been no doubt about the state's right (if not the duty) to enact criminal laws which protected human life in the womb. The Code of Hammurabi, which is probably a compilation of much older laws, when promulgated about 1728 B.C., contained prohibitions against abortion.[73] In the twelfth century, B.C., the Assyrian King Tiglath-Pileser I codified certain of their laws, which also contained prohibitions against abortion.[74] The Hittites had somewhat similar laws.[75]

There is a unique continuity between those ancient statutes, the development of laws concerning abortion, and the existence and nature of present abortion statutes. For example, it is sometimes argued that the therapeutic exception in the 1828 New York abortion statute (that abortion may be performed when necessary to save the life of the mother) was the unique creation of the revisers of the New York criminal law in 1828.[76] However, Avicenna taught that abortion may sometimes be necessary where birth would endanger the life of the mother.[77] His medical text, which was translated by Gerard of Cremona about 1150 A.D., became the standard text in European medical schools until the seventeenth century.[78] Thus, the "unique" creation of the New York revisers may, in fact, have been a mere repetition of a medical tradition centuries old.

Anglo-Saxon law before the Norman conquest in 1066 provided both civil penalties and ecclesiastical penalties for abortion.[79] Henry De Bracton, the Chancellor of Exeter Cathedral and a Justicer of the Court, which was soon to become the Court of the King's Bench, in the mid-thirteenth century wrote:

If there be anyone who strikes a pregnant woman or gives her a poison whereby he causes an abortion, if the foetus be already formed or animated, and especially if it be animated, he commits homicide.[80]

According to Aristotelian embryology, animation, or the infusion of the rational soul into the form of the body, occurred at forty days of gestation in the male and at eighty days of gestation in the female.[81] His embryology became the basis for many philosophical opinions through the ages.[82] Based upon Aristotelian embryology, the theory of late animation or late hominization was accepted by some philosophers.[83] Under this theory, the rational soul was infused into the embryo at some time during its development.[84] Nonetheless, during many centuries when the distinction between civil and ecclesiastical law was slight or nonexistent, both religion and society condemned abortion at any stage of embryological development.[85] Thus, in the mid-thirteenth century when Bracton was writing, abortion after animation or after the early weeks of pregnancy was a homicide even in the modern sense of our use of that word: the killing of a human being.

At the time of Bracton any killing of a human was a homicide.[86] There were no degrees of murder, but only defenses (as we would say now) to the act of homicide.[87] Approximately one century later a commentator on Bracton known as Fleta stated:

One is rightly a homicide who has pressed on a pregnant woman or has given her a poison, or struck her to produce an abortion ... if the foetus was already formed and ensouled....[88]

Between 1248 and 1350 these were apparently the only two extant comments on abortion in what was to become the civil, as distinguished from ecclesiastical or canonical, law. If these comments prove anything, they prove that abortion was practically nonexistent, but that where it existed it was condemned. After ensoulment it was condemned both by canonical and "common law" authorities as a true homicide. It was not a true homicide prior to ensoulment because of the Aristotelian theory of embryological development. That Aristotelian theory became for Lord Coke in the seventeenth century the theory of "quickening."

In 1650 Coke wrote:

If a woman be quick with child and by a potion or otherwise kills it in her womb, or if a man beat her, whereby the child dies in her body, and she is delivered of a dead child, this is a great misprison and no murder, but if the child be born alive, and dies of the potion, battery or other cause, this is murder; for in law it is counted as a reasonable creature in rerum natura when it is born alive.[89]

It is often said of this passage from Coke, that prior to quickening (under Coke's understanding) the common law did not consider abortion to be a crime.[90] This is apparently seen from some of the early American cases which considered abortion under the common law,[91] although other American courts strongly disagreed.[92] It is difficult to understand how it can be said that abortion in the early weeks was not "considered" a crime when the first English statute on the subject made abortion at any time after conception not only a crime but a *felony*.[93] Statutes do not spring whole from nothing. They reflect what is generally the common sentiment of thinking persons of that time. Perhaps the explanation for the strict common-law approach to abortion in the early weeks reflects nothing but the procedural difficulty of proof at a time when the criminal law, at least in the courts, was nothing but highly technical warfare.

It is clear from a reading of Blackstone that the common law considered life to be infused at the time of quickening.[94] Since you could not kill what was not alive, there could be no crime for the destruction of a non-living being. Certainly, under this theory the forming human in the womb prior to quickening was considered nothing other than tissue of the mother, which was a very common idea of courts until this century.[95] For example, Blackstone wrote:

In case this plea [reprieve] is made in stay of execution, the Judge must direct a jury of twelve matrons or discreet women to inquire the fact, and if they bring in their verdict "quick with child" for barely, "with child" unless it be alive in the womb is not sufficient. . . .[96]

As can be seen from that passage, "with child" was not sufficient to stay execution of a pregnant felon since the foetus was not considered to be alive, whereas "quick with child" was sufficient to stay execution since the foetus was alive and the law would not take the lives of two people where only one had committed the crime.

There was no question in Blackstone's mind, but that at quickening not only was life infused into the child in the womb, but so were all of the rights that belonged to a person. For example, Blackstone stated:

Life is the immediate gift of God, a right inherent by nature in every individual; and it begins in contemplation of law as soon as an infant is able to stir in the mother's womb.[97]

Modern science, as demonstrated in this book, has proven the absurdity of the common-law notion that "life" is suddenly infused into the fetus at the time of quickening or at about fifteen or sixteen weeks of gestation. Individual human life is a continuum which commences with conception and progresses by orderly biological development until the time of death. There is no point along this continuum where a cellular change can be identified as at one moment non-human and the next human.

Hawkins said that abortion in ancient times of a quickened fetus was murder without regard to the distinction made by Coke as to whether or not the fetus must be born alive before it dies.[98] Any confusion concerning the nature of the crime of abortion at the common law was clarified in 1803 when the English Parliament passed the first English and first modern statute on abortion.[99] This statute removed the requirement originated by Coke and enunciated by Blackstone that the crime of abortion occurred only if the fetus was quickened.

There has been much philosophical debate on the historical purpose of abortion statutes without considering at the same time simple problems in the criminal law. Until 1803 it was very easy for a defendant to win an abortion case because of the difficulties that the state faced in proving that the fetus was alive, or quick, at the time of the abortion.[100] The statute of 1803 cured that difficulty because it made abortion at *any time* a felony. The statute kept a distinction that had grown up in the canonical courts by punishing abortion before quickening less than after quickening.[101]

The important thing to understand, though, is that the statute of 1803 did not in any way change the nature of the crime, which was always considered to be a crime *against the child*. The procedural criminal difficulty of winning a conviction when the woman testified that she had felt no quickening was such an impossible burden that the 1803 statute was passed to correct this situation.[102] Thus, such a similar correction was made in many states where the abortion was a crime even if the woman is not pregnant.[103] This is not to say that the statute was to protect the health of the woman, or that common-law sensitivities were pro-abortion, but was merely to correct the criminal difficulty of proving an attempt at abortion since it is the intent of the performer of the abortion that is the crime.[104] If he or she intends the destruction of the unborn child, then he is guilty of the crime of abortion. Whether or not the woman is pregnant when he makes that attempt is irrelevant under many state statutes.[105] Far from being an argument in support of the unconstitutionality of present-day abortion laws (on the theory that they were originally passed only to protect the woman and not the child), the lack of a pregnancy requirement shows conclusively that abortion laws were created to protect the child's life.[106] Such laws show that the purpose of the abortion statutes was to halt even an attempt at abortion. A necessity to prove the pregnancy could be as difficult a procedural problem as the necessity to prove that the fetus had quickened. Therefore, many abortion statutes do not require even proof of pregnancy.[107] Thus, even these statutes reflect the states' historical purpose to protect unborn life.

Connecticut was the first American state to enact a statute dealing directly with abortion. In 1821 it adopted Section 1 of Lord Ellenborough's Act.[108] Connecticut did not extend the crime to pre-quickening until 1860, at which time abortion was also allowed if necessary to save the child and also when necessary to preserve the life of the woman.[109] Illinois passed its first statute in 1827 and made no distinction with regard to quickening.[110]

In 1803 Thomas Percival, M.D., published his very famous medical juris-prudential text in which he stated:

To extinguish the first spark of life is a crime of the same nature, both against our Maker and society, as to destroy an infant, a child, or a man; these regular and successive stages of existence being the ordinances of God, subject alone to His divine will. . . .[111]

Percival's book was the standard work in medical ethics throughout the nineteenth century.[112] Such a work was probably the reason that the American Medical Association repeatedly, during the nineteenth century, urged legislators to pass laws protecting the child in the womb from the moment of conception.[113] For example, a review of the *American Medical Association, 1846-1952 Digest of Official Actions* (edited by F.J.L. Blasingame, 1959), at p. 66, lists the repeated attacks by the American Medical Association on the crime of abortion. It will be seen that the great medical battle of the nineteenth century was to persuade legislators to eliminate the requirement of quickening and to condemn abortion from conception. The Association unanimously condemned abortion as the destruction of human life. It was this pressure, during the nineteenth century, on state legislators that did away with the requirement of quickening in many abortion statutes.[114]

Thus it is that American legislators throughout the nineteenth century passed laws protecting life within the womb. Not for any narrow sectarian religious point of view, but because developing human life in the womb was entitled to the law's protection just as is an adult.

By 1967 every state in the union, under its criminal law, protected incipient and developing human life in the womb from destruction. The purpose of these criminal statutes was to protect the life of the child. Certainly there was a concomitant protection for the health of the mother, but that was not the main intent when legislators passed laws against abortion. All of the criminal abortion statutes of the states and territories absolutely prohibited or severely restricted abortion. Several absolutely prohibited it. Most prohibited it unless necessary to preserve or save the life of the mother, although there was an occasional variation in the verbal formula.[115] For example, Maryland proscribed abortion unless ". . . no other method will secure the safety of the mother."[116] New Jersey prohibited abortion done ". . . without lawful justification."[117] Pennsylvania proscribed abortions done with the "unlawful" use of any instrument.[118] In a few states the necessity to save the child's life was an additional authorizing exception.[119] Eventually the District of Columbia and Alabama prohibited abortion unless necessary to preserve the life or health of the mother.[120] Until 1967, when Colorado liberalized its law,[121] the Alabama and District of Columbia statutes were the most liberal in the balance struck between the life of the child and the life of the mother.

In forbidding abortions except when necessary to preserve the life (or health) of the mother, the states were striking a standard of due process and equal protection to protect the life of the unborn child. To be sure, it was a minimal balance, but nonetheless it was a balance struck in measuring life against life—not a mere additional protection of the mother. In effect, the states were enacting a minimum norm of due process and equal protection for the unborn by specifically forbidding killing them unless necessary for the preservation of the mother's life (or health). There is nothing unusual, arbitrary or vague in the states' exercising their inherent legislative authority to protect the civil rights of the unborn.

The Humanity of the Unborn Offspring of Human Parents Has Been the Critical Issue in Lower Federal Court Abortion Cases

The immediate and intended consequence of an induced abortion is the destruction of life of the unborn. It is in the light of this reality that courts must consider and decide the profound and far-reaching issues in these abortion cases.

Certain courts have decided abortion cases without considering whether the victim, i.e. the unborn, of the abortion has constitutionally protected rights. For example, in *Roe* v. *Wade*,[122] the U.S. District Court for the Northern District of Texas, without once mentioning, discussing or considering whether the unborn is a "person" under the

Fifth and Fourteenth Amendments, or otherwise has legally protected interests involved, concluded that the "Texas Abortion Laws must be declared unconstitutional because they deprive single women and married couples of their right, secured by the Ninth Amendment, to choose whether to have children."

In *Doe* v. *Bolton*,[123] the U.S. District Court for the Northern District of Georgia touched, but only in passing, upon the primary issue in this litigation, i.e. the legal "personality" of the unborn for constitutional purposes. At one point in the opinion, the court wrote that it did not ". . . (posit) the existence of a new being with its own identity and federal constitutional rights, . . ."[124] Elsewhere in the opinion the court, in denying a reconsideration of the court's previous order revoking another's appointment as *guardian ad litem* for the unborn person, wrote that ". . . the court does not postulate the existence of a new being with federal constitutional rights at any time during gestation."

The *Bolton* court was thus able to conclude that, while procedures for obtaining an abortion may be controlled, the "reasons for which an abortion may be obtained" may not be regulated "because such action unduly restricts a decision sheltered by the constitutional right to privacy."[125]

The *Bolton* court did point out that once conception has occurred and the embryo has formed, ". . . the decision to abort its development cannot be considered a purely private one affecting only husband and wife, man and woman."[126]

Other three-judge federal courts presented with the same clash of "rights" between mother and the unborn have not ignored the developments of many areas of the law which have found rights in the unborn. For example, in *Steinberg* v. *Brown*,[127] the majority gave careful consideration to both the rights of the woman and the unborn, and concluded that ". . . the state has a legitimate interest to legislate for the purpose of affording an embryonic or fetal organism an opportunity to survive."[128] This court concluded that the state did have that right" . . . and on balance it is superior to the claimed right of a pregnant woman or anyone else to destroy the fetus except when necessary to preserve her own life."[129]

In *Rosen* v. *Louisiana State Board of Medical Examiners*[130] the court recognized that it was not dealing merely with the question whether a woman has a generalized right to choose whether to bear children ". . . but instead with the more complicated question whether a pregnant woman has the right to cause the abortion of the embryo or fetus she carries in her womb."[131] Without deciding whether the unborn per se is a person protected by the Constitution, since that was not the issue that court faced, the *Rosen* court concluded that the State of Louisiana had intended to and could legitimately protect fetal life against destruction.[132]

In *Corkey* v. *Edwards*[133] the court concluded also that the issue involved ultimately a consideration of more than just the issue of whether a woman has a right not to bear children:

The basic distinction between a decision whether to bear children which is made before conception and one which is made after conception is that the first contemplates the creation of a new human organism, but the latter contemplates the destruction of such an organism already created.[134]

Finding protection to fetal life an adequate state interest in invading the woman's claimed right to privacy, the *Corkey* court concluded:

To determine the state interest we shall not attempt to choose between extreme positions. Whether possessing a soul from the moment of conception or mere protoplasm, the fertilized egg is, we think, "unique as a physical entity," Lucas, Federal Constitutional Limitations of the Enforcement and Administration of State Abortion Statutes, 46 *N.C.L. Rev.* 730, 744 (1968), with the potential to become a person. Whatever that entity is, the state has chosen to protect its very existence. The state's power to protect children is a well-established constitutional maxim. See *Shelton* v. *Tucker,* 364 U.S. 479, 485, 81 S. Ct. 247, 5 L. Ed. 2d 231 (1960); *Prince* v. *Massachusetts,* 321 U.S. 158, at 166–168, 64 S. Ct. 438, 88 L. Ed. 645. That this power should be used to protect a fertilized egg or embryo or fetus during the period of gestation embodies no logical infirmity, but would seemingly fall within the "plenary power of government." *Poe* v. *Ullman,* 367 U.S. 497, at 539, 81 S. Ct. 1752, 6 L. Ed. 2d 989 (Harlan, J., dissenting). That there is a state interest has until recently been taken for granted. History sides with the state.[135]

Even this brief review of five federal decisions involving the constitutionality of state abortion laws makes it clear that whether or not courts consider the developing humanity of the unborn is critical in its resolution of the issues.[136]

An expansion of the right to privacy to include the right of a woman to have an abortion without considering the interests of the unborn person decides this question against the unborn. The necessary consequence of that expansion would be a direct and unavoidable conflict between the unborn person's right to life and the woman's extended right of privacy. Assuming such a conflict, it is our position that the more fundamental and established of the conflicting rights must prevail where they clash. The right to life is most certainly the most fundamental and established of the rights involved in the cases facing the courts today.

The Unborn Offspring of Human Parents Is a Person within the Meaning of the Fifth and Fourteenth Amendments of the U.S. Constitution

The Standard for Decision

The U. S. Supreme Court has considered the constitutionality of legal classifications numerous times. Under the due process clause of the Fifth Amendment, and the "equal protection" clause of the Fourteenth Amendment, the strictness of the standard for decision in cases involving classifications made by legislative bodies varies according to the nature of the right placed in jeopardy; the more fundamental the right involved, the greater the judicial requirement to "carefully and meticulously scrutinize"[137] the classification in light of the following principles:

a. As the right in jeopardy becomes more fundamental, the more perfect must be the relationship between the classification excluding a human group from the enjoyment of the right and the purpose for which the classification is made.[138]

b. As the right involved becomes more fundamental, the more "compelling" the state or governmental interest must be in making a classification excluding certain human groups from the enjoyment of the right.[139]

In addition, classifications affecting fundamental rights are said to be "especially suspect"[140] or, to use Mr. Justice White's expression, such classifications are "constitutionally suspect."[141]

The Courts Must Apply This Same Standard to Themselves

The court, in interpreting laws, performs a quasi-legislative or a subordinate legislative function.[142] It performs this interstitial legislative function by supplementing the written law with definitions.[143]

In these cases the courts must construe, interpret and define the expression "person" in the Fifth and Fourteenth Amendments. In fixing the limits of the word "person" in the Fifth and Fourteenth Amendments, the courts will, in essence, perform a classificatory function; in other words, the courts must decide, on the basis of some established criteria whether, for the cases at bar, the unborn person belongs to the class of persons encompassed, and therefore protected, by the term "person" as used in the "due process" clause of the Fifth Amendment and "equal protection" and "due process" clauses of the Fourteenth Amendment.

The "due process" clause of the Fifth Amendment and the "equal protection" clause of the Fourteenth Amendment to the United States Constitution require that "Cities, States and the Federal Government . . . exercise their powers so as not to discriminate between their inhabitants except upon some reasonable differentiation fairly related to the object of the regulation."[144] Expressed differently, the Constitution prohibits "invidious discrimination" by the State.

The concepts of "State" and "Federal Government," as used above, refer to the different agencies through which the "State or Federal Government" may act. And this includes judicial authorities[145] as well as legislative and executive authorities. The courts have, therefore, a constitutional duty equal to that of Congress and the various state legislatures to avoid "invidious discriminations" in the course of making classifications in the exercise of their interpretive and quasi-legislative functions.

Application of the Standard for Decision: The Rules of Construction Applied

By attempting to strike down the criminal abortion statutes of some states, the courts are implicitly deciding whether unborn off-spring of human parents are "persons" within the meaning of the Fifth and Fourteenth Amendments, and thereby classifying such offspring as to whether they may be "deprived of life." Since this is the most fundamental of all rights[146] the courts are bound by their own teachings to apply the most strict of standards.

Likewise because of the fundamental nature of life, the most compelling of all interests would have to be shown on the part of a court in order to carve out such a classification, which would exclude the lives of unborn humans from the protection of the law.

Proponents of abortion-on-demand argue that a "compelling state interest" must be shown to justify the restrictions imposed by those criminal abortion statutes on their freedom to have the unborn killed, or their freedom as physicians to perform the abortions. We argue that the "compelling" state interest doctrine instead limits the right of either State or Federal Government to classify the unborn as "non-person" and thereby permit the deprivation of their lives.

Consequently, in interpreting and construing the word "person" as used in the Fifth and Fourteenth Amendments, courts must be constantly aware (1) that the right in jeopardy is the most fundamental of all legal rights, being necessary and basic to the enjoyment of all other legal rights; (2) that no compelling governmental interest in excluding the unborn from constitutional protection under the Fifth and Fourteenth Amendments has ever been shown, and that classifications affecting fundamental human rights are "especially" or "constitutionally suspect." Based on these rules of construction, the unborn offspring of human parents are to be given every benefit of doubt, to be afforded every advantage.

These standards for decision considered in light of the *scientific fact* that the unborn offspring of human parents is an autonomous human being,[147] and in light of the *legal fact* that the unborn is a legal person in numerous other areas of the law,[148] compel the conclusion that the word "person" as used in the Fifth and Fourteenth Amendments includes unborn persons.

The Fifth Amendment protects all persons against arbitrary action by the State. "No person shall be deprived of life, liberty or property without due process of law." If the word "person" in the Fifth Amendment is construed to mean only born "persons," then all unborn persons who have vested property rights (subject to divestiture if they are not born alive)[149] would have no protection against an arbitrary taking of such property rights by the Federal Government. This would leave an absurd gap in the scope of constitutional protection of individual rights. The unborn person would have legal protection against everyone except the State.

If the unborn offspring of human parents is a "person" within the meaning of the Fifth Amendment for the purpose of protecting its property interests against arbitrary action by the government, it must follow that the life of that "person" is also protected against arbitrary interference by the State.

As Professor Dallin H. Oaks has said:

The guarantees of due process extend to such rights and to such persons. The due process clause surely protects at least as much "property" as the law recognizes. If an unborn is a legal entity or person for purposes of acquiring property or a cause of action, it is surely a "person" who qualifies to have his property or cause of action protected by the due process clause. And his life as well. The due process clause would be a proper object of ridicule if it allowed the guardian of an unborn child to protect the unborn's right to property but left the guardian powerless to prevent the destruction of its life.[150]

It is submitted that the unborn is a "person" within the meaning of the Fifth and Fourteenth Amendments. Consequently, the unborn's life can be taken only with due process of law, and its life is entitled, like all other persons' lives, to equal protection under law.

The voidance of state abortion statutes by court or legislature is governmental action which deprives the innocent unborn of the right to life, and therefore deprives them of equal protection and due process. Courts should therefore protect the unborn's constitutional rights in any decision they render.

THE UNBORN PERSON IN INTERNATIONAL LAW

Although international protection of human rights is still in the developing stages and the jurisprudence of international tribunals is consequently limited, there are persuasive indications that international law requires that the unborn person's right to life be recognized and protected by law.

UNITED NATIONS DOCUMENTS

Aritcle 6 (1) of the International Covenant on Civil and Political Rights provides that "every human being has the inherent right to life." The term "human being" is most certainly broad enough to include unborn as well as born human beings. If "human being" is interpreted in the light of paragraph 5 of Article 6 of this Covenant, which provides that "Sentence of death . . . shall not be carried out on pregnant women," it appears that the drafters intended to protect the right to life of unborn human beings as well as those already born.

Further support for this position can be found in the Declaration of the Rights of the Child, proclaimed by the General Assembly of the United Nations on 20 November, 1959. Paragraph 3 of the Preamble provides:

Whereas the child, by reason of his physical and mental immaturity, needs special safeguards and care, *including appropriate legal protection, before as well as after birth.* [emphasis added]

The proclamation paragraph of the Preamble provides:

Proclaims this Declaration of the Rights of the Child to the end that he may have a happy childhood and enjoy *for his own good* and for the good of society the rights and freedoms herein set forth, and calls upon parents, upon men and women as individuals, and upon voluntary organizations, local authorities and national governments to recognize these rights and strive for their observance by legislative and other measures progressively taken in accordance with the following principles: [emphasis added]

The fourth of the principles listed in the Declaration of the Rights of the Child provides that "special care and protection shall be provided to [the child] and to his mother, *including adequate prenatal and post-natal care* [emphasis added]."

ORGANIZATION OF AMERICAN STATES

Article 4 (1) of the American Convention on Human Rights of 1969 provides:

Every person has the right to have his life respected. This right shall be protected by law and, in general, from the moment of conception. No one shall be arbitrarily deprived of his life.

Paragraph 5 of this same article provides that "capital punishment" shall not "be applied to pregnant women."

It is clear from this article that the term "person" includes the unborn and that the unborn's right to life is to be protected by law from the moment of conception.

To be emphasized is that the United States may some day become or desire to become a party to both the International Covenant on Civil and Political Rights of 1966 and the American Convention on Human Rights of 1969. United States Constitutional theory should not be allowed to become at variance with both universal and regional international human rights theory.

REFERENCES

1. *Mills* v. *Commonwealth of Pennsylvania,* 13 Pa. St. 631 (1850).
2. *Steinberg* v. *Rhodes,* 321 F. Supp. 741 (N.D. Ohio 1970).
3. *Griswold* v. *Connecticut,* 381 U.S. 479, 85 Sup. Ct. 1678.
4. E.g., see note 115.
5. Biondi, *LaPatria Potestas,* II *Diritto Romano Christiano* (1954), Vol. 3, p. 13.
6. Buckland and McNair, *Roman Law and Common Law,* p. 35 (1936).
7. Kempe, *"The Battered-Child Syndrome,"* 181 *American Medical Association Journal,* 17 (1962).
8. 16 Am. Jur. 2d, Constitutional Law, Sec. 60, pp. 687 and 688.
9. Ibid., pp. 688 and 689.

10. *Rosen* v. *The Louisiana State Board of Medical Examiners,* 318 F. Supp., 1717 (E.D.La. New Orleans Div. 1970).
11. *Doe* v. *Clarke,* 2 H.Bl. 399, 126 Eng. Rep. 617 (1795).
12. *Thelluson* v. *Woodford,* 4 Ves. 227, 31 Eng. Rep. 117 (1798).
13. Ibid., at p. 322.
14. *Hall* v. *Hancock,* 15 Pick. 255 (Mass. 1834).
15. *Wallis* v. *Hodson,* 2 Atk. 117.
16. Ill. Rev. Stat., 1969, Ch. 3, §13.
17. *Tomlin* v. *Laws,* 301 Ill. 616, 134 N.E. 24 (1922); *Barr* v. *Gardner,* 259 Ill. 256, 106 N.E. 287 (1913).
18. Ill. Rev. Stat., 1939, Ch. 30, §13.
19. Ill. Rev. Stat., Ch. 111-1/2, §73-1(5).
20. Ill. Rev. Stat., Ch. 111-1/2, §73-12.
21. Ill. Rev. Stat., Ch. 111-1/2, §73-20.
22. *Prosser on Torts,* 3d Edition, 1964, Sec. 56.
23. *Dietrich* v. *Northampton,* 138 Mass. 14 (1884).
24. *Scott* v. *McPheeters,* 33 Cal. App. 2d 629, 92 P. 2d 678 (1939), petition for re-hearing denied, 93 P.2d 562 (1939).
25. *Bombrest* v. *Kotz,* 65 F. Supp. 138 (D.D.C. 1946).
26. *Prosser on Torts,* 3d Edition, 1964, p. 355.
27. Gordon, *The Unborn Plaintiff,* 63 Mich. L. Rev. 627 (1965).
28. *Amamn* v. *Faidy,* 415 Ill. 422 (1953).
29. *Daley* v. *Meier,* 33 Ill. App. 2d 218 (1961).
30. *Sinkler* v. *Kneale,* 401 Penn. 276, 164 A. 2d 93.
31. *Smith* v. *Brennan,* 31 N.J. 353, 157 A. 2d 497.
32. At the common law the unquickened fetus was not considered alive. In 4 Blackstone, *Commentaries on the Laws of England* (concerning reprieves) 394-395 (1769), it is said: "... and if they bring in their verdict 'quick with child' (for barely, 'with child' unless it be alive in the womb, is not sufficient)." In other words "with child" was not sufficient to stay execution of a pregnant felon because the fetus was not considered to be alive; whereas "quick with child" was sufficient to stay execution since the fetus was alive and the law would not take the lives of two people where only one had committed the crime. Blackstone also said: "Life is the immediate gift of God, a right inherent by nature in every individual; and it begins in contemplation of law as soon as an infant is able to stir in the mother's womb." Blackstone, Book I, Chap. I, Sec. I.
33. *Prosser on Torts,* 3d Edition, 1964, Sec. 56.
34. Ibid.
35. *Gullborg* v. *Rizzo,* 331 F. 2d 557 (3rd 1964; Penn. Statute); *Todd* v. *Sandidge Construction Co.,* 341 F. 2d 75 (1964); *Hatala* v. *Markiewicz,* 26 Conn. Supp. 358, 224 A. 2d 406 (1966); *Worgan* v. *Greggo & Ferrara, Inc.,* 50 Del. 258, 128 A 2d 557 (1956); *Porter* v. *Lassiter,* 91 Ga. App. 712, 87 S.E. 2d 100 (1955); *Wendt* v. *Lillo,* (1960, D. C. Iowa), 182 F. Supp. 56 (applying Iowa law); *Hale* v. *Manion,* 189 Kan. 143, 368 P. 2d

1 (1962); *Mitchell* v. *Couch,* Ky, 285 S.W. 2d 901 (1955); *Valence* v. *Louisiana Power & Light Co.,* La. App. 50 So. 2d 847 (1951); *Odham* v. *Sherman,* 234 Md. 179, 198 A. 2d 71 (1964); *Verkennes* v. *Cornea,* 229 Minn. 365, 38 N.W. 2d 838, 10 ALR 2d 634 (1949); *Rainey* v. *Horn,* 221 Miss. 269, 72 So. 2d 434 (1954); *Poliquin* v. *MacDonald,* 101 N.H. 104, 135 A. 2d 249 (1957); *Stidam* v. *Ashmore,* 109 Ohio, App. 431, 11 Ohio Ops. 2d 383, 167 N.E. 2d 106 (1959); *Kwaterski* v. *State Farm Mut. Auto Ins. Co.,* 34 Wis. 2d 14, 148 N.W. 2d 107 (1967).

36. *Glona* v. *American Guarantee & Liability Insurance Co.,* 391 U. S. 73 at 75-76, 88 S. Ct. 1515 at 1516-17 (1968); see also *Levy* v. *Louisiana,* 391 U. S. 68, 88 S. Ct. 1509 (1968) and *Munn* v. *Munn,* 450 P. 2d 68, 69 (Colo. 1969).

37. In *Zepeda* v. *Zepeda,* 41 Ill. App. 2d 240, 249-250, 190 N.E. 2d, 849 853 (1963) the court said: "How can the law distinguish the day to day development of life? If there is human life, proved by subsequent birth, then that human life has the same rights at conception as it has at any time thereafter. There cannot be absolutes in the minute to minute progress of life from the sperm and ovum to cell, to embryo, to foetus, to child."

38. The issue as to whether or not a stillborn child can maintain an action for wrongful death is now pending in the Illinois reviewing courts.

39. *Prosser on Torts,* 3d Edition, 1964, Sec. 56.

40. Edwin W. Patterson, *Law in a Scientific Age* (1963), at p. 35.

41. Liley, *Modern Motherhood,* Random House, p. 48 (1969).

42. 42 N. J. 421, 201 A. 2d 537 (1964) cert. denied 377 U. S. 985, 12 L. Ed. 2d 1032, 84 S. Ct. 1894 (1964).

43. Ibid, at 538.

44. See also *Hoener* v. *Bertinato,* 67 N. J. Super., 517, 171 A. 2d 140 (1961).

45. 38 C. A. 2d 122, 100 P. 2d 806 (1st District 1940).

46. See also *Wagner* v. *Gardner,* 413 F. 2d 267 (5th Cir. 1969).

47. *Prince* v. *Massachusetts,* 321 U. S. 158, 166, 64 S. Ct. 438, 88 L. Ed. 645 (1944); *State* v. *Perricone,* 37 N. J. 463,181 A. 2d 751 (1962) cert. denied 371 U. S. 890, 83 S. Ct. 189, 9 L. Ed. 124 (1962); *People ex rel Wallace* v. *Labrenze,* 411 Ill. 618, 104 N.E. 2d 769 (1952).

48. 1 Blackstone, *Commentaries,* 456 (W. Jones ed. at 561, 1916); 2 Hale, *Pleas of the Crown,* 413-14 (1st Am. ed. at 412-13, 1847).

49. Such as the California Penal Code, Secs. 3705-06 (West's California Statutes 1954).

50. General Assembly of the United Nations, "Declaration of the Rights of the Child," adopted unanimously in the plenary meeting on November 20, 1959 (Official Records of the General Assembly, 14th Session, pp. 19-20).

51. *Winters* v. *New York,* 333 U. S. 507, 92 L. Ed. 840, 852, (1947).

52. 402 U.S. 62, 28 L. Ed. 2d 601, 91 S. Ct. 1294 (1971).

53. 22 D.C. Code 201.

54. 458 P. 2d 194, 80 Cal. Rep. 354 (1969).

55. *State* v. *Moretti,* 52 N. J. 182, 244 A. 2d 499 (1968), cert. denied 393 U. S. 952 (1968).

56. *Kudish* v. *Board of Registration of Medicine,* 248 N.E. 2d 264 (Mass. 1969).

57. *Babbitz* v. *McCann,* 310 F. Supp. 293 (E.D. Wis. 1970).

58. On the other hand, it appears that no reputable physician has been prosecuted for performing an abortion in a reputable hospital; see Lucas, *Federal Constitutional Limitations on the Enforcement and Administration of State Abortion Statutes,* North Carolina Law Rev., 46:749 (1967-68).

59. See *Iowa* v. *Abodeely,* 179 N.W. 2d 347 (Ia. Sup. Ct. No. 66-53864, 1970); *Vermont* v. *Bartlett* (Vermont Sup. Ct., No. 137-69, 1970); *Rosen* v. *Louisiana State Board of Medical Examiners,* 318 F. Supp. 1217 (E.D. La. No. 70-1304, 1970); *Steinberg* v. *Rhodes,* et. al., 321 F. Supp. 741 (N.D. Ohio No. 70-289, 1970).

60. *Nash* v. *United States,* 229 U. S. 337, at p. 377.

61. *United States* v. *Wurzbach,* 280 U. S. 396, at p. 399.

62. Where the statute involved makes no distinction between the quick and unquickened fetus, it is clear that the life referred to under the statute is the fetus itself. See Means, *The Law of New York Concerning Abortion,* 14 N.Y.L.F., 411, 508 (1968). Means says: "The Common Law protects the quickened (but not the unquickened) fetus as a being with its own right to life, immune to destruction at maternal will"; at p. 508.

63. *State* v. *Howard,* 32 Vt. 380 (1859).

64. *State* v. *Cox,* 197 Wash. 67, 84 P. 2d 357, 361 (1939).

65. *Anderson* v. *Commonwealth,* 190 Va. 665, 58 S.E. 2d 72, 75 (1950).

66. *State* v. *Siciliano,* 21 N.J.S. 249, 121 A. 2d 490, 495 (1956).

67. *State* v. *Hoover,* 252 N.C. 113, S.E. 2d 281, 283 (1960).

68. *Nash et ux* v. *Meyer,* 54 Idaho 283, 31 P. 2d 273, 276 (1934).

69. *Bowland* v. *Lunsford,* 176 Okla. 115, 54 P. 2d 666 (1936).

70. *Miller* v. *Bennett,* 190 Va. 162, 56 S.E. 2d 217 (1949).

71. *State* v. *Siciliano,* 21 N.J.S. 249, 121 A. 2d 490, 495 (1956).

72. *Steinberg* v. *Rhodes, et al.,* 321 F. Supp. 741 (N.D. Ohio 1970).

73. The Code of Hammurabi, in James B. Pritchard, *Ancient Near Eastern Texts Relating to the Old Testament,* 2d ed. (Princeton: Princeton Univ. Press, 1955) at p. 175.

74. The Middle Assyrian Laws in Pritchard, Id. at 181, 184-85.

75. The Hittite Laws, in Pritchard, Id. at 190.

76. See Cyril Means, "The Law of New York Concerning Abortions and The Status of the Foetus, 1664-1968: A Case of Cessation of Constitutionality," *New York Law Forum* 14:411, 451 Fall 1968.

77. Avicenna, "De regimine abortus," book 3, Fen 21 tract 2, C. 12 of *Canon Medicine,* trans. Gerard of Cremona (Venice, 1608).

78. Charles Signer and E. Ashworth Underwood, *A Short History of Medicine* 76 (Oxford, 2d ed. 1962).

79. Palomo Gonzalez, *El Aborto en San Agustin* (Salamanca: Calatrova, 1959) pp. 285–288; Bernard M. Dickens, *Abortion and the Law* (Bristol: MacGivvon & Kee, 1966) pp. 18–20.

80. 2 Bracton, *De Legibus et Conseutudinibus Angliae* 278 (Twiss ed. 1879).

81. Aristotle, *History of Animals* 7.3.583b.

82. For example see Silvester Prieras (Mazzolini), *Summa summarum* (Venice, 1501), "De Aborsu"; "Medicus" 4, 2; "Homicidium" 1, 3. And even more recently philosophers continue to "solve" the abortion problem by reference to Aristotelian embryology. E.g., see J. Donceel, S.J., "Abortion Mediate v. Immediate Animation," *Continuum*, 5 (Spring 1967), pp. 167–171.

83. E.g., see Donceel, op. cit., note 82.

84. See Means, op.cit., at p. 411.

85. J. T. Noonan, Jr., "An Almost Absolute Value in History" in *The Morality of Abortion, Legal and Historical Perspectives*, ed. John T. Noonan (Cambridge, Mass.: Harvard University Press, 1970), pp. 1–59.

86. Plucknett, *Concise History of the Common Law*, pp. 444–446.

87. Ibid., pp. 444–446.

88. 2 Fleta 60–61 (Selden Society ed. Richardson & Sayles eds. 1955).

89. Coke, *The Third Part of the Institutes of the Laws of England*, ch. 7 (3d ed. 1660); commenting on Coke, Sir James F. Stephen wrote: "I now come to Coke's *Third Institute*, a work which not by reason of its own merits, but, because of the reputation of its author, may be regarded as the second source of the criminal law, Bracton being regarded as the first."—3 Stephen, *History of the Criminal Law of England*, 52 (1883).

90. See Means, op. cit., at p. 420. See also Lucas, "Federal Constitutional Limitations on the Enforcement and Administration of State Abortion Statutes," *North Carolina Law Review* 446:730–778 (1967-68).

91. *Smith* v. *Gafford*, 31 Ala. 51 (1857); *Commonwealth* v. *Parker*, 50 Mass. (9 Met) 263, 265–66 (1845); *Commonwealth* v. *Bangs*, 9 Mass. 387, 388 (1812); *State* v. *Cooper*, 22 N.J.L. 52, 58 (Sup. Ct. 1849). It is interesting to note that many of these cases were decided long after the respective legislatures had passed criminal statutes regulating abortions. For example, in 1840–41 Alabama condemned abortion without regard to quickening, so that any comment by its court on the common law was the purest dicta.

92. *State* v. *Slagle*, 83 N.C. 630 (1880); *Mills* v. *Commonwealth*, 13 Pa. 631 (1850).

93. Miscarriage of Women Act, 1803, 43 Geo. 3 C. 58.

94. 4 Blackstone, *Commentaries on the Laws of England*, 394–395 (1769).

95. Gordon, The Unborn Plaintiff, 63 *Mich. L. Rev.* at 627 (1965).

96. 4 Blackstone, *Commentaries on the Laws of England*, 394–395 (1769).

97. 1 Blackstone, *Commentaries on the Laws of England*, p. 124 (1769).

98. William Hawkins, *Pleas of the Crown,* Vol. 1, p. 121.

99. 43 Geo. 3, C 58 (1803).

100. See *Rex* v. *Phillips,* 3 Campbell 73 (1812) Nisi Prius, which was a case decided under the statute, but the reasoning is applicable to our point. The woman testified that she had not felt the child move yet and the court directed an acquittal.

101. For a compilation of ecclesiastical punishments which probably influenced the problem, see Germain Grisez, *Abortion: The Myths, the Realities and the Arguments* (New York: Corpus Books, 1970), pp. 150-155.

102. Part of the preamble reads: " . . . And whereas the Provisions now by Law made for the Prevention of such offenses have been found ineffective for that Purpose;"

103. See 46 ALR 2d 1407, sec. 13.

104. See *Rex* v. *Phillips,* 3 Campbell 73 (1812) Nisi Prius where it was said: "Lawrence, J.—It is immaterial whether the drug was savin or not, or whether or not it was capable of procuring abortion, or even whether the woman was actually with child. If the prisoner believed at the time that it would procure abortion, and administered it with that intent, the case is within the statute and he is guilty of the offense laid to his charge."

105. See 46 ALR 2d, 1407, sec. 13.

106. The sentence quoted at note 104 from the Preamble seems to indicate that perhaps abortion before quickening was "considered" a crime also, in spite of Coke.

107. Ibid.

108. Conn. Stat., tit. 22, sec. 14, 16 at 152, 153 (1821).

109. Conn. Pub. Acts, Ch. LXXI, sec. 1 at 65 (1860).

110. Ill. Rev. Code, sec. 46 at 131 (1827).

111. Thomas Percival, *Percival's Medical Ethics,* ed. Chauncey D. Leake (Baltimore: Williams and Wilkins, 1927) pp. 134-135.

112. Grisez, op. cit., at p. 190.

113. Isaac M. Quimby, "Introduction to Medical Jurisprudence," *Journal of American Medical Association,* Aug. 6, 1887, Vol. 9, p. 164.

114. See H. C. Markham, "Foeticide and Its Prevention," ibid., Dec. 8, 1888, Vol. 11, p. 805. See also American Medical Association, Minutes of the Annual Meeting, 1859, *The American Medical Gazette 1859,* Vol. 10, p. 49.

115. For a compilation of abortion laws see Eugene Quay, "Justifiable Abortion: The Medical and Legal Foundations," *The Georgetown Law Journal,* Winter 1960, Spring 1961, Vol. 49, Nos. 2 and 3, at pp. 447-519.

    This seems the proper time to pay our homage and respect to a great legal scholar and seer, Eugene Quay. Certainly his compilation of state abortion laws is unsurpassed in the literature, and a scholarly tool without which work in this area might well be overwhelming. As Cyril Means has said: "For citations and texts consult the monumental collection of American statutory materials on abortion in Appendix 1 of Quay.... Every subsequent scholar in the abortion field must acknowledge a keen debt of gratitude to Mr. Quay for this meticulously researched compendium, which is the nearest thing that now exists to a complete collection of the American statutes."—Means, op. cit., at p. 507.

116. Md. Laws, Ch. 179, sec. 2 at 315 (1868).
117. N.J. Laws at 266 (1849).
118. Pa. Laws No. 374, secs. 87, 88, 89 (1860).
119. E.g. Minn. Stat. at Large, Vol. II, Ch. 54, Sec. 29, sec. 1-4 at 987 (1873).
120. D.C. Code 31 Stat. 1322 (1901) Ala. Code tit. 14, sec. 9 (1940).
121. Colorado was the first state to adopt an American Law Institute type of abortion statute. For a criticism of the American Law Institute Model Penal Code concerning abortion see Quay's article in *The Georgetown Law Journal:* Quay, idem, note 115.
122. *Roe* v. *Wade,* 314 F. Supp. 1217 (1970) at 1221 (N. D. Tex. 1970).
123. *Doe* v. *Bolton,* 319 F. Supp. 1048 (N. D. Ga. 1970).
124. Ibid., p. 1055.
125. Ibid., p. 1076.
126. Ibid., p. 1055.
127. 321 F. Supp. 741 (N. D. Ohio 1970) (J. Green dissenting).
128. Ibid., p. 746.
129. Ibid., p. 746.
130. 318 F. Supp. 1217 (E. D. Louisiana 1970) (J. Cassibry dissenting).
131. Ibid., p. 1223.
132. Ibid., p. 1225.
133. *Corkey* v. *Edwards,* 322 F. Supp. 1248 (N. D. North Carolina 1971).
134. Ibid., p. 1252.
135. Ibid., p. 1253.
136. Even the *Bolton* court preserved the Georgia statute after alluding in its decision to the creation of a new life after conception, thus making any decision involving abortion one affecting the state since it involved developing human life.
137. *Reynolds* v. *Sims,* 377 U.S. 533, 84 S. Ct. 1362, 12 L. Ed. 2d 506 (1964) at 1303; see also *Harper* v. *Virginia State Board of Elections,* 383 U.S. 663, 86 S. Ct. 1079 (1966).
138. See *Railway Express Agency* v. *New York,* 336 U. S. 106, 93 L. Ed. 533, 96 S. Ct. 463 (1949); *Skinner* v. *Oklahoma,* 316 U. S. 535, 86 L. Ed. 1655, 62 S. Ct. 1110 (1942); *Loving* v. *Commonwealth of Virginia,* 388 U. S. 1, 87 S. Ct. 1817 (1967); *Shapiro* v. *Thompson,* 394 U. S. 618, 89 S. Ct. 1322 (1969); see also Tussman & Tenbrock, 37 Calif. L. Rev. 341 (1949), Selected Essays on Constitutional Law 789 (1969).
139. The "compelling governmental interest" doctrine has developed in sev-

eral recent cases. See *Shapiro* v. *Thompson,* 394 U. S. 618, 89 S. Ct. 1322 (1969), particularly Mr. Justice Harlan's dissent; see also Mr. Justice White's concurring opinion in *Griswold* v. *Connecticut,* 381 U. S. 479, 85 S. Ct. 1628 (1965).

140. *Loving* v. *Virginia,* 388 U. S. 1, 87 S. Ct. 1817 (1967).

141. *McLaughlin* v. *Florida,* 379 U. S. 184, 85 S. Ct. 282 (1964).

142. See M. R. Cohen, "The Process of Judicial Legislation," in *Law and the Social Order* (1933); also collected in Cohen, *Readings in Jurisprudence and Legal Philosophy;* Pound, *An Introduction to the Philosophy of Law* (Yale University Press), page 53; Grey, *The Nature and Sources of the Law* (2d ed., 1921), pp. 172-173; Fuller, *The Morality of Law* (Yale University Press), p. 81H.

143. See Cohen, supra.

144. *Railway Express Agency* v. *New York,* 336 U. S. 106, 93 L. Ed. 533, 69 S. Ct. 463 (1949), con. opinion by Mr. Justice Jackson.

145. See, e.g., *Virginia* v. *Rives,* 100 U. S. 313, 25 L. Ed. 667, where the Court said: "It is doubtless true that a State may act through different agencies, either by its legislative, its executive, or its judicial authorities; and prohibitions of the amendments extend to *all action* of the State denying equal protection of the laws, whether it be action *by one of those agencies or by another,"* 100 U.S. at 318. (emphasis added). See, more recently, *Shelley* v. *Kraemer,* 334 U. S. 1, 92 L. Ed. 161, 68 S. Ct. 836 (1948), and *Barrows* v. *Jackson,* 346 U. S. 249, 97 L. Ed. 1586, 93 S. Ct. 1031 (1953).

146. *Raleigh Fitkin-Paul Memorial Hospital* v. *Anderson,* 42 N. J. 421, 201 A. 2d 537 cert. denied 377 U. S. 985 (1964).

147. See this Brief, infra.

148. For a survey of the rights which have been granted the unborn by the Courts, see 3 S. L. R. 225, "Abortion, the Law and Defective Children: A Legal-Medical Study," *Suffolk University Law Review* (Vol. III, Spring 1969, pp. 225-276). Also see this Brief, infra.

149. In many states the unborn's intestate rights of succession to property *vest* immediately upon the death of the decedent subject to divestment if the child is not born alive, e.g., see *Tomlin* v. *Laws,* 301 Ill. 616, 134 N.E. 24 (1922); *Deal* v. *Septon,* 144 N. C. 110, 56 S.E. 691 (1907).

150. Dallin H. Oaks, "Abortion and Due Process" in *Res Ipsa Loquitur,* Vol. 23, No. 1, pp. 5-7.

• 7 •

COERCION IN LIBERATION'S GUISE

Victor G. Rosenblum

Let me assert at the outset that these are subjective views. I have not striven for a consensus or for a survey of professional opinion. I know that my beliefs are rooted in that inner self that is the composite of my genes, environment, experiences, conscience, and consciousness. I'm not sure whether my level of consciousness is I, II or III on Professor Reich's "Greening of America" scale, but I take pride in its being there and in my being able to be here. I think it would be the apogee of egocentricity and hypocrisy to revel in my being while advocating through it a quick end to the being and beginnings of being of others.

About a year ago, my youngest daughter, then a high school senior, told me about a discussion with her classmates over the population explosion. She was asked at one point how her mother and father, who were assumed to be reasonably intelligent people, could have had eight children when the world hovers on the brink of destruction by Professor Ehrlich's population bomb. I took no comfort in the answer Laura reported she gave initially: "I guess my parents just didn't know any better." She added, however, that she would hate to have had parents so committed to the new Malthusianism that she would have been among those omitted from or remitted after conception.

Norman St. John-Stevas, in a paper on Law and the Moral

Reprinted from *Child and Family,* Vol. 9, No. 4, 1970.

Consensus given at a Reed College symposium in 1966, concluded with a statement with which I'd like to start:

In an age which has placed, through technology, unprecedented power in the hands of man, a view of man's nature is not less necessary and relevant, but more so. Man may know more, but he has never been in greater danger of being dehumanized. Every layman knows that today drugs can control or alter human personality, that life or reproductive functions can be easily destroyed, that radiation and fallout threaten the future of the human race. If power is there, why should it not be used? My personal belief is that only the Christian doctrine of man can effectively moderate the tyranny of scientific techniques. The Christian view is that man is not absolute master of his own fate, but holds his life and body in trust for other purposes. If this concept places limits on man's independence by stressing that he is the user not the proprietor of life, it also preserves his humanity by erecting barriers beyond which technology cannot pass. Yet faith is given to few, and modern secular man must, it seems, do without it. In this predicament he could do worse than be guided by the wisdom of the Common Law, with its centuries-old recognition of man's dignity and freedom. An intrinsic constituent of that recognition is respect for the sanctity of human life.

I have the same belief that man holds his life and body in trust, that he is the user rather than the proprietor of life, and that we must not yield to the tyranny of scientific techniques. As the realistic potentials emerge—both benign and bizarre—of the biocrats, the cloners, and the proponents of Dr. Delgado's ESB (electrical stimulation of the brain) in bringing man to an evolutionary turning point, it becomes all the more essential that we channel and control the power of science through human priorities. Such priorities are crucial to protect us from what Paul Ramsey termed "the corrosive influence of the view that what *should* be done, is largely a function of what technically *can* be done."

I differ with Mr. St. John-Stevas in what is perhaps a small respect. For although I believe the Common Law has accorded vital recognition to man's dignity and freedom, legal history in the United States is not without indicators that some strands of the law strayed from that noble conception. Our law has not always been at its best, especially when dealing with the poor and alienated. It has had some of its worst moments when, in construing particular manifestations of policy, it has applied arbitrary or oversimplified criteria, such as freedom of contract.

Let me cite some examples of what I regard as the best and the worst, drawing first on some dimensions of relationships between process and justice and then on several cases that denigrated man's dignity and freedom. The denigrations, while not bearing on questions of life per se, allow us—if they do not require us—to ask if some of the recent decisions on abortion are not as insensitive to human need or as nonperceptive of realities of pressure and coercion as the decisions in *Dred Scott* in 1857, *Coppage* v. *Kansas* in 1915 and *Adkins* v. *Children's Hospital* in 1923.

The inscription above the entrance to the U.S. Supreme Court building reads "Equal Justice under Law." In thinking about the quest for its fulfillment, I recalled a visit to the Court in March 1953 when the case of *Shaughnessy* v. *U.S. ex rel Mezei* was decided. In 1948, Mezei, a resident alien who had lived in Buffalo, New York, for twenty-five years but who had never taken out United States citizenship papers, was granted a visa by Rumania to visit his dying mother. For reasons never quite clear, he didn't get beyond Budapest. After waiting some nineteen months for an exit visa to leave Hungary, he returned to Ellis Island only to be held in custody there for the next three years. He was denied admission to the United States on the basis of allegations by the Department of Justice that he was a security·risk by virtue of information of a confidential nature, the disclosure of which would be prejudicial to the public interest. He tried to leave Ellis Island for some other country, but could find none. The Supreme Court of the United States ruled on that day that Mezei was not entitled even to a hearing. The majority argued that, having left the United States without permission while merely a resident alien, his subsequent petition for re-entry had to be classified as that of any other alien seeking admission for the first time, who would not by law be entitled to a hearing before exclusion. The Court ruled that the Department of Justice could not be compelled to disclose the confidential information on which it relied.

As soon as the majority decision had been read, Justice Robert Jackson rose from his seat and delivered an impassioned dissent without even looking at his notes.

If it be conceded that in some way this alien be confined, does it matter what the procedure is? Only the untaught layman or the charlatan lawyer can answer that procedures matter not. Procedural fairness and regularity are of the indispensable essence of liberty. Severe substantive laws can be endured if they are fairly and impartially applied. Indeed, if put to the choice, one might well prefer to live under Soviet substantive law applied in good faith by our common law procedures than under our substantive law enforced by Soviet procedural practices. . . .

Process is not to be equated simply with etiquette or ritual. It is the major instrument in the objective search for truth that must underlie justice.

Buber observed that

The lie is the specific evil which man has introduced into nature. . . . The lie is our very own invention, different in kind from every deceit that the animals can produce.

This proclivity of man is seen as the product, not of intransigence, but of the fact that often man does not know and cannot distinguish. Development of "the lie" as a uniquely human form of deceit placed a premium on the formulation and utilization of mechanisms that could maximize the objective discovery of truth. The ordeal and the utilization of oath helpers were important but inadequate early devices for discovering truth. The trouble with them was that rigging the outcome in favor of the dominant custom or ideology of the times was too easy and attractive. Verbal confrontation between disputants along with the right to cross-examination were more significant and effective means for testing the accuracy of rival allegations. The determination of truth was an objective but not abstract function of the judicial process. For the goal of discovering and asserting truth was not merely to perceive accurately what had occurred or was occurring, but to enhance the congruence between the "is's" of behavior and the "ought's" of equity and justice. The task was not simply to correct acts of injustice on the part of acknowledged scoundrels; it was also to avoid the perversion of justice by those who should know better.

> Do horses run upon rocks?
>   Does one plow the sea with oxen?
> But you have turned justice into poison,
>   and the fruit of righteousness into wormwood—
> O you who turn justice into wormwood,
>   and cast down righteousness to the earth!
>   (Amos 6:12; 5:7)[1]

At best, it would be a delusion to see justice as the *guaranteed* output of process; for process can become sterile or corrupt or both. Despite Justice Jackson's eloquent dissent, Mezei lost his case in the Supreme Court. We must note also, however, that although the Supreme Court's ruling in the case might legally have consigned him for life to the fate of a man without a country, the Immigration Service relented and the Attorney General finally approved Mezei's readmittance. Thus procedures that recognize the rights and status of the disputants, that foster within an objective setting the tests and challenges of the adversary system, and that separate the impulse to act from the opportunity to act may not always be effective; but they provide spurs to reason and conscience that facilitate justice.

Extension of procedural safeguards to the poor who must deal daily with governmental bureaucracies provides further illustration of the functionality of process in the pursuit of justice. Industries subject to regulation by state and federal administrative agencies have long been protected against procedural abuse. The potential and actual injustices of benevolent despotism or of uncontrolled governmental parentalism are not confined to the worlds of business and finance, however. Agencies such as Housing and Welfare bodies have crucial powers over the daily lives of the disadvantaged.

In a landmark decision of the U.S. Supreme Court, *Goldberg* v. *Kelly,* Justice Brennan made it clear for the first time that a state agency which terminates public assistance payments to a particular recipient without affording him the opportunity for an evidentiary hearing prior to such termination denies the recipient procedural due process and violates the Fourteenth Amendment.

Residents of New York City receiving financial aid under the federally assisted program of Aid to Families with Dependent Children had alleged in their complaint that New York City and State officials administering these programs terminated their aid without prior notice and hearing. For example, Mr. Juan DeJesus had his payments terminated allegedly because he refused to accept counseling and rehabilitation for drug addiction. He maintained that he did not use drugs. But he had no prior hearing and his payments were not restored until after his complaint was filed in court. The crucial factor cited by Justice Brennan as necessitating a pretermination hearing was that canceling aid, pending resolution of a controversy over eligibility,

may deprive an eligible recipient of the very means by which to live while he waits. Since he lacks independent resources, his situation becomes immediately desperate. His need to concentrate upon finding the means for daily subsistence in turn adversely affects his ability to seek redress from the Welfare bureaucracy.

The Court explicitly rejected the view that the considerations of due process must be outweighed by countervailing governmental interests in conserving fiscal and administrative resources. The Supreme Court's 7-1 decision was a victory for the legal system's commitment to process as an instrument of justice.

President Edward Levi of the University of Chicago has stated eloquently the function of law as commitment.

If there is any validity to the concept of a commitment of law as a whole upon the workings of society, then law does relate to political realities and to policy, not as an equivalent of social policy, but with special purposes which it seeks to implement. These special purposes, particularly during a period of anomie and unrest, go beyond the support and disciplining of legitimacy; they include the guidance of the society into a direct discussion and understanding of values, policies, and their consequences.

This commitment . . . is to develop concepts and to maintain and operate procedures which enable a sovereign community to be governed by rule for the common good, the attainment of human values, and to make that rule effective.

Virtually the antithesis of President Levi's conception of law as a commitment that includes guidance of the society into discussion and understanding of values, policies, and their consequences was present in the *Dred Scott, Coppage* and *Adkins* cases. They were models of prejudice, elitism, and indifference to human needs.

Can you believe that the Supreme Court of the United States could respond with hostility to the plea of a human being that his dignity and freedom as a man be recognized? In disposing of Dred Scott's suit, Justice Taney ruled that the Declaration of Independence did not apply to the "enslaved African race" when it said:

We hold these truths to be self-evident: that all men are created equal, that they are endowed by their Creator with certain inalienable rights, that among these are life, liberty, and the pursuit of happiness—that to secure these rights, governments are instituted among men, deriving their just powers from the consent of the governed. . . .

Taney described the Negro race as one which "by common consent had been excluded from civilized governments and the family of nations and doomed to slavery."

Slaves were "property," the ownership of whom (or of which, if one wants to run true to Taney's opinion) could not be interfered with by Congressional legislation. Furthermore, even "free persons of color" were not citizens of the United States within the meaning of the Constitution and laws. The Court majority could see black people only as objects, not as persons or citizens entitled to constitutional protection against the deprivation of life or liberty without due process of law. Since blacks were in essence property, not constitutional "persons," the Court could conclude it "too plain for argument" that Scott's plea for recognition must be dismissed. Ostensibly, the *Dred Scott* case's distinction between property and persons has been discredited and abandoned. But we must ask ourselves whether there is not a resurgence of its smug and inhuman tone in the contention voiced by some today that a fetus in the womb is merely property to be disposed of according to the wishes of its owner, who is the possessor of the body that houses it.

Coppage v. *Kansas* takes us back to the early days of the labor union and to the requirement by many employers that employees, as a condition of their employment, agree that they would not join a union. When Congress had sought to outlaw such so-called "yellow dog" contracts as conditions of employment on interstate railroads, the Supreme Court struck down the legislation under the due process clause of the Fifth Amendment. The Court ruled in 1908 that "the employer and the employee have equality of right, and any legislation which disturbs that equality is an arbitrary interference with the liberty of contract."

The *Coppage* case involved a Kansas law of 1903 that prohibited all employers within the state from requiring that employees agree as a condition of employment "not to join or become or remain a member of any labor organization." Ruling the law unconstitutional, the Court stressed that the right to make contracts is part of the right of personal liberty and private property. The Kansas Supreme Court had upheld the statute, noting that it was common knowledge that

employees as a rule are not financially able to be as independent in making contracts for the sale of their labor as are employers in making contracts of purchase thereof.

The U.S. Supreme Court's response, through Justice Pitney, observed piously

... no doubt wherever the right of property exists, there must and will be inequalities of fortune, and thus it naturally happens that parties negotiating about a contract are not equally unhampered by circumstances. It is from the nature of things impossible to uphold freedom of contract and the right of private property without at the same time recognizing as legitimate those inequalities of fortune that are the necessary result of the exercise of those rights.

Justice Holmes was one of three dissenters. He noted succinctly that "in present conditions a workman not unnaturally may believe that only by belonging to a union can he secure a contract that shall be fair to him."

Justice Day wrote a more extensive dissent, emphasizing the element of coercion. "It is constantly emphasized," he said,

that the case presented is not one of coercion. But in view of the relative positions of employer and employed, who is to deny that the stipulation here insisted upon and forbidden by the law is essentially coercive? No form of words can strip it of its true character.

As a result of the 6–3 vote, the aspiring trade union member could know that his freedom not to agree that he would not join a union could keep him in the ranks of the principled and, not incidentally, the unemployed for years to come. It took another quarter of a century before the Courts began to look at the nuances of coercion and to rule that a worker's right to join a union could be protected. The special irony of the *Coppage* case was that the Court based its ruling on the workers' "freedom of contract."

Adkins v. *Children's Hospital* had similarities to *Coppage* in tone and content. At issue this time were not questions surrounding union membership but of minimum wages for women and children. Congress in 1919 had established a minimum wage board for women and children in the District of Columbia

in order to protect the women and children of the District from conditions detrimental to their health and morals resulting from wages which are inadequate to maintain decent standards of living.

Elaborate procedural requirements including notice, hearing and participation in conferences by employers were part of the statute.

Among the disputants in the case was a woman twenty-one years of age, employed by the Congress Hotel Company as an elevator operator, at a salary of $35 per month and two meals a day. She alleged that

the work was light and healthful, the hours short, with surroundings clean and moral, and that she was anxious to continue it for the compensation she was receiving, and that she could not earn more.

The Supreme Court ruled that the employee's freedom of contract had been unconstitutionally infringed by the minimum wage legislation. While recognizing that there is no such thing as absolute freedom of contract, Justice Sutherland, writing the majority opinion, found as the feature of the statute which puts upon it the stamp of invalidity its exaction from the employer of

an arbitrary payment for a purpose and upon a basis having no causal connection with his business or the contract or the work the employee engages to do.

As a matter of principle, the Court held, "there can be no difference between the case of selling labor and the case of selling goods." Again, as in *Dred Scott,* the concept of property was paramount; the concept of humanity secondary.

In the course of this 1923 case, Justice Sutherland also concluded that, as a result of adoption of the Nineteenth Amendment, the ancient inequality of the sexes has

now come almost if not quite to the vanishing point. . . . We cannot accept the doctrine that women of mature age, sui juris, require or may be subjected to restrictions upon their liberty of contract which could not lawfully be imposed in the case of men under similar circumstances.

Taft and Holmes dissented, Taft noting that

employees, in the class receiving least pay, are not upon a full level of equality of choice with their employer and in their necessitous circumstances are prone to accept pretty much anything that is offered. They are peculiarly subject to the overreaching of the harsh and greedy employer.

Holmes said:

It will need more than the Nineteenth Amendment to convince me that there are no differences between men and women and that legislation cannot take those differences into account.

As to the freedom of contract argument of the majority, he observed that "pretty much all law consists in forbidding men to do some things that they want to do and contract is no more exempt from law than other acts."

The *Dred Scott, Coppage* and *Adkins* cases all paid lip service to man's dignity and freedom but then reached decisions, through the ostensible application of constitutional rights, that sanctioned, in the first instance, a literal regime of human slavery and, in the others, forms of economic coercion incompatible in practice with the freedom of contract principle.

I would like now to examine the trend of recent judicial opinions

Legal

on abortion and to raise with you the question whether there are not oversights or misperceptions of realities here too that will sanction, in the guise of privacy and freedom, equally dangerous forms of coercion.

Three recent cases evince a pattern for challenging long-standing anti-abortion statutes on grounds of vagueness and especially of invasion of privacy. The cases are *People* v. *Belous,* decided by the California Supreme Court in September 1969, *U.S.* v. *Vuitch,* decided by the Federal District Court for the District of Columbia in November 1969; and *McCann* v. *Babbitz* decided by the Federal District Court for the Eastern District of Wisconsin in March 1970.

In the *Belous* case, a split California Supreme Court voided for being vague and overbroad the 1850 California statute prohibiting abortions not "necessary to preserve" the mother's life. The case arose prior to the 1967 changes in the California law. Dr. Belous was convicted of criminal abortion and abortion conspiracy under provisions of the California penal code based on the 1850 statute.

Judge Peters, writing for the majority, concluded that the term "necessary to preserve" was not susceptible of a construction sufficiently certain to satisfy due process requirements without improperly infringing fundamental constitutional rights. Peters also maintained that if "necessary to preserve" were held to require immediacy or certainty of the mother's death, such a definition would "work an invalid abridgment of the woman's constitutional rights to life and to choose whether to bear children."

In *U.S.* v. *Vuitch* the district court held that the 1901 statute that authorizes abortion only when "necessary for preservation of the mother's life or health" was too vague to meet constitutional standards. Judge Gesell was particularly concerned with the amorphousness of the term "health," maintaining that a jury's acceptance or rejection of an individual doctor's interpretation of "health" should not determine whether he stands convicted of a felony facing ten years' imprisonment. Judge Gesell added:

As a secular matter a woman's liberty and right of privacy extends to family, marriage, and sex matters and may well include the right to remove an unwanted child at least in early stages of pregnancy.

In *Babbitz* v. *McCann,* a three-judge federal district in a *per curiam* decision ruled that the language of the Wisconsin anti-abortion statute, which was similar to the other statutes we have been considering, was not unconstitutionally vague. The language "necessary to save the life of the mother" could be understood and construed without jeopardizing constitutional rights.

The statute was ruled unconstitutional, however, on the ground that the Wisconsin statute violates the Ninth Amendment by depriving a woman of "her private decision whether to bear her unquickened child." Citing the *Belous* and *Vuitch* cases for support on the privacy theme, the court maintained explicitly that

a woman's right to refuse to carry an embryo during the early months of pregnancy may not be invaded by the state without a more compelling public necessity than is reflected in the statute in question. When measured against the claimed rights of an embryo of four months or less, we hold that the mother's right transcends that of such an embryo.

The mother's interests were held to be superior to those of an unquickened embryo "whether the embryo is mere protoplasm as the plaintiff contends or a human being as the Wisconsin statute declares."

In construing the trend exhibited by these cases, an observation by Daniel Callahan in his volume on *Abortion: Law, Choice, and Morality* is initially appropriate:

The credibility of advocates of legalized abortion under the banner of female freedom and "the wanted child" is weakened when the zeal for change in the abortion laws is not matched by a comparable zeal to change those social conditions which force many women to choose abortion.[2]

I believe that economic pressures and social stigmas related to childbearing today are as much instruments of force and coercion in ostensible choices of abortion as were the economic pressures and fears in ostensible choices not to join unions or to work at less than minimum wages in times past.

It is not without significance that the strongest advocates of abortion-on-demand are members of the higher strata in our social and political system. Few voices of the poverty-stricken and downtrodden are heard.

My oldest daughter, who has begun her graduate study in social work at the University of California, sent me some excerpts from the June 1970 issue of *California's Health* in which a number of people were asked how they felt about the population problem. Dr. Price Cobbs, an eminent black psychiatrist, said that he believed the possibility of the world becoming overpopulated is "an overexaggerated issue, particularly in this country." He felt that many people are using the population issue to keep from directing their energy towards solving things like racism, war, and more important problems.

Particularly interesting were the observations of Mrs. Laura Anderson, a black social worker who is Program Coordinator for Comprehensive Family Planning of the Berkeley City Health Department:

The current issue of population, in my mind, displaces an emerging American conscience for human dignity and eradication of poverty and hunger. I see population control or overpopulation as a political issue which diagnoses our society ills as one of too many people with problems by reducing the people as opposed to reducing the problems. In my opinion, when we attempt to solve problems by getting rid of people or potential people who will have these problems, like welfare recipients and those who will be poor or hungry, that's genocide. And I join with many people in making this charge against the move toward population control.

Some supporters of Zero Population Growth might seek to dismiss Mrs. Anderson's concerns as a possible paranoia of blacks about genocide. But we must bear in mind Professor Abraham Kaplan's observation that

in our time there is a cult of death that provides the backdrop against which we must view the problems of the sanctity of life. Our technology never seems to reach greater heights than when it is put to the service of destruction.[3]

I was thinking of Mrs. Anderson's and Professor Kaplan's words recently as frustration and confusion marred the humanitarian efforts to provide assistance for the beleaguered survivors of the tidal wave in East Pakistan. Man has managed to become scientifically efficient and precise in waging war, but the samaritan's work remains fraught with inefficacies and obstacles.

The May 1970 issue of the *Houston Law Review* contains an article on "the right to die" that further sustains Professor Kaplan's observations. The author, William P. Cannon, contends that the law should not interfere

as long as the individual himself is the only person to be harmed by his decision in favor of death. . . . An individual should have the right to die.[4]

Preoccupation with and rationalization of death and destruction and the fear that our environment is inadequate to sustain life dull us to human suffering and inhibit massive organized humanitarian responses to nature's own acts of violence. Our task is not to succumb to the cult of death but to accept as our first priority developing ways to enhance the significance and interdependence of life.

Amidst the otherwise depressing logistics of the season comes the kind of news item which helps remind us that scarcity of resources is not an overriding problem. In November 1970 the *Wall Street Journal* reported in a headline: "Flood of Florida Orange Juice Threatened Amid Forecast of Mammoth Citrus crop."[5] One citrus grower at a meeting of the Florida citrus commission was quoted as lamenting, "We could all drown in orange juice." The potential "glut" was reported to be so great that "even unloading it could be a problem." But as prices went down, people weren't drowning in orange juice; they were drinking more of it. Consumer purchases from the end of September 1970 averaged more than two million gallons a week, up more than 10% over the year earlier and down 3¢ a can in price.

Our need is not to lament the bounties of which nature is capable but to learn to distribute them more equitably; not to impose or accept a cult of death but to assert and enhance the dignity and vitality of human life and achievement; not to isolate ourselves in sleek new models of Plato's cave but to perceive and implement the vision of a community of mankind.

Our judicial models for these roles are not the cases that elevated property over humanity; not those that coerce labor from the economically oppressed under the meretricious banner of "freedom of contract"; and not those that allow coercion for abortion in the guise of "right to privacy."

There is no setting of privacy for decision-making when fear of being labelled unpatriotic or subversive of ecological factors leads a woman to remit the life within her. There is no setting of privacy when fear of a husband's job layoff impels a pregnant wife to seek an abortion. There is no setting of privacy when fear of being removed from the rolls of Aid to Dependent Children over producing another illegitimate child compels a pregnant woman to destroy that child.

The judicial models are found in the opinions that have recognized the need to separate the impulse to act from the opportunity to act, that accord the protection of full and impartial hearings before official action may be taken, that recognize the vulnerability of the disadvantaged, especially to the multiple and subtle forms of social, political, and economic coercion.

One opinion I haven't discussed, but which is perhaps more significant in these respects than Jackson's in the *Mezei* case or Brennan's majority opinion in *Goldberg* v. *Kelly*, was Douglas's majority opinion in *Skinner* v. *Oklahoma* in 1942. Pursuant to the Oklahoma Habitual Criminal Sterilization Act, a person convicted twice for felonies said to involve moral turpitude in any state and then convicted a third time in Oklahoma could be rendered sexually sterile by vasectomy or salpingectomy. Skinner was convicted in 1926 of stealing chickens and of robbery with firearms in 1929 and 1934. He was subsequently ordered to be sterilized and appealed on the ground that his Fourteenth Amendment rights were in jeopardy. In ruling the statute unconstitutional, Douglas pointed out that

marriage and procreation are fundamental to the very existence and survival of the race. The power to sterilize, if exercised, may have subtle, far-reaching and devastating effects. In evil or reckless hands it can cause races or types which are inimical to the dominant group to wither and disappear.

Let us rid ourselves of the false pieties with which we have often invaded human freedom while pretending to expand it. I urge that we reaffirm simple but crucial choices. I urge that we choose compassion over indifference, affection over gratification, sharing over insularity, giving over demanding, life over death. The technical skill to provide fuller and more meaningful lives for all is within our grasp. Let that quest be our priority, our prayer and our act.

REFERENCES

1. *The Holy Scriptures,* copyrighted 1955 by the Jewish Publications Society of America.
2. New York: Macmillan, 1970, p. 505.
3. Abraham Kaplan, "Social Ethics and the Sanctity of Life: A Summary," in *Life or Death: Ethics and Options* (Seattle: University of Washington Press, 1968), p. 156.
4. "The Right to Die," *Houston Law Review,* 7 (1970), p. 670.
5. November 16, 1970, p. 20.

SOCIAL

▪ 8 ▪

IS ABORTION NECESSARY
TO SOLVE POPULATION
PROBLEMS?

Arthur J. Dyck

It has become rather fashionable to blame spiralling population growth for almost every human ill and national problem. The popular literature abounds with examples of social ills attributed to rapid population growth like those cited by Representative Morris Udall in a recent article:

The numbers of people jammed into our large cities are increasingly ominous. Crime rates soar. Freeways and airports are overloaded with traffic. Some schools are in double sessions. There is poverty, racial strife, the rotting of our central cities, the formless and ugly sprawl of urbanization.[1]

Pollution is another of the serious problems very often directly linked to population growth. A full-page ad in the *New York Times* showed a picture of a beautiful baby and accused this baby of being a dangerous polluter.[2]

Population growth is not only linked to many kinds of social problems but is also depicted as a threat to human survival. And so one speaks of a population crisis. If population growth threatens human survival, then measures to curtail such growth would obviously be urgent. It is not surprising, therefore, that alarm about population growth has influenced some people to take a more tolerant view of abortion or even to advocate its increasing availability. Some

have even suggested that abortion be compulsory under certain circumstances.[3]

If we are to decide in an intelligent and well-informed manner
whether abortion is necessary to solve population problems, we will
need first of all to be clear about the kinds of problems that are
actually linked to population growth and how serious these are.
Equally important for our decision is some educated estimate as to
whether population growth rates are going to increase or decrease,
now and in the long run.

But our decision regarding the necessity of abortion will have to
take into account other important facts as well. Abortion is one
method among others by means of which people can control the size
of their families. How significant is abortion as a method of birth
control? How are birth rates affected by it? What is the relationship
between resort to abortion and the use of contraceptives, and conversely, the use of contraceptives and the resort to abortion?

Any society that is contemplating the inclusion of abortion in its
population policy would also want to consider what impact that
would have on the public good. Would policies that encourage abortion, whatever effect they might have on birth rates, increase or
decrease the welfare and humaneness of society?

In order, therefore, to come to some reasonable conclusion about
how abortion policy relates to population policy, it is essential to
consider at least the following four topics: the nature and seriousness
of problems associated with population growth; the relation between
abortion and birth rates; the relation between abortion and other
birth control methods; and the implications of making abortion a
part of population policy.

The Nature and Seriousness of Population Problems

A number of the links between certain serious social problems
and population size are tenuous conjectures. As Ansley Coale, the
noted Princeton demograper, has observed:

Most of the social and economic problems ascribed to our excessive population in the U. S. or to its excessive rate of growth are affected more by *how*
our population has chosen to distribute itself than by its *size*. . . . The density
of population is much higher in France, the United Kingdom and Nether-
lands. Yet pollution, traffic jams and delinquency are no worse in those
countries than here . . . We must attack the problems of pollution, urban

deterioration, juvenile delinquency and the like directly, and if sensible programs are evolved, continued population growth in the order of one percent annually would not make the programs tangibly less effective.[4]

It should be noted that at the present time, the rate of population growth in the United States is less than one percent.

There are those who would argue that poor people would be much better off if they had considerably fewer children. Such a view entirely misses the point—namely, that people who are less poor are the ones who will have fewer children. A direct attack on poverty is a way of reducing birth rates, if reducing birth rates is one's goal. Poverty, of course, should be attacked in its own right for humane and social reasons. Lower fertility is, however, a by-product of increased social and racial justice.[5] For the alleviation of discrimination makes available to disadvantaged minorities the kinds of educational and employment opportunities enjoyed by couples who have small families.

Some have tried to link population density and conditions of rapid population growth to social unrest and revolution. Here again, there is no proved relationship. An extensive survey of the voluminous literature on the political consequences of population growth conclusively demonstrates the lack of any evidence for such an association.[6]

There are three problems that are often cited as posing a real crisis for the future of mankind. Since population growth is related to these problems, it is worth exploring how critical they are and how important a role population growth plays in bringing them about. We refer here to environmental deterioration, starvation, and poverty.

Population Growth and Environmental Deterioration. Environmental deterioration can be seen as an imminent threat to human survival. In the *Population Bomb,* Paul Ehrlich declares that our environment is sick, and that the disease is overpopulation. The remedy for this illness is population control to achieve zero population growth rates, using coercive methods as necessary.

But Ehrlich's reasoning is too simple. Our environment may be sick, but zero population growth will not by itself cure it.[7] Roger Revelle in a testimony given before the Reuss Committee, a Congressional Committee on Conservation and Natural Resources, made the following analysis:

The lack of utility of any simple correlation between environmental deterioration and population growth can be demonstrated by calculating the size of the population of the United States which, with the same per capita income and dirty habits as the average U. S. citizen in 1965, would have produced no more pollution than the country experienced in 1940.

Other things being equal, the number of automobiles and the amount of gasoline and paper consumed would have remained about constant over the quarter century if our population had declined from 133 million people in 1940 to 67 million in 1965. To maintain a constant flow of sulfur dioxide in the air from electric power plants, the population would have had to decrease to only 40 million people. Presumably the amount of nitrogen fertilizers would not have increased, if all but 17 million Americans had re-emigrated to the homes of their ancestors. Only 17 million people in the country would use the same amount of nitrogen in 1965 as we used in 1940. The national parks would have remained as uncrowded in 1965 as they were in 1940 if our population during the interval had gone down from 130 million people in 1940 to 30 million people in 1965, instead of going up to 195 million, as, of course, it actually did.

These unlikely speculations emphasize the uncertainties of the relationships between population, gross national product, and the quality of life, of which environmental deterioration is one aspect.[8]

From this analysis, we can readily see that pollution is a way of life and must be attacked in its own right. We cannot accept this way of life as the price of affluence. For if environmental deterioration is accepted as an inevitable by-product of affluence, then it would be foolish to urge non-affluent countries to reduce their population. One major argument for asking non-affluent countries to reduce their population is that such a reduction would stimulate economic development, and if affluence and environmental deterioration inevitably accompany each other, environmental deterioration will increase as populations decrease. This applies to affluent countries like the United States as well. If we do not change our habits of polluting, we could greatly reduce population growth, as indeed we are at present doing, and not only fail to reduce environmental deterioration, but increase it.

Nothing we have said should be misconstrued. Population growth does affect the demands we make upon our environment, but what we have tried to show is that environmental deterioration of crisis proportions is not tied to sheer numbers of people.[9] In any event, no nation can solve the problems of pollution simply through reductions in population, whether by greater resort to abortions or by other means.

Population Growth and Starvation. Another dire prediction in some of the population literature is that of widespread famines caused by present population growth rates. *Famine 1975* is what the Paddocks assert.[10]

The favorite example for famine prophecies is India. In a careful analysis of famines in his country, the Indian scholar B. M. Bhatia found that famines in the nineteenth century were due to genuine shortages of food; in the twentieth century, they occur because people either fail to receive in time the food that is available, or else they cannot pay for it.[11] As in so many developing countries, food supplies in India continue to increase at a faster rate than population growth, and there is currently enough food in India adequately to nourish its citizens.[12]

But people starve even where there is sufficient food. In some localities it is largely due to the way in which infants are fed. This cause of death could be greatly curtailed by minimal instruction in the nutritional needs of infants.[13] Within the United States, high rates of infant mortality, maternal death, and generally lower life expectancies occur because of malnourishment. Quite clearly, however, malnourishment in the United States is a problem of social injustice, not lack of food.

Again, our view should not be misunderstood. We are not asserting that a given population could not exhaust its food supply. Our point is simply that there is no current necessity for people to starve because of the unavailability of food. Experts differ as to when time would run out for feeding the population of the world, should it continue to grow at its present rate.[14] At the same time, we must bear in mind that growth rates in many countries are declining, and other countries appear poised to follow suit.[15]

Population Growth and Poverty. The relationship of economic gains and population growth are very ambiguous. We know that rapid population growth can and has been accompanied by increases rather than decreases in per capita income. This is true of India, for example. Furthermore, there are respected economists who argue that population growth provides an incentive for economic development insofar as it brings with it increased motivation, imagination, and productivity.[16]

It is not at all axiomatic that choosing to have fewer children will increase one's wealth or the opportunities for oneself and one's children. For many people throughout the world and for some in the United States, there are situations where children are a source of farm labor and of security in one's old age. Under these circumstances, it is as unrealistic as it is unjust to expect these people to be persuaded that economic benefits will follow from reducing the size of their families.

For those who are extremely poor, a reduction in the number of one's children does not by itself alleviate the conditions and sources of poverty. As one poverty-stricken Black mother in the United States put it, "Even without children, my life would still be bad . . . they are not going to give us what *they* have, the birth control people."[17] Whatever other benefits may accrue to mothers who have a small, rather than a large family, the elimination of extreme poverty is not guaranteed to be one of them. This is particularly so for disadvantaged minority groups.

Our conclusion, then, with respect to the relationship between population growth and threats to the human species, such as environmental deterioration, starvation, and poverty, is that none of these dangers, however imminent, ensue directly from present population growth rates. Concern over space and the use of space in a finite world, another genuine concern, is again something that is not solved simply by decreasing numbers.

Is there no reason to be concerned about population growth, some of our readers may well ask at this juncture? Yes, population growth is a genuine human concern, and because our world and the space in which we live is finite, zero population growth would appear to be a necessity at some point in our history. This means that it is important to observe and think about the ways in which population decreases occur and what role abortion, and other modes of limiting birth, have to play. However, as we have tried to show, there is no justification for fanaticism or haste when considered reflection would better serve us.

Now, agreeing that zero population growth is at some point an apparent necessity is not to say that government policies specifically designed to influence or regulate brith rates are inevitable or essential in any or every country. We should realize that in a country like the United States, we are now very close to zero population growth. During the first quarter of this year, *before* the nation or its government had heard or tried to implement the policy suggestions made by the Commission on Population Growth and the American Future, birth rates in the United States fell below 2.29 children per woman; 2.11 per woman is the figure required for zero population growth.[18] It is also important to note that there are a number of developing countries around the world that appear to be going through the demographic transition more rapidly than was the case for Western countries.[19] The demographic transition is the name that demographers give to the shift from a situation of high death rates accompanied by high birth rates to a situation where low death rates and low birth rates prevail. Low birth rates only occur in societies where low mortality rates, particularly low infant mortality rates, have been achieved. The switch to lower birth rates as a response to lower mortality rates is occurring much faster now than it ever has before in the history of mankind.[20] This phenomenon is a further reminder of the relation between justice and fertility behavior: those who have high infant mortality rates will not have small families. Small families occur where couples have reasonable opportunities for attaining health and the conditions that sustain it, such as education and satisfying employment.

The decline in birth rates in the United States is being recorded not only in states that have permissive abortion laws but also in states that have restrictive laws.[21] Moreover, much of this continuing decline in birth rates over the past decade has come about in a nation where most of the states have restrictive abortion laws, and before permissive abortion laws of the New York variety were passed. The relation of abortion policies to fertility behavior, therefore, is not self-evident: it bears scrutiny.

ABORTION, BIRTH RATES, AND CONTRACEPTIVE PRACTICES

In the study of abortion, little, if anything, is known with certainty. Moreover, there are very few studies of the effects of abortion policies upon birth rates.

One reason why studies of the demographic effects of abortion are inconclusive and few in number is that it is difficult to know just how many abortions, both legal and illegal, actually occur. This lack of solid information has been an unfortunate part of the abortion debate in the United States, where people have based their opinions on extremely unreliable figures.

For example, the great majority of commentators in recent American law journals accept that 1,200,000 is a plausible estimate of the number of abortions *per annum* in the United States. But on examination it appears that this figure is based on a study published in 1934—according to which it may be assumed that there is one illegal abortion for every 3.55 live births. And this latter figure is an extrapolation from the case histories of 10,000 women who attended the Margaret Sanger birth control clinic in New York City between 1925 and 1929! Another widely accepted figure for the United States is

600,000 *per annum*—this by extrapolation from the case histories of the women who volunteered the information in Kinsey's famous study of female sexuality (a group which included a negligible proportion of blacks and Catholics, and which was unrepresentative even of urban white women). The statistics committee at a 1958 conference called by Planned Parenthood agreed that the number may be between 200,000 and 1,000,000, and that there is no way of determining the number more closely than that.[22]

One should not assume that the lower limit of 200,000 is a sacred figure. Consider, for example, the study done in Indianapolis in 1941-42, involving married, white Protestant couples: 1.9 percent of their pregnancies ended in illegal abortions. If we were to extrapolate this figure and apply it to the United States for the year 1940, it would have meant that there were 48,000 illegal abortions in the United States in that year. If we were to increase this number by 50 percent to allow for population growth up to the year 1969, we would be estimating the number of illegal abortions per year in the United States as roughly 72,000.[23] Clearly, this also is an unrepresentative sample, but it serves to indicate the range of extrapolations based on unrepresentative samples that could be used to sway public opinion.

Are there any generalizations that one can make about the relation between permissive abortion policies, on the one hand, and birth rates and contraceptive practices, on the other? First of all, it seems fair to say that permissive abortion policies generally facilitate and accelerate a downward trend in fertility, but not always.[24] At the same time, restrictive abortion policies do not prevent the achievement of a low level of fertility, nor do they prevent a downward trend in fertility even where fertility is already low. The United States is a good example of a country very near to zero population growth, the trend toward which began a number of years before there were permissive abortion policies in any of its states. This trend continues and holds also for states with restrictive abortion policies.

The Commission on Population Growth and the American Future was well aware of all this. Indeed, this Commission acknowledges that the potential effect of permissive abortion policies on the birth rate in the United States would be minimal. Its argument for abortion is largely an argument to leave the option for abortion in the hands of individual women and physicians.[25]

In countries where contraception is already practiced by the vast majority of the population, permissive abortion policies tend to contribute more to the diminution of the effective practice of contraception than to a reduction of the birth rate below the level already obtained by contraception.[26] Conversely, when contraception is introduced into a country where abortion is widely practiced, declines in abortion rates may accompany declines in pregnancy and fertility rates.[27]

Japan is a country in which permissive abortion policies were introduced at a point where contraception was not widely practiced, and in which major efforts to introduce contraception were undertaken once abortion was widely practiced. The immediate result of the permissive abortion law of 1948 was a sharp increase in the number of legal abortions. This increase reached a peak of 1,170,000 in 1955 and declined to less than 900,000 in 1964. Contrary to what happened in countries like Bulgaria and Hungary, the total pregnancy rate as well as the total fertility rate declined in Japan during this period. This means that contraception also contributed to the decline in birth rates that occurred in Japan in the early 1950's. Since there is little correlation between increases in abortion rates and decreases in birth rates, it would appear that contraception and delayed marriage were important factors in the decline in birth rates in Japan.[28]

There is, therefore, no evidence that abortion has to be part of any policy designed to bring about zero population growth.[29] In countries where contraceptives are widely used, permissive abortion policies exact an immediate price. They lead to the neglect of careful contraception. This price of permissive abortion policies has been well-documented in England.

Studies in England reveal that contraceptive use among women who seek abortion is declining. Of 1,000 women studied between 1964 and 1969, 30 percent normally used no method of birth control, and 48 percent used none on the occasion of the unwanted conception. More recently, women obtaining lawful abortions through the Birmingham Pregnancy Advisory Service normally used no method in 45.8 percent of the cases and none at the time of conception in 73.5 percent of the cases. Among the first 500 women aborted through the offices of the London Pregnancy Advisory Service, 42 percent normally used no method and 70 percent used none at the time of conception. In the last-mentioned study, it was found that 60 percent of the women were single, but that only 8 percent of the pregnancies resulted from a casual union. Many intelligent, young, unmarried women expressed the view that taking oral contraceptives was a degree of commitment for which they were not prepared.[30] Pregnancy counseling services, such as those in Boston, report similarly high percentages of single women who are not practicing contraception even though a high proportion of them have a college education. Furthermore, Abdel Omran has warned us that

Many studies from various countries indicate that women who have experienced one or more induced abortions have a proclivity to continue this method of birth control even when effective contraceptives become available. This group of vulnerable women may continue to rely on induced abortion as a "tried and true" method of family planning.[31]

Someone may ask why, if abortion sometimes facilitates reduction in fertility rates, don't we make it available as one more method among others for bringing about this result? Recently, a study has shown that Europe nearly doubled its population between 1750 and 1850, but the practice of infanticide contributed to keeping population growth rates lower than they might have been.[32] Clearly, one can argue that the practice of infanticide would facilitate trends toward lower fertility. However, modern Europe has now achieved considerably lower birth rates than it had in the period of 1750 to 1850, and this was accomplished without infanticide as a policy. The question regarding abortion, then, is like the question regarding infanticide: do we want to use this particular method to facilitate lower fertility when there are other methods available for accomplishing the same thing? The question, then, is strictly a moral one and not a question of necessity.

While, as we have argued, abortion is not needed to solve population problems, there are individuals who experience a genuinely felt need for abortion when contraceptives have failed them. Our best hope for these couples lies in the development of fail-safe contraceptives. But here we are assuming that a policy encouraging contraception is to be preferred to a policy encouraging abortion. Why?

ABORTION AS A POLICY

In the recent advocacy of more permissive abortion policies, there has been a distinct tendency to take the view that the decision whether or not to resort to abortion is a private, moral decision and is not to be legislated. Many of these same advocates have also stressed the failure of restrictive abortion laws to deter people from having abortions. Both of these points need to be challenged.

Increasingly through research in psychology, more is being learned about moral development and its stages.[33] One of the most significant findings of this research is that most adults in any culture are at a stage in moral development where existing laws and customs are the most important bases for deciding what is right and wrong. Public policies and laws, therefore, have a definite role in guiding moral decisions and teaching what is right and wrong. Private morality is influenced as much by permissive abortion policies as it is by restrictive abortion policies. The choice is one of deciding which of two different moral viewpoints we want to encourage.

Although it is true that restrictive abortion laws never succeed in preventing all abortions, as criminal laws generally never succeed in preventing all crime, they have a demonstrable deterrent effect. Wherever highly permissive laws have been instituted, the data available show that the total abortion rates have been increased thereby.[34] Our question, then, is a moral one—namely, what difference does it make to have a permissive abortion policy rather than a restrictive one? The difference revolves around two issues: the protection of individual human life, and the protection of the welfare of the community.

The Protection of Individual Human Life. In the Preamble to the Declaration of Independence, the right to life is declared to be an inalienable right. One of the clear advantages of retaining strict abortion laws is that this policy in no way erodes or abrogates that kind of public commitment. For the kind of restrictive abortion policy that we have in mind permits abortion in instances where the life of a pregnant woman is endangered by carrying her fetus to term. Here the principle by which life is taken is that of self-defense. We would not, and we do not, deny people the right to defend themselves against genuine threats to their own lives, even when this means taking another life.

But what happens if we shift to permissive abortion policies? Surely abortion advocates do not wish to decrease the right to life and the sanctity that attaches to life. Their hope is that permissive abortion policies will not have that effect. What are the facts?

New York State since July 1, 1970, has a law that permits abortion to be performed at the request of the pregnant woman and with the compliance of a physician unless the fetus is more than twenty-four weeks old. The principle behind this policy is to leave decisions about fetuses, provided that they are no more than twenty-four weeks old, in the private sphere, and to invoke public sanctions against this decision when this fetus is more than twenty-four weeks old. Presumably, therefore, one could preserve the inalienable right to life of every individual by claiming that individuals acquire that right when they are more than twenty-four weeks old. In practice this is not the way it works. Why not?

Women who do not want to bear the child that is developing in their wombs often resort to abortion because their fetus has been diagnosed as abnormal or likely to be abnormal, or because they project a bad life for this child on other grounds. The argument here is that there are some lives that are not worth living. This argument applies logically to developing human life at any stage. A life that is considered unworthy to live at twenty-four weeks because it will be a life of blindness, deafness, mental retardation, or whatever, is logically as unworthy at twenty-five weeks as it is at twenty-three, and is as unworthy at birth.

Now you might say that all of this is true, but hypothetical. Isn't it true that in practice you can make a dividing line between a living entity that will be treated as an individual human life and one that will not? Unfortunately, this is not the case. In New York State today, there are aborted fetuses who are delivered alive, and yet no effort is made to keep them alive. Why not? Because, among other things, the process by which they have been aborted has greatly increased the risks that they will not be normal.[35] Also, some physicians simply honor the intent of the pregnant woman, which is that this child is not wanted, and the presumption is made that no one else, in that case, can have it. These are clear instances of moral infanticide, which are not legally recognized as such. However, we also have cases of infanticide that should be tried as murder and are not. There are physicians in New York who will do an abortion for a pregnant woman whose fetus is known to be more than twenty-four weeks old.[36] Not only should these abortions be looked upon as clear instances of infanticide, but they should also be added to the total number of illegal abortions that persist in New York despite, or because of, a permissive abortion policy.

As if these cases were not enough, there is another kind of tragedy occurring in the United States, being justified by the very arguments by which fetal life is taken under permissive abortion laws. Let me cite just one example. At Johns Hopkins University Hospital, a couple gave birth to a child who was alleged to be mongoloid. This child needed an operation, an operation which normally succeeds, and would more or less assure this child of the attainment of its potentialities, whatever these might have been. The couple refused to grant permission for the operation on the grounds that it did not want this child since it would probably be mentally retarded, how severely could not be known. (Mongoloids range from those who are severely retarded to those who are quite educable, even to the point of becoming published authors.) The hospital authorities, as in the abortion cases in New York, honored the wishes of the parents and did nothing to question them. The child was then ordered to be given "nothing by mouth" and, after fifteen days with nothing to eat or drink, died.[37] For any of our existing statutes, this is murder. It has not been tried as such. Hence, the principle that you can dispose of unwanted life, and of lives deemed to be unworthy of sustenance, is being applied even when that life is living and breathing outside the womb. This is not the only case of its kind in the United States.

If a fetus is unwanted because in prospect its life would be burdensome to those who would rear it, there is no way of assuring that those who are unwanted at any stage will be protected from being considered burdensome, and hence dispensable. This is not a prediction; this is simply what is happening. And we know, also, from our history that human beings who, for whatever reasons, are seen to be less than what they might or should be, will become victims of cruelty and neglect. This has been the history of our treatment of Black people. As we strive mightily to redress our victimization of Blacks, it would be ironic to develop new categories of individual human lives that are not worthy of protection under our laws and customs. It would be equally ironic and unfortunate to change the role of physicians and nurses from that of saving lives to that of taking lives. No wonder some of the nurses who must dispose of fetuses living and dead, in New York and elsewhere, have resigned in protest, reaffirming their professional pledge to save, rather than to destroy, lives.

Protection of the Welfare of the Community. Where a permissive abortion policy is adopted on the principle that abortion is an individual decision, certain consequences result for the familial life and for the life of the whole community. These deserve to be examined and assessed.

One of the apparent benefits of permissive abortion policies is that individual freedom, particularly of women, would seem to be increased. However, a great deal depends upon the rationale for one's policy to make abortion accessible on request. If the argument is that voluntary abortion on request is essential for bringing down birth rates, then this policy would become a candidate for compulsion if this voluntary abortion policy proved unsuccessful. Such a policy would not only fail to protect nascent life but would directly assault the freedom and bodily welfare of women.[38]

Let us examine, however, permissive abortion policies whose purpose is solely to enhance freedom and not to achieve certain birth rates, since as we have shown, abortion is not necessary for this latter purpose anyway. A circuit court in Washington, D.C., has recently ruled that it is the constitutional right of any woman to have an abortion without the consent of her husband or her sexual partner. The Commission on Population Growth and the American Future has asked that abortion on request apply also to minors. These moves are made in accord with the principle of complete individual freedom and privacy in reproductive decisions. Is this what we want? The effect of completely individualizing reproductive decisions is to drive a considerable wedge between husband and wife, and, for that matter, between all sexual partners. Family planning on such a principle would be a totally euphemistic expression.

A similar split and strain in communication occurs between parent and child. Where minors decide reproductive matters for themselves, physicians would, by default, be their parents in such privileged communication. Here again family planning would be a euphemism.

Since the family is the only predictable way in which children can be socialized and brought to maturity in an atmosphere of love, one cannot treat lightly any policy that would further undermine its effectiveness and stability. In saying this, we are not making a brief for the nuclear family as such, but we are underlining the point that, whatever familial structures a society adopts, the possibility for loving relationships among adults, and between adults and children, needs to be fostered not undermined. The implications of adopting the principles behind permissive abortion policies, therefore, portend great harm and no benefits for familial life.

But the principle that reproductive decisions are purely individual decisions has other, perhaps even more ominous, implications. Consider, for example, one of the reasons why Japan moved rapidly to reduce its birth rates. There was a strong feeling in Japan that the future of that community would be jeopardized by continued rapid population growth. The Japanese culture and religion, with its strong emphasis on obligations to one's parents and ancestors, and obligations to do what is good for the race, did not think of reproduction as a purely individual matter.[39] If one's culture is threatened by excessive rates of growth, then one has an obligation to do something about it. The Japanese people did what they felt morally obligated to do.

In a situation, however, where reproductive decisions are not made with an eye to the welfare of one's community, one's parents, one's spouse, or one's sexual partner, the response to any threat to one's community because birth rates are too high or too low is utterly unpredictable. This is ironic because it means that the quest for freedom in reproduction could lead precisely to a situation in which coercion may be the only way of achieving a birth rate, whether higher or lower, which would secure the continuation and future of a community or culture.

Pure individualism is unpredictable because no one really knows whether people see it as in their self-interest to have children. During the depression years, when the birth rates in the United States fell to almost the very low levels we now have, sociologists with a certain view of self-interest and of the consequences of urbanization predicted that the United States would certainly be depopulated. It would be depopulated because people in large cities would not want to be married and would not want to have children. This is what they felt self-interest would dictate. Given the delays in publication and in doing research, these books and articles came out during the time the baby boom in the United States began.

Now, as the country returns to low birth rates, and young people do not as uniformally expect to marry and have children, one could, as these sociologists did, predict again that the effect of completely individualizing reproductive decisions would be the disappearance of this nation. Whether this is what would happen, I do not know. It could happen if the desire to have children is purely a matter of acculturation, and if our culture were totally to succeed in linking self-interest with childlessness and selfishness with having children. Some people are inclined to go this way, but how they will be received remains uncertain.[40]

On the other hand, if self-interest is linked with childbearing so that having children is a highly gratifying sort of experience, then completely individualizing such decisions may mean that it will be difficult to keep birth rates low and to maintain eventual zero population growth. Societies which have zero population growth, such as the recently studied hunter-gatherers, have a strong sense of community, along with a highly positive attitude toward children. This is the same combination that we find among American Jews, who have the lowest birth rates in our country.[41]

Surely those who are concerned for the welfare of human communities and the human species will want to foster attitudes of responsiveness to these communities and to the species. The concern for population policy is, after all, a concern that mankind live and flourish. Any policy that would subvert that aim is not worthy of it. Permissive abortion policies, on balance, would threaten the future both of individual lives and of the human community much more than they could ever hope to benefit it.

REFERENCES

1. Morris K. Udall, "Standing Room Only on Spaceship Earth," *Reader's Digest,* December 1969.
2. Blaming environmental problems on "overpopulation" is a view popularized by the biologist Paul Ehrlich in *The Population Bomb* (New York: Ballantine Books, Inc., 1968).
3. For the suggestion that abortions be required for illegitimate pregnancies, see Paul Ehrlich and Ann Ehrlich, *Population, Resources, Environment* (San Francisco: W. H. Freeman and Co., 1970), p. 254, and Kingsley Davis, "Population Policy: Will Current Programs Succeed?" *Science,* Vol. 158, pp. 730-739.
4. Cited by R. Elliot, L. C. Landman, Richard Lincoln and Theodore Tsurnoka, "U. S. Population Growth and Family Planning: A Review of the Literature" in Daniel Callahan (ed.), *The American Population Debate* (New York: Doubleday & Co., Inc., 1971), p. 192.
5. College-educated black women, for example, have the lowest fertility rates among college-educated women.
6. Myron Weiner, "Political Demography: An Inquiry into the Political Consequences of Population Change," in *Rapid Population Growth: Consequences and Policy Implications* (Baltimore: The Johns Hopkins Press, 1971), pp. 567-617.
7. Ehrlich's diagnosis of the seriousness of environmental problems is sometimes faulty and exaggerated. See Roger Revelle, "Paul Ehrlich: New High Priest of Ecocatastrophy," *Family Planning Perspectives,* Vol. 3, No. 2, April 1971, pp. 66-70.
8. Roger Revelle (testimony), *Effects of Population Growth on Natural Resources and the Environment;* Hearings before the Reuss Subcommittee on Conservation and Natural Resources (Washington: U. S. Govt. Printing Office, 1969).
9. For a very balanced account of the consequences of population growth, see *Rapid Population Growth: Consequences and Policy Implications,* Vol. I, chapter 3.
10. W. Paddock and P. Paddock, *Famine 1975* (Boston: Little Brown and Co., 1967).

11. B. M. Bhatia, *Famines in India: 1860 to 1965* (New York: Asia Publishing House, 1967).

12. Private communication, Roger Revelle. See also note 9 above and the President's Science Advisory Committee, Panel on the World Food Supply, *The World Food Problem* (three volumes, The White House, May 1967). The total number of malnourished people in the world may be smaller than it was thirty to forty years ago. (See note 8 above.)

13. How this can be done is spelled out in J. B. Wyon and J. E. Gordon, *The Khanna Study* (Cambridge: Harvard University Press, 1971).

14. For careful research in this area, see Roger Revelle, "Projected World Population and Food Production Potentials," in *The Land-Grant University and World Food Needs* (University of Illinois College of Agriculture) and T. W. Schultz, "The Food Supply-Population Growth Quandary," in *Rapid Population Growth: Consequences and Policy Implications*, Vol. II, chapter 7.

15. Dudley Kirk, "A New Demographic Transition?" in *Rapid Population Growth: Consequences and Policy Implications*, Vol. II, chapter 2.

16. A balanced account of the economic advantages and disadvantages of population growth is given by Harvey Leibenstein, "The Impact of Population Growth on Economic Welfare—Nontraditional Elements," in *Rapid Population Growth: Consequences and Policy Implications*, Vol. II, chapter 4.

17. Robert Coles, *Children of Crisis* (Boston: Atlantic-Little Brown, 1964), p. 368. See also the essay in this book by Erma Clardy Craven, p. 231.

18. The 2.29 figure is the average number of children per woman born in the last six months of 1971 and the first six months of 1972. It was calculated by the Harvard demographer David Heer, based on data from the Bureau of the Census and vital statistics; the 2.11 figure is a calculation made by demographer Ansley Coale of Princeton.

19. Kirk, op. cit.

20. Ibid.

21. Reported by the U. S. Bureau of the Census.

22. J. M. Finnis, "Three Schemes of Regulation," in J. T. Noonan, Jr. (ed.), *The Morality of Abortion* (Cambridge: Harvard University Press, 1970), p. 181.

23. Reported in D. W. Louisell and J. T. Noonan, Jr., "Constitutional Balance," in Noonan, *The Morality of Abortion*. Using deaths from illegal abortions, one would estimate that there are 50,000 illegal abortions per year in the United States.

24. Data from Eastern European countries and Japan are widely cited as evidence that permissive abortion policies contribute to lower fertility rates. But it is important to take note of the following facts: there is no evidence that increases in the uses of contraceptives would not have yielded similar results; in Bulgaria the increase in the total abortion rates far outstripped the decline in the total fertility rate; in East Germany a

more permissive abortion policy resulted in higher fertility rates, while a return to a restrictive policy lowered fertility rates; in Japan delayed marriage and contraception greatly facilitated decreases in fertility rates; and Sweden's fertility rate did not decline after more permissive abortion laws were enacted. See the careful study by Harald Frederiksen and J. W. Brackett, "Demographic Effects of Abortion," *Public Health Reports,* Vol. 83, No. 12, December 1968, pp. 999-1010.

25. *Population and the American Future* (New York: The New American Library, Inc., 1972), pp. 172-178.

26. See Frederiksen and Brackett, op. cit.

27. Ibid.

28. Ibid.

29. Some would argue that permissive abortion policies are needed to substitute legal abortions for illegal abortions and greatly reduce the latter. Uniformly, however, total abortion rates greatly increase when permissive abortion policies are introduced; sometimes illegal abortions rates remain constant or even rise. See ibid. and also Finnis, "Three Schemes of Regulation," op. cit., pp. 208-219.

30. See Finnis, op. cit., p. 212.

31. A. R. Omran, "Abortion in the Demographic Transition," in *Rapid Population Growth: Consequences and Policy Implications,* Vol. II, chapter 13, p. 512.

32. W. L. Langer, "Checks on Population Growth: 1750-1850," *Scientific American,* Vol. 226, No. 2, February 1972, pp. 92-99.

33. For a brief introduction to this research, see Lawrence Kohlberg, "The Child as Moral Philosopher," *Psychology Today,* Vol. 2, No. 4, September 1968, pp. 25-30.

34. See Frederiksen and Brackett, op. cit.

35. Numerous cases have been reported in newspapers and at abortion conferences. One case was dramatized in *Look Magazine,* February 9, 1971. In this article, the troubled responses of nurses are also reported. At least two, perhaps more, aborted fetuses have been saved and subsequently adopted.

36. Communicated to me by reliable sources working in New York hospitals where this occurs.

37. The Johns Hopkins case has been put on a film, "Who Should Survive?" sponsored by the Joseph P. Kennedy, Jr. Foundation.

38. Encroachments on women's freedom occur also under permissive abortion policies. See the essays in this volume by Jill Knight, M. P., p. 215, and Audra Stevens, p. 267. Note also the pressures from those who favor abortions for defective fetuses to make abortion compulsory. "Should not the abortion of a seriously defective fetus be obligatory?" writes Bentley Glass in "Heredity and Ethical Problems," *Perspectives in Biology and Medicine,* Winter 1972.

39. Unpublished essay by Steven Tipton.

40. See, for example, Davis, op. cit.

41. R. Freedman, P. K. Whelpton, and A. A. Campbell, *Family Planning, Sterility, and Population Growth* (New York: McGraw-Hill Book Co., Inc., 1959).

■9■

IS ABORTION THE BEST
WE HAVE TO OFFER?
A Challenge to the
Aborting Society

Thomas W. Hilgers, M.D., Marjory Mecklenburg, B.S.,
Gayle Riordan, R.N.

Why does a "civilized" society become so threatened by its own offspring that it seeks the violence of human abortion to relieve its anxiety? Why do innocent children become such a threat that parents are moved to destroy them? Why does a society which attempts to promote peace and justice continue to advocate the mass slaughter of unborn children? These questions are not easy for anyone to answer. And yet, that alone does not detract from the reality of their implication: the reality of a society which is rapidly engulfing itself in fear—a fear which could eventually mean its dissolution.

This fear, deeply rooted and multicentric in origin, is aiming the fullness of its grip toward our women and children. It is amply manifest, day in and day out, by the members of today's so-termed "affluent society" in their unwillingness to give of themselves to others. For some strange reason (one which is shortchanging more and more people as time passes), we have become, in a very striking way, a society in which one's own personal self takes total precedence over the selves of others. We have reached a state of self-orientation while ignoring—and sometimes eliminating—the other.

As in the case of any new mode of behavior, rationalizations are being devised for our actions. Like the Negro slavery of the nine-teenth century and the Black discrimination of the twentieth, we are collectively crying "unwanted!"—and again, it finds its base in the "less than human" penultimate rationale.

Must we not accuse ourselves of actively fostering a new preju-dice; one involving a future generation, with its focus on the children of the present generation? Isn't this new prejudice quite as deep in its roots as those of the past and potentially just as destructive? We now callously, and often flippantly, refer to our offspring as "unwanted"; almost as if we never really thought about what it means to *be unwanted* nor paused long enough to recognize *who is doing the unwanting!* Isn't there a strong parallel between the unquestioningly accepted notion of "every pregnancy a planned pregnancy" and the degree to which "unwantedness" has spread in the last decade? Cer-tainly, it is now easy to accept automatically any unplanned preg-nancy as an unwanted child. This, to the ultimate abuse of the child—abortion.

Perhaps we must again perceive the creeping nature of bias and the role it has played in this latest development, the "unwanted prejudice." Doesn't this euphemistic categorization of a newly created "unwanted class" of human beings really represent a subtle shift in our national and individual discriminations? In a time when so much progress has been made in re-establishing the rights of the minority— rights which have always been theirs, but through subtle persuasion (and sometimes not so subtle) were denied them—we have, for the lack of a prejudicial target, refocused our discrimination toward the child, his mother and his family. We are literally abandoning women and children, as we abandoned the Indians, the Blacks and others, in the past.

When Garrett Hardin, Professor of Biology at the University of California, Santa Barbara, and one of the leading proponents of abortion, declares, in an article entitled "We Need Abortion for the Children's Sake," that to rid society of "unwanted" children "we must more and more emphasize the *non-right*" (emphasis his) "of the individual woman to continue a pregnancy in utter disregard of the interests of the significant persons in her life" (her husband, parents or friends?), and that, to achieve this, "we might emphasize the social sin of a girl's becoming pregnant without considering the interests of everyone else concerned,"[1] isn't he really advocating the abandon-ment of women? And when Keith B. Russell, M.D., past president of the American College of Obstetrics and Gynecology and also a leading pro-abortionist, refers to pregnancy as a "complication" of "sexuality,"[2] isn't he really abandoning both the women and the children? These kinds of statements, publicly made and widely distributed (cf. *The Death Peddlers:War on the Unborn*, St. John's University Press, 1971), can only add fuel to this new tragedy. To the careful observer, these prejudice-provoking statements are a reflection of the deeply entrenched puritanism which is inherent in the plastic attitude of the pro-abortionists.

The faithless abandonment of women and children, which is so overtly promoted in today's society, is rapidly becoming a part of "Americana." People unthinkingly promote and advocate it as much as they were all for Mom and apple pie in times past. Even the women themselves have undertaken this battle for abandonment, and all under the guise of "liberation"! What will eventually come from this growing irresponsibility is the awareness that it only expands and deepens the abortion of peoples. What gradually begins with the violent abortion of the unborn child, before long becomes de facto "social abortion." Women who seek abortion of their "unwanted child" find themselves "socially aborted" themselves, long before they seek the medical abortionist. They are aborted, rejected and unwanted by those close to them—their husbands, parents and friends. (The unwanted grandchild syndrome is already well known.) By the time these same women reach the abortionist (who at least identifies himself) they are already isolated and afraid; they feel literally trapped.

And this is not all. The woman involved begins to reject and destroy herself—"self-abortion." Instead of accepting herself and the responsibility she has for her helpless child, she turns away from the reality of life and the expectation that she, too, can play a role in the ultimate direction in which she moves. She fails to recognize that she is at least partially independent of her circumstances and begins to close herself off from the constructive solutions to her dilemma and the opportunity for human dignity. A woman must value herself before she can value her child, and society must value women before they can value their unborn children.

The medical-technical abortion is one problem in the abortion controversy, the problem of absolute destruction of new life; but the rejection of a woman by those close to her ("social abortion") and the refusal of a woman to enter into her life situation ("self-abortion") are ever-expanding, new problems which compose the eventual substance of societal break. "Social abortion" represents a not so subtle prelude to the "unwanted child" prejudice, while the woman's "self-abortion" represents her own unique decision to destroy.

How do we abolish the aborting society—one which turns its back on those who need assistance and incites people to turn their backs on themselves and their own lives? Certainly, *the hearts of men must change!* Man must open himself up to those around him—the people of his everyday existence. He must also open himself up from within. He must not be afraid to help, to be helped, or to help himself. Indeed, he must once again be reawakened to that joy which is inherent in giving. A certain lack of joy is substantive to the whole abortion problem, and a reawakening to this joy is essential if we are to ever again open ourselves to new life.

In order to begin our own participation in this change of heart, we must begin by recognizing that we are all, in one way or another, part of the aborting society (how many people have you rejected or been destructive to today?). Not until we as individuals begin to recognize our own participation in the aborting society—that we, everyday, close ourselves off from people around us and from ourselves; that we are, indeed, part of the problem—will we ever be able to become part of the solution. Our recognition of our participation in the aborting society must be on a deeply personal level; so personal, that it compels major attitudinal changes in our own self-extension.

Certainly, our society cannot accept the "unwanted prejudice," nor can it justly allow the mass slaughter of the unborn. What we can, and must, do is change our hearts, open our hands, extend our help and begin to deeply care. This is really the basis of an active love—an involvement in life, its beauties and its difficulties. This *is the very best* we have to offer the woman pregnant and distressed. And this is the only thing that will abolish the aborting society.

Both those who favor and oppose abortion can agree that a woman with a problem pregnancy needs help. The suggestions which follow represent new ideas and an extension of the old. The list is limited only by imagination and creativity and is admittedly a mere beginning. Its presentation serves primarily as a *call to action*.

COUNSELING

It goes without saying that medical, legal, psychiatric and spiritual counseling should be *immediately available* to any woman and her family who find a particular pregnancy distressful. And yet, the medical, legal and religious professions have been grossly negligent in providing this kind of care. Obstetricians, in general, have left unrecognized their awesome potential to guide women and their families toward proper care during the prenatal visit. The non-medical difficulties which may confront a woman in pregnancy should be of as much concern to the physician as the medical complications which may be encountered. For here, the physician, while not trained to deal directly with many of these problems himself, can refer the person involved to those who can be of help.

Counselors who work with pregnant women will relieve some of their own anxiety if they keep several facts in mind. First of all, it is not uncommon for women who can become good mothers to react to their pregnancy with resentment, frustration and depression—only to express strong, genuine, positive feelings of acceptance as the pregnancy advances and fetal movements are detected.[3] Secondly, most women who are refused abortion will be glad that they carried the pregnancy to term.[4] Finally, it has been shown that by the support given pregnant women throughout their pregnancy, the pressures to abort can be remarkable reduced, and in fact the pregnancy that is carried to term may be a positive factor in the mother's return to normalcy.[5]

1. A number of emergency crisis counseling services have sprung up all across the United States and Canada in the last couple of years. These services are now immediately available in most cities. There are now 175 such crisis centers in the United States and Canada and the list is rapidly expanding. With names like BIRTHRIGHT, LIFELINE, HEARTBEAT and CHOOSE LIFE, these organizations have helped thousands of girls in the last few years (see Appendix II for a complete listing of pregnancy crisis centers). These facilities are service-oriented and offer a compassionate "listener" who projects the warmth of human understanding to meet the individual's need as long as that need exists. They make available various professional services (medical, psychiatric, financial, legal, social and spiritual) to which the individual with a specific problem can be referred.

It should be emphasized that these services are *available now*. One does not have to wait for needed social reform to obtain the kind of personalized care that these services offer.

2. It is becoming apparent that increased professional care must be delivered to the woman pregnant and distressed. The professions must begin seriously to consider and act upon the formation of

multidisciplinary *birth centers* which would bring together professions from many areas to work primarily with these difficulties. This would be, in essence, the concept of "intensive care," which is not new to the medical profession. The emphasis here, however, is on *care;* for, if these centers are not motivated by a sense of dedication, then they will provide only the sterile and static service which is at present available.

3. Very few cities have established liaison between the police departments and mental health facilities of that city. Victims of rape and incest are, therefore, not provided with the immediate and long-term care which they require. This should be made available, for certainly the majority of rape victims, while they don't become pregnant, will need some degree of help to allow them adequate adjustment.

4. Genetic counseling has become available, in narrow application, to those in need; but it demands further implementation. The genetics counselor elicits and analyzes all relevant genetical data and informs prospective parents concerning the probability of an abnormal child being born from the union of their biological backgrounds. It is within the counselor's province to advise avoidance of parenthood, but not his function to authorize or forbid the procurement of abortion.[6] The question of abortion because of the probable genetic risk should never arise. The matter should have been thrashed out before the pregnancy occurred—perhaps even before the marriage. If at that stage the genetic risks are unacceptable to the prospective parents, suitable advice about contraception and child-adoption should be given.

THE UNWED MOTHER

Approximately seventy-five percent of all of the abortions performed in the United States are performed on unwed mothers.[7] This statistic indicates the largest area where direct involvement is needed. Unfortunately, this recent trend toward medically aborting the unwed mother is proving only to undo all that has been so constructively accomplished in the area of help for these women. It is here that "social abortion" is rapidly taking over; where care is being replaced by rejection.

The pregnant unwed girl is at a crisis point in her life. We in society can help her survive this experience and regain self-esteem or we can reject both her and her baby, to the aggravation of existing problems. We have a unique opportunity to rescue the girl at this point by showing her that we value her and have confidence in her. We can provide her with services which will help her be successful and well-adjusted whether she keeps her baby or not. We can intervene in young people's lives to make crisis an experience for growth. Healthy, well-adjusted mothers and their babies are an asset to society, and it is worth considerable time, effort and money to give them the assistance they deserve.

Any approach to the unwed mother must be aimed at eliminating the social stigma normally attached to unwed motherhood. It should be noted that this can be accomplished while at the same time promoting responsible interpersonal relationships between man and woman. Acceptance and help for people with problems need not in any way condone or foster the behavior which led them to have their problem. In fact, the more aware people become of the struggle and hardship it means to be unmarried and pregnant or to be an unmarried parent raising a child alone, the less likely will people be to put themselves into that position.

1. Many school administrators refuse to allow a pregnant schoolgirl to remain in school. This denies reality and at the same time rejects the girl and her problems. School boards, superintendents and principals must be alerted to the importance of continuing her education.

Whenever possible, an opportunity should be available for the girl to choose homebound education, to remain in the regular school curriculum with special class needs met within the school, or to attend a special school with others in the same situation. The basic emphasis should be to ensure that pregnant schoolgirls can remain in the school system and that they are encouraged to keep up with their studies.

2. Both federal and individual state legislation must be enacted providing that pregnancy cannot constitute grounds for denial of education. The more we can normalize the life of the unwed mother, the better expectation we can have for adjustment.

3. Special living arrangements need to be available for some unwed mothers. Group homes for the unwed mother who cannot for some reason return to her own family, or who has multiple problems solvable within a group-living environment, must be provided.

4. Work-wage homes, where unwed mothers can receive guidance and care in a private home while contributing to and receiving from that family unit, should be encouraged. Screening of these homes so that the girl is not exploited and has a clear understanding of her own responsibilities is desirable.

5. The development of day-care centers would help the young unmarried mother finish her education or become self-supporting. However, these care centers must be more than just custodials for children. If the mother is required to spend some time at the center and become involved in the program, then she, too, while caring for the children, can learn more about parental skills. The centers could be combined with the school program so that the girls could assume as much responsibility for the child as possible, learn child-care skills and finish their education concurrently. Other students could also learn child development and care through inclusion of such a nursery.

6. Insurance companies issuing hospitalization coverage must be legislatively regulated in provisions concerning maternity benefits. Time lapse of pregnancy after marriage or marital status should no longer provide a basis for denial of payment. Many insurance programs do deny payment for these reasons. This should be corrected.

7. A continuing program of publicly funded research, inquiring into the needs of unmarried mothers, fathers and their children, would vastly benefit future projections of help for these people.

8. The unwed father and his unique dilemma has all too frequently been ignored by society. He, too, requires our attention and care in helping work out his feelings and responsibilities. This is an area which needs much more study; for, to date, the unwed father has been thought of as practically nonexistent.

9. Premarital counseling is necessary for the young unwed mother and father who plan to marry in the future (whether before or after the child's birth). This facility could not fail to strengthen the potential new family unit and in turn strengthen society.

10. In some states, the word *illegitimate* appears on the birth certificates of children born out of wedlock. This, in essence, implies that, by state proclamation, the child is for some reason inferior. Such provision in our state law must be erased.

THE UNWANTED CHILD

To speak of unwanted children is, in reality, somewhat of a myth, for certainly the number of couples who apply for adoption each year in the United States far outweighs the number of children actually available. In fact, for Caucasian babies there are ten applicants for every available child.[8] This overabundance of prospective parents is so clear that six states on the East Coast have closed their adoption intake, and throughout the country the waiting period is getting very long; in many states it is now reaching the 3-5 year period.[9] This baby shortage is leading many would-be parents to turn to independent, or "gray market" adoptions arranged quickly by private lawyers at high fees.[10]

Those children who are unwanted by their natural parents are not unwanted by potential adoptive parents. The adoption of these children, rather than their abortion, will never become a reality, however, as long as the prevalent attitude is one where it is considered worse to give up a child who is living than to destroy the living child. Perhaps nowhere in this abortion debate is the abandonment of children seen so vividly.

There are, of course, some difficulties with adoption. The single most gnawing dilemma is the placement of minority race children and children with various physical and mental handicaps. But even here, there is at present a surplus of families available for Indian children of any age and for the Black child under two years of age.[11] Furthermore, through the help of the Adoption Resource Exchange of North America and their publication "Children's Home Finder," parents who specifically request handicapped children are listed. When these children become available, they are placed with the listed families who want them. At present, there is a surplus of families available for handicapped children, and perhaps with greater public knowledge of this service, no handicapped child will be left unadoptable.[12]

The adoptive psychology, perhaps one of the most significant contributors to a strong national concept of family life, can be promoted even further, if only we as a nation assume the attitude that *no child is unwanted*. Some states have written legislation to help financially those parents who wish to adopt handicapped children. Still other states have allowed adoption expenses to be tax-deductible. Truly, these steps, along with many others yet untried, can move our nation closer to abolishment of that aborting society.

Reappraisal of the Physically and Mentally Handicapped

Retardation is *not* the cause of unhappiness in its victims. With acceptance in the family and the community, retarded children happily attend school, join activities appropriate to their level of functioning and interest, receive vocational training and become contributing members of society. Eighty-five percent can be completely independent and another eleven percent semi-independent.[13]

1. In 1961, the President's Panel on Mental Retardation was appointed, consisting of a widely representative group of experts in the field who were given the mandate to prepare a national program to combat mental retardation. Emphasis was placed upon the complex and social nature of this question. They wrote:

Clearly, ... the evidence of mental retardation is heavily correlated with a lack of maternal and perinatal health care, which in turn is closely associated with the unfavorable socio-economic status of families or whole neighborhoods or groups in the population. ... Whether the causes of retardation in a specific individual may turn out to be bio-medical or environmental in character, there is highly suggestive evidence that the root causes of a great part of the problem of mental retardation are to be found in bad social and economic conditions as they affect individuals and families, and that correction of these fundamental conditions is necessary to prevent mental retardation successfully on a truly significant scale.[14]

The President's Panel concluded that, "Like other citizens, the mentally retarded must be assumed to have full human and legal rights and privileges. The mere fact of retardation should never be considered in and of itself sufficient to remove their rights."[15]

2. Eunice Kennedy Shriver proposed in 1968 that we consider the possibility of *birth insurance* to protect families from the financial burden which comes with the addition of a mentally or physically handicapped child.[16] This insurance could be provided through private insurance companies, a government agency or a combination of the two. If this plan were instituted, every family would have the means to see to it that their baby had the proper care and attention. The other children in the family would not then be deprived of educational or other advantages because of their handicapped brother or sister. Such a program should be granted careful consideration.

3. Working with the mentally and physically handicapped child

could become a very valuable area of endeavor and reward in the life of the senior citizen. By means of such involvement, those who are growing old and often lonely, could, with their extra time, grasp again at the love of life, and, at the same time, vitally participate in a changing society.

EDUCATION

To better understand the whole abortion controversy, people must become educated as to all of its dimensions. This educational effort must be carried out with everyone from the man-in-the-street to the most powerful of intellectuals. As to those who feel that the controversy will be settled once and for all in the ivory towers of state capitals or in the Halls of Justice, they are mistaken. The educational effort is just beginning, and for the truth to be seen by all, much more must be done.

1. Somebody once said that "hell hath no fury like a pregnant woman scorned." Unfortunately, this scorn is all too often seen reflected in the physician when he is confronted by a woman who is pregnant and distressed. An excellent example of this is related by Louise Summerhill from her BIRTHRIGHT experience:

A young girl of twenty who had an abortion talked to me on the phone. She sobbed quietly as she talked, "I gave up. I went to the doctor, not because I wanted to be told I was pregnant, I already knew this. I went because I just wanted to talk to someone about it and to find out if I could receive some help somewhere. When he told me I was pregnant, I started to cry and he seemed uncomfortable. I got the idea he was busy. I wanted to tell him that I'd like to have my baby if only I knew where to go, what to do. Instead, I left. I felt so alone and discouraged and deserted that I went out and had an abortion. What else could I do?"[17]

The abandonment of women, so typified by this story, is more prevalent than we wish to admit. But through it, it becomes increasingly more apparent that medical education has been placing an overwhelming emphasis upon the scientific and technological aspects of medicine to the neglect of the communicative and personal approaches necessary to the practice of good medicine. As the young medical student ages, he realizes that his medical education has not prepared him to cope with the human condition. The subsequently ill-equipped doctor frequently feels powerless and threatened; unable to meet his patient's needs.

We should *demand* that our medical schools (most of which are run by state and federal monies) begin to take another look at the art of medicine (i.e., the treatment of the patient as a whole person), so that that aspect of medicine can again be incorporated into the patient-doctor relationship.

2. It is becoming alarmingly clear that our medical institutions are, for the most part, beehives of anti-life activity (this trend, incidentally, is very reminiscent of the direction the German medical profession adopted in the 1930's). The number of doctors who are pro-abortion, pro-euthanasia, pro-forced-sterilization and pro-infanticide is staggering. This is at least a direct result of medical education's less-than-token participation in any open discussion of medical ethics. It is important to realize that medical ethics are for the protection of the patient and not the physician. Likewise, a lack of medical ethics (discussion of which is totally absent in the overwhelming majority of American medical institutions) will only result in increased disservice to the patient—not the physician.

3. Education regarding the use of acceptable family-planning techniques should be made available to those who voluntarily request them. It should be noted that abortion and contraception are not the same thing. Contraception prevents the beginning of new life and abortion kills a human life already present.

4. There are many agencies and individuals who are already involved in helping the woman and her family. These range from publicly funded welfare groups to sectarian and nonsectarian private ones. Unfortunately, the doctors, lawyers and clergy of villages and cities are all too often unaware of their existence. These professionals need to be re-educated. It is to be hoped that this kind of re-education will come from within the profession or denomination. However, if this doesn't occur, then citizens within the community will have to provide a liaison between the professions. An example of such a liaison is the Problem Pregnancy Research and Advisory Committee of Minnesota. Many social agencies that help women are represented (city welfare agencies, Lutheran Social Service, Catholic Charities, Children's Home Society, Booth Memorial Hospital, etc.), as well as professionals who work in state and city school systems with the unwed mother and medical people who specialize in counseling women. Because individual participants have varying positions on

abortion, this topic is excluded. It is their function to evaluate the programs existent in the state and educate the public, including the legislature, Board of Education, Housing Authority, etc., to what is now available and additionally needed.

FAMILY LIFE EDUCATION

We must begin to realize that family life is disintegrating in the United States. The growing divorce rate is testimony enough for this. If we understand that *the family is the basic social unit of society,* then we can begin to appreciate that the society is only as strong as the individual family. To do other than to declare the disintegrating family a crisis of gigantic proportions would be to ill-serve the societal complex. Only when we face this can we begin to act in a crisis-like way to re-establish the basic values and principles of family life.

1. Marriage and parenthood classes—infinitely more discussive and in-depth than fringe sex education—should be offered in our schools. They should take into account that many children do not have an adequate model in their parents' relationship or in their own home life upon which to build a successful marriage or become adequate parents. These classes must place emphasis not only on the joys of marriage and parenthood but also upon those difficulties, and their likely solutions, which will be encountered in a relationship so intimate and profound. When this subject matter is presented as a total experience, rather than a fragmentalized educational requirement, awareness of the immense possibilities for individual growth and commitment will be unavoidable.

When, in Keokuk, Iowa, a family-life education program of the dimension proposed above was put into effect in 1947, it had a profound impact. The course, programmed for a public high school, approached the subject with a firm grounding in the moral code. Twenty years later, when its effects were partially analyzed, the following was noted: 60% of the girls who took the class had produced 8.4% of the children born out of wedlock for the whole community; while the 40% not taking the course had produced 91.6% of the children born out of wedlock.[18] This experience shows what can be done through education alone and the importance of it in the school curriculum.

2. The young adults in our schools should be given the opportunity

to work with preschool children—perhaps as part of their marriage and parenthood class—so that they can learn correct child care.

3. The value of family-life education for *adults* should be more seriously considered, so that the already married may grow in their mutual commitment.

4. Those couples who are at present involved in a stable family relationship and who have some perception of what they are experiencing should see their responsibility to share this with others; especially the young. This can be done in small group discussions, as part of the school curriculum, in connection with the church or civic organizations.

PUBLIC HEALTH MEASURES

Many of the current problems which lead women to seek abortion could be solved if large-scale public health programs could be instituted along certain lines. We have seen the elimination of many diseases as the result of these kinds of programs in the past; therefore, there is good reason to expect that these same kinds of programs could eliminate certain other of the medical and social diseases.

1. The problem of criminal abortion has been a long-standing one, while the legalization of abortion-on-demand has never been shown to eliminate it. This is an area where we can positively reject a program which has been known to fail in the past and embark in a new, more constructive direction. It would seem that public health education programs aimed at informing the public of the dangers of criminal abortion, combined with an educational program designed to bring the solutions to problem pregnancies closer to the woman in need, might make inroads into this problem.

2. There should be increased attempts made to provide health manpower. The foundation of new medical schools in order to provide more doctors to meet the current shortage is a serious need and of national importance. Further, the widespread use of nurse-midwives, pediatric nurse assistants and physicians' assistants should be thoroughly explored, so that ample personnel are trained in the health sciences.

3. Vaccination programs for rubella (German measles) should be

implemented in order to prevent infection of the unborn and in this way eliminate, once and for all, rubella as a cause of birth defects.

4. With the advent of the anti-Rh-negative immunoglobulin (Rhogam), mothers who are Rh negative can be immunized against the possibility of having future children damaged by Rh disease. This immunization should be made available to everyone. Interestingly enough, those women who are being so generously "helped" by the abortionists are, in fact, not being given this treatment (see above, chapter 4, pp. 57-85, section on complications—transplacental hemorrhage, p. 74). This subtle irresponsibility should be immediately corrected before many babies are hurt for life.

The Need for a Strong Anti-Poverty Program

When one carefully examines the poverty-stricken mother-to-be, one can't help but see the connection between poverty and the abortion problem. The connection is more than just economic, it is multifactoral. Women in the ghetto generally lack proper nutrition, not because they have too little food to eat, but because they eat too much of the wrong kinds of foods. Their diets are deficient in calcium, protein, riboflavin and Vitamin C. This leads to generally lower blood levels as the rule rather than the exception. In combination, all of this allows for increased difficulties with infection, toxemia of pregnancy and hemorrhage.[19]

The prematurity rate in poverty-stricken areas runs about twice what it is in non-poverty areas.[20] This, too, reflects the poor care they are given. Dr. Augusta Webster, Chief of Obstetrics at Cook County Hospital (a Chicago hospital located in one of the largest urban ghettos in the United States)—and a woman with a wealth of experience in treating the medically indigent—has stated: "It has long been my observation that race is not the pertinent factor in either infant or maternal mortality or morbidity. Poverty, however, with all its attendant evils, is the basis of deaths of both mothers and babies."[21]

These factors, which the poverty-stricken family must face, along with obvious economic difficulties, put tremendous pressures on them to abort their unborn children. It seems somewhat of a paradox that in the richest nation in the world the best solution we have been able to offer so far to poverty has been the introduction of abortion. Is it too much to ask for people to see through this less-than-symptomatic relief? The time has come for the war on poverty to become a national commitment, similar to our man-on-the-moon commitment, so that the war on poverty can become more than just a backyard skirmish and a war on the unborn.

1. A revision in our governmental welfare program is desperately needed. Any such revision would best serve the individual and the community if it were directed toward the family unit.

2. Exploring a family income maintenance program with built-in incentives would be a start at reforming the failing welfare system.

3. Continuing efforts at providing adequate job training and retraining programs should be widely encouraged.

4. President Johnson in his 1967 State of the Union message encouraged action in both the areas of crime in the streets and maternity care.[22] It may be that many of our problems, whether crime in the streets or the troubles which are engulfing our big cities, will find their ultimate solution in a national effort to promote and stabilize family life.

5. The Volunteers in Service to America (VISTA) program, or some similar involvement program, should be considerably expanded, so that more people can become engaged in helping the poor on a deeper personal level.

6. Obvious difficulties must be removed in order that the poor can seek and obtain proper care. These include:

Transportation to and from clinics and hospitals;

Baby-sitting services as an active part of the out-patient clinic, relieving the mother of the need to find someone to care for her children while she seeks professional help;

Social services, readily available to deal with financial and social problems;

Nutritional services to meet the dietary educational requirements of the community;

Neighborhood clinics to insure the availability of adequate care;

Area drug abuse centers and alcoholic treatment centers to provide the purposeful handling of these problems which are so prevalent in the poverty-stricken areas.

Above all else, there must be developed within the institutions which deal with the poor a climate of human dignity, with emphasis placed upon the inherent right to respect of each person as a human being. It would be appalling to many to witness the subhuman treatment often accorded these people.

Lest anyone feel that the poor already receive care equal to that of the middle class, let us take a careful look at what is happening today in Cook County Hospital, Chicago.

1. While pregnant women are receiving more and more prenatal care (mostly from the Chicago Board of Health), the extent of it usually amounts to little more than a urinalysis and blood pressure check at each visit. There is little attempt being made at an ongoing educational effort to teach the young mother and her husband the essentials of pregnancy, labor and delivery, nutrition and/or child care.

2. The "labor ward" at Cook County is made up of several large rooms holding between three and fifteen beds. It is here that the woman in labor stays prior to delivery of her baby. While in labor, she is not allowed (except in unusual circumstances) any visitors whatsoever. This includes husband, relatives and friends. Cook County Hospital does not even have a fathers' waiting room. Finally, there is no provision for the husband and new father to visit either the new mother or the newly born during their three-to-four-day stay in the hospital. In the case of operative deliveries (like caesarean section) this may extend to longer than one week. This experience for those involved is truly a several days' journey of loneliness and fear. At a time when the new mother needs care and support and someone to share the ecstasy of the arrival of the new child, she has no one.

3. Finally, Cook County Hospital has no facilities for the treatment of either drug addiction or alcoholism.

If any real progress is to be made in the poverty battle, there must be a recognized program for the cultivation of leadership from the people who live within the poverty-stricken area with emphasis on their active participation in any effort to promote community growth. If leadership can be encouraged to initiate from within the poverty-stricken community rather than impose upon it from the outside, then the people of that community can be expected to respond to the authority of that leadership.

PLAN OF ACTION

If any of the above outlined programs and others like them, but yet unexplored, are ever to become a reality, then the immediate and primary need is obvious: the interested and loving dedication of people who are willing to become involved. This involvement requires imagination, foresight and initiative. For those possessed of such desire, the following is offered to complete this call to action:

1. A committee composed of lay and professional people concerned about problem pregnancies should be formed in each state. They should begin by surveying existing help available to pregnant women and then decisions should be reached on ways to improve that help (see Minnesota Problem Pregnancy Research and Advisory Committee).

In addition to providing leadership for new services and educating the public about existing programs, the committee could give professionals from different fields concerned with the same group of people a unique opportunity to interact and enter into dialogue. Through this, a greater degree of cooperation can be achieved between individuals, agencies and institutions as they begin to work together to solve problems.

2. Proposals should be introduced into state legislatures to provide for interim legislative hearings on the solutions to problem pregnancies. This interim process can serve to educate and sensitize the legislator as to the need for action. If the legislature is in continuous session, perhaps a special commission or committee could be set up to hear testimony. After these hearings, specific legislation can then be written and introduced.

3. State and national medical societies should form committees to study solutions to problem pregnancies in greater depth and then set out positively to enact them.

4. Individuals can offer resolutions at various political and civic group meetings calling for supportive services for pregnant women. Letters-to-the-editor of local newspapers and letters to representatives on a local, state and national level should also be written in support of such services. All this not only serves to educate the public and your representative, it also provides an impetus for action.

5. The emergency pregnancy counseling service in your city can always use help. If there is no such service present, then one can be started. A complete listing of these centers is given in Appendix II.

These facilities offer immediate service to anyone in distress, and if a girl has a problem, they can be contacted.

6. There are a number of organizations around the country who have been actively involved on a state and national level to promote solutions to problem pregnancies. All of these organizations need your support. For further information call or write:

ALTERNATIVES TO ABORTION, INC.*
Hillcrest 827
Madison and 16th Streets
Toledo, Ohio 43624
419-248-4471

NATIONAL RIGHT TO LIFE COMMITTEE
P.O. Box 9365
Washington, D.C. 20005

AMERICANS UNITED FOR LIFE
422 Washington Bldg.
Washington, D.C. 20005
202-737-7668

CLERGY CONCERNED FOR LIFE, INC.
1414 N. Dearborn Parkway
Chicago, Illinois 60610

EPISCOPALIANS CONCERNED ABOUT ABORTION
1919 East Fifth Street
Tucson, Arizona 85719

MINNESOTA PROBLEM PREGNANCY RESEARCH
AND ADVISORY COMMITTEE
1219 W. 51st Street
Minneapolis, Minnesota 55419
612-827-4973

* This organization provides the following services:
1. A monthly bulletin "AAI-Heartbeat."
2. A quarterly directory of emergency pregnancy services with an international supplement.
3. An "open-ended" manual to provide practical help in the establishment, operation and expansion of all such services.
4. Promotion of local, regional and national meetings to provide for an enhancement of services.

NATIONAL YOUTH PRO-LIFE COALITION
20 Adeline Rd.
Cleveland, Ohio 44111
216-251-1391

SOUL (SAVE OUR UNWANTED LIFE)
Box 14185
Minneapolis, Minnesota 55414

MINNESOTA CITIZENS CONCERNED FOR LIFE, INC.
4803 Nicollet Avenue
Minneapolis, Minnesota 55409
612-825-3611

CONCLUSION

It has been said that if one is honestly in opposition to abortion, he then must be willing to extend his hand to those who need his help. If this is true, and we think that it is, then the extension of this statement is even more true; it is even more meaningful. If you allow yourself to become sensitized to the most diminutive of human beings, the unborn child, then you must also allow that sensitization to work deeply within you. You must allow it to sensitize you *to all of human life:* the old and the senile, the mentally retarded and the physically unrehabilitatable, the wanted and the unwanted, the white, black, yellow and red, the theist and the atheist, and the woman and her family who find a particular pregnancy distressful.

The paradox of modern man is his assumption that he can turn on and turn off, seemingly at will, the respect for human life. He assumes that he can offer a woman the very best while denying her child the very least. These assumptions are invalid because they are inconsistent. Human life is a continuum; and to be consistent in its respect, we must value the whole of this continuum. We cannot promote the quality of life while arbitrarily denying any aspect of our common humanity. We cannot kill a child and then say that this is the best we have to offer the mother.

The time has come for some real self-examination of ourselves as a people. We have been endowed with tremendous gifts and we possess enormous power; whether we use these gifts for good or for evil now depends on us. Will we passively submit to man's inhumanity to man, or will we silence the abortion cry with love and concern for our suffering neighbor?

REFERENCES

1. In *Abortion and the Unwanted Child,* ed. C. Reitermann (New York: Springer Pub. Co., 1971), p. 4.
2. Editorial introduction to "Abortion: A Legal Fact," *Audio-Digest Obstet. Gynec.,* Vol. 18, No. 15, August 3, 1971.
3. S. H. Gardiner, "Psychosomatic Aspects of Obstetrics," in *Williams Obstetrics,* 13th ed. (New York: Appleton-Century-Crofts, 1966), p. 335.
4. P. Kolstad, "Therapeutic Abortion: A Clinical Study Based Upon 968 Cases From a Norwegian Hospital, 1940-1953," *Acta. Obstet. Gynec. Scand.,* 36: Suppl. 6, 1957.
5. K. M. Murdock, "Experiences in a Psychiatric Hospital," in *Abortion in America,* ed. H. Rosen (Boston: Beacon Press, 1967).
6. H. Gordon, "Genetical, Social, and Medical Aspects of Abortion," *S. A. Med. J.,* July 20, 1968, pp. 721-730.
7. *Abortion Surveillance Report—Hospital Abortions, Jan.-June, 1970* (distributed by the U. S. Dept. of H. E. W., Center for Disease Control, Atlanta, Georgia 30333).
8. "Adoption Re-Examined," *Hospital Administration Currents* (Ross Laboratories, Columbus, Ohio), Nov.-Dec. 1969.
9. R. Toogood, ACSW (Executive Director, Children's Home Society of Minnesota, 2230 Como Avenue, St. Paul, Minnesota 55108): Personal communication.
10. W. King, "Adoption Agencies Report Shortage of White Infants," p. 1; *The New York Times,* December 7, 1970.
11. Toogood, op. cit.
12. Ibid.
13. Sr. Mary Patricia, "A Mental Retardation Expert Views Abortion," *Child and Family* (Reprint Booklet Series; The Case Against Abortion), p. 18.
14. President's Panel on Mental Retardation, "National Action to Combat Mental Retardation," Washington, D.C., October 1962.
15. Ibid.
16. E. K. Shriver, "When Pregnancy Means Heartbreak . . . Is Abortion the Answer?" *McCall's,* April 1968.
17. L. Summerhill, *The Story of Birthright,* 1968 (obtainable from Birthright, Inc., Toronto, Canada).
18. J. O. Lockett, "Sex Education Pays Off in Keokuk Senior High School." Mr. Lockett is instructor in Marriage and Family Living in Keokuk Senior High School, Keokuk, Iowa.
19. A. Webster, "Some Comments about Maternal and Child Welfare at Cook County Hospital," *Chicago Medicine,* 7:485-488, June 8, 1968.
20. Ibid.
21. Ibid.
22. *Briefs,* the official publication of the Maternity Center Association; *Social Pathology and Maternity Care,* 33:19-23, Feb. 1969.

▪ 10 ▪

STALEMATE OF RHETORIC
AND PHILOSOPHY

David Mall

Within the context of fundamental social change, the question what is man has been asked and answered many times in human history. Slavery and prohibition are but two outstanding examples within the American experience.

Today, the question of man's nature is being asked again in the drive to modify existing abortion laws. How this question is being answered is a matter of substantial public concern and, it would appear, a fit subject of inquiry.

What follows is an attempt to analyze the ideological matrix of abortion as it relates to rhetoric and philosophy. Without intending an awkward dichotomy, the rhetorical component will be viewed largely through the parameter of semantics, and the philosophical component largely through analogue.

IDEOLOGY

To understand any social movement one must first take note of the basic ideological conflict. Toch maintains that "the most important appeals of a social movement are contained in its *ideology*" (author's italics) which he describes as follows:

The term "ideology" denotes a set of related beliefs held by a group of persons. The ideology of a social movement is a statement of what the members of the movement are trying to achieve together, and what they wish to affirm jointly. Such a statement points down the road along which the

199

social movement is moving, and specifies the principles and objectives that guide its journey.

He then considers how ideology is manifested. It may be formalized in an official platform, scattered in written and oral messages, or simply inferred. "However recorded," he concludes, "the ideology of a social movement *defines* [author's italics] the movement. . ."[1]

Of the many possible sources for an ideological analysis of abortion, the most carefully thought out are probably contained in a number of legal briefs.[2] These documents must stand the test of time and close scrutiny and so are prepared with utmost diligence. The investigator could read them with profit along with any legislative debates.[3] Another extremely important source would be the statements of the chief movement ideologues. Regarding abortion, the investigator would gain substantial insight by inspecting the written and oral prouncements of Fletcher and Hardin. These men, without intending to omit others who are as outspoken, have probably attained the most prominent and/or persistent recognition as theoreticians within the abortion movement. A representative sample of the former's thinking follows.[4]

Joseph Fletcher, the situation ethicist, in a paper presented at a symposium banquet early in 1971, laid out the basic ideological position of the abortion movement. Addressing himself mainly to the question of ethics, Is abortion intrinsically wrong? he prefaced his theme by considering briefly four other problems constituting in his judgment "a complete and logical package." They were: Should anyone be compelled against her will to bear a child? Is abortion a form of homicide? Does God have a monopoly control of life which allows no stewardship to man? and Is embryonic life human? With respect to his last question, the key issue of prenatal life, he said:

Now in terms of realistic biology, none of this is meaningful; we cannot check off some arbitrary point as the beginning of life on a conceptional or gestational continuum in a dynamic and continuous process. Life is a process and not an event. Just as one can say there is no moment of death, so one cannot say there is any one moment of life. We must apply symbolic logic at both ends of life and death.

This may be uncomfortable for those still locked in conventional wisdom. When people talk about changing their minds, they're really only rearranging their prejudices, someone once said. But biomedical scientists brought us to a point where we need not only rearrange our mental furniture but actually throw it out and put in new furniture.

This means a tremendous philosophical, theological revolution in anthropology and in theories about man and his nature; it is unfair and imperialistic to impose a model of metaphysics like the one I've been discussing negatively on those who do not happen to believe it. That's what many of our laws in the states concerning abortion do.

After stating the case for situation ethics within a medical setting and asserting that with abortion "there are no universally applicable moral principles involved," Fletcher continues:

Now when it is a question of contagious illness, we do not have full control over ourselves, because it involves others. Likewise, we may not use our bodies as living bombs. Humanistic liberty and social democracy are based on the ethics of selfhood within self-possession: We should be in control of our own bodies. So the real issue is compulsory pregnancy and not abortion.

And because we believe in personal freedom and social pluralism and democracy, we contend for repeal of abortion laws rather than reform. The concept of therapeutic abortion is archaic and unethical. Therapeutic abortion as a phrase carries the suggestion that non-therapeutic abortion is somehow immoral or wrong or unacceptable or unpreferable. But the real issue is between legal and illegal abortion, not between elective and therapeutic abortion.

A section of his conclusion is also worth quoting.

First, consistency may be the virtue of petty minds. While not radically Emersonian on that score, I was asked by a Duke professor why society condemns ending a life in the uterus but not *in terminis*. In creative and constructive medical ethics, the question is, what does it mean to be human? This question arises at both ends of the life cycle. When is the *humanum* here and when is the *humanum* gone? I suspect there is no answer. The ethics of medical initiative is at stake in both abortion and euthanasia, whether in its direct or indirect form, and the problem ethically is the same, and the two are inextricably associated.[5]

An inspection of the above passages would appear to yield a number of salient points. To begin with, Fletcher admits that the abortion controversy deals with what it is to be human. He speaks of discarding a dominant metaphysic concerning man's nature and substituting another. Presumably, the substitution is a relative valuation on human life instead of an absolute one. A theological justification for such a substitution is that selfhood should be entirely self-possessed, the woman should have complete control over her reproductive capacity. In short, the basic ideological conflict raised by Fletcher seems reducible to a single contention, the primacy of choice behavior over an alleged right-to-life.

Ideologically, the basic conflict raised in the abortion controversy represents a struggle for dominance between alternative synthesizing concepts. And since Fletcher admits that ethically abortion and euthanasia are inextricably associated, it would be helpful to consider his views on this latter subject as well. In 1960, he wrote:

The biggest obstacle to a compassionate and honest understanding of this problem is a superstitious concept of "nature" inherited from an earlier, prescientific culture. People often feel that death should be "natural"—that is, humanly uncontrolled and uncontrived. Sometimes, they say that God works through nature; therefore any "interference" with nature by controlling what happens to people in the way of illness and death interferes with God's activity. This argument has a specious aura of religious force. For example, one doctor with an eighty-three-year-old patient, paralyzed by a stroke and a half-dozen other ailments, tells the compassionate family that he will do nothing, "leave it to God." But God does not cooperate; their mother goes on gasping. Maybe the doctor needs a better and more creative theology.

For the fact is that medicine itself is an interference with nature. It freely cooperates with or counteracts and foils nature to fulfill humanly chosen ends. As Thomas Sydenham said three hundred years ago, medicine is "the support of enfeebled and the coercion of outrageous nature." Blind, brute nature imposing an agonized and prolonged death is outrageous to the limit, and to bow to it, to "leave things in God's hands," is the last word in determinism and fatalism. It is the very opposite of a morality that prizes human freedom and loving kindness.

The right of spiritual beings to use intelligent control over physical nature rather than submit beast-like to its blind workings, is the heart of many crucial questions. Birth control, artificial insemination, sterilization and abortion are all medically discovered ways of fulfilling and protecting human values and hopes in spite of nature's failures or foolishnesses. Death control, like birth control, is a matter of human dignity. Without it persons become puppets. To perceive this is to grasp the error lurking in the notion—widespread in medical circles—that life as such is the highest good. This kind of vitalism seduces its victims into being more loyal to the physical spark of mere biological life than to the personality values of self-possession and human integrity. The beauty and spiritual depths of human stature are what should be preserved and conserved in our value system, with the flesh as the means rather than the end. The vitalist fallacy is to view life at any old level as the highest good. This betrays us into keeping "vegetables" going and dragging the dying back to brute "life" just because we have the medical know-how to do it.[6]

Adding, then, to the previous summary of Fletcher's views on abortion, we have here another aspect of the basic ideological conflict, namely that nature is not good. To label nature "beast-like" is to consider nature evil.

Anticipating analysis we shall give in detail later, facsimiles of the choice behavior/nature-is-evil concepts were present in both the slavery and prohibition movements. Regarding choice behavior and slavery, the ideological conflict as clarified in the Lincoln-Douglas debates of 1858 pitted the ideal of popular sovereignty (the doctrine that each state or territory should determine within its jurisdiction what status the Negro could have) against the principle that slavery was inherently wrong. Regarding choice behavior and prohibition, the ideological conflict prior to the Volstead Act involved the attempt to strike down the principle that a person had the right to pursue what was at the time considered a common and normal form of happiness, the consumption of alcoholic beverages in moderation. As a patterned response, therefore, the abortion movement ideology amounts to the internalizing of a new social value.[7] How this goal is to be accomplished and how resisted can be approached from a number of perspectives. The following approach is limited to semantics.

SEMANTICS

Language usage in the abortion controversy represents for the critic an interesting study of how idiom advances ideology. This usage relates generally to the utopian nature of the movement and more specifically to the stasis issue, the humanity of what has been conceived. In the absence of overwhelming contrary evidence, the best assumption would seem to be that words are selected by either side with great care. There may be some truth, however, in the observation that with a certain mind-set or *weltanschauung,* language patterns itself automatically. People may use words as their presuppositions dictate. At any rate, the point to be emphasized is that the abortion controversy exhibits language that is inherently attitudinal.

A convenient frame for a semantic analysis of the abortion controversy is that offered by Weaver.[8] His description of ultimate terms seems to have a special relevance because these terms represent certain values which a society has endorsed. They are words which reflect social consensus, an almost subconscious social understanding. They enhance a course of action by making it more attractive, or conversely they weaken it by engendering rebuke. An ultimate term above all is trusted. It literally becomes a god of the national household. In fact, Weaver refers to good ultimate terms as "god terms" and their opposites as "devil terms." He underlines their danger because they validate ideas in an uncritical way.

Weaver considers the most powerful god term in use today to be "progress." So powerful has this term become that it would not be an undue exaggeration even to label it Western man's secular salvation. To the nonevaluative mind it seems almost unassailable, for in a world of rapid technological change it rests on the premise that every change so certified must therefore be an improvement. Such an appeal confirms the scholar's observation that "Dissatisfaction with the world in which we live and determination to realize one that shall be better are the prevailing characteristics of the modern spirit."[9]

Viable societies are said to be goal-oriented. These goals are usually assumed tacitly and help form national aspirations or priorities. In America the impartial observer would probably notice an earnest striving for the good life which, when translated accurately, seems to imply the hedonistic opposites of maximized pleasure and minimized pain. There is also a rich overlay of secular and religious humanism in America which generates compassion for those less fortunate. They too should share in the good life. In the realm of social concern the ultimate term of "progress" reflects an unfulfilled expectancy. It becomes an implied coordinator of effort to put a man on the moon, to build a better mousetrap, or to deal with problem pregnancies.

"Progress" and words associated with it become rhetorical trump cards in the abortion debate. Efforts are made to "reform" the abortion laws. Somehow this sector of the legal code has gotten untidy through neglect. The "modern, up-to-date" approach to the problem is a simple termination of pregnancy. Abortion laws are characterized as "archaic, outmoded, Nineteenth-Century anachronisms," which is the antonymic way of using the ultimate term. Those who favor change in the law employ a verbalized approach—avoidance psychology which maximizes the appeal.

According to Weaver the contemporary handmaid of "progress" is its methodological tool called "science." In a world that appears ever more capricious, the god term "science" represents a constancy people can trust. It gives an aura of certitude to anything it touches, including the abortion controversy. Often the word "therapeutic" is used to describe the abortion process. With this label everything seems neat and antiseptic. Science is applied through the healing art of medicine and human suffering is relieved.

Scientific terminology has a more significant role in the abortion debate, however. It assists the user in dehumanizing the object in dispute, the unborn offspring. In addition to calling abortion "a crime without a victim," life *in utero* is described as a "product of conception," an "embryo" or a "fetus." The cold, impartial language of science tends to dehumanize, and the message receiver is made to feel that the sender is being scrupulously objective.[10] After all, it is subconsciously argued, in the face of the tremendous good that science has accomplished, how can anyone resist the petition to abort? Intensifying the scientific appeal is the frequent reference to polls of doctors favoring abortion. Those who apply science to solve human health problems testify in science's behalf and the association becomes exoneration.

The procedures and implements of science, which the abortion movement emphasizes, add yet another dimension to the scientific appeal, the dimension of efficiency.[11] If there is anything that smacks of progress, it is an easier way of doing things. Not only is it the scientific way but, like the well-equipped kitchen, it is above all the American way. "Amniocentesis" becomes a dependable method for detecting fetal defects and the "vacuum aspirator" one of the more efficient methods for eliminating them. The machine thus comes to man's rescue once again. It does the job well, even in sterile conditions, and removes all guilt.

One would have to agree with Weaver's analysis in a final respect; the most efficacious ultimate term now used is that of "freedom." Because this term has broken away almost completely from its denotative moorings, it guarantees instant charisma. A feature of the gospel of Western man seems to be that only the completely unfettered life is worth living. If sheer self-sacrifice is needed, this term finds legions of dedicated people marching to its banner. Some of them march to war to make the world safe for democracy while others become lifetime members of the American Civil Liberties Union. In the case of abortion, the woman is characterized as having the inherent right to "reproductive autonomy," or doing whatever she wants with her own body. This doctrine, of course, finds receptive ears in a permissive society currently in the process of liberating its women. "Compulsory pregnancy" becomes a devil term. Expectant women are forced to "endure nine months of unwilling pregnancy," and we are asked, by implication, what greater emancipation can there be than removing the chains of pregnant servitude?

Those favoring modification of abortion laws are not alone in the use of ideologically oriented language. In response to the new value internalization, those opposed to abortion-law change reply aggressively in kind. Liberalizing or reforming abortion laws becomes "relaxing" or "loosening" abortion laws. Restrictive abortion becomes "easy" abortion. Progress becomes "regress." Abortion-on-request becomes "abortion on demand." Reproduction becomes "procreation." Reproductive autonomy becomes "sexual irresponsibility." The curette becomes an "instrument of death" and the salting-out process,[12] "pickling alive." Regarding the existence of intra-uterine life, one finds an insistent use of such labels as "unborn child, baby" or "infant." Termination of pregnancy becomes "murdering," or at best "killing." A potential human being becomes "a human being with potential." In short, the semantic component is prejudiced in favor of life.

A strictly objective analysis of the language used in the abortion controversy reveals few truly neutral terms, or to quote Minnick's corrective, "few people who do not respond with some kind of value judgment to the terms they hear or read."[13] Even the supposedly objective media coverage seems to load and unload the semantic component. The point to be stressed, of course, is that each side attempts to structure the ambiguity of intra-uterine life through language. As a result, arguments are often discarded for mere verbal attachments which advance ideology without advancing rationality. The message receiver is urged semantically to view the proposed activity in an uncritical way.

Any critical examination of the abortion controversy as projected rhetorically will disclose an attempt by both sides to align their respective positions with former social crises. The denial of abortion is often equated with the denial of alcohol and the dehumanization of abortion with the dehumanization of slavery. Such associations are made so earnestly and arise in the mind so naturally, that they would appear to demand a closer scrutiny. The next section explores these associations to uncover common philosophical presuppositions. It is assumed that the resulting analogue will yield a clearer understanding of abortion's ideological matrix.

ANALOGUE

America has been characterized as an intensely idealistic nation, one of the most idealistic in history. The utopian vision permeates the national thinking and was the generating force behind two of the greatest movements to consume the reformer's energies—slavery and prohibition. That there is a fundamental connection between these movements and that of abortion is more than coincidental. All three involve the same philosophical presuppositions diffused by the same rhetorical methods.

A utopian-dystopian rhetorical configuration was the dominant diffusion technique in both the slavery and prohibition movements. In each social crisis society attempted to restructure or extend an existing institution to relieve a perceived discrepancy involving basic values. An ideal-real gap compelled each period to match what was with what ought to be. The result was a clash of utopian-dystopian visions and of similar rhetorical motifs.

A one-alternative chamber-of-horrors motif appeared in both the slavery and prohibition movements. Each side, when its world view had gained rhetorical momentum, pictured for itself and for the rest of society a subconscious blind alley. Cherished behavior patterns seemed threatened by an alien philosophy and a feeling of entrapment became the fixed mental set. This chamber-of-horrors was peopled with heroes and villains in a surrealistic way. Events of a highly dramatic nature were related by movement leaders and spread by all the carriers of change. These events often depicted such inhibitors of change as the ruthless slave merchant and the conniving saloon keeper in the darkest of colors. By the same token, the facilitators of change received the opposite treatment and a new set of minor culture heroes emerged. Appeals to those communal emotions of pity and fear were made on a grand scale.

From the depths of Western Civilization there evolved a rank order of values recognized, it might be argued, in both nature and custom. Jefferson, with the help of Locke, memorialized them at the beginning of the *Declaration of Independence*. Life, liberty, and the pursuit of happiness (property) thus became enshrined as the American value trilogy, and they have become even in shifting contexts a sometimes unstated if not unrecognized part of nearly every major social movement. In fact, it would not be unfair to say that this same trilogy contains the motive energy necessary to sustain the Edenic myth.[14] New additions to the city on the hill are built whenever the hierarchy is disturbed. Such was no less true of the agony of slavery than of the folly of prohibition.

Philosophically, certain social movements proceed from definition. In the case of slavery and prohibition, the definition involved the completeness of the ideal man. A person because he was black or took a drink was inherently incomplete and could not measure up.

The response, therefore, was a simple negation: take away his liberty and his happiness (alcohol). In 1924 Nicholas Murray Butler, the President of Columbia University, might have noted this relationship when he said: "My own feeling toward prohibition is exactly the feeling which my parents and my grandparents had toward slavery. I look upon the Volstead Act precisely as they looked upon the Fugitive Slave Law."[15]

Now, it may be asked, what does all this have to do with the abortion controversy? The answer is to be found in completing the logical circuit. The Negro (since he is black) does not have all the qualities of the ideal man; the drinker (since he imbibes) does not have all the qualities of the ideal man; and the being *in utero* (since he is unborn) does not have all the qualities of the ideal man. Stated another way: the Negro cannot handle liberty, so make him a slave; the drinker cannot pursue happiness properly, so deny him alcohol; and the being *in utero* cannot cope with life satisfactorily, so abort him. In each case a basic right is denied and a simple negation becomes the accepted social response.

To some this tripartite analogue may seem exaggerated, and to others altogether invalid.[16] The cause, perhaps, can be traced to the logical relationships having been blurred by the intensity of the value being threatened and by how one views the initiation of change. As one moves down the pre-potent value scale, the key argument becomes masked. It is easy to recognize the definition of a complete man in the abortion controversy and to see it less sharply in slavery. With prohibition, however, since the value in question shades off into the region of social norms, the presence of the argument is almost imperceptible. For assistance in recognizing it one can turn to the writings of Lincoln. In a speech before the Washingtonian Temperance Society he observed for the benefit of his audience that humans with a drinking problem were not inferior specimens of the race but "will bear an advantageous comparison with those of any other class."[17] Mr. Lincoln was known as a careful student of human nature.

The tendency to dehumanize is an almost universal human failing. In some quarters the word "pig" is used to describe a policeman and in others the word "monkey" a member of the Viet Cong. These are contemporary manifestations of the phenomenon. That which is held in low esteem suddenly takes on the nomenclature of the subhuman. Hitler's *untermenschen* had no monopoly in history. In truth, the heart of the current controversy over women's rights and the rights of homosexuals involves once again the definition of the whole person. The women's and gay liberation movements are essentially protesting an implied definition of inferiority.

Those who propose change are not always to be identified as the affirmative in the standard debate pattern. Prior to the Civil War, for example, the abolitionist sentiment in the North for eliminating slavery was matched by a nearly equally strong sentiment in the South for extending its scope. The two movements clashed over the status of slavery in the new states west of the Mississippi. In the Dred Scott Decision the Negro was declared a piece of chattel property to be transported at will into free territory. Paradoxically, an analogous situation faces the United States Supreme Court with regard to abortion. In a very important sense, any decision which affects the alleged humanity of intra-uterine life is in essence a second Dred Scott Decision, for it defines a human being.

Social movements oftentimes have shifting protagonists. Both aggressors and defenders can change places and the final outcome of the ideological conflict is not always with the side that alters the law. From a purely argumentative standpoint, those who are *against* something can also be *for* its opposite. As Cronkhite observes:

The idea that the status quo always has the presumption and the individual who attacks the present system always has the burden of proof ... creates some real problems when applied to "real-life" argument, however, since the status quo cannot always be identified.[18]

He argues that the burden should sometimes be in proving one's assertions.[19]

The confusion in identifying protagonists can be seen in comparing the prohibition and abortion movements. Initially, those who advocate change in these areas assume the same argumentative position. Both challenge an accepted norm or value. The hard-core prohibitionist tried to sell the American public on the idea that Western Civilization's acceptance of moderate drinking was wrong. The hard-core pro-abortionist is saying that Western Civilization's acceptance of intra-uterine humanity is also wrong. Thus both ideologies attack a commonly held belief.

With all three movements the ideological core contains a trace of Manicheism, the attachment of evil to matter. In prohibition, slavery, and abortion the attachment of evil to an amoral entity is inversely related to the strength of the value being altered. This attachment is most easily seen in prohibition. Here the substance alcohol became an evil and was separated from the person. In slavery, the evil was the color black.[20] In abortion the evil is size and location as related to the pregnancy process. To understand these philosophical relationships is to understand the rhetoric of the movements. As will be pointed out shortly, there is an affinity between Manicheism and the mind-body duality.

It is no accident that certain spiritual segments of the Judeo-Christian tradition banded together at least informally on prohibition and are now doing so with abortion. Sacramental Christianity (Lutheran, Catholic, Episcopalian, Orthodox, etc.) and Orthodox Judaism for the most part opposed prohibition just as they have tacitly befriended one another in the abortion controversy. These segments of the Judeo-Christian tradition have usually taken a more relaxed attitude toward the relationships between religion and culture. Furthermore, and what ultimately may be more important, they all possess a rather fully developed theology of nature.

Susceptibility to blind-alley thinking can be traced to a mind-body dualism. *Cogito ergo sum,* the classic Cartesian distinction, epitomizes this mind-in-the-body separation. A wholistic view of man, on the other hand, provides a psychological defense. The spirit-flesh unity (signified by the Incarnation) is emphasized in sacramental Christianity as well as in the teachings of Orthodox Judaism. Significantly, an existentialist no-exit philosophy does not appear quite as attractive to the true Judeo-Christian believer, irrespective of sect.[21] "And the word was made flesh" has an important bearing upon the rhetoric of social movements.

According to psychoanalytic theory, there resides beyond the threshold of the conscious a region dominated solely by the pleasure principle. It is here that wish-fulfillment assumes the guise of large-scale metaphor. Freud recognized it partially in dreams of convenience, or what those who oppose abortion have recognized as the primary motivation behind the abortion movement. Abortion-on-demand can ultimately have no other justification for an impartial investigator.

Conveniently getting rid of the ugly or less than ideal has been the secret wish of man since time began. In fact, a subconscious purification metaphor can be detected in all the social movements under discussion. Pro-slavery sentiment feared a potential deterioration of the Caucasian majority through intermarriage with Negroes if slavery were abolished. With prohibition a portion of the argumentation concerned the connection between alcohol and mental and genetic defects. With abortion the tendency to eliminate the unfit is most clearly seen. Pro-abortion rhetoric assumes the unstated premise that defectives, including the potential unwanteds, should have no place in a well-ordered society. In short, every movement stressing purification taps a subconscious yearning and provides a motivational symbolism for conscious behavior. Such can also be said for every religious purification ritual and exclusive social grouping. The unclean in many societies are unacceptable.

This analogue should now enable us to get to the heart of the present abortion controversy. How each side views *in utero* generation is a sign of how each side views human beings in general. The key issue which involves the humanity of the offspring brings a dynamic vs. static concept into sharp focus.[22] To assume that man is a creature immersed in time who is open to the future is to contradict the sudden acquisition of humanity at any point other than the true biological beginning.[23] Pro-abortion rhetoric emphasizes a static determinism which those in opposition contend is a scientific cul-de-sac. Dynamism produces hope, which is the philosophical counterthrust of the self-styled "pro-life" position. It is a major generalization of this paper, then, that any rhetoric which fosters a static determinism must eventually contend with the counter-evolution of human awareness.

In summary, the ideological matrix of the abortion controversy involves a conflict between two modes of collective behavior. America's social heritage has provided alternate and opposing justification for dealing with problem pregnancies—the right-to-life versus personal choice. Rhetorically, these justifications are defended and attacked by both sides of the dispute. Given the assumption of humanity *in utero,* those who favor abortion-law change use a semantic of denial, while those who oppose it a semantic of affirmation. Through the use of ultimate terms the intra-uterine being becomes subservient to the overriding demands of individual freedom.

The type of ideological conflict seen in the abortion controversy is not new to the American experience. Similar conflicts involving an intended rearrangement of the societal value structure can be seen in the controversy over slavery and prohibition. In all three conflicts the fundamental question concerns the definition of the acceptable human being. The conclusion of this inquiry, therefore, may be found in its beginning. Shakespeare phrased the question poignantly through his character King Lear. "Who is it that can tell me who I am?" is a

212   *Social*

lament echoed in the abortion controversy and at some time by all
men who dare to think deeply.

REFERENCES

1. Hans Toch, *The Social Psychology of Social Movements* (Indianapolis:
   The Bobbs-Merrill Company, Inc., 1965), p. 21.
2. Among the many legal briefs available a representative sample would be
   those concerning *U. S.* vs. *Vuitch* and *Minnesota* vs. *Hodgson.*
3. The debate in the British Parliament would be particularly helpful. For
   an analysis of the argumentation see David Mall, "Trial-by-Exhaustion:
   The 1967 Abortion Debate in the House of Commons," *Today's Speech,*
   XVII, No. 4 (November, 1969), 16.
4. For biologist Garrett Hardin's views, which correspond essentially with
   those of Fletcher, the reader is referred to the following representative
   articles: "Abortion and Human Dignity," *Per/Se,* I, No. 1 (Spring, 1966),
   16; "Blueprints, DNA, and Abortion: A Scientific and Ethical Analysis,"
   Medical Opinion and Review, III, No. 2 (February, 1967), 74; "Semantic
   Aspects of Abortion," *ETC.: A Review of General Semantics,* XXIV,
   No. 3 (September, 1967), 263; "Abortion-or-Compulsory Pregnancy?"
   Journal of Marriage and the Family, XXX, No. 2 (May, 1968), 246. The
   reader may also wish to consult Alan F. Guttmacher, ed., *The Case for
   Legalized Abortion Now* (Berkeley: Diablo Press, 1967).
5. The full name of the symposium held at the International Hotel in Los
   Angeles, January 22-24, 1971, was *Therapeutic Abortion: A Symposium
   on Implementation.* It was sponsored as an educational course by the
   UCLA University Extension School of Nursing and School of Medicine
   with the cooperation of the California Committee on Therapeutic Abor-
   tion.
6. Joseph Fletcher, "The Patient's Right to Die," in *Euthanasia and the
   Right to Death,* ed. A. B. Downing (New York: Humanities Press, 1970).
   This essay first appeared in a special supplement to *Harper's Magazine,*
   CCI, No. 1325 (October, 1960), p. 139. Copyright © 1960, by Minneapolis
   Star and Tribune Co., Inc. Reprinted from the October, 1960, issue of
   Harper's Magazine by permission of the author.
7. An excellent passage, too lengthy to quote here, which clearly spells out
   this internalizing objective can be found in the official journal of the
   California Medical Association. See "A New Ethic for Medicine and
   Society," *California Medicine,* CXIII, No. 3 (September, 1970), 68.
8. Richard Weaver, *The Ethics of Rhetoric* (Chicago: Henry Regnery Company, 1953), p. 211.
9. G. Lowes Dickinson, *The Greek View of Life* (New York: McClure,
   Phillips & Company, 1905), p. 233.
10. The reader, if adequately steeped in the rhetoric of the abortion move-

ment, may wonder why those who favor abortion sometimes use the unscientific terms "blobs" and "pieces of tissue" to describe that which has been conceived. Apparently, the abortion rhetoric can dehumanize without being highly denotative.

11. Weaver defines efficiency as "a good adaptation of means to ends, with small loss through friction." Weaver, *op. cit.,* p. 217.

12. This term refers to an abortion procedure whereby a needle is stuck through a pregnant woman's abdominal wall and into the amniotic sac. After some fluid is withdrawn a sterile salt water solution is injected. Labor starts in about twenty-four hours.

13. Wayne C. Minnick, *The Art of Persuasion* (Boston: Houghton Mifflin Company, 1968), p. 191.

14. America's principal values seem weighted in the manner of Maslow's prepotent needs. See A. H. Maslow, "A Theory of Human Motivation," *Psychological Review,* L, No. 4 (July, 1943), 370.

15. From an address at the Annual Dinner of the Missouri Society, April 29, 1924. Quoted in Andrew Sinclair, *Prohibition: The Era of Excess* (Boston: Little, Brown, and Company, 1962), p. 369.

16. An observation by Perelman is helpful in aligning the three movements properly. He maintains that challenges to commonly held opinions emphasize the *locus communis* of quality as opposed to quantity. In other words, the timeless struggle between the romantic and classic outlook is operative within the three movements considered. The romantic outlook implies that the born are preferable to the unborn, the white man to the black man and the non-drinker to the drinker. The classicist says that the born and the unborn, the white and the black man, the non-drinker and drinker are equally preferred. In short, the advocates of abortion, slavery, and prohibition stress "some" while their opponents stress "all." See Chaim Perelman, *The New Rhetoric: A Treatise on Argumentation* (Notre Dame: University of Notre Dame Press, 1969), pp. 83-99.

17. Charles T. White, *Lincoln and Prohibition* (New York: The Abingdon Press, 1921), p. 52. It should be noted that the right of the individual to abstain from alcohol and to persuade others to do so is acknowledged. When this persuasion takes the form of law binding on other individuals, however, such law ultimately denies a traditionally accepted right, i.e., the pursuit of happiness (property) via the consumption of alcohol.

18. Gary Cronkhite, *Persuasion: Speech and Behaviorial Change* (Indianapolis: The Bobbs-Merrill Company, Inc., 1969), p. 39.

19. Gary Cronkhite, "The Focus of Presumption," *Central States Speech Journal,* XVII, No. 4 (November, 1966), 270.

20. The contemporary Black Power movement has reacted to this aspect of the nature-is-evil ideology by sloganizing that "Black is beautiful."

21. A helpful distinction might be made between "explicit" and "implicit" sacramentalists with the latter including all those Judeo-Christians who are not formally a part of sacramental Christianity.

22. In general, the writer agrees with Dubos that medical utopias are essentially static. For an explanation of this attitude see René Dubos, *The Dreams of Reason* (New York: Columbia University Press, 1961).

23. Fletcher's earlier ideological statement may seem to contradict this assertion. The problem is again philosophical. Most life scientists believe that life begins at fertilization. The value to be attached to this life, if it is conceived of human parents, is another matter. An honest judgment would appear to be that when the premeditated decision is made to abort, the doubt concerning *in utero* humanity has been satisfactorily resolved. To argue otherwise is to argue against common sense. For a scholarly treatment of the abortion argument see B. Z. Brody, "Abortion and the Law," *The Journal of Philosophy,* LXVIII, No. 12 (June 17, 1971), 357, and Roger Wertheimer, "Understanding the Abortion Argument," *Philosophy and Public Affairs,* I, No. 1 (Fall, 1971), 67.

· 11 ·

NOW WHY NOT ASK
A WOMAN?

Jill Knight, M.P.

I am not a member of Women's Liberation, nor do I seek to escalate the battle between the sexes, but I must say at the outset that, to my mind, abortion is really a *woman's* subject. How can any man guess what it is like to start a pregnancy when one doesn't know how on earth one is going to be able to care for the baby: the anguish or fear or worry when the first signs are unmistakable? The male of the species doesn't vomit all the time, or get cumbersome, or have to figure out how he is going to keep on working in the later months, or plan how he is going to earn *and* look after the baby at the same time.

There are other factors. Take my case: my children are almost grown up; I have succeeded, after years of work and preparation, in a fascinating job which I enjoy thoroughly. If I were to start another baby, that would go, and my whole life would have to alter drastically.

So let's say I do understand, perhaps more basically than my respected and erudite male colleagues, why pressure has grown up for abortion to be legalized.

On the other hand, fully understanding all this, I am 100% against abortion—unless there are incontrovertible medical reasons why it must be done. If the terrible choice has to be made between the *life* of the mother and the life of the child, I think the mother should be saved because she probably has a husband, perhaps other children, and possibly parents, too, who love her and rely upon her. But abortion because the baby is inconvenient, or the mother doesn't happen to want one—never.

I used not to feel so strongly; like most people, I had never really examined the subject. But I did oppose the Abortion Bill, when it was first introduced in the British House of Commons, and my opposition led me to study the ramifications of this intensely complicated matter. The more I studied it, the more against abortion I became.

A lot of well-meaning people join the pro-abortion lobby because they have been revolted by horrendous tales of back-street abortions. Grisly talk about unsavory operators, grubby kitchen tables, coat-hangers, hooks or knitting needles used as instruments on terrified girls, leads the kindly listener to vehement opposition—and the entirely wrong assumption that all this will be brought to an end if abortion is lwgalized. In point of fact, as we in Britain have discovered, back-street operations continue however many legal abortions go on. This is because the cost of an abortion in a private clinic is generally high, and because in a National Health Service (free) hospital, the woman will have to give her name and address, which she is often reluctant to do; after all, there is no operation for which a woman wants to have greater anonymity than abortion.

Nevertheless, there is less social conscience about having the operation than there used to be. After all, even Parliament doesn't appear to think there is anything very wrong in having an abortion, and this attitude has certainly contributed to the astronomical rise in the number of abortions in Britain. Before the Act, we had about 10,000 per year—now the figure is 138,000 per year, and still rising.

As any doctor knows, depression and rejection of the child is quite a normal phenomenon of early pregnancy. Perhaps the mother-to-be feels sick, perhaps she regrets spoiled holiday plans, perhaps she did not intend to start a baby just then. However, before the Abortion Act it would never have entered he head to go along to her G.P. and ask to have the pregnancy ended. Within a few weeks she would not only accept her condition, but usually begin to look forward with pleasure to her baby. Now, with the possibility ofabortion firmly before her, the knowledge that the highest authority in the land has sanctioned it, and the fact that her temporary period of rejection coincides with the "best" time to have an abortion, medically speaking, off she goes.

This huge rise in the number of abortions has meant that the gynaecological units in our hospitals are grossly overworked, and women who need obstetrical care, other than an abortion, are finding that they are pushed to the bottom of the queue endlessly, because "abortion patients cannot wait." The recent concern expressed in a report from the Royal College of Gynaecologists and Obstetricians on this matter went on to state that two of the women who had been constantly relegated to the bottom of the list for entry to hospital were found, when finally admitted, to have been suffering from early cancer of the cervix.

Many women suffer from varying forms of gynaecological disorder which are distressing and/or painful. How can it be right that they should have their suffering doubled or trebled because the beds they need are constantly occupied by abortion patients?

Any country or State which is contemplating making abortion available on demand had better ask itself whether it has the medical facilities, and the medical staff, to take on what is going to be a very heavy case-load indeed. Pro-abortionists say, "But if a woman is going to have a baby, she will have to go into hospital anyway, so why should there be any more pressure on hospital services if she goes in for an abortion instead?" But maternity cases are almost always straightforward: the doctors and nurses have usually looked after hundreds, and the process goes smoothly. Abortion cases are different—in the *time* at which the operation is being carried out (just how pregnant a woman is makes a lot of difference), in the circumstances surrounding the case, and in the psychological state of the patient. Reputable doctors take far longer in assessing abortion patients than they do in dealing with normal pregnancies. Besides, as we have found in Britain, it is possible to go into hospital two or three times for an abortion in the time it takes to have one baby.

Another thing about the situation which has arisen in Britain is the way in which, all too often, a woman who is in hospital because she either wants a baby very much, and is being given treatment which may bring this about, *or* because she has just lost a baby through miscarriage, is put in the next bed to an abortion patient. Sometimes she is sandwiched between two. The Royal College of Nursing, in the week in which I write this chapter, has made a statement deploring this, and the heartbreak it causes. Because of the pressure under which gynaecological wards are working, it is administratively impossible to avoid this happening.

Our nurses are clearly very distressed—or the vast majority are—at several other angles, too. There is no limit to the time after which an abortion may be performed in Britain. In the first 3 years after the Abortion Act went through, 528 babies were aborted at over 24 weeks gestation. Remember, many babies born prematurely at six months have been reared successfully—I have a very good friend who boasts of being a "six-month baby."

We had one case in Britain where a baby who had been aborted cried pitifully as it was about to be put into an incinerator by a hospital orderly. That baby was a seven-month baby. The figures show that there must have been many, many other babies killed or left to die after abortion, for when they are as late as that, I understand the abortion takes the form of a caesarian section.

A nurse came to see me recently to tell me that her experiences since the Abortion Act had now driven her to give up nursing. She told me that she had been ordered to dispose of a six-month baby boy, after an abortion. In the premature baby unit in her ward, they had a six-month baby boy, born too early. "We are doing everything we can for him," she said. "He is a lovely little chap, and I think he is going to make it. But how can I square it with my conscience that I do all in my power to save one baby, and kill off the other—*for no better reason than that the mother of the first wants him, and the mother of the second does not.*"

Women's Lib, which strongly supports abortion on demand, says a woman has a right to do what she wants with her body. So she does; what she has no right to do is to destroy *another* body. Pro-abortionists hate to admit there is any question of a baby being destroyed in an abortion. "Why do you make such a fuss?" they cry. "It's only a blob." Yet, by the time a woman knows beyond all doubt that she is pregnant, she has a quite recognizable baby inside her.

The less the woman knows about the actual abortion, the better the pro-abortionists are pleased. After all, it takes a pretty strong stomach to accept the fact that many abortions are carried out by the insertion of an instrument into the womb, and the pulling out of separate bits of the baby at each insertion. Not nice, really: first an arm, then a leg, then a bit of head or shoulder, lying in a sterile dish in the operating theater.

But the point that Women's Lib misses is that freely available abortion can make women *more* enslaved, not less.

Parents, husbands, doctors more anxious to make money than to give their patient time and care—all these groups, in their separate ways, can and do exert pressure on a frightened or bewildered girl to have an abortion. I will quote from just two of the letters I have in my file, to illustrate my point.

The first is from a married woman in the London area who writes:

I had an abortion last July, and did so under pressure from my husband. It was emotional pressure, I suppose, for I had just become pregnant quite accidentally when my third baby was just two and a half months old. I feel so mixed-up and find it hard to understand how such a thing could ever have happened. The simple truth is that I signed the form, and therefore it is perhaps my fault for not having the strength of character to do what I know to be the right thing. The abortion itself was obtained very easily. I saw the doctor alone for less than five minutes; I gave him no reasons whatsoever that could possibly have justified him in granting the abortion so readily. He did in fact send me to see the medical social worker who told me that I had been sent to her because the doctor did not feel I had sufficient reason for an abortion. But during my conversation with her the telephone rang and it was the doctor, who had re-read my notes and discovered that my husband was quite prepared to pay for it.

It all seems so complicated and difficult to put on paper. I had the abortion and feel that much of the blame must lie with me. Since it happened I have been depressed and no one seems to care. I am supposed to forget and forgive but I feel nothing but bitterness and hatred towards those people who allowed it to happen. If this letter will help in any way, I shall feel I have done something to protect unborn babies from being conveniently disposed of.

The second letter is from a young girl of eighteen who is not married:

I am about to complete a Sixth Form course at Grammar School. I have been going steady with a boy for two years, and he attends the same school. I have just discovered that I am five weeks pregnant and I feel I am in a desperate situation. My boy friend, and his parents, want me to have an abortion. My father and mother have told me I must get an abortion and they will not allow me in the house otherwise. My father has heart trouble and my mother and sister say I am slowly killing him and if I keep the baby they say he will probably die of a heart attack.

I feel very selfish about the whole situation and I would hate to see my mother and father unhappy. I want to discuss the whole situation with someone but my mother will not allow me out of the house. They take and collect me from school.

I understand how my parents feel, but to me to get an abortion would be the end of the world. I could never forget the fact that I had once been pregnant. I desperately want to keep the baby, but I am constantly being reminded that at the moment it is only a cell. This cell is the living nucleus of a potential human being and already I love it and feel it is part of me. I would do all in my power to keep the baby. I know it would mean great sacrifices on my part, but to me it would be worth every penny and every ounce of effort. I know I would love the baby and do everything possible to make it happy. I have weighed up both sides of the argument for and against an abortion, but I feel an abortion would be a disaster for me. I am a healthy eighteen-year old; I feel an abortion would be heartbreaking and unnecessary.

We tried to help that girl, but her parents, his parents, and the boy himself, won. I have not heard from her since.

Some of the worst letters I have had have come from women who had had an abortion many years previously, but have never been able to forget it. Particularly if she is not able to have a baby when she *does* want one (and this is frequently what happens) the woman tends to feel ashamed and guilty. "God has paid me back," wrote one woman.

Of course, many women who have abortions do not feel like this at all. The harder a woman is, the less an abortion bothers her; but the sensitive ones experience anguish of which no one warned them— no one asked them to stop and think.

I am not a Catholic, but my Catholic friends usually share my view that responsible family planning, not abortion, is the answer. The tragedy is that the overwhelming majority of women who seek abortions in Britain today admit that they were following no form of contraception when they became pregnant. This seems to me quite appalling. In my book of rules there is all the difference in the world between not starting a baby, and getting rid of the one you have started.

Before the Abortion Act went through in Britain, all the public communications media, and thus public opinion, was vociferously in favor of making abortion easily available. Now, after four years, the reverse is generally true. We have seen what a tiger we have by the tail. We now know the many evils of abortion-on-demand. The soaring abortion figures; the lack of care for the patient in the mushrooming abortion clinics where cash takes inevitable priority over care; the strain on hospitals, nurses and reputable doctors; the people who tout for some of the private clinics, getting money for each patient they bring; the effect on women who want other hospital care; the psychological kick-back of abortion; the lack of babies for adoption.

A Labour Government spokesman congratulated that Government about two years after the Abortion Act went through because there were 120,000 less illegitimate babies than there would have been. I think he was wrong—that no congratulations were in order at all. I think one should work towards removing the stigma of illegitimacy, not kill the babies off. Many people want babies who cannot have them: once they could adopt a baby, but now there are none in Britain to adopt.

Abortion is a complex subject. Those who take the trouble to investigate it thoroughly hardly ever campaign for it. Those who have learned what it means to a country, when abortion legislation gets into the Statute Book, are sadder and wiser people.

· 12 ·

THE SEXUAL REVOLUTION
IS YET TO BEGIN

Mary R. Joyce

So many people, including professionals, think that what is happening today in human sexuality is revolutionary. But there can be no revolution until certain basic assumptions are radically changed. The most crucial of these assumptions might be addressed by the question, "When is a human person sexually active?" No revolution has ever occurred in the way people would respond to this question. Most, if not all, would respond to it by saying that a person is sexually active when he engages in genital stimulation of one kind or another. And they would say that if the person is continent, or honestly a virgin or celibate, he is then sexually inactive. It is my purpose to show how unenlightened and unrevolutionary this almost universal view really is.

First of all, genital stimulation is sexual activity. But how genito-centric is human sexuality? There is a great difference, not a separation, between sexuality and genital expression in human beings. The difference is much less in animals. In the human dimension, it is possible that the most sexually *active* person might be one who has not engaged in genital expression. He might also be one who does so frequently. Furthermore, it is possible that the most sexually *inactive* person has not engaged in genital expression. He might also be one who does so frequently. The fact to be assimilated before the revolution actually begins is that neither genital stimulation nor its absence is essential to an active sexuality in human beings. Genital intercourse, regarded entirely as an option, and not as a necessity, is perhaps the most revolutionary indication of an authentic sexual freedom.

This is a hard saying! Freedom is not easy. Freedom is not comfortable. But freedom is tremendously exciting. The question is now delivered, "What is sexual activity?"

We are conditioned to think that overt, dramatic behavior is also the most active form of behavior. For example, we tend to regard the orchestral conductor who dramatically flings his arms, head and upper body in every direction as extremely active in the production of fine music. Until we experience the near-motionless power of a conductor like the late Fritz Reiner of the Chicago Symphony Orchestra! One could not believe his eyes and ears while listening to such exquisitely magnificent and electrifying music coming from an orchestra directed by what seemed to be an inert man. Reiner was impressively dynamic without being dramatic. His love for the music, his insight into the composer's inspiration, and his dedication communicated so much power to his musicians that a wildly moving baton would have been incongruous. Human activity need not be overt and dramatic in order to be dynamic.

Similarly, human sexuality need not be passionately erotic, or dramatically expressed, in order to be intensely dynamic. A strong sense of self, a vibrant love for life and reverence for the life of others, an intense insightful and feelingful life, characterize a person who is highly active sexually whether or not this person chooses to express himself in a genital manner. A growing ability to see and accept this radical shift in perspective would signal the beginning of the first sexual revolution in history. Its effects would be utterly liberating both for human pleasure and human joy.

The sexual energy of man and woman is probably about ninety percent other than genito-centric. This estimate certainly is not based on human behavior as it has been, or now is, but rather on an insight into the human potential. Psychologists are just beginning to say that the main sexual organ of the human person is the brain. Interpreters of Teilhard de Chardin's view of evolution are saying the same. Meanwhile, other scientists are declaring that the brain of the normal adult person is only about five to ten percent developed. This would indicate, then, that with all the genital fluency of people, most of them have been and still are sexually quite inactive.*

We have come to the point in our self-awareness where we are called upon to recognize that our sexuality is much more cerebro-centric than genito-centric. While we are loudly claiming that our sexuality is different from the animal's sexuality in not being primarily ordered toward reproduction, we need to insist just as strongly that, unlike animals, our primary sexual organ is the brain. But, then, we will be confronted by the great impotence and frigidity that exists in the primary center of our manhood and womanhood. Many people, rather than facing up to this startling revelation, will turn away and deny their potential for new development. This is one thing that can be predicted infallibly.

Many voices will be heard to say that there is no evidence for the claim that our human sexuality is largely inactive, or that we are so massively underdeveloped as men and women. What is the evidence? Is the claim supportable?

We have only to consider the worldwide plague of venereal disease resulting from what is badly misnamed as "sexual freedom." The rampant use of veterinarian means of birth control is no compliment to the humanity of the person's sexuality. And most tragically of all, the great number of human lives destroyed by abortion is a dramatic statement in innocent human blood about the impoverished condition of man-woman relationships.

How can all this degradation result from acts of love? Is love so diseased? Is it so mechanically, chemically or surgically conditioned; so destructive of human life? It is obvious, then, that the real revolution is yet to come.

"Make love, not war," young people cry. Then, many of them "make love" only to make war on the children they conceive.

Young people often berate their parents for evils of the older generation. Do these young think their own children will find no fault with them? Those in the womb who survive the abortion era will have much to say to the "now" generation. These survivors are likely to be too small in number to bear the social burden of an increasingly

---

* People generally understand the role of the brain in the fantasizing necessary for erection and stimulation of erotic passion. This is just the beginning of an insight into the primacy of the brain in human sexuality. Without dynamics of freedom, meaning and love internal to its very essence, human sexuality is grotesquely truncated. These dynamics transcend, while including, the erection, orgasm and other aspects of genitality. The brain, as the organ of freedom, meaning and love is, then, the main *physical* center of a largely trans-physical energy. This is not to imply that all human energy is sexual, but that sexuality is an important aspect of all human energy.

geriatric population, and they might be easily tempted to use the same expediency tactics on the "unwanted aging" as these latter used upon "unwanted pregnancies." Young people, however, can also begin to break the expediency-cycle that grips our culture. They can initiate on the face of this planet a revolution in love. The promise is already evident in college-age students. Some of them respond immediately when they hear the news and the challenge of the revolution that is yet to begin.

But too many young people still accept the new wave of violence against human life in the name of love. If it is true that there are over fifty million abortions in the world each year (this is probably only "the tip of the iceberg"), there is no body-count in history as extensive as this one. We are cutting down on men's killing in land, air and sea wars, but stepping up women's killing in the war on preborn children. This latter war is the most terrible because the victims are incapable of self-defense, as are all small children.

And women are saying that this war is their way to liberation! They say they want to control their own bodies. But destroying the body of another is not controlling one's own body. Most liberationists seem oblivious of the pre-genital zone of human control. And they fail to ask men to control *their* own bodies, too. Without a man no woman has a pregnancy she does not want. Men seeking profit perform most abortions, legal and illegal. In recent statistics, more men than women favor easy abortion. Why?

Women are still big business for men. Abortion now provides a new multi-million-dollar business in another kind of feminine prostitution. In the first form of prostitution women are paid by men. But when women prostitute themselves to what is called the "baby scrambler," the suction machine for abortion, they give the money to men more often than not. In New York alone, doctors and hospitals are reported to have made $139,061,000 in a year and a half on abortion. If women were not so intellectually passive, they would be able to see through this so-called liberation very clearly.

Before the Nazis began their direct slaughter of the Jews, they allowed abortion for Jewish women, but not for other German women. Why should they want the women they despised to have such a "noble and liberating right"? One does not necessarily care about women when he wants them to have easy abortion. He might despise them, want to "clean them up" and be rid of their problem. The easiest riddance is often the most care-less. And besides, these women are much more available for sexual exploitation both by themselves and by men. They can easily be led to believe that this condition is one of love and liberation. Women have been blind much too long that they should suddenly become wise.

There are a few rare women, however, who are beginning to see the light. Quoted by Dr. Jessie Bernard in *The Futurist* (April, 1970), one woman says, "The hangup to liberation is the supposed need for sex. It is something that must be refuted, coped with, demythified, or the cause of female liberation is doomed. We are programmed to crave sex. It sells consumer goods." In spite of the fact that this woman seems to be limiting human sexuality to its genital meaning, she senses the authentic direction of liberation. Dr. Bernard, a woman, says further that some women are oriented toward a new revolution. "This is not the now stale revolution—the work-harder-to-achieve-orgasm revolution—but one that transcends it."

In *Life* (Nov. 6, 1970), Derek Wright echoes the same theme when he says, "Sexual motivation is to a very large extent cultivated. We could, therefore, progressively decondition ourselves and considerably reduce our sexual desire if we wished . . . liberation in sex means being able to take it or to leave it." Again, sexuality is limited to its genital meaning by Mr. Wright, but the direction of liberation is seen. This direction is not away from sexuality, but deeper within it, so that genitality is finally in context and in perspective.

As the person develops his deeper, cerebro-centric, sexuality, his genito-centric sexuality becomes more imbued with freedom, less driven by compulsion. This authentic sexual freedom does not lessen the value of genitality, but increases its value—intensifying its quality while moderating its quantity. (Cf. *New Dynamics in Sexual Love* by Robert and Mary Joyce.)[1]

The deeper sexuality of the human person is centered in his most powerful ability to express his total human energy—his creative awareness. The organ of this awareness, the brain, is by far the most complex, agile and amazing organ of the human body. Since the person, however, is not reducible to any one of his organs, nor to all of them together, his being-energy, of which his body is an internal concretization, transcends while including his brain. The person's total awareness of himself and of the world is the main outlet for his being-energy. And, since most of his sexual energy is ontodynamic, that is, an aspect of his being-energy, the main outlet for his sexual energy is also his awareness of himself and the world.

The human being is designed to assimilate his reality and his sexuality into his self-awareness, increasing the dynamic quality of his manhood or her womanhood along with the dynamic quality of his or her personhood. Cerebro-centric sexuality is not cool, aloof and removed from flesh and blood responses; instead it is an interior marriage of insightful feeling and feelingful insight. This deeper sexuality is intensely vital, both intellectually and emotionally. On the other hand, the mental and emotional apathy of many persons who are genitally involved is evidence of a deep sexual apathy in spite of their genito-centric activity.

Before the deeper sexuality of the person is relatively well developed, genital involvement is premature. This is true even in marriage. In fact, most coital activity is premature. The result is genito-centric fixation.

An example of fixation following upon premature behavior appears in primitive tribes where five-year-old children set traps for hunting, and handle their own canoes. This is advanced behavior for children so young, but then they fail to develop much further. Similarly, genital involvement (including premarital coition) before considerable maturation in the deeper dynamics of human sexuality strongly tends to fixate people in a genito-centric sexuality. As a result, they tend to remain sexually retarded.

Our culture provides numerous mind-binders that lock people in a condition of sexual retardation. One of these is the ancient and still fully pervasive idea that man is some kind of animal. Man is rock-like in falling, plant-like in growing physically, animal-like in his senses and God-like in his creative awareness. But he is in no sense a rock, a plant, an animal or a god. He is entirely a human person. Everything within him, including his animal-like functions, is person-al, belonging to a person. Human evolution through the animal kingdom does not mean that the evolved being is an animal any more than an animal is a plant.

The ancient definition of man as a rational animal is totally incorrect. Man is neither an animal, nor is his intellect basically rational. The human intellect, as the intellect of a person, is primarily intuitive and secondarily rational. Man must be defined, if at all, on the basis of his personhood and not by substantizing his likeness to animals. Until we liberate ourselves from all identification with animal life, realizing how radically we are human persons and nothing else, we will remain humanly, as well as sexually, retarded.

By identifying sexuality with a supposed animal nature in man, earlier thinkers of the Western world identified the purpose of human sexuality with that of animal sexuality: the preservation of the species. Contemporary awareness of sex as an interpersonal relation has triggered a partial reaction against this view. However, the human generative power is still regarded as a simply biological function, as it is in animals, and sexuality is still identified with genitality, as it is in animals. Something specifically human is lacking in the present interpretation both of the human generative power and of human sexual energy.

Man's sexual energy is entirely *personal*, and not, in any sense, simply biological. In the human being, sexuality is an energy of personality, a relational energy for giving and receiving. This energy of personality is expressed primarily in attitudes, feelings, meanings and motives that distinguish the individual uniqueness of a man or a woman. The most primordial sexual act is the deeply interior act of receiving one's being in gratitude for the gift of existence, and in giving one's being toward others. In receiving one's being as a man or a woman, the person's sexual reality becomes dynamic in all of his attitudes, meanings and values. There develops in the person an interior marriage of insight and feeling, of giving and receiving. This interior marriage is different in men and women. A certain kind of receiving quality is accentuated in women; giving in men. Receiving is not passive, however; it is just as active as giving, but differently so. The marriage within the person reveals a dimension of sexuality that is much more than, though not exclusive of, impulse and passion. Sexual energy is meant to become a powerfully creative energy for love in the world. This creative love may be expressed in a genital manner in marriage, but most of it is oriented toward other than coital expression.

We need to abandon fear of our great potential for life, and deepen our understanding of sexuality, so that the liberation of man and woman from the phallic tyranny will become possible. Men, perhaps, will feel most threatened by this call to liberation. But women are most involved. Women must respond if they want to neutralize the forces that pressure them into genital fixation with the consequent frustration that turns them upon their innocent children with intent to kill. When all the energy of human sexuality is vested by a culture in one avenue of expression, sex and violence go hand in hand.

The way to liberation is the friendship of man and woman. But there is barely any cultural precedent for such a relationship. It needs to be created almost out of nothing. People think that men can be friends and that women can be friends. But men and women? Friendship requires a kind of sexual freedom so that persons may share meanings, values and feelings without erotic urgencies nagging the depths of their awareness. And people still wonder how this can be possible for men and women. Physical and psychological attraction and repulsion tend too strongly to interfere.

We are faced inescapably with the need to activate our deeper sexual energies so that men and women can become friends, sexually free in the most authentic sense. True sexual freedom transcends the urge to possess and be possessed; it gives people the disposition necessary for discovering and living their mutual independence. Men and women become liberated from within so that they are able to listen to each other and share thoughts they never dared to think before.

The ability to be alone is the condition for the freedom of attitude that makes friendship possible. Especially between men and women!

> Sing and dance together and be joyous,
>   but let each one of you be alone,
> Even as the strings of a lute are alone
>   though they quiver with the same music.[2]

In aloneness (not at all the same as loneliness), the person listens to his own meanings, values and feelings, so that he becomes free to listen to another person. While his inner unheard voices confuse him in his relationship with another, he cannot hear what the other person is trying to say, nor freely invite the other to share what he or she really thinks and feels.

A man who has received his own sexuality into the depths of his consciousness does not feel basically possessive toward a woman. And a woman who has received (assimilated) her own sexuality does not feel basically possessive toward a man. Both can understand and live these words, even in marriage:

> Give your hearts, but not into each other's keeping.
>   For only the hand of Life can contain your hearts.
> And stand together yet not too near together:
>   For the pillars of the temple stand apart,
> And the oak tree and the cypress grow not in each
>   other's shadow.[3]

The revolution yet to begin is all in what we think about our sexuality. Meanings ought to lead feelings, or else feelings lead us into meaninglessness. "As a man thinks in his heart, so is he." If the word "sex" necessarily evokes erotic meanings, the problem is in the mind, in the brain. But if men and women begin to think freedom, and think creative friendship, they *will* become free; they *will* become friends.

True sexual freedom is possible for human persons. It cannot be easy. It cannot be comfortable. But true sexual freedom is deeply exciting. The revolution is about to begin.

REFERENCES

1. Collegeville, Minn.: St. John's University Press.
2. From "On Marriage," by Kahlil Gibran. Reprinted from *The Prophet,* by Kahlil Gibran, with permission of the publisher, Alfred A. Knopf, Inc. Copyright 1923 by Kahlil Gibran; renewal copyright 1951 by Administrators C.T.A. of Kahlil Gibran Estate, and Mary G. Gibran.
3. Gibran, op. cit.

• 13 •

ABORTION, POVERTY AND BLACK GENOCIDE:
Gifts to the Poor?

Erma Clardy Craven

I am somebody.... I can see, I can hear, I can feel, I can touch! ...
I am—

—Rev. Jesse Jackson
Spring, 1969

Throughout the course of American history, the quality of human life has always been improved at the expense of the weak and oppressed. The tragic awareness of this reality leads one to the inexorable conclusion that the quality of life has never been a *universally* applied concept. This has never been so true as it is today in the move toward human abortion. It takes little imagination to see that the unborn Black baby is the real object of many abortionists. Except for the privilege of aborting herself, the Black woman and her family must fight for every other social and economic privilege. This move toward the free application of a non-right (abortion) for those whose real need is equal human rights and opportunities is benumbing the social conscience of America into unquestioningly accepting the "smoke screen" of abortion. The quality of life for the poor, the Black and the oppressed will not be served by destroying their children.

Held in bondage for decades, the Black man served the master society. His humanness was *ruled out of existence* by the law and social "norms." His only function was to advance the slave owners' prestige and economic gain. Every effort was made to destroy the Black family; knowing that with its destruction, the Black man remained powerless. But we hung on, and in the 1960's the civil rights legislation brought some equality to those who were already equal. While all seemed good and power seemed imminent, the plight of the Black man, woman and child did not improve, but only changed from the plantation to the ghetto, and the chains of slavery took on newer, more subtle and sophisticated forms. Prejudice and poverty now kept the Black family in a powerless state. Now, the womb of the poor Black woman is seen as the latest battleground for oppression. In times past, the Blacks couldn't grow kids fast enough for their "masters" to harvest; now that power is near, the "masters" want us to call a moratorium on having babies. When looked at in context, the whole mess adds up to blatant *genocide.*

Genocide has come to mean

acts committed with the intent to destroy, in whole or in part, a national, ethnical, racial or religious group as such; by killing members of the group; causing serious bodily or mental harm to members of the group; deliberately inflicting on the group conditions of life calculated to bring about its physical destruction in whole or in part; imposing measures intended to prevent births within the group; or forcibly transferring children of the group to another group.[1]

So when Adolph Hitler sent 6 million Jews to the gas chambers and ovens, it was genocide. When the Turks slaughtered 1.2 million Armenians in 1915, it was genocide. When the ancient Romans fed Christians to the lions in a conscious effort to wipe out Christianity, it was genocide. These are all very open and very blatant acts. But there are more subtle forms of genocide, and these are occurring in America, at an ever increasing rate, every day.

The substandard housing of the poor in this country where heat, water and plumbing facilities are lacking, and adequate public services such as garbage removal are withheld, is genocide. The poor food found in the ghetto supermarkets, the absence of health services, and the fires which consume the run-down houses and the little kids who live in them is genocide. The fact that Blacks die six years earlier than whites and the infant mortality rate is twice as high for Blacks is genocide. The conditions of ghetto schools and the quality of public education in Black communities is genocide. Government family planning programs designed for poor Blacks which emphasize birth control and abortion with the intent of limiting the Black population is genocide. The deliberate killing of Black babies in abortion is genocide—perhaps the most overt form of all.

Black genocide is so subtly, insidiously and deeply woven into the fabric of American society that it is little wonder that the United States has still not ratified the 1948 United Nations Genocide Convention which made the crime of genocide a part of international law.[2] Russia, China and seventy-three other countries have done so, but not the United States.[3] It seems that the Congress has certain "reservations," and it seems that these fall in line with other "reservations" that this nation perpetuates.

As a Black, Protestant social worker of thirty-four years experience in the rat-infested ghettos of the United States, I am calling for an immediate halt to this genocide. The time has come for our nation to bury its prejudices and open its doors to *everyone*. Only when this occurs will true equality become a reality and the fullness of our humanity be experienced.

Certainly there are many who may feel that I am grossly exaggerating; that I am making accusations out of bitterness. While I may have all the reason in the world to be bitter, it is not from this that I speak. The evidence speaks for itself—loud and clear!

REASONS FOR CONCERN

The move toward genocide in the United States has been most powerful, although generally unrecognized. In a brilliant exposé of this movement,[4] Samuel F. Yette, formerly with OEO (Office of Economic Opportunity), the Peace Corps, and *Newsweek* magazine, has told how (1) sterilization and birth control programs have been aimed against Blacks while masquerading under the name of hunger relief, (2) the "rice cup" bloc in Congress has worked to turn Black ghettos into exploited colonies, (3) state, county and local governments have refused "socialistic" programs to feed Black poor, while grabbing millions in federal aid for wealthy, nonproducing farmers, and (4) in a study made for the National Commission on the Causes and Prevention of Violence it was concluded that "the overwhelming majority of white Americans would be 'good Germans' if the government turned to massive racial repression" (Rodney Stark and James McEvoy III, "Middle-Class Violence," *Psychology Today*, November 1970).

While many southern states have relaxed their abortion statutes, I have not found one piece of truly progressive social legislation which the South as a whole has been willing to give to Blacks. On the other hand, the same year that North Carolina relaxed its abortion law, it refused to legislate equal employment opportunities for Blacks.

Many politicians have openly endorsed abortion as part and parcel of their political philosophy. Most significant among these is the abortion-on-demand stand of Senator George McGovern,[5] the Democratic nominee for President in 1972. In addition to this, Senator McGovern has set as a "firm national goal" the year 1976 as a target date for achieving zero population growth in the United States.[6] Since most white Americans have already achieved this, it can only be interpreted as having its most significant impact on the Black poor. To kill an unborn child because it may be unwanted, or deformed, or simply does not measure up to someone's standard of excellence is the same as destroying a Vietnamese village in order to save it. For Senator McGovern, who has made his name as a peace candidate, to strongly support abortion is totally inconsistent with any reasonable concept of the value and dignity of human life.

New York City Mayor John Lindsay, himself a strong advocate of abortion on demand,[7] implemented his prejudices when he appointed Mr. Gordon Chase as administrator of New York City's Health Services Administration. On November 29, 1969, Mayor Lindsay quietly asked for the resignation of Dr. Bernard Bucove, the former administrator who had won the confidence of many neighborhood groups. Mrs. Letitia Diaz of the East Harlem Health Council called the move "a blow to community participation in health planning and the setting of health priorities," and George Goodman, Chairman of the Committee on Health Priorities for Harlem, stated that Chase's appointment "has caused grave concern in the community."[8]

One of Mr. Chase's principal advocates was the city's budget director, Frederick O'R. Hayes.[9] As budget director, Mr. Hayes could be expected to exert some influence on Mayor Lindsay in the direction of cost-effective birth control programs. Gordon Chase's own qualifications include budgeting, auditing, accounting, personnel, and office services,[10] and he is also a member of the CIA.[11] To some, such qualifications eminently suited him to run the health program for the nation's largest city. To others it is obvious that Gordon Chase (a strong advocate of abortion) was appointed by Mayor Lindsay to run the New York City abortion program efficiently—one that is destroying Black babies at an unbelievable rate (see below).

While President Nixon has strongly defended the unborn's right to exist,[12] his administration policies toward the delivery of family planning programs to the Black poor are highly suspicious and, I think, can be strongly indicted. In a terribly illogical move, he proposed, in his opening remarks to the White House Conference on Hunger, held in 1969, that the Commission on Population Growth and the American Future be established. What this had to do with hunger is still to be determined. However, he made it quite clear that this was aimed at the poor: "In proposing the commission I also declared that it would be the goal of this administration to provide adequate family planning services within the next five years to all those who want them but cannot afford them. There are some five million women in low-income families who are in that situation. But I can report that steps to meet that goal have already been taken within the administration and the program is underway."[13] While efforts in this direction have been gigantic, similar efforts to feed and house the poor are hardly off the ground.

At the same Conference on Hunger, a panel on "Pregnant and Nursing Women and Infants" headed by Dr. Charles U. Lowe of HEW's National Institutes of Health recommended: (1) *mandatory* abortion for any unmarried girl found to be within the first three months of pregnancy and (2) *mandatory* sterilization of any such girl giving birth out of wedlock for a second time.[14] Passage of this proposal was virtually assured when Dr. Alan Guttmacher, President of Planned Parenthood-World Population and a member of the panel, gave it his strong support.[15] However, through the quick action of Mrs. Fannie Lou Hamer, a Black lady from Ruleville, Mississippi, and a strong civil rights leader, the inane proposal was withdrawn.[16] It was never explained what all of this had to do with hunger.

Dr. Guttmacher's strong support of this proposal has been characteristic of Planned Parenthood's approach over the last several years. Generally, Planned Parenthood's policies are made by upper-middle-class white people who have a fetish about controlling the reproductive capacities of others, especially those who are poor and Black. They are joined by many others of even greater wealth: John D. Rockefeller, III; Nelson A. Rockefeller; the Rockefeller Foundation; the Ford Foundation; the Carnegie Foundation; the Commonwealth and Community Funds; the Mott Trust; the Population Council (a Rockefeller baby); the World Bank; the Hugh Moore Fund; General Draper; Robert McNamara; J. Patrick Moynihan; the Kellogg Foundation; Clifford Hardin; Stuart Udall; Robert Packwood; Paul Erhlich; and the Agency for International Development (AID).[17]

In addition to these, the medical profession in the United States has been a potent power in bringing abortions to the poor. While they have sadly neglected the delivery of health care to the underprivileged, they have responded to the "make-a-buck" philosophy of the American system in their push for legal abortion.[18]

Those who openly propose abortion as a solution to almost any problem openly deny that it has racial or genocidal implications. However, recent testimony before the Minnesota State Legislature by a pro-abortionist social worker gives insight into the subtleties of prejudice. She cites the following case as an example of why abortion should be available on demand: A teenage girl came home from a boarding school pregnant. She and her parents were very sensitive people. They spent hours together planning on how the girl would go away to have her baby, place it out for adoption, and then come back home. Until—until she told her parents that the baby's father was Black. On hearing this the parents were horrified. They then chose abortion as the only way out.

This case was cited as an example to our legislators that abortion-on-demand is necessary to make it possible for white folks to kill some unborn children simply because they are Black. This is a form of racism that reaches all the way to the gutter.

Reason for concern? YES! But why this trend? With an ever increasing awareness of the morality of equal rights, why the put-down? Well, it is socially undesirable today to chain the Black man up or to reintroduce slavery. With the persistence of the Black family, the Blacks may one day make our society see where we have been deeply wrong and deeply prejudiced all these years. It will be difficult to handle when that day comes. Extermination is the one way out (?).

EVIDENCE OF COERCION

If family limitation programs were truly grounded in free choice, in voluntary acceptance or rejection, one could have little quarrel with their availability. However, there is mounting evidence to suggest that coercion is being used; that the freedom to say no has been lost.

Chicago's Planned Parenthood Association has been known to sponsor birth control "coffee parties" all over the poorer sections of the city,[19] a policy unheard-of in the suburbs. Dr. Charles Greenlee, a respected Black physician in Pittsburgh, contends that the birth control information and "propaganda" of federally financed family planning programs are carried into the homes of poor Blacks by "home visitors" and public assistance workers, who allegedly coerce indigent Black women into visiting the clinics. Greenlee says that intimidation takes the form of implicit and explicit threats that welfare payments will be cut off if the recipient has more children.[20]

The Senate Finance Committee, chaired by Louisiana Senator Russell B. Long, recently rewrote the Administration's Welfare Reform and Social Security Bill. This Bill, which has now become law, applies pressure on states to step up birth control programs for the poor. While coercion has been denied, those states which fail to set up "adequate" birth control programs for the poor will lose up to two percent of their total federal welfare payments for families with dependent children.[21] If this isn't coercion, I don't know what it is. In New York City, the fear of losing appropriations has led one health center to play a recording in waiting rooms every five to ten minutes urging women to visit the local family planning agency.[22] This is not only coercive, it is genuinely dehumanizing.

The Federal Government has financed a true confessions-type magazine, called *True to Life*, to sell contraception to women. The magazine is produced by the staff and students of the Emory University family planning program. More than 130,000 copies of the first issue have been produced. The project is based on the premise that lower-income women identify with the characters in the confession magazine. *True to Life* has been distributed free to schools, OEO centers, post-partum wards, and similar places; but nowhere does the magazine tell the reader that it is financed by the government.[23]

The South Carolina Legislature recently heard a proposal to begin mandatory sterilization of all welfare mothers after they have had two children out of wedlock. Similar legislation has been spoken of in the Delaware State Legislature; and in New York, judges offer women the choice—either be sterilized or receive no welfare. These actions would acquire a markedly different political cast if "welfare" were defined to include the five- and six-figure federal subsidies paid to wealthy Southern agriculturists.

At Cook County Hospital in Chicago, some physicians attempt to "make sterilization appeal" to women who are in the pains of labor. How coercive can one get?

PREVALENT BLACK ATTITUDES

The prevalent Black attitude toward birth control and abortion is distinctly in opposition. A summary of these attitudes was presented by Charles V. Willie, Ph.D., Chairman of the Department of Sociology at Syracuse University, in his testimony before the Commission on Population Growth and the American Future. He said:

I must state categorically that many people in the Black community are deeply suspicious of any family planning program initiated by whites. You probably have heard about, but not taken seriously, the call by some male-dominated Black militant groups for females to eschew the use of contraceptives because they are pushed in the Black communities as a "method of exterminating Black people."

The genocidal charge is neither "absurd" nor "hollow," as some whites have contended. Neither is it limited to residents of the ghetto, whether they be low-income Black militants or middle-aged Black moderates. Indeed, my studies at white colleges indicate that young educated Blacks fear Black genocide.[24]

This attitude has been expressed in many ways. Not long ago, a family planning center in Cleveland was burned to the ground after militant Blacks labeled its activities "Black genocide."[25] Following this, the antipoverty board of Pittsburgh became the first in the nation to vote down OEO appropriations to continue Planned Parenthood clinics in six of the city's eight poverty neighborhoods. The move resulted from intense pressure applied by Blacks, who again charged genocide.[26]

At the First National Congress on Optimum Population and Environment, held in Chicago, Black psychiatrists and other delegates vigorously dissented. They saw such schemes as genocidal. Dr. Alyce Gullattee, staff psychiatrist at St. Elizabeth's Hospital in Washington, D.C., after walking out, said: "I think that whites are into a psychological state of denial of their own fears and anxieties about their annihilation. Therefore, what they are talking about represents the survival of all peoples but at the expense of certain people, and those certain people just happen to be Black people. So we perceive it as a genocidal attempt."[27]

In writing about this incident, Carl Rowan, the well-known Black syndicated columnist and former ambassador to Finland, said:

However irrational these fears of trickery and worries about genocide may seem, they are real in many minds. We must take care not to intensify them by sending bureaucrats into Black neighborhoods to push birth control, or wealthy white "do-gooders" into impoverished ghettos to beat the drums for family planning.

The challenge is to illustrate every day that rats, roaches and hunger pains are viewed by all society as more of a menace than an accidental pregnancy.[28]

At the National Conference on the Status of Health in the Black Community, held in Nashville, Tennessee, December 11, 1971, and sponsored by Mehary Medical College, Howard University School of Medicine, the National Dental and Medical Associations and the Congressional Black Caucus, it was unanimously voted to condemn family planning programs and urge better maternal and child health care.[29]

Many studies of Black attitudes reflect the strong support of the above actions. In a study conducted by the Bowman Gray Medical School on poverty-level Blacks, 79% of 776 poverty-level Black females, 86% of 500 of their sex partners, and 70% of 215 low-middle-income Black females were found to be "not in favor of abortions under any circumstances."[30] Similarly, when 990 urban Black females were studied, 77% were found to be opposed to abortion under any circumstances, and this opposition was found to be manifest in their actions of actually carrying their children to term.[31] When Black males under 30 were studied, 88% of them were found to be in opposition to abortion as a means of birth control.[32]

THE REALITY OF BLACK GENOCIDE

Although Blacks are strongly opposed to various family planning programs and especially to abortion, there is incontrovertible evidence that they are being eliminated against their wishes. While birth rates have dropped for nearly every sector of the United States population over the last decade, births to poor women dropped by 32 per thousand, compared with a drop of 17 fewer per thousand among the rest. For Black poor women, the fall was even greater; they produced 49 fewer babies per thousand.[33] Government-sponsored birth control clinics, supported strongly by men and organizations with money and power, are slowly achieving their aims.

The evidence is even more striking when one reviews the abortion experience of New York City. During the first 15 months' experience with abortion in New York City, *43.4%* of all abortions performed on New York City residents were performed on "non-whites" (90% of whom are Black).[34] This is put into even more tragic perspective when one realizes that only *18.1%* of New York City residents are "non-white" (90% of whom are Black).[35]

To make the point clearer, Bellevue Hospital, a large metropolitan hospital whose patients are mostly Black, is now aborting 2.3 babies for every live birth.[36] And this hospital has not filed an official report to the Health Services Administration since the enactment of the New York law, in July 1970.[37]

Black women are being aborted at a rate 2.5 times greater than any other ethnic group in New York City. WHY? They are not being given the freedom to say no! They are being coerced into destroying their children! THIS MUST COME TO AN IMMEDIATE HALT! Then, an investigation should be carried out, and those responsible should be brought to trial for one of the most ghastly crimes of this century.

AN UNTRIED APPROACH TO POVERTY

Blacks have every right to be offended by a policy that tries to solve the dilemmas of poverty and swelling relief roles by urging Blacks to have fewer children. President Johnson, in his March 16, 1964, message on poverty to Congress, said: "... I have called for a national war on poverty. Our objective: Total Victory." The jobs, decent housing, healthy environment, adequate food, clean water and sanitation and improved education that haven't been provided as part of this "total victory" show that the "war on poverty" has been a dismal failure.

It has been amply demonstrated that discrimination against Blacks, Indians, Latin Americans and Puerto Ricans has reduced their employment opportunities. But discrimination does more than that. It instills in minority groups a hopelessness that inhibits ambition and limits educational advance.

What does poverty mean to those who endure it? It means a daily struggle to secure the necessities for even a meager existence. It means that the abundance, the comforts, the opportunities they see all around them are beyond their grasp. Worst of all, it means hopelessness for the young. Anyone who feels that family limitation, especially abortion, will alleviate these problems is sadly mistaken.

Poverty prevents man from realizing his humanity to the fullest degree. Abortion only knocks him down another step. One can only help the poor effectively to rise above their subhuman condition by attacking the structures of their impoverishment from which the rich profit, even if they do not realize it or do not desire it. One can only serve them when one has judged and eliminated that natural feeling of superiority which causes people to use other people for their affluence and profit.

It is impossible to hoist the poor out of their state of malnourishment if one refuses to touch in any way the living standard of the rich, or the economic system which, by itself, works for increasing impoverishment of the poor.

Our response must be:

1. We must develop a concrete program to get at the root causes of poverty. Any effective response demanded of us by the poverty of others implies on our part the acceptance of a certain impoverishment of our own.

2. We must help the poor eliminate their subhuman condition by providing them with the means to vanquish this poverty. This implies education, instruction, planning, the training of technicians and teams. This must be based in a conscientious loyalty and dedication to truth and justice at all costs.

3. We must recognize the necessity to fight the mechanisms and structures that tend to consolidate and even worsen the impoverishment of the poor.

The recognition of the mechanism by which the rich exploit the poor; the denunciation of everything that encourages misery and prevents millions of human beings from receiving the instruction, dignity, welfare and freedom to which a man is entitled; and, lastly, the fight against the worship of money—all this is our duty, who belong to a world of security and affluence and so are involved in the abuses of the system.

The effective commitment to the fight against the misery and subhuman condition of the poor demands that we revise our outlook on things, that we criticize clearly and courageously many ideas to which we are accustomed, and that we accept beforehand a revision of the privileged situation we enjoy.

This all takes a great deal of courage, and it may be for this reason that it has never been tried before, anywhere in the world. But since abortion, poverty and Black genocide are hardly gifts to the poor, the time to begin is now!

CONCLUSION

Mrs. Grace Olivarez, Vice-Chairman of the Commission on Population Growth and the American Future, in a dissenting statement on abortion, expressed my views completely:

I am not impressed nor persuaded by those who express concern for the low-income woman who may find herself carrying an unplanned pregnancy and for the future of the unplanned child who may be deprived of the benefits of a full life as a result of the parents' poverty, because the fact remains that in this affluent nation of ours, pregnant cattle and horses receive better health care than pregnant poor women.[38]

Poverty and Black genocide are realities in the United States. The introduction of abortion has poignantly brought this into clear perspective. IT MUST NOT BE ALLOWED TO GO FURTHER!

If we are truly a nation who speak of civil human rights, then we must prove that we carry no prejudices. The abortion issue, with its gnawing ability to make one honest, may very well be the ultimate test. If we can openly admit our prejudice, then perhaps we can begin to move forward. If we cannot, then we will move one step further down into the valley of death.

The blood-and-guts problem is our lack of compassion and our lack of concern. More and more, women are being seen as wombs to be deactivated rather than human beings with lives to be fulfilled. Only when this impoverishment is eliminated can we fully expect to enter the new frontier.

REFERENCES

1. D. Gregory, "My Answer to Genocide," *Ebony*, Oct. 1971.
2. Ibid.
3. Ibid.
4. *The Choice: The Issue of Black Survival in America* (New York: G. P. Putnam's Sons, 1971).
5. *Congressional Record*, S7155-6, May 3, 1972.
6. Ibid.
7. "Federal Abortion Law Urged by Lindsay," *New York Times*, March 7, 1972.
8. *New York Times*, Dec. 16, 1969.
9. Ibid.
10. *New York Times*, Dec. 16, 1969.
11. Julius Mader, *Who's Who in the CIA* (Berlin: Julius Mader, 1968), p. 98.
12. "Nixon Abortion Statement," *New York Times*, Sunday, April 4, 1971.
13. Yette, op. cit., pp. 109-110.
14. Ibid., p. 112.
15. Ibid.
16. Ibid., p. 113.
17. S. Weissman, "Why the Population Bomb Is a Rockefeller Baby," *Ramparts*, May 1970.

18. J. Eisenberg, "The Mad Scramble for Abortion Money," *Med. Econ.,* Jan. 4, 1971.
19. *America,* Nov. 6, 1965, p. 511.
20. R. Z. Hallow, "The Blacks Cry Genocide," *The Nation,* April 28, 1969, p. 535.
21. *New York Times,* June 7, 1972.
22. J. Short, Nassau County Social Welfare Department: Personal communication.
23. *National Catholic Reporter,* June 23, 1972, p. 2.
24. "Syracuse Sociologist Gives Black Population Viewpoint"; Statement presented by Charles V. Willie, Ph.D., at the hearings of the Commission on Population Growth and the American Future, *Ob. Gyn. News,* June 1, 1971, p. 26.
25. Hallow, op. cit.
26. Ibid.
27. Yette, op. cit., p. 246.
28. "Does Population Control = Zero Black Children?" Statement by Naomi Gray at the hearings of the Commission on Population Growth and the American Future, *Ob. Gyn. News,* June 1, 1971, p. 32.
29. W. Greenberg, "Blacks Condemn Family Planning"; Special to the *Washington Post,* Dec. 12, 1971.
30. C. E. Vincent, C. A. Haney, and C. N. Cochrane, "Abortion Attitudes in Poverty-Level Blacks," *Semin. Psychiat,* 1970, pp. 309-317.
31. R. Michielutte, C. A. Haney, C. E. Vincent, and C. N. Cochrane, "Outcome of Illegitimate Conceptions in a Black Population," *Obstet. Gynec.,* 38:583-588, Oct. 1971.
32. "Family Planning Physicians Answer Abortion Critics," *American Medical News,* April 9, 1971, p. 9.
33. "Why the Poor Are Fewer," *Newsweek,* March 13, 1972.
34. G. Chase, *Complications Rate Drops by More than 50% for the Last Six Months; Proportion of Early Abortions Increases; Death Rate Declines, While 278,122 Legal Abortions Performed in NYC in First 18 Months of Law;* News release, Health Services Administration, City of New York, February 29, 1972.
35. *The New York Times Encyclopedia Almanac, 1970,* ed. Seymour Kurtz (New York: The New York Times), p. 305.
36. G. W. Douglas, "Complications of Saline Abortions"; Talk presented at Cook County Hospital, Chicago, Illinois, Dec. 16, 1971.
37. *Bulletin on Abortion Program,* Health Services Administration, New York City, March 1972.
38. Separate Statement of Grace Olivarez, "Childrearing and Childbearing," *Population and the American Future: The Report of the Commission on Population Growth and the American Future, Part II,* March 18, 1972.

· 14 ·

PRIVATE INDIVIDUAL
VS.
GLOBAL VILLAGE

Marshall McLuhan

**CHICAGO (Reuter): 11-year-old Chicago girl
receives abortion in N. Y. (July 21, 1972)**

"Not with a bang, but a whimper"
—T. S. Eliot

One way to put the question of abortion in perspective is to look at our Western assumptions concerning man. In his *Pentagon of Power,* Lewis Mumford has pointed to individual man as "his own supreme artefact." Individuality and private identity have not been the typical concerns of non-Western peoples. It may be that, under conditions of electronic culture, Western man is ceasing to have a separate, substantial psyche or a private personal existence. The *figure* of the Western individual seen against the new *ground* of the all-inclusive electronic information environment—this figure may be undergoing modification or even abolition. Abortion as a tactic for tailoring populations seems to assume this new electronic ground of the awareness of world resources and world population problems. This new urgent concern with relating the unborn infant to the newly born global village is a confrontation which seems to inspire some, at least, of the abortion discussion. There seems to be a new assumption

245

that the good of the private individual cannot be put in the balance with the good of the global village. Electrically, men are now so much closer together that we can no longer admit that there is anything that is of merely private concern.

The great popularity of the idea of "For Whom the Bell Tolls" occurred in the radio age. John Donne's admonition not to ask for whom the bell tolls, since "it tolls for thee," was in Hemingway a kind of literary experience which has since become entirely existential through TV. The growing idea of the totality of man and the inclusive consciousness has increasingly belittled the individual to the point of insignificance. If all people have become interfused with one another in a single tribal family, under conditions of the instantaneous-information environment, then the mere individual no longer looms as a significant entity. Electrically, we begin to think of mankind as the individual and of the private person as of a merely historical memory. That is one aspect of the figure-ground of group and person relationship under electric conditions. It may be that the subject of abortion has become a kind of test case for the even greater issue of individual man in relation to society. Viewed atomistically, the individual man presents a very small case indeed, vis-à-vis society. In the same way, the developing foetus or embryo appears to present a very small case compared to the individuality and rights of the mother. Likewise, if the rights of the individual are to be measured quantitatively against the needs and pressures of society, there can be no serious disagreement. The individual must go. If the good, private or corporate, is to be measured quantitatively, the lesser must always yield to the greater. (In Christianity at least, there is no question of quantity. Human rights are grounded in a divine source which overcomes all mere quantitative differences.)

Since all current secular discussion of abortion takes place on quantitative assumptions relating to human convenience, there can be no question that the arguments in favor of abortion apply with equal validity to the status of all other living beings. The same assumptions of more or less convenience, or inconvenience, must apply to the decisions about continuing or suppressing the existence of any members or groups of all human or nonhuman populations.

The quantitative argument, when applied to the foetus as part of the mother's individuality, points to the fact that the unborn have no individuality and therefore do not present a moral problem for the abortionist. At another level, there is the existential argument that it is consciousness itself that is the mark of the human condition—that which is not conscious is not human, and therefore the unborn child again presents no problem to the abortionist. *But the same argument applies to individuals and groups that might be considered to be characteristically of a very low level of consciousness.* Thus, the great proportion of mankind has always seemed to lead a somnambulistic kind of life, and to deal with such groups as if they were types of an irresponsible foetus, would be entirely justified according to the current and popular existential philosophy.

In figure-ground terms, one can look at the entire drive toward abortion-as-social-planning in the light of other mass tendencies of our time. It would be a mistake to think of abortion as exceptional or unconventional behavior on our part. Siegfried Giedion devoted a large study *(Mechanization Takes Command,* Oxford University Press) to the twentieth-century mechanization of all the organic functions, whether of agriculture, bread-making, or meat-packing. Buchenwald and Auschwitz are literal applications and extensions of the techniques and procedures of the most highly developed arts of our twentieth-century world. Giedion's theme is that it is difficult to live in a totally mechanized way without having some of these methods invade the world of spiritual values. It is not surprising that the anti-life methods of mechanical industry and of the work patterns celebrated in Charlie Chaplin's *Modern Times* should have intruded upon the worlds of education and procreation.

When the mechanization of death occurs on a vast scale, the minds of civilized people are numbed. Decent and well-meaning people, acting as if in a corporate somnambulism, are engaged today in repeating in abortion centers the patterns of life-processing which worked so well in meat-packing and death camps. The abortion centers are impelled by "humane automatism" to resonate and to re-enact patterns of death and indignity seen and felt in quite different areas of commercial activity. One precedent begets another by echo of remorseless logic and quantified statistical reasoning. If meat-packing and death camps can resonate in a way that makes abortion centers a familiar and acceptable pattern, the abortion centers themselves constitute a further precedent for the repetition of further violence to human dignity and compassion.

To take a stand, therefore, about abortion as a moral issue is also to take a stand against the principal currents and trends which we have inherited from nineteenth-century industry. Our motor highways, for example, are centers of programmed mayhem, set at statistical levels of psychic tolerance. As much as any abortion mill, our schools are programmed as centers of psychic mayhem for the imposing of nineteenth-century patterns on twentieth-century living.

It is, however, precisely the massive forms and patterns of nineteenth-century industry which are called in question by the new electric technology of the twentieth century. Whereas mechanized industrial processes have been based on hardware and the specialism both of production and managerial functions, the information environment of the electric age suddenly favors software as against hardware, and design as against quantity in living style. Likewise, it favors in work and life styles, the human scale and personal involvement as opposed to quantitative standards of measurement and value. The plight of Howard Hughes as a man caught between these two worlds, as a man possessing the hardware and the quantity but seeking privacy and personal significance—his plight besets all aware people in our time, when we are caught between industrial fragmentation and electric wholeness. The outlook and the methods of the abortionists are borrowed from the preceding industrial age where significance was to be found in efficiency and in quantity. It is the decline of the human significance resulting from industrial goals and methods that now confronts both the exponents and the victims of abortion. Caught between the industrial quantitative values and the new life values of the electric age, many people are unable to perceive why they feel so unhappy about abortions while at the same time thinking that it is a plausible and enlightened program for the relief of man's congested estate.

As Peter Kelvin has said: "In principle we may say that 'facts speak for themselves'; in practice they do so only when accompanied by a chorus of approval."

·15·

ABORTION WITHOUT ETHICS

Charles Carroll

Six years ago when I became involved in the abortion controversy, I could not have dreamed that it would assume the proportions which it has. Nor could I have foreseen the implications that the same controversy would have for the life scientist's application of his newly won knowledge.

When asked by a physician friend where I stood—shortly after my return from Berlin after a year's study in suicide prevention—I refused to commit myself until I had some knowledge of the proposal presented to the California legislature.

The proposal would have permitted abortion for any one of five conditions: threat to the physical or mental health of the mother, rape, incest, and potential deformity of the fetus.

The proposal appeared to be motivated by the most humane considerations and genuine charitable concern. Many people with impeccable credentials, among them leaders of the Christian community, announced their support of the measure. A clergyman who was one of the most outspoken advocates of "reform" issued invitations to a "Service of Witness" sponsored by the California Council of Churches at a church near the capitol in the spring of 1967.

Still something within me said, "Wait." Something within me asked, "What precedents are we destroying? What precedents are we establishing? Will our children and children's children find the decisions which we are now making irreversible? Are we not dividing humanity, as we have so many times before, into 'human' and 'subhuman'? Had not the Black man been legally designated as a half-man shortly after the founding of the republic? Had the Chicano and Latino not been similarly treated even if they had not been similarly designated? Had the Orientals in our midst not been similarly degraded and dehumanized by the Exclusion Acts which limited their immigration to our country while encouraging that of Europeans? What people had coined the phrase, 'The only good Indian is a dead Indian'? Who, in Viet Nam had coined the phrase, 'The only good Dink is a dead Dink'?"

A conversation which I had had with a German psychiatrist came to mind. A consultant to the American Military Tribunal at Nuremberg at the time of the Nazi Doctors' Trials *(U.S.* v. *Brandt, et al.),* she and I had spent many hours one summer night in 1947 discussing the war years. I had asked, "How did it happen? How can one so benumb another's conscience that he can kill without remorse, even with pride in having done his duty?"

Perceptive as she was and had been trained to be, she may have anticipated what was and would remain—for me—the fundamental theological problem of my life, "How? Auschwitz?"

Her answer came in carefully measured tones. "You need only take those principles a people hold most dear and distort them *just enough.* Take 'Fatherland,' 'Kultur,' 'Duty.' Then provide these cherished symbols a mortal enemy: in this case, 'the' Jew.

" 'Fatherland' represents a place of residence, home and family; 'Kultur,' the language and values of the nation which give its life coherence and meaning; and 'Duty,' those responsibilities which each citizen must assume if he is to enjoy his rights as citizen of such a country with such ideals. Once these are attacked, the group, as the individual in the group, feels attacked. Those who attack become 'they.' Those who are attacked become 'we.' And 'we,' if we are to eliminate 'them,' must first reduce 'them' to subhuman status. Then we can justify our liquidation of them. Then and only then can we continue to live with ourselves."

Whatever books a man may read or not read; whatever experiences he may have or not have; whatever faith he may proclaim or deny, few men could forget such an exchange at such a time in our recent history. The gradualism by which man moves and can be moved towards a denigration of life (other than his own) is too evident to be refuted.

It was at this point—in recalling this conversation—that I began to realize that I, too, was susceptible to this same gradualism that is so erosive of every human value. I, too, had to be at one with myself. But I, too, wanted to be one of the group. I, too, found it hard to discriminate between love and sentiment; freedom and license; progress and welfare; knowledge and wisdom; cult and culture.

LOVE AND SENTIMENT

Surely, incest seemed good and sufficient cause to "terminate a pregnancy." But then, when would the two parties to an incestuous relationship seek abortion on that ground—at risk of the attendant publicity?

Rape seemed a reasonable ground. But then why was there no discrimination between statutory and criminal rape? Why was there no mention of the simple and obvious fact that immediate medical treatment could free the rape victim of fear of pregnancy? Why did no one rise to question the validity of this claim when presented weeks—if not months—later in order to gain an abortion?

Why had I been so naive? Why had I not recognized the use of incest and rape as reasons for abortion—more because of their emotional value in debate than from real concern for the woman?

Potential deformity seemed such a charitable reason. Still, several questions forced themselves upon me, gnawed at me, and would not let me go. Would acceptance of this reason lead to medicine's abandonment of its attempts to understand, treat and correct intra-uterine diseases and abnormalities? What about the rubella vaccine? If potential deformity were to be allowed as just cause for an abortion, what were we saying to *and* about—the retarded? the totally disabled victim of automobile or industrial accident? the totally disabled veteran of our wars? the incurable (whether mentally or physically ill)? and, finally, the senile and the aged? They, too, could be regarded as "burdens" on society, the welfare budget and hospital-bed resources.

Threat to the physical health of the mother seemed, of all reasons, the most valid—until I reflected upon the enormous advances in medicine, the minimal risk that pregnancy now poses, and the more than adequate provision made by the law of most states to allow the physician to terminate the pregnancy (another euphemism now employed to avoid use of the word "abortion") if, in those increasingly rare instances, he confronted the ugly choice of saving one life rather than losing two.

Threat to the mental health of the mother seemed hardly less valid—until I asked myself how this would be defined, by whom the appraisal would be made, how long a period of time would be required for the appraisal, what psychiatric indications would be considered valid, and then reflected upon the easy, tempting but temporary answer which abortion might provide while compounding the patient's problems *and* the difficult, time-consuming and permanent answer which compassionate care and competent therapy rather than abortion would provide.

It was in the midst of these thoughts that I first became conscious of the appeal made to my emotions by these proposals. And the way in which the truth of love was being equated with shallow sentimentality and, in turn, being used to subvert the love of truth.

FREEDOM AND LICENSE

Then, I began to see how the rhetoric of the abortionists had confused freedom with license; how those who insisted that women have sovereignty or dominion over their own bodies would—by implication—argue that suicide is a constitutional right; so, too, is euthanasia; and the unborn child within them, their property, and thus subject to their whims, whether suicidal or homicidal. No less interesting was the abortionist's insistence that the man—who could be charged, tried, sentenced, fined and/or imprisoned when found guilty of (1) statutory rape, (2) criminal rape, (3) delinquency in alimony or child support payments, even if denied visitation rights with his children; or in (4) a paternity action—had *no* rights in the abortion decision even when he was the woman's husband *and* the child's father. Indeed, once a "therapeutic" abortion statute was passed by the California legislature, the California Supreme Court in the case of *O'Beirne* v. *O'Beirne* so decided, denying a hearing to the petitioner-father by a five to two vote. This threat to the husband-wife relationship (which would deny the husband, like the unborn, any rights whatsoever) has now been joined by another; this, to the parent-child relationship. Now many abortionists insist that pregnant, unwed minors be "emancipated" from parental control.

PROGRESS AND WELFARE

If these "advances" are to be equated with "progress," then we had best ask what progress means when motherhood is robbed of its dignity; parenthood, of its sense of privilege; and family life, of any meaningful hope for the future—at a time when the prospect for *absolute* separation of sexual enjoyment from sexual reproduction with the fabrication of "test tube babies" and "retort man"[1] looms as a distinct *probability.*

How real this prospect is becomes clear in many recent writings.[2] How intimately it is linked to the abortion controversy becomes incontrovertible in reading *The Biological Time Bomb* by Gordon Rattray Taylor. There, in discussing the future of genetic "engineering" and the mistakes which are bound to occur, he writes: "The necessity of destroying the defective embryos, which constitutes abortion under present law in many countries, will no doubt arouse resistance. Those countries which do not consider destruction of the embryo to be abortion until after the fifth month of pregnancy, or some other stated period, will then be at an advantage."[3] These words immediately precede his sub-chapter on "The Spectre of Gene Warfare."

KNOWLEDGE AND WISDOM

If wisdom is to be distinguished from knowledge, then women particularly had best ask themselves what these developments mean, as I have asked and continue to ask what they mean for us all. Men and women, we have been motivated by fear of a population explosion to accept changes in our laws and our thinking. And unfortunately what we make legal we tend to make moral. Still more unfortunately, we have been induced to accept unsubstantiable statistics; some clothed in academic robes; some with the prestige of government agencies.

When the abortion debate began, no one really knew how many "criminal" or "illegal" abortions were committed in this country every year. Certainly they were not reported; and certainly many of the deaths which were caused by them were attributed to other "complications" and other reasons. No one, even now, knows how many "legal" abortions are performed or how many deaths can be attributed to them. Given the emphasis upon new "techniques" and the increasing speed with which they can be done, many of the "clinics" which have been established to meet the demand doubtlessly allow many to go unreported for what to them are good and sufficient reasons. The prestigious United States Bureau of the Census, with all the computers and computer scientists available to it, admitted in August 1970 that its 1967 forecast of the American population in the year 2000 may well have been an *over*estimate of

100,000,000.[4] If statistics are to be used to sway us in making our moral and ethical decisions, then we had best make sure of them rather than allow ourselves to be seduced and entrapped by them.

Still more important, however, are the consequences of an all too glib acceptance of these fears and statistics. When fear of a "genetic apocalypse" is added to those already created; when "Parenthood: Right or Privilege?" can be openly discussed in scientific journals;[5] when the physician can write unreservedly and unashamedly of "Our Role in the Generation, Modification and Termination of Life"[6] assuming that "they" who are to be "generated," "modified" and "terminated" play, if any, at best a secondary role; when a leading picture magazine offers its multi-million readership to a scientific journalist to write that "Compassion Has Sacrificed Man's Quality";[7] when scientists talk openly of "enforced contraception," "conception license," "cleansing the gene pool," "improving the gene pool," "negative eugenics" and "positive eugenics" (all of which simply means that some men and women will be denied the right to reproduce while others will be required to "participate" in the process whether through contribution to "sperm banks," artificial insemination, artificial inovulation or other ways including cloning, the asexual reproduction of an exact genetic type), then we would have to suffer from that blindness that glories in being blind if we were *not* to see the move from the voluntary to the mandatory in all this; if we were *not* to realize that abortion and sterilization on demand of the individual can easily become abortion and sterilization on demand of the state. Society need not trouble to deprive its citizens of rights which the individuals within society are all too willing to forfeit. Let us hope it is not yet too late to ask: "Who is to make policy? Who is to draft the laws necessary to its implementation? Who is to enact them? Who is to enforce them?"

At this point, I began to ask, "If laws are sought to allow destruction of defective embryos in the laboratory, what then should prevent destruction (or conception) of embryos that are presumed to be defective (whatever that may mean) in the womb?" Then I remembered the proposal drafted by Professor Clauberg for Gestapo Chief Heinrich Himmler on May 30, 1942. I read my notes of the trial again. Clearly *quantity and quality* control were very much in mind. The proposal read:

the possibility must be provided—

a. for most intensive treatment of women hitherto sterile but desirous of child-bearing. . . .

b. to evaluate the method of sterilization without operation (bloodless steril-ization) on women unworthy of propagation.[8]

The records of that trial proved time and again who were thought "unworthy of propagation" in the Third Reich and who were encour-aged time and again, in and out of marriage, to be "desirous of child-bearing" in order that the Fatherland have an ample supply of sol-diers and workers, and the "demographic problem" be resolved in Germany's favor. Eugenics had not alone "negative" and "positive" overtones. It had political, social, economic *and* racial implications. It was not mere coincidence that William L. Shirer, on the prefatory page of *The Rise and Fall of the Third Reich,* chose to quote the words of George Santayana: "Those who do not remember the past are condemned to relive it."

The greatest tragedy—beyond the wanton destruction of life and the anesthetization of a nation's conscience—that these develop-ments, past and present, imply is the present-day "liberated" wom-an's enslavement of herself in abdicating her absolute power in the ongoing process of creation (compared to which man's has always been relative) and, by default, becoming herself a "love machine" (whatever mechanized love may mean). Yet this is where she and he to whom we so long referred as "Man" are headed.

As the years have passed and the relationship of the abortion issue to all other issues in the field of the life sciences has become clear, it might not be inappropriate to conjecture whether the penis envy of the woman described by Freud has not given way to the womb envy of the man to the point that the geneticist, in his eagerness to fabri-cate man and improve the race and the "quality of life," could well eliminate the need of woman altogether.

"Man," as Reinhold Niebuhr stated in *The Nature and Destiny of Man,* "has always been his most vexing problem."[9] Man still does not know who he is or what he wants to be.

We have demeaned our brothers. We have demeaned ourselves. At times, it would appear that we have a death wish. We are so bent on reducing ourselves—to things.

A Nobel Laureate of my acquaintance, in discussing the popula-tion "explosion" and the needs for controls, spoke of the problem as one "not of sentiment but mathematics."

Jacques Monod, the French Nobel Laureate, in his recent work

Chance and Necessity,[10] describes man as little more than a molecular system. Dismissing Jew and Greek, Christian and Marxist as animists, he calls for an end to the value systems that have guided men through their recorded history and for establishment of one, based on scientific evidence, by scientists—apparently without consultation with any of their colleagues in any other discipline.

This, in a far less scholarly, far less subtle way, the California Medical Association did in an editorial which appeared in its official journal, *California Medicine,* in September 1970. Openly admitting what many of its most prominent members had carefully concealed in the course of the abortion debate, it affirmed "the scientific fact, which everyone really knows, that human life begins at conception and is continuous whether intra- or extra-uterine until death." Then, it insisted that "no other discipline" (than the life sciences, obviously) "has the knowledge of human nature, human behavior, health and disease, and of what is involved in physical and mental well-being."[11] The word "spiritual" was conspicuously absent.

Nothing made the real issues clearer to me than that editorial. Church and synagogue had not made them clear. Bench and bar had not made them clear. The social "sciences" had not made them clear. The chastening of the physical sciences that had come with the discovery of atomic energy and the bombing of Hiroshima and Nagasaki had not made them clear. Even the written record of the gnawing afterthoughts of Max Planck, Otto Hahn, Albert Einstein, J. Robert Oppenheimer, Max Born and Harold Urey had not made them clear.

The life scientists while they, like Konrad Lorenz, pleaded for "the virtue of humility" upon the part of others, proudly proclaimed the uniqueness of their insights, the priority of their knowledge, and the superiority of their method to that of any other disciplines. Corrupted by their newly won power, they became models of arrogance.

Still Lorenz, in writing that "the functions of reason and moral responsibility . . . first came into the world with man,"[12] admits that "the origin of life is still the most puzzling of all natural phenomena,"[13] and Lederberg, in stating that "there is no gene that can ensure the development of a child's brain without reference to tender care and inspired teaching,"[14] retreats from an absolute biological determinism of man, and thus of human history.

For all their brilliance as zoologist and geneticist, they share the same fate as all great thinkers who, at one time or other in their reflections, are tempted to see man from one perspective alone. Plato was right in his view that man is a political animal; Aristotle, in his claim that man is a social animal; Hobbes, in his assertion that man formed and accepted the authority of the state because of his fear of a "violent death"; Darwin, in his insistence that man is immanent in nature; Marx, in his contention that man and human history are fashioned by economic forces; Freud, in his argument that man is propelled by primordial sexual drives; and Jung, in his opinion that man is pulled forward, motivated by a desire to find meaning and purpose in life. All were right. All were wrong. They were right in assuming that what they believed to be a determinant of human conduct did indeed determine human conduct. They were wrong in assuming that what they believed to be a determinant of human conduct *alone* determined human conduct.

Theology was once called "the queen of the sciences." Today, Lorenz calls medicine the "queen of the applied sciences."[15] Be that as it may, humility would be becoming to us all. Galileo was right in emphasizing the place of the earth in the universe. Darwin was right in emphasizing man's immanence in nature. But man is also transcendent over nature. And that transcendence can be used for good or evil, as the masters of Auschwitz demonstrated on the one hand; and Father Maximilian Kolbe, who volunteered to take the place of a father of five assigned to the ovens of Auschwitz, demonstrated on the other.

If *reason* and *moral reponsibility* first came into the world with man, as Lorenz claims, then evil is a reality against which man must contend, and no study on the natural history of aggression can be justly entitled *So-Called Evil,* as Lorenz chose to label his work in German—particularly when its author, in spite of his many allusions to the follies and nobilities of man, *never once* mentioned Hitler, Auschwitz or Lidice in either the German or the quite different version to appear in English translation.

The wise man accepts two simple truths. We are not totally subjective or totally objective. We are not totally bound or totally free. With Ian Ramsey, the late Bishop of Durham, England, "I do not know what a 'purely subjective' experience is—all experience is *of* something."[16] With Langdon Gilkey, the Chicago theologian, I find that "all thought is 'theory laden.' "[17] As with the organist, there are so many registers, so many manuals, so many pedals available to each and every one of us. But within the limits imposed upon us by the organ (or to use another analogy, the living organism) which is at the disposal of each and every one of us, we are free and we have power. And while power when exercised is never neutral, we exercise that power for better or for worse, by virtue of our reason, according to our sense of moral responsibility, whether that sense springs from "right reason," "revealed truth," the "collective unconscious" or the existentialism of Camus.

The wise man faces the fact that being precedes thought and, examining Descartes' popularly accepted dictum, *Cogito, ergo sum,* he wonders if the truth is not more likely reflected in *Sum, ergo cogito,* or better yet in *Sum, ergo cogito, ergo aestimo*—"I am, I think, I value." [18] Surely, being precedes thought; and being and thought precede value.

When Theodosius Dobzhansky, the geneticist, contends that "what is established as a biological adaptation is the ability to 'ethicize,' not the nature or the content of the ethical tenets,"[19] he denies neither man's immanence in nature nor his transcendence over nature.

In this, he would appear to claim, like Johann Georg Hamann, the philosopher, that "knowledge of self and knowledge of the world are inseparable,"[20] and like Langdon Gilkey, the theologian, that "most books of the science of man, in their 'scientific' sections, portray man as determined by ... forces that determine his behavior ... and that of his group, and that make his ideals epiphenomenal at best. But in their 'prophetic' sections at the ends of their books, when they discuss human destiny and the possible uses scientific knowledge can offer toward the eradication of human evil and the improvement of the human situation, these same authors tend to see man as rationally motivated by their own liberal ideals. . . ."[21] Unfortunately, as Gilkey observes, "Few books of evolutionary or social science put these two models of man together."[22]

Admittedly, they may be put together in many ways. The sense of moral responsibility may issue from the "divine law" of Heraclitus, the "general law" of Aristotle,[23] the "right reason" of Cicero,[24] the "natural law" of St. Thomas Aquinas;[25] the "revealed truth" of the Old Testament (the Torah) and the New Testament (the new Law implicit in the new commandment that "you love one another, as I have loved you" [St. John 15:12b]); the "collective unconscious" of Carl Jung (which led Joseph Campbell to his monumental four-volume work on *The Masks of God,* its theses of cultural diffusionism as opposed to cultural parallelism, and may well account for German scholars' current interest in the compilation of a Sumerian-Akkadian dictionary, as we may well be spiritually Sumerians) or the existentialism of Albert Camus. As John Macquarrie, Lady Margaret Professor of Philosophy at Oxford, has said: "One may think of Albert Camus, who visualized man's position to be as hopeless and absurd as that of the mythical Sisyphus, rolling a great stone up a slope over and over again, only to see it crashing back down. Yet Camus saw this godless situation as a challenge to greater moral effort."[26] Indeed, it may be in the rediscovery of our moral obligation to one another that we rediscover our common humanity.

Martin Golding, professor of philosophy at Columbia University, in relating the absence of moral concern toward the unborn to discussion of a genetic utopia, put it succinctly: "If someone finds it difficult to think of having an obligation towards his unborn child, then he should find it difficult to think of having an obligation toward a community of humans (humanoids?) fifty generations hence." And with him, "I must confess to finding it odd when the same people who put biological engineering for the future on ethical grounds also defend abortion of a foetus on the ground that we have no obligation in respect of an unborn child."[27]

The moment men become concerned for the *quantity of life,* it is only natural that they would become concerned for the *quality of life.* That is why population control, euthanasia and genetic engineering (whether the emphasis falls on "negative" or "positive" eugenics) cannot and will not be divorced from one another.

Whenever a society begins to count the number of those to be fed on one hand and the amount of food available to feed them on the other, a greater value is bound to be placed on some lives; a lesser value, on others; the gradation of humanity begins; and each individual's claim to membership in the *humanum* becomes subject to review.

Reading my records of the doctors' trials, I recalled the "Professional Order for the German Physicians" of November 5, 1937. It read: "The physician is called upon to serve the health of the individual and the German people, and all German physicians are called upon to work for the welfare of the people of the Reich, for the maintenance and improvement of the health, heredity and race of the German people."[28]

Innocent in appearance, seemingly innocuous in its language, that order had been preceded as early as 1933 by the disappearance of any real canon of ethical rules for the medical profession and the gradual supplantation of an oath of loyalty to the Weimar Constitution by one of sole loyalty to the Fuehrer.[29] The explanation of official motivation for state intervention was given as "love for our neighbor and care for the future generations."[30]

Then it all came back to me: the letter of SS Colonel Brack to Heinrich Himmler on June 23, 1942, when the real aims of German demographic (quantitative) and eugenic (qualitative) policy were revealed. "Among 10 millions of Jews in Europe," he wrote, "there are, I figure, at least 2-3 millions of men and women who are fit enough to work. Considering the extraordinary difficulties the labor problem presents us with, I hold the view that those 2-3 millions should be carefully selected and preserved. This can, however, only be done if at the same time they are rendered incapable to propagate."[31] (To you who think that love is the question and the answer, think on these things!)

Then, I remembered still another letter, that of Gund, deputy Gauleiter of Lower Austria, to Himmler, of August 24, 1942, in which the aims became more specific, swifter implementation was urged and secrecy in "research" advised. "Since the prevention of reproduction by the congenitally unfit and racially inferior belongs to the duties of our National Socialist racial and demographic policy ... castration and sterilization are not sufficient in themselves," he contended, "to meet expectations."

Then he continued: "It is quite clear that such research must be handled as a nationally important secret matter of the most dangerous character, because enemy propaganda could work tremendous harm all over the world by the knowledge of such research, should it come by such knowledge."[32]

All that was then needed was Hitler's decree of December 23, 1942, in which he relieved "physicians, medical practitioners and dentists of their pledge to secrecy"[33] in the patient-doctor relationship. With that decree the confidentiality of that relationship had been abrogated and that of the state-doctor relationship firmly established. It had all become "a point of law."

My final thoughts at the time turned to the final statement of one of the defendants, SS Colonel Poppendick. He contended—and I do not for a moment doubt the sincerity with which he made the claim—that "the oath of Hippocrates ... has nothing to do with the problem."[34] As Thomas Merton said of Adolf Eichmann, he was sane; he simply was not in his "right mind." At about this time, the representative of the American medical community made a prophetic remark: "The moral imperative of the Oath of Hippocrates ... is necessary for the survival of the scientific and technical philosophy of medicine."[35]

Today, when the Hippocratic Oath gradually disappears from the commencement exercises of American schools of medicine and neither the Nuremburg Code nor the Helsinki Declaration replaces it, it might be wise to ponder those words and ask if they are any less relevant today.

What happened to the *liquidated* (all six million of them) is a matter of record. What happened to the *liquidators* is not so well known.

After my lecture at the Harvard Divinity School on April 19, 1971, I invited discussion from the floor. During the hour that followed, Dr. Leo Alexander, a distinguished Vienna-born and -educated neurologist and psychiatrist who had served as consultant to the U. S. Chief of Counsel at the War Crimes and Doctors' Trials, arose to tell of an exchange he had had, during the trial, in the cell of the chief defendant, SS Lieutenant General (and Professor) Karl Brandt, personal physician to Hitler and Commissioner General of the Reich for Health and Sanitation.

"Why are you persecuting and prosecuting us?" Brandt began. "Countless physicians have used radiation therapy and other techniques to destroy cancer cells in the human body. We have simply liquidated the cancer cells in the body politic of our German Fatherland." So, the denigration of human life that begins gradually comes to its inexorable end. So, the benumbed conscience accepts the Big Lie as the Big Truth. So, the society without an ethic blindly accepts law and obedience to authority without thought of justice. So, love when undefined and structureless *sacrifices the other* rather than *sacrifices for the other.*

What had begun in 1933 with a "Law for the Prevention of Congenitally Ill Progeny" which permitted sterilization of those suffering from

1. Congenital Imbecility
2. Schizophrenia
3. Circular (Manic Depressive) Psychosis
4. Congenital Epilepsy
5. Congenital St. Vitus Dance (Huntington's Chorea)
6. Congenital Blindness
7. Congenital Dumbness
8. Bad Congenital Physical Malformation *and*
9. Chronic Alcoholism[36]

was amended five times in the next two years; supplemented by two other laws in 1935; and culminated in Hitler's secret order authorizing mass sterilization on the first day of World War II—September 1, 1939.

What happened in the years 1939-45 is also a matter of record. Still, many are unaware that Brandt in 1942 suggested that this mass sterilization policy be extended to include 3,000,000 Russian prisoners of war and that, in addition to the abortion, sterilization and liquidation of the Jews and the Reich's other "enemies," German doctors also liquidated 240,000 of 300,000 German mental patients in the war years in specially constructed carbon monoxide chambers in some of the best German hospitals.[37] Many good men who refused to speak out against the destruction of others found themselves at last destroying their own. What was legal, what was disallowed, had become their sole concern. The road from morality to immorality had led them finally to total amorality.[38]

In Brandt's Final Plea to the American Military Tribunal, his counsel claimed that "what is to be done is decided not by the physician but by the political leader";[39] and "Voluntariness is a fiction; the emergency of the state hard reality."[40] In his Final Statement, he could say: "I know things that disturb the conscience of a medical man and I know the inner distress that afflicts one when ethics of every form are decided by an order or obedience."[41] Yet these were essentially the same arguments made on behalf of his co-defendant, SS Major General Karl Gebhardt: "A deed offending the recognized principles of medical ethics does not necessarily constitute a crime. Only the cogent precepts of the law can be used as the basis for a verdict." And again: "One thing is certain, that the state has more and more taken possession of the individual and limited his personal freedom. This is evidently one of the accompanying facts of technics and the modern mass-state."[42]

CULT AND CULTURE

There is a difference between sin and crime that is perceptible to the man who is true to his cult (religious faith or community of worship) that is sometimes hidden from the man whose first loyalty is to his culture (that style of social and artistic expression common to a society or class).

Eugen Rosenstock-Huessey wrote of the difference with real acuity of vision:

The clever thing about the sins of the . . . Medical Society is not that they can be committed without breaking our laws. For sin is not a crime of the penal code, although some people seem to think so. Sins and crimes are different in nature. Long before an act or an omission becomes defined as a crime, it may be gross sin. And something defined as a crime by the law may have ceased to be sin. Our law codes certainly travel in the same direction as sins, trying to transform them into crimes. But sin is always far ahead of them. Hence, a new nature of sin is not defined in the penal code. To the contrary, our laws urge this sin upon us. The only trouble is that this new nature of sin saps our vitality and dwarfs us.[43]

Ethics have need of law if they are to be more than empty abstractions. Law has need of ethics if it is to achieve equal justice. Things have not changed so much since St. Augustine's times (354-430). A kingdom or a state without justice is still like a band of robbers.

Crane Brinton, in *The Anatomy of Revolution*,[44] describes the English, American, French and Russian revolutions as ones in which the moderates, in the main, gain control in the initial stages only to have the extremists wrest control from them. Extremists act decisively, without hesitation and without concern for anyone or anything other than the seizure of power. Then comes that moment when even they must bow before the truth so eloquently articulated by Jean-Jacques Rousseau in *The Social Contract*, "The strongest is never strong enough to be always the master, unless he transforms strength into right, and obedience into duty." Gradually they, too, are replaced, and as the revolution grows older, the revolutionaries grow more moderate.

The Nazi revolution died in its thirteenth year. Yet, in the years in which the Nazis were in power, it is difficult to believe that they could have committed greater excesses or more barbarous crimes. These, however, sprang from small beginnings.

When in the film *Judgment at Nuremberg*, the American Judge Haywood visited his German colleague Judge Janning in his cell, the one-time Nazi judge said of the deaths of millions of men, women and children in gas ovens: "I did not know it would come to that. You must believe it. You must believe it."

Haywood stood staring at the man before him: then, almost without thinking, he said the words as though he were speaking to a child: "Herr Janning. It came to that the first time you sentenced to death a man you knew to be innocent."[45]

We, as a people, may have to experience the consequences of our own capacity for self-deception before we regain our "right mind." Today, we and our World War II allies who conquered Hitler are liqudating life in the womb every year at as great a rate—if not greater—as he liquidated life in the ovens of Auschwitz.

The "silent spring" we have yet to experience is more awesome than that contemplated by Rachel Carson, though she has asked many of the right questions:

Who has made the decision that sets in motion these chains of poisonings, this ever-widening wave of death that spreads out, like ripples when a pebble is dropped into a still pond? . . . Who has decided—who has the *right* to decide—for the countless legions of people who were not consulted, that the supreme value is a world without insects, even though it be also a sterile world ungraced by the curving wing of a bird in flight?[46]

We shall not hear the song of the birds. We also shall not hear the fumbling attempts of the retarded to speak; the faltering step of the disabled in their efforts to walk; the cry for help of the irreversibly ill and the aged. Scientific Man will give. Scientific Man will take away. And we shall be called upon to withhold our questions and bless his name.

It can't happen here? It can—here or anywhere.

Unless—before we destroy the balance of nature; earth and sky, beast and bird, fish and insect, *man and woman*—we hear the Voice that Elie Wiesel heard as he entered Auschwitz:

Think of your soul and you'll resist better. The soul is important and the enemy knows it; that's why he tries to corrupt it before destroying us. Do not let him. The soul counts for more than the body. If your soul maintains its strength, your body too will withstand the test. I tell you this because you have just arrived; you are still capable of listening. In a month it will be too late. In a month you will no longer know what having a soul could possibly mean.[47]

REFERENCES

1. K. Rahner, "Menschenzüchtung. Das Problem der genetischen Manipulierung des Menschen," ed. F. Wagner, 2d ed. (Munich: C. H. Beck Verlag, 1970), pp. 135-167.
2. J. Dukeminier, Jr., "Supplying Organs for Transplantation," *Michigan Law Review, 68,* 5, April 1970 (especially pp. 846-847); T. Dobzhansky, *The Biology of Ultimate Concern* (New York: The New American Library, 1967): J. Fletcher, "Ethical Aspects of Genetic Control: Designed Genetic Changes in Man," *New England Journal of Medicine, 285,* 14, September 30, 1971; M. Golding, "Ethical Issues in Biological Engineering," *UCLA Law Review, 15,* 267, February 1968; G. Hardin, "Parent-

hood: Right or Privilege?" *Science, 49,* 3944, July 31, 1970, p. 427; J. Lederberg, "Experimental Genetics and Human Evolution," *Bulletin of Atomic Scientists,* October 1966, pp. 4-10; J. Macquarrie, *Three Issues in Ethics* (New York, Evanston and London: Harper and Row, 1970); I. Ramsey, ed., *Biology and Personality* (Oxford, England: Basil Blackwell, 1965); P. Ramsey, *Fabricated Man* (New Haven and London: Yale University Press, 1970) and *The Patient as Person* (New Haven and London, Yale University Press, 1970); G. Stebbins, "Prospects for Spaceship Man," *Saturday Review,* March 7, 1970, pp. 48-50, 64-66; G. Taylor, *The Biological Time Bomb,* Signet Book (New York: The New American Library, 1968); T. Thompson, "The Year They Changed Hearts," *Life, 71,* 12, September 17, 1971, pp. 56-70; R. Williams, "Our Role in the Generation, Modification and Termination of Life," *The Archives of Internal Medicine, 124,*2, August 1969, pp. 215-237; "A New Ethic for Medicine and Society," *California Medicine* (Official Journal of the California Medical Association), *113,* 3, September 1970, pp. 67-68; "The Biologist's Dilemma," *Nature Magazine, 228,* December 5, 1970, pp. 900-901.

3. Taylor, *The Biological Time Bomb,* supra, p. 183.

4. "U. S. Population Forecast Cut," *San Francisco Chronicle,* Times-Post Service, August 13, 1970, pp. 1 and 30.

5. Hardin, "Parenthood: Right or Privilege?" supra.

6. Williams, "Our Role in the Generation, Modification and Termination of Life," supra.

7. R. Ardrey, "Control of Population," *Life, 68,* 6, pp. 48-60.

8. Nuernberg Military Tribunals, Trials of War Criminals: *U.S.* v. *Brandt et al., I,* pp. 726-727.

9. R. Niebuhr, *The Nature and Destiny of Man* (New York: Charles Scribner's Sons, 1945), I, 1.

10. J. Monod, *Chance and Necessity* (New York: Knopf, 1971).

11. "A New Ethic for Medicine and Society," supra, p. 68.

12. K. Lorenz, *Das Sogennante Böse. Zur Naturgeschichte der Aggression,* 17th-20th printing (Vienna: Verlag Dr. G. Borotha-Schoeler, 1966), p. 317; id., *On Aggression,* trans. Marjorie Kerr Wilson (New York: Harcourt, Brace and World, 1966), p. 225.

13. Ibid. (German ed.), p. 320; ibid. (Engl. trans.), p. 227.

14. J. Lederberg, "Humanics and Genetic Engineering," *1970 Yearbook of Science and the Future* (Encyclopedia Britannica).

15. Lorenz, op. cit. supra, pp. 324-325, German; p. 230, English.

16. I. Ramsey, *Religious Language: An Empirical Placing of Theological Phrases,* 2d ed. (New York: Macmillan, 1967), p. 35.

17. L. Gilkey, *Naming the Whirlwind: The Renewal of God-Language* (Indianapolis and New York: Bobbs-Merrill Co., 1969), p. 432.

18. Ibid., see p. 443.

19. Dobzhansky, *The Biology of Ultimate Concern,* supra, p. 86.

20. W. Leibrecht, *God and Man in the Thought of Hamann* (Philadelphia: Fortress Press, 1966), p. 136.
21. Gilkey, *Naming the Whirlwind,* supra, p. 387, note 14.
22. Ibid.
23. Aristotle, *Rhetoric,* bk. 1, ch. 9, *Basic Works of Aristotle,* ed. Richard McKeon (New York: Random House, 1941), p. 1359.
24. Cicero, *De la Republique des Lois,* bk. iii, ch. 22, Traduction nouvelle de Ch. Appuhn (Paris: Librarie Garnier, 1940), p. 162.
25. Aquinas, *Summa Theologica,* q. 91, 2, *Basic Writings of St. Thomas Aquinas,* ed. Anton C. Pegis (New York, 1945), II, pp. 749-750.
26. Macquarrie, *Three Issues in Ethics,* supra, p. 23.
27. Golding, "Ethical Issues in Biological Engineering," supra, p. 457.
28. Nuernberg Military Tribunals, Trials of War Criminals, supra, *I,* 6.
29. Ibid., *I,* 59.
30. Ibid., *I, 58.*
31. *Ibid., I,* 721.
32. Ibid., *I,* 717.
33. Ibid., *II,* 192.
34. Ibid., *II,* 156.
35. Ibid., *II,* 86.
36. Ibid., *II,* 60; cf. Reichsgesetzblatt 1933, *I,* 529.
37. F. Wertham, *A Sign for Cain* (New York: Paperback Library, 1962), pp. 150-186.
38. P. Marx, *The Death Peddlers: War on the Unborn* (Collegeville, Minn.: St. John's University Press, 1971). Cf. this symposium report for parallels.
39. Nuernberg Military Tribunals, Trials of War Criminals, supra, *II,* 127.
40. Ibid., *II,* 129.
41. Ibid., *II,* 138.
42. Ibid., *II,* 72.
43. E. Rosenstock-Huessy, *The Christian Future or The Modern Mind Outrun,* A Harper Torchbook (New York: Harper and Row, 1966), p. 31.
44. C. Brinton, *The Anatomy of Revolution,* Vintage Books (New York: Random House, 1965).
45. A. Mann, *Judgment at Nuremberg,* Signet Books (New York: The New American Library), p. 136.
46. R. Carson, *Silent Spring* (Boston: Houghton-Mifflin Co., 1962), p. 127.
47. E. Wiesel, *One Generation After,* trans. Lily Edelman and the author (New York: Random House, 1970), pp. 79-80.

· 16 ·

BUT NOBODY SAID
"THINK"

Audra Stevens

The problems I've had with my mother go back farther than I can remember. Things really started getting bad, though, when I was a freshman in high school. That's when my oldest brother and his girlfriend had to get married. I remember how broken up my mom was. Bob had always been her favorite son, and she felt that somehow she had failed him as a mother.

After my brother's marriage, I began to go steady with Darrel. My folks never gave me a moment's peace the three years I dated him. Almost every night Mom would come into my room and yell at me. She was really worried that something would happen. I was too young, she said, and too serious. I finally broke up with Darrel because of her constant nagging.

My senior year in high school I met Bill. He was two years older than I was, and I found that very flattering. We got along really well, right from the start; so well that I didn't pay much attention to his progressively friendlier advances. My loneliness was working against me too. One night about four months after we had begun dating, I was especially weak, and Bill didn't stop. I felt like something beautiful had been ruined, and I wanted Bill to reassure me that everything was still all right. But he said he didn't want to talk about

Audra Stevens is a pseudonym. Because all of her problems have not yet been resolved, the young woman writing this story has asked to remain anonymous. All personal names have been changed at her request, but actual names of the organizations mentioned have been used.

it. It was over and we should forget it. But I couldn't forget it. I'd never wanted that to happen.

When I missed my period I really began to worry. After five weeks of crying and hoping, I went to the free clinic for a pregnancy test. It came out negative. The technician told me that it may have been too early, and I should try again in a couple of weeks if I didn't get my period. Two weeks later, I went to my own doctor. This time the test was positive and I felt panic as I had never felt it before. The only thing the doctor told me, assuming that Bill wouldn't marry me, was abortions were available; but the decision was up to me.

When I told Bill I was pregnant, he was furious. He said it was all my fault, it wasn't his problem, and he walked out. Then I was completely alone, knowing I couldn't tell my parents. That word the doctor had said—abortion—kept running through my head. Oh, so quick, so simple. And presto! The whole mess never happened.

I put that out of my mind and called the Underground Switchboard. They have doctors and other professional people who try to talk kids down off bum trips, and things like that. Well, I was on a real bummer, but all the Switchboard could offer me was a New York telephone number. Again the word abortion cropped up, and it was sounding more and more like I had no other choice. Even a medical student friend of Bill's offered himself to do the abortion, but this was one thing that I knew I could never go through.

Bill had another friend who had been researching New York abortion clinics as some kind of hobby. Bill got a telephone number and began to set up an appointment for me. He reminded me of what my parents would do if they found out. Right now I think they could have handled it, but just then I was in no condition to argue with him. I was deathly afraid of letting anyone know!

Things began to happen very quickly from that point on. Bill gave me the phone numbers to call, then bowed out. Making all the necessary arrangements didn't leave me with much time to think, and when I did have time I just thought about how scared and alone I was. I desperately needed a friend, but there weren't many around just then. There was one girl, a nurse, who listened to my problem, then told me a little of what to expect from the abortion. Abortion! I swear that's the only word I heard for two weeks.

My nurse friend drove me to the airport the morning of the appointment. I arrived in New York at 9:00 A.M. and waved down a taxi to take me to the clinic. If I'd only listened to that taxi driver, my story would be a lot different now. He was in his late twenties and fairly good-looking. After I gave him the address of the clinic, he asked if I wanted to go to a hockey game with him. I told him I wasn't going to be in New York long.

"Can I ask why you're going to Long Island?" He had obviously guessed.

"Yes, I am," I replied.

He turned to me with a look of genuine concern. "Is this really what you want?" Funny, but no one had bothered to ask me that before. He said that if I wouldn't go through with it he would take me to a counselor friend of his who helped another girl find a job in New York, have her baby and place it for adoption. If he had been at the other end of the flight, I would have turned back. But I was already in New York, and I had a notion I would be wasting money if I didn't do what I had come there to do. I was afraid Bill would hate me if I were still pregnant when I got home.

The cab driver wouldn't take the full twenty-two-dollar fare. He said I would need some extra money. "If you change your mind, I'll take you back to the airport free and get you help." He knew what was going on in my head better than I did. I'd like to return to New York and thank him now for being the only one who cared enough to offer some real help.

The clinic was a plain, square, cement building, nicely decorated inside. The receiving nurse handed me a card to fill out. I had to give my name and address and indicate anything that might be bothering me. I skipped over concern about the procedure, and a couple of others, and marked the one about my parents finding out. A short time later I was called into the counseling office. I saw a big room, a big desk, and a big man in a suit. He handled the counseling like my dad would sell a car. His manner was so stiff he seemed to be reading words off a sheet. He never asked me if I was sure I wanted an abortion. He reassured me that my parents couldn't possibly find out, since the records were strictly confidential.

I then went downstairs to the prep room where two nurses gave me some pre-operative medication and outlined the abortion procedure for me. They explained different forms of contraception, and asked me if I wanted a prescription for the Pill. I said definitely not; I wouldn't be needing anything like that. They smiled a "sure, we know" smile at each other, then tried to sell me the Pill idea again. They never even asked about my boyfriend, or how we were getting along. They just assumed I was that kind of girl, and I would need a little "protection" to make sure I wouldn't have to come back to New York.

After a very short time the medication began to work, and I soon didn't care about anything. While I was on the operating table, the doctor talked to me about my home state. One nurse assisted him while the other held my hand. There was no pain until he turned on the suction machine. Then for a three-minute eternity the cramps were excruciating. Afterwards, I was very weak. The nurse led me into a room where another girl sat. My stomach felt terrible, and I couldn't eat a thing. Finally, the nurse sat me down and I ate a small bowl of soup. A few minutes later I felt strong enough to leave the clinic.

By this time the clinic was just about ready to close, and the director and nurses were standing in the corridor as I was leaving. The director knew I didn't have any money, so he gave five dollars of my money back for carfare to the airport. He said I could mail it back to him anytime. One of the nurses gave me another five dollars and drove me to the airport limousine stand. She told me I could just include her five dollars with the money I sent back to the director.

The flight home seemed endless. My stomach was upset and I was having the chills. Five times during the trip I asked for a glass of water so I could take the medicine the clinic had given to me, but my request was completely ignored. Twelve hours after my trip had begun, my nurse friend picked me up again. The propaganda hadn't lied. It was quick and easy—the abortion, that is. I soon learned that the future would not be quite that simple. The old problems hadn't been removed with the pregnancy, and several new ones lie ahead.

Bill called that night. He had left the city on vacation with his parents three days before. He asked me how I was feeling, but before I could mention anything about the abortion, he launched into a long speil about what he had done the night before. From then on our relationship became more and more strained. We saw each other several times, but I felt strangely distant from him. He refused to talk things out, and changed the subject whenever I mentioned the abortion.

Later that spring a doctor spoke in our school about contraception and abortion. I picked up a book on fetology and began looking through it. I was amazed to see how perfectly formed the developing baby is. I then began having vicious cramps starting a week before my period. They doubled me over in pain at times, but my doctor couldn't find anything wrong. Physically I was healthy, but the cramps didn't go away. I began to lie awake nights thinking about the abortion. The picture of the eight-week child haunted my mind. I knew then it was a human life I had been playing with, and I finally admitted to myself what I had done was wrong.

Guilt wreaked havoc with my mind from then on. I looked for someone else to blame, and picked out each person along the way who hadn't told me what it was that was growing inside me. The thought that my child could be alive and loved, if not directly by me, then by a couple that had been waiting for years for a baby, drove me into a deep depression. I felt I never deserved another chance to give life. Why hadn't someone told me? Why had my first pregnancy been like a disease, something too horrible to tell anyone about? The injustice of it nearly drove me to suicide.

We moved to another city the following summer, but the guilt and the cramps came along. When the fall arrived, I met a very sensitive and understanding guy. Not long after I began dating Mike I had a vicious bout with my cramps one evening. He wanted to know what the problem was, so in desperation I told him. Not in one big crash, but little by little, letting him piece it together and fill in the details. He didn't judge. He didn't condemn. He took me where I was at, and started helping me face myself. He told me that punishing myself wouldn't do anyone any good. I should do something to help someone else. I talked. He listened. It was a brand-new beautiful experience to be treated as a person.

To be treated as a person! I can see, with increasing clarity, how this is so essential. In my case, there were many opportunities for someone close to me to accept me as a person; to love me in spite of my condition, in spite of what I had done and in spite of what my future held. My parents had never allowed me to open myself to them. My boyfriend, with his "after my body" mindset, literally rejected me. My close friends seemed afraid. The Underground Switchboard used the cookbook approach as they gave me a telephone number to solve my problem. I have always felt that my doctor could have helped in some way, but as I think back he didn't try to understand me or my dilemma; he didn't try to explain the child within me to me and he didn't hesitate to direct me to abortion as the solution to my problem. The abortionists themselves seemed friendly enough, but their attitude lacked real depth. The only person was the taxicab driver. He cared. But who would expect one so distant to care so much when those so close cared so little?

After the abortion there lingered the same alienation, loneliness, and lack of communication with Bill and especially my parents. The death of my baby, a tragedy that can never be undone, was of no help in solving these difficulties. My abortion served only to temporarily avoid confronting the basic problem with my mother and father.

Since the abortion, I have always expected to be damned by everybody, but beautiful people have since touched me, cared for me as a person, helped me work through my memories of the abortion, and muster courage to face my parents. I am hopeful that with sensitive professional direction, many tears and time, the years of estrangement from my parents will be reconciled.

Mike and I have become involved in BIRTHRIGHT and SOUL—a youth pro-life group—helping other girls who might be faced with the loneliness and confusion of pregnancy. I now want to be a maternity nurse. The thought of working in a delivery room thrills me. Not only do I want to help other women have their babies, but I want to be a mother myself.

I have realized the forces that pushed me into abortion—forces that affect many girls. Student newspapers, radio, television, magazines and freeway advertisements all depict the glory of abortion. The sterile, efficient, prefabricated solution of abortion has saturated our society. This may be satisfactory for one-step floor waxes and TV dinners, but with problem pregnancies, it is destructive to human beings.

I hope maybe someone reading this may see herself and think for a moment of the kind of help both she and the delicate human infant within her deserve. Many people are waiting to care for them both. People who believe that every human life at any stage is valuable, and that there is just no such thing as the life not worth living.

APPENDIXES

GLOSSARY OF MEDICAL TERMS

ABORTION: The premature expulsion from the uterus of the products of conception—of the embryo, or of a nonviable fetus. *Artificial* a., induced abortion; an abortion which is brought on purposely. *Criminal* a., an abortion which is not justified by the circumstances. *Induced* a., abortion brought on intentionally. *Therapeutic* a., abortion induced to save the life of the mother.

ACCOUCHER: One skilled in midwifery.

ALKALOSIS: A clinical term commonly used to indicate an increase in blood pH.

AMNIOTIC FLUID: The fluid which surrounds and protects the baby while still in the womb.

ANALGESIA: Pain relief.

ANOXIA: Reduction of oxygen in the body tissues below physiologic levels.

ASPHYXIA: Suffocation.

ATELECTASIS: Incomplete expansion of the lungs at birth.

ATRESIA: Absence or closure of a normal body orifice.

BENIGN: Not malignant; not recurrent; favorable for recovery.

BRAXTON-HICK'S CONTRACTIONS: Intermittent contraction of the uterus after the third month of pregnancy.

BREECH: The buttocks.

CAESAREAN SECTION (CESAREAN SECTION): Delivery of the fetus by an incision through the abdominal and uterine wall.

CELLULITIS: Inflammation of cellular tissue; especially purulent inflammation of the loose subcutaneous tissue.

CEPHALIC: Pertaining to the head.

CERVIX: The mouth of the womb.

CHROMOSOME: A small rod-shaped body which is within the nucleus of a cell and contains the genes, or hereditary factors, and these are constant in number in each species.

CONGENITAL: Existing at, and usually before, birth.

CONSTITUTION: The make-up or functional habit of the body, determined by the genetic, biochemical, and physiologic endowment of the individual, and modified in great measure by environmental factors.

CONSUMPTION COAGULOPATHY: A pathologic state of consuming of blood-clotting factors, resulting in a deficient clotting system and bleeding tendency.

CURETTE: A kind of scraper or spoon for removing growths or other matter from the walls of cavities.

DECIDUA: The uterine lining of pregnancy, thrown off after delivery.

DIALYSIS UNIT: Artificial kidney machine.

DILATATION: The condition of being dilated or stretched beyond the normal dimensions.

DYSMENORREAH: Painful menstruation.

ECTOPIC PREGNANCY: A pregnancy which exists outside the womb, usually in the tube; but it may be in the abdominal cavity, on the ovary or on the cervix.

ELECTROCARDIOGRAM (ECG, EKG): A graphic tracing of the electric current produced by the contraction of the heart muscle.

ELECTROENCEPHALOGRAM (EEG): A graphic recording of the electric currents developed in the brain.

EMBOLISATION: The sudden blocking of an artery or vein by a clot or obstruction which has been brought to its place by the blood current.

EMBRYO: The developing human being from the moment of conception (or one week after conception) to the end of the second month.

ENDOCARDITIS: Inflammation of the lining membrane of the heart and the connective tissue bed on which it lies.

ENDOCRINE: Applied to organs whose function is to secrete into the blood or lymph a substance that has a specific effect on another organ or part.

ENDOMETRIOSIS: A condition in which tissue more or less resembling the uterine lining occurs aberrantly in various locations in the pelvic cavity.

ENDOMETRITIS: Inflammation of the uterine lining.

EUGENIC: Serving in the production of physically and mentally improved offspring.

EUTHANASIA: The putting to death of a person suffering from an incurable disease. This definition is a strict one. Many deaths have been accorded to euthanasia in which no such incurable disease actually existed.

FETOLOGY: That branch of medicine that treats diseases of the unborn.

FETUS (FOETUS): The scientific name for the developing human being from two months after conception until birth.

GENE: The biologic unit of heredity, it is located in a definite position on a particular chromosome.

GYNECOLOGY: The specialty of medicine involved in the diagnosis and treatment of diseases of the genital tract of women.

HEMATOCRIT (HAEMATOCRIT): The number of red blood cells within the total volume of blood and expressed as a percentage.

HEMATOPOIETIC (HAEMATOPOIETIC): The formation of blood cells.

HOMOGRAFT: A piece of tissue transplanted from one individual to another individual of the same species.

HYPERTENSION: High blood pressure.

HYPERTONIC: Pertaining to a solution that has a higher concentration than the fluid system with which it is compared.

HYPOFIBRINOGENEMIA: Abnormally low fibrinogen (a serum protein important to normal clotting) content of the blood.

HYPOXIC: Decreased oxygen content.

HYSTERECTOMY: Surgical removal of the uterus.

HYSTEROTOMY: A cesarian section-like operation performed early in pregnancy (but usually after 3 1/2 months) to deliver the child with the purpose of allowing his death.

INCEST: Sexual intercourse between persons too closely related to contract a legal marriage.

IMMUNE: Resistance against disease.

INTERVERTEBRAL: Between the vertebrae.

INTRA-UTERINE: Within the confines of the womb.

INTRAVENOUS: Solutions given through a needle directly into a vein.

LAPAROTOMY: Surgical incision into the abdominal cavity.

LIE: The relation of the long axis of the fetus to that of the mother; it is either longitudinal or transverse.

LOBOTOMY: In psychosurgery, the surgical incision of all the fibers of a lobe, usually the frontal lobe of the brain.

LORDOSIS: Curvature of the spinal column with a forward convexity.

LUMBAR: The part of the back between the thorax and the pelvis.

MALIGNANT: Tending to go from bad to worse; usually refers to the destructive nature of cancer.

MANIC DEPRESSIVE: Denoting a mental disorder in which periods of depression alternate with periods of excitement.

MENSES: The menstrual period.

METABOLISM: The sum of all the physical and chemical processes by which living organized substance is produced and maintained; and also, the transformation by which energy is made available for the uses of the organism.

MICTURITION: The passage of urine.

MISCARRIAGE: The lay term for spontaneous natural abortion.

NEOPLASTIC: A new and abnormal growth any place in the body; it may be benign or malignant.

OBSTETRICS: That specialty in surgery which deals with the management of pregnancy, labor and the puerperium.

OLIGOHYDRAMNIOS: The presence of less than 300 cc of amniotic fluid at term.

OSMOMETRIC: Pertaining to osmosis or the passage of pure solvent from the lesser to the greater concentration when two solutions are separated by a membrane which selectively prevents the passage of solute molecules, but is permeable to the solvent.

OVUM: The female reproductive cell which, after fertilization, develops into a new member of the same species.

OXYTOCIN: One of the two hormones secreted by the posterior lobe of the pituitary gland. It stimulates the uterine musculature to contract, and is used to induce active labor or to cause contraction of the uterus after delivery of the placenta.

OXYTOCINASE: An enzyme in the blood whose job it is to de-activate oxytocin.

PARACERVICAL: Adjacent to the cervix; in paracervical block anesthesia, the anesthetic is injected adjacent to the cervix at the 3 and 9 o'clock positions.

PARALYTIC ILEUS: An inhibition of the normal peristaltic action of the bowels resulting in clinical bowel obstruction.

PARAMETRITIS: Inflammation of the surface of the uterus and the other closely adjacent structures.

PATENT DUCTUS ARTERIOSUS (PDA): An open vessel between the pulmonary artery and the aorta that usually closes immediately after birth; however, in a few people it remains open and needs repair.

PATHOGENESIS: The developmental process of disease.

PATHOLOGICAL: Indicative of a morbid condition.

PERINATAL MORTALITY: The combined infant mortality during pregnancy, labor and the puerperium.

PERINATOLOGY: A new branch of medicine restricted to the treatment of the infant from conception to one year after birth.

PERITONEUM: A serous membrane lining the abdominal walls and enclosing the viscera.

PERITONITIS: Inflammation of the peritoneum; a condition marked by exudations in the peritoneum of serum, fibrin, cells, and pus. It is attended by abdominal pain and tenderness.

PHONENDOSCOPE: A stethoscope that amplifies sound.

PHYLOGENETIC: Pertaining to the complete developmental history of a race or group of animals.

PLACENTA: The cakelike organ within the uterus which establishes communication between the mother and child by means of the umbilical cord. *P. previa.,* the placenta covers the mouth of the womb.

POLYHYDRAMNIOS: The presence of more than 2,000 cc of amniotic fluid at term.

POSTNATAL: Occurring after birth.

PREMATURITY: Underdevelopment; occurring before the proper time.

PRESENTATION: In labor, that part of the fetus which comes first through the mouth of the womb; usually the head, but may be the breech, feet, hands, shoulder, etc.

PROGENY: Offspring.

PSYCHOCHEMICALS: Chemicals used as drugs to alter one's mood or behavior.

PSYCHONEUROSIS: Neurosis. Functional nervous disorder of psychogenic origin, like obsessive-compulsive and many others.

PSYCHOTIC: Pertaining to the deeper, more far-reaching and prolonged behavior disorders, such as schizophrenia and manic-depression.

RENAL: Pertaining to the kidney.

RUBELLA: German measles.

SALINE: Containing salt.

SALPINGITIS: Inflammation of the fallopian tube.

SCHIZOPHRENIA: A condition which represents a cleavage of the mental functions.

SEPTIC EMBOLI: An embolus in which the dislodged particle is infectious and as a result usually carries the infection to another part of the body.

SEPTICEMIA: A morbid condition due to the presence of bacteria and their associated poisons in the blood. It is accompanied by chills, profuse sweat, irregularly remittent fever and great prostration.

SEROLOGIC: Pertaining to the study of antigen—antibody reactions of the human serum in the laboratory.

SOLUTE: A substance dissolved in a solution.

SPERMATOZOON: Sperm. A mature male germ cell. It is the generative element of the semen which serves to impregnate the ovum.

STERILE: Not fertile; infertile; barren; not capable of producing young.

TERATOGENIC: Pertaining to the production of anatomical anomalies.

TERM: A pregnancy which has reached its culmination; generally 40 weeks after the last menstrual period.

THROMBOCYTOPENIA: Decrease in the number of blood platelets (a factor in the clotting mechanism) which may lead to bleeding tendencies.

THROMBOPHLEBITIS: A condition in which inflammation of the vein wall has preceded the formation of a clot within the vein.

TOXEMIA: Toxemia of pregnancy; preeclampsia; eclampsia. A pathologic disorder, complexly metabolic in origin, which is found in the last three months of pregnancy, more often in young women pregnant for the first time. It is characterized by increased blood pressure, protein in the urine and peripheral edema.

TRIMESTER: A period of three months; thus pregnancy is divided into the first, second and third trimesters.

UTERUS: The womb.

VASCULAR: Pertaining to or full of blood vessels.

VASODILATATION: Dilation of a blood vessel.

VERSION: May be external or internal. Change of position of the fetus artificially with reference to the body of the mother, in order to convert an abnormal or relatively abnormal relation into a normal or relatively normal relation. Classically, external version is carried out by manipulating the baby through the mother's abdominal wall in order to convert a breech presentation to a cephalic, or head, presentation.

ZYGOTE: The fertilized egg.

▪ II ▪

LIST OF EMERGENCY PREGNANCY COUNSELING CENTERS

The following facilities offer help to *any* woman who is pregnant and distressed.

ALASKA

BIRTHRIGHT
Anchorage, Alaska
907-277-5433

ARIZONA

ALTERNATIVES TO ABORTION
1825 W. Northern Avenue
Phoenix, Arizona 85021
602-943-7231

BIRTHRIGHT
155 W. Helen St.
Tucson, Arizona 85705
602-622-3631

CALIFORNIA

Route 1, Box 48
Courtland, California 95615

BIRTHRIGHT
354 S. Church St.
Grass Valley, California 95945
916-273-2738

LIFE-LINE
301 S. Kingsley Dr.
Los Angeles, California 90005
Life-Line Central Office
213-380-8750

LIFE-LINE
Long Beach, California
213-831-4357

LIFE-LINE
Newhall-Saugus-Valencia,
California
805-252-7777

LIFE-LINE
Orange County, California
714-541-5522

LIFE-LINE
Palmdale Lancaster, California

LIFE-LINE
San Fernando Valley, California
213-981-4357

LIFE-LINE
San Gabriel Valley, California
213-444-4357

LIFE-LINE
Whittier-East L.A., California
213-724-6436

BIRTHRIGHT
Box 16064
San Francisco, California 94116
415-863-0800

St. Elizabeth Infant Hospital
415-567-8370

BIRTHRIGHT
21 Santa Margarita Dr.
San Rafael, California 94901
415-456-4500

BIRTHRIGHT
609 East Haley
Santa Barbara, California 93103
805-963-2200

BIRTHRIGHT
Santa Rosa, California
707-546-7777

COLORADO

BIRTHRIGHT
2215 N. Cascade
Colorado Springs, Colorado 80903
Margery Reed Prof. Bldg.
303-471-9633

BIRTHRIGHT
P.O. Box 20144
Denver, Colorado 80220
303-321-3780

CONNECTICUT

BIRTHRIGHT
Bridgeport, Connecticut
203-333-3888

BIRTHRIGHT
1303 Chapel Street
New Haven, Connecticut 06511
203-776-5395

BIRTHRIGHT OF
GREATER HARTFORD
134 Farmington Ave.
Hartford, Connecticut 06105
203-233-6666

DISTRICT OF COLUMBIA

BIRTHRIGHT
2800 Otis St., N.E.
Washington, D.C. 20018
202-526-3333

DELAWARE

42 Kings Hwy. East
Dover, Delaware 19901

FLORIDA

2215 Chippewa Trail
Maitland, Florida 32751

6001 S.W. 46th St.
Miami, Florida 33101

BIRTHRIGHT
646 W. Colonial Dr.
Orlando, Florida 32804
305-841-2223

8601 Pennsylvania
Sarasota, Florida 33580

GEORGIA

BIRTHRIGHT
316 Ivy St., N.E.
Atlanta, Georgia 30303
404-688-4496

BIRTHRIGHT
No. 9 Campbell Bldg., 8th
Augusta, Georgia 30902
404-722-4367

HAWAII

291 Uluniu St.
Kihei Maui, Hawaii 96753

ILLINOIS

204 S. Russell
Aurora, Illinois 60506

BIRTHRIGHT
11055 South St. Louis Ave.
Chicago, Illinois 60655
312-233-0305

BIRTHRIGHT
310 Bridge St.
Joliet, Illinois 60435
815-727-2222

18053 Oakwood
Lansing, Illinois 60438

BIRTHRIGHT
2201 Fifth Ave.
Moline, Illinois 61265
309-797-3305

BIRTHRIGHT OF
ROCK ISLAND CITY
Rock Island, Illinois
309-797-3305

THE SOCIETY FOR THE
PRESERVATION OF
HUMAN DIGNITY
(P.H.D.)
4518 Kings Walk
Rolling Meadows, Illinois
312-359-4919

HELP-LINE
P.O. Box 463
Skokie, Illinois 60076
312-359-4919

BIRTHRIGHT
Box 593
Springfield, Illinois
217-523-1328

INDIANA

BIRTHRIGHT
617 Court Building
Evansville, Indiana 47708
812-424-2555

BIRTHRIGHT
919 Fairfield Ave.
Fort Wayne, Indiana 46802
219-422-7511

St. Elizabeth's Home
2500 Churchman Ave.
Indianapolis, Indiana 46203
317-787-3412

BIRTHRIGHT
Kokomo, Indiana 46901
800-328-8860

R.R. 2, Box 171
Thornton, Indiana 46071

IOWA

BIRTHRIGHT OF AMES
Ames, Iowa
515-232-6240

BIRTHRIGHT
316 Fifth St., N.W.
Cedar Rapids, Iowa 52401
319-398-3543

BIRTHRIGHT
115 W. 6th St.
Davenport, Iowa 52803
309-797-3305

BIRTHRIGHT
P.O. Box 2545
Des Moines, Iowa 50315
515-288-7785

BIRTHRIGHT
1349 Prairie St.
Dubuque, Iowa 52001
319-556-1991

BIRTHRIGHT OF
BLACKHAWK CITY
2705 East 4th St.
Waterloo, Iowa 50703
319-232-3553

KANSAS

BIRTHRIGHT
526 West 34th St.
Wichita, Kansas 67204
316-838-4255

123 Barberry Lane
Lexington, Kentucky 40503

BIRTHRIGHT
2544 Kings Hwy.
Louisville, Kentucky 40243
502-452-2949

LOUISIANA

NEW-LIFE
P.O. Box 13632
New Orleans, Louisiana 70125
504-581-5433
581-LIFE

MAINE

BIRTHRIGHT COUNSELING
519 Ocean Ave.
Portland, Maine 04103
Maine Tollfree 800-442-6018
207-773-5678

MARYLAND

BIRTHRIGHT
320 Cathedral St.
Baltimore, Maryland
301-323-7444

BIRTHRIGHT
Route 97
Cooksville, Maryland 21723
301-323-7444

BIRTHRIGHT
7224 Old Gate Rd.
Rockville, Maryland 20852
301-526-3333

MASSACHUSETTS

902 East Pleasant
Amherst, Massachusetts 01002

PREGNANCY GUIDANCE
637 Cambridge St.
Brighton, Massachusetts 02135
617-787-4400

BIRTHRIGHT OF CAPE COD
31 Blueberry Hill Rd.
Hyannis, Massachusetts 02601

LIFE-LINE
56 Prospect St.
Shrewsbury, Massachusetts 01545
617-791-9128

LIFE-LINE
2 Granite St.
Worcester, Massachusetts 01604
Marillac Manor
617-791-9128

MICHIGAN

PROBLEM PREGNANCY HELP
400 S. Division
Ann Arbor, Michigan 48104
313-971-1827

BIRTHRIGHT
123 Main St. S.
Royal Oak, Michigan 48067
(Detroit area)
313-547-4600

Farmington, Michigan 48024
Marillac Hall
313-742-0660

HEARTBEAT
221 W. Fifth St.
Flint, Michigan 48502
313-742-0660

66 Lothrup
Grosse Point, Michigan 48236

252 S. Howell
Hillsdale, Michigan 49242
517-439-9307

BIRTH-LINE
526 Lansing Ave.
Jackson, Michigan 49203
517-784-9187

BIRTHRIGHT
1214 Hays Park Ave.
Kalamazoo, Michigan 49001
    616-349-4673
        349-HOPE

PREGNANCY COUNSELING
300 N. Washington St.
Lansing, Michigan 48933
    517-372-1560

328 Scott
Monroe, Michigan 48161
    313-242-2797

MINNESOTA

BIRTHRIGHT
Box 862
Albert Lea, Minnesota 56007
    507-373-7026

BIRTHRIGHT
510 Fifth Ave., N.W.
Austin, Minnesota 55912
    507-437-2373

BIRTHRIGHT OF DULUTH,
INC.
704 N. 19th Ave. E.
Duluth, Minnesota 55812

BIRTHRIGHT
Grand Rapids, Minnesota
    218-326-2843

BIRTHRIGHT
100 North 7th St.
Minneapolis, Minnesota 55403
Produce Bank Building
    612-333-2397

BIRTHRIGHT
215 8th Ave. N.W.
Rochester, Minnesota 55901
    507-288-9374

BIRTHRIGHT
1406 N. 6th Ave.
St. Cloud, Minnesota 56301
    612-253-4848

BIRTHRIGHT
355 Marshall Ave.
St. Paul, Minnesota 55101
Seton Center
    612-227-9894

HELP, INC.
Box 362
Worthington, Minnesota 56187

MISSOURI

BIRTHRIGHT
1026 Forest Ave.
Kansas City, Missouri
    816-474-4676

BIRTHRIGHT
118 N. Meramec
St. Louis, Missouri 63108
    314-862-5141

MONTANA

BIRTHRIGHT
1116-19th Ave. S.W.
Great Falls, Montana 59404
    406-453-4508

NEBRASKA

BIRTHRIGHT
215 South 15th St.
Lincoln, Nebraska 68501
    402-477-8021

GUIDELINE
Omaha, Nebraska
    402-536-6749

PERSONAL CRISIS SERVICE
Omaha, Nebraska
402-342-6200

NEW HAMPSHIRE

BIRTHRIGHT
215 Myrtle St.
Manchester, New Hampshire 03103

NEW JERSEY

BIRTHRIGHT
110 Atco Ave.
Atco, New Jersey 08804

BIRTHRIGHT
Atlantic City, New Jersey
609-348-6010

BIRTHRIGHT
Hwy 66 & Greengrove Rd.
Neptune, New Jersey 07753
201-922-9333

BIRTHRIGHT
290 Mt. Prospect Ave.
Newark, New Jersey 07102
201-485-1677

BIRTHRIGHT
94 Somerset St.
New Brunswick, New Jersey 08901
201-247-5445

BIRTHRIGHT
475 High Mountain Rd.
North Haledon, New Jersey
201-427-5142

BIRTHRIGHT
2 Allen Ave.
Allenhurst, New Jersey 07711
(Red Bank area)
201-922-9333

BIRTHRIGHT
76 Drake Rd.
Somerset, New Jersey 08873

BIRTHRIGHT
18 Euclid St.
Woodbury, New Jersey 08096
609-848-1818

NEW YORK

BIRTHRIGHT
1949 East 33rd St.
Brooklyn, New York 11234

ALTERNATIVE INC.
116 West Buffalo St.
Ithaca, New York 14850
607-273-5433

CHOOSE LIFE
790 Ridge Rd.
Lackawanna, New York 14218
(Buffalo area)
OLV Infant Home
716-824-4700

BIRTHRIGHT
122 East 22nd St.
New York City, New York 10010
212-260-2700

BIRTHRIGHT
Plattsburg, New York
518-563-4300

BIRTHRIGHT
23 Haggerty Rd.
Potsdam, New York 13676
315-265-4510

BIRTHRIGHT
Box 8473
Rochester, New York 14618
716-328-8700

Rt. 3, Box 304AA
Saugerties, New York 12477

BIRTHRIGHT
240 East Onondaga St.
Syracuse, New York 13202
   315-455-5871

BIRTHRIGHT
P.O. Box 13
New Hartford, New York 13513
(Utica area)
   315-797-1160

NORTH CAROLINA

BIRTH CHOICE, INC.
Durham, North Carolina
   919-544-3267

NORTH DAKOTA

BIRTHRIGHT
Berlin, North Dakota 58415

BIRTHRIGHT
210 West Custer Park
Bismarck, North Dakota 58501

BIRTHRIGHT
143-7th St. East
Dickinson, North Dakota 58601

BIRTHRIGHT
Box 1334
Fargo, North Dakota 58102

BIRTHRIGHT
901-3rd St. N.W.
Mandan, North Dakota 58554

OHIO

BIRTHRIGHT
Akron, Ohio
   216-253-4531

BIRTHRIGHT
408 East Ford St.
Barberton, Ohio 44203
   216-753-6108

BIRTHRIGHT
Canton, Ohio 44701
   216-455-7063

BIRTHRIGHT
5th and Walnut
Cincinnati, Ohio 45202
Tri-State Building, Room 412
   513-241-5433
      AH-1-LIFE

BIRTHRIGHT
14700 Detroit Ave.
Cleveland, Ohio 44107
   216-228-5998

BIRTHRIGHT
481 E. Town St.
Columbus, Ohio 43215
   614-221-0844

BIRTHRIGHT
1727-13th St.
Cuyahoga Falls, Ohio 44223
(Akron area)
   216-253-4531

BIRTHRIGHT
221 Rockhill Dr.
Kettering, Ohio 45429
(Dayton area)
   513-299-7917

HEARTBEAT
Madison and Huron
Toledo, Ohio 43604
1038 National Bank Building
   419-241-9131

BIRTHRIGHT
563 McDonald
Wooster, Ohio 44691
   216-264-9327

BIRTHRIGHT
5020 Market St.
Youngstown, Ohio 44501
   216-782-3377

OREGON

BIRTHRIGHT
8830 S.W. Woodside Dr.
Portland, Oregon 97225
   503-292-0812

PENNSYLVANIA

BIRTHRIGHT
2809 Bellaire Dr.
Allentown, Pennsylvania 18101
215-432-2222

BIRTHRIGHT OF
GREATER HARRISBURG
Box 492
Harrisburg, Pennsylvania 17108
717-236-1661

BIRTHRIGHT OF
LANCASTER, INC.
213 E. King St.
Lancaster, Pennsylvania 17602

304 James St.
Mechanicsburg, Pennsylvania 17055

BIRTHRIGHT
Box 12559
Philadelphia, Pennsylvania 19151
215-667-3910

BIRTHRIGHT
4612 Bayard St.
Pittsburgh, Pennsylvania 15213
412-621-1988

1259 Old Bolsburg
State College, Pennsylvania 16801
814-237-7546

RHODE ISLAND

BIRTHRIGHT COUNSELING
433 Elmwood Ave.
Providence, Rhode Island 02904
401-467-4545

SOUTH CAROLINA

1228 Hobard Dr.
Florence, South Carolina 29501

SOUTH DAKOTA

BIRTHRIGHT
220 S. Tyler
Pierre, South Dakota 57501
605-224-7672

BIRTHRIGHT
Rapid City, South Dakota

TENNESSEE

1049 Sunset Dr.
Signal Mt., Tennessee 37377

TEXAS

BIRTHRIGHT
8215 Westchester
Dallas, Texas
Preston Doctors Center
214-691-8881

BIRTHRIGHT
2903 West Salinas
San Antonio, Texas 78207
512-434-7288

VERMONT

VERMONT BIRTHRIGHT
CHAPTER
Box 953
Burlington, Vermont 05401
802-862-1160

R.D. 2
North Bennington, Vermont 05259
AVON MEADOWS FARM

VIRGINIA

BIRTHRIGHT
3901 Woodburn Rd.
Annandale, Virginia 22003
703-280-3960

BIRTHRIGHT
401 Colley Ave.
Norfolk, Virginia 23501
703-627-8100

WASHINGTON

PREGNANCY AID
536 Medical Dental Center
Everett, Washington 98201
206-353-7351

WISCONSIN

BIRTHRIGHT COUNSELING
939 Liberty Ave.
Beloit, Wisconsin 53511
    608-365-2844

LIFERIGHT
1400 75th St.
Kenosha, Wisconsin 53140
    414-658-8681

BIRTHRIGHT
Madison, Wisconsin

BIRTHRIGHT
1004 North 10th St.
Milwaukee, Wisconsin 53233
    414-272-5860

BIRTHRIGHT
Milladore, Wisconsin 54454

BIRTHRIGHT
Stevens Point, Wisconsin
    715-341-4357

BIRTHRIGHT
3177-92nd St.
Sturdevant, Wisconsin 53177

WYOMING

BIRTHRIGHT COUNSELING
414 S. 13th St.
Laramie, Wyoming 82070
    307-742-2223

CANADA

ALBERTA

BIRTHRIGHT
106-803 First S.E.
Calgary, Alberta, Canada
    403-262-7402

BRITISH COLUMBIA

BIRTHRIGHT
3371 Linwood St.
Victoria, B.C., Canada
    604-384-1431

NOVA SCOTIA

BIRTHRIGHT
1544 Barrington St.
Halifax, N.S., Canada
    902-422-4408

ONTARIO

BIRTHRIGHT
Hamilton, Ontario
    416-527-3677

BIRTHRIGHT
London, Ontario
    519-432-7197

BIRTHRIGHT
Oshawa, Ontario
    416-579-2336

BIRTHRIGHT
Sudbury, Ontario
    705-673-7393

BIRTHRIGHT
Toronto, Ontario
    416-469-1111

BIRTHRIGHT
Waterloo, Ontario
    519-579-3990

BIRTHRIGHT
Windsor, Ontario
    519-252-3322

QUEBEC

BIRTHRIGHT
Montreal, Quebec
    514-679-6722

▪ III ▪

ABORTION PROCEDURE

Human abortion can be carried out in many ways. In the first twelve weeks of pregnancy two methods are generally used in the United States: Dilatation and Curettage (D&C) and Suction Curettage (Vacuum Aspiration). When the pregnancy advances beyond twelve weeks gestation, the child is much too large and his skeleton too well developed for either of these two procedures to be performed without tremendous hazard to the mother. Between twelve and sixteen weeks the abortion procedure is usually not performed because the child is too large for curettage and too small to get at by saline injection. After sixteen weeks, however, salting out is the most commonly used procedure (1). If this fails, or if the pregnancy is far advanced, hysterotomy is performed. These four techniques of bringing death to the child are described below.

1. *Dilatation and Curettage*

The patient is premedicated and then placed on her back with her legs elevated and separated, exposing the vaginal area to clear vision. A standard "delivery" table is used to accommodate this. Her bottom is washed with an antiseptic solution and a weighted retractor is inserted into the vagina to expose the cervix. She may be given general anesthesia, local anesthesia (by injections alongside the cervix) or no anesthesia, depending on the size of the uterus and the age of the fetus (2,3,4). The mouth of the womb is then forcibly dilated with a special instrument designed for this purpose. A sharp curette, which is a spoon-like, knife-like instrument, is then inserted and the baby is methodically scraped in pieces from its support system. Following this procedure, the patient is often given medicine which will stimulate her uterus to contract and thus help prevent excessive bleeding. The results of this operation are shown in Plate One.

2. *Suction Curettage*

In this procedure, the patient is prepared and positioned in the same way as in the D&C. The mouth of the womb is forcibly dilated as in the D&C. After this, a clear plastic tube, larger in size than the bore of a soda straw, is inserted through the mouth of the womb into the uterus. This suction curette is attached to a machine which creates an extremely high negative pressure. The curette is worked in and out, while slowly rotated. Through a process working like a vacuum cleaner, the child is sucked from its support system. The mutilated parts rush through the tubing and eventually are trapped in a glass jar so that the parts will not interfere with the machinery(3). This procedure very often has to be followed by sharp curettage to ensure that no remnants of the child are left behind(5). The results of this operation are shown in Plate Two.

3. *Saline Injection*

The technique of salting out was originally developed in the concentration camps of Nazi Germany. Today it is used as a "sterile and efficient" technique of "modern" medicine. After the abdomen is cleansed with antiseptic solutions, the area of injection is locally anesthetised. A long #18 gauge needle is inserted through the abdomen into the fluid that surrounds and protects the baby. Approximately 200 cc. of fluid is withdrawn and then replaced by 200 cc. of 20 percent saline solution. This solution is so unphysiologic that the Food and Drug Administration has never officially approved it for human use. After the toxic solution is injected, studies have shown that within 1-1 1/2 hours, the child's heartbeat gradually slows down and stops (6). From 12 to 72 hours after injection the mother begins to have labor pains and delivers the dead child, usually in bed, as if she were delivering a living child. It is noteworthy that the mechanism through which 20 percent salt initiates labor is not yet known(7,8). A New York physician who does saline abortions has said of this procedure, "I hate to do saline injections—when you inject the saline you see an increase of fetal movements—it's horrible"(9). This increase in movement is the convulsive activity of the child as he moves towards his death.

This procedure was abandoned by the Japanese because it was extraordinarily dangerous(2). In accord with this, the mortality rate from saline injection doubled from the first year to the second in New York City(10). The results of this operation are shown in Plate Three.

4. *Hysterotomy*

Hysterotomy is a "small caesarean section." The abdomen is cleansed and the patient is given a general anesthetic. The abdomen and womb are then surgically incised. The child is removed and, just as in caesarean section, the child moves, cries and breathes. If the child is alive before the operation is performed, he then will be born alive. In New York State 1,802 of these live-born "abortions" were performed during the first year of weak legislation(10). The mortality rate from this operation in New York City increased from 230.4/100,000 in the first year to 356.5/100,000 the second year(11). The results of this operation are shown in Plate Four.

BIBLIOGRAPHY

1. Pathak, U. N. Intra-Amniotic Saline Induction for Termination of Early Pregnancy. *West Indian Med. J.,* 15:89-93, 1966.
2. Alpern, W., et al. Hypertonic Solutions for Termination of Pregnancy. *Am. J. Obstet. Gynec.,* 100:250-254, 1968.
3. Kerslake, K., et al. Abortion Induced by Means of the Uterine Aspirator. *Obstet. Gynec.,* 30:35-45, 1967.
4. Wu, P. The Use of Vacuum Bottle in Therapeutic Abortion—A Collective Survey. *Chinese Med. J.,* 85:245-248, 1966.
5. Peketz, A., et al. Evacuation of the Gravid Uterus by Negative Pressure (Suction Evacuation). *Am. J. Obstet. Gynec.,* 98:18-22, 1966.
6. Schaeffer, G. Technique of Dilatation and Curettage for Abortion. *Clinical Obstet. Gynec.,* 14:85-98, 1971.
7. Manabe, Y. Artificial Abortion at Mid-Pregnancy by Mechanical Stimulation of the Uterus. *Am. J. Obstet. Gynec.,* 105:132-146, 1969.
8. Schiffer, M. S. Induction of Labor by Intra-Amniotic Installation of Hypertonic Solutions for Therapeautic Abortion or Intrauterine Death. *Obstet. Gynec.* 33:729-736, 1969.
9. Edmiston, S. A Report on the Abortion Capital of the Country. *New York Times Magazine,* April 11, 1971.
10. Bulletin on Abortion Program. Department of Health, Health Services Administration City of New York. March 1972.
11. Ingraham, H. S. Report of Selected Characteristics on Induced Abortion Recorded in New York State. July 1, 1970-June 30, 1971, New York State Dept. of Health, October 1971. Tables 7 & 15.

COLOR PLATES

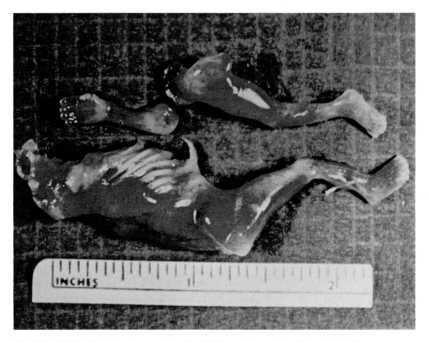

PLATE ONE. This is the result of a D&C performed in New York State at ten to twelve weeks gestation. The picture shows the right side of the chest cage with the right leg attached to the trunk. The left leg and right arm are shown above the trunk.

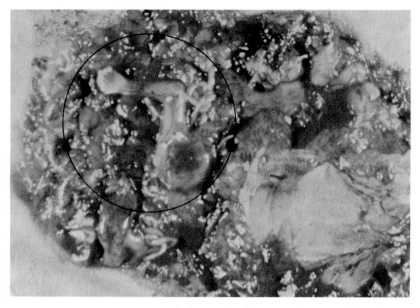

PLATE TWO. This is the result of a suction curettage at approximately ten weeks gestation. The left shoulder girdle and left arm are circled.

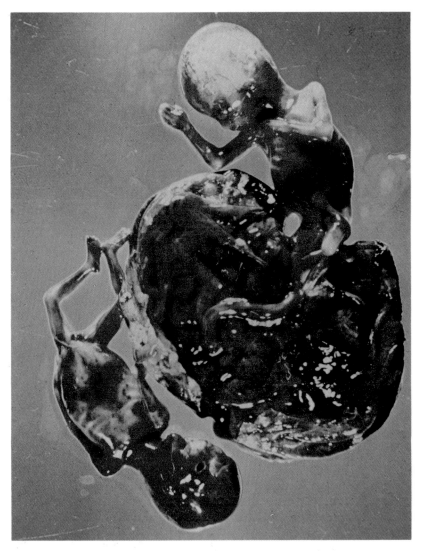

PLATE THREE. This set of twins was destroyed by saline injection at an estimated age of fourteen to sixteen weeks gestation. The skin is severely burned because of the corrosive action of the hypertonic salt.

PLATE FOUR: This beautiful child was killed by hysterotomy at twenty weeks of age.

EPILOGUE

ABORTION AND THE SUPREME COURT: DEATH BECOMES A WAY OF LIFE

Dennis J. Horan, John D. Gorby
Thomas W. Hilgers, M.D.

"Thoughtful men have long known that the campaign for the technological conquest of nature, conducted under the banner of modern science, would someday train its guns against the commanding officer, man himself."

—Leon R. Kass[1]

On January 22, 1973, we entered a brave new era of constitutional interpretation. On that date the United States Supreme Court decided the Texas and Georgia abortion cases[2] without the unborn child being represented in the litigation. Obviously the court did not consider this ex parte hearing unfair nor did it consider a few briefs and affidavits and two hours of oral argument inadequate to the task. Such procedure can only be evidence, if evidence is needed, that the court approached these cases with preconceived notions, one of which was *not* that human lives weighed in the balance. Having subliminally so concluded, legal, historical and medical precedent fell, like Downy Liquid, softly into place.

Prior to this decision it was universally held that the purpose of the Bill of Rights was to protect basic and absolute rights of individuals against incursions by tyrannical governments (even though where rights clash balancing must ensue); now, because these decisions have accepted the "spoilage of earth by man" theory[3] we are seeing the beginning of the shifting of the focus of those basic and fundamental rights from the individual to the tribe.[4] Abortion is the area where this fundamental change is taking place. Not revolution but evolution.

The argument is this: the word "person" in the Bill of Rights or, indeed, anywhere in the Constitution, includes only those whom we define it to include. It may or may not include the unborn; it certainly does not include the mongoloid or the severely mental retardate; it probably does not include the senile, or the incurably mentally or physically ill. With the exception of slavery,[5] this novel approach to human life problems is a drastic departure from the developing norms of traditional Anglo-American jurisprudence which cannot be explained, as some would, by reference to the calamitous need for population control or cleansing of the gene pool. Nor is it akin to the invasion of privacy necessitated by the need for universal vaccination. There, though the communal good demands that the individual's privacy be invaded for the good of all, that good includes also the good of the one vaccinated, who is thus protected from the same evil he may cause. On the contrary, abortion as the solution to any social problem demands that the developing life of one person be ended because of the problems of the other. This permanent invasion of the privacy of the unborn does not benefit him/her and cannot be corrected by the hopeful solution of the same social problem in the future, since the child's life has ended.

In the Texas and Georgia cases the Supreme Court sought to avoid or delay recognition of these consequences by seemingly avoiding the question of when human life begins, but it then prohibited the states from passing any law which declared that human life began prior to six months.[6]

Of even more significance was its citing with approval a New York case where there were judicial findings of fact that abortion was the taking of human lives.[7] In the New York case, even though the trial and appellate courts had found it to be undisputed in the evidence that the unborn child was "a live human being,"[8] a "child [with] a separate life,"[9] a "human who is 'unquestionably alive' and 'has an autonomy of development and character,' "[10] the highest court in New York said that the profound life-and-death issues presented by the New York abortion law "are not legal or justiciable," for "the constitution does not confer or require legal personality for the unborn."[11]

In his dissent in the *Sierra*[12] case, Justice Douglas argued that the law ought to confer legal personality on a "valley, an alpine meadow, a river or a lake" just as it does on corporations and ships in order to allow legal redress of pollution problems. The wilderness is sacred, but human life is not.

Yet Justice Douglas voting with the majority concurred that "the word 'person' as used in the Fourteenth Amendment, does not include the unborn."[13]

Thus, what has been and remains an imperceptible attitude in mental health and aging problems, has become the law of the land in the womb: We can by definition exclude from the law's protection those humans who do not qualify as persons. The next step is obvious. We need only define the word "person" to include the desired quality of life and we can exlude from the law's protection the unwanted of any age.

The notion that man may by definition exclude those who are unwanted from the human community and thereby exclude them from the law's protection has already been favorably entertained and promulgated by others. Perhaps the most succinct statement evidencing this position was given by Daniel Callahan:

Abortion is an act of killing, the violent, direct destruction of potential human life, already in the process of development. That fact should not be disguised or glossed over by euphemism and circumlocution. It is not the destruction of a human person—for at no stage of its development does the conceptus fulfill the definition of a person, which implies a developed capacity for reasoning, willing, desiring and relating to others—but it is the destruction of an important and valuable form of human life.[14]

Under this definition, human life that does not have "a developed capacity for reasoning, willing, desiring and relating to others" does not qualify as a "person" and, therefore, does not qualify for the law's protection since only persons may receive such protection. Garret Hardin has said:

Whether the fetus is or is not a human being is a matter of definition, not fact, and we can define it any way we wish.[15]

There seems to be no logical reason why this definitional jurisprudence is applicable only in the womb.

THE CIVIL RIGHT TO LIFE

The Declaration of Independence states that all men are created equal and are endowed with certain inalienable rights, among which is the right to life. In speaking of the first official action of this nation which declared the foundation of our government in those words, the United States Supreme Court has said that "... it is always safe to read the letter of the Constitution in the spirit of the Declaration of Independence."[16] Then, commenting upon the basic function of government, the court said:

No duty rests more imperatively upon the courts than the enforcement of those constitutional provisions intended to secure that equality of rights which is the foundation of free government.[17]

We are concerned today with the attempt to secure that equality of civil rights on behalf of the unborn child in a society which, where it has not abolished the child's civil right to life altogether, has made such inroads on its exercise as to make the mention of it a mockery. For what difference does it make to protect human life in the third trimester, since every individual must first pass through the unprotected first and second trimesters?

Writing for the majority of the court, Justice Brennan, in one of history's ironic statements, in speaking for the abolition of the death penalty for convicted felons, said:

The country has debated whether a society for which the dignity of the individual is the supreme value can without a fundamental inconsistency follow the practice of deliberately putting some of its members to death.[18]

Death is a unique punishment in the United States. In a society that so strongly affirms the sanctity of life, not surprisingly the common view is that death is the ultimate sanction.[19]

Professor Cyril Means, an ardent proponent of abortion, who has undertaken exhaustive studies in the legal history of abortion, has admitted:

The common law protected the quickened (but not the unquickened) fetus as a being with its own right to life, immune to destruction at maternal will.[20]

In his *Commentaries on the Law,* in a section entitled, "The Rights of Persons," Blackstone states that the primary aim of law is to maintain and regulate the absolute rights of individuals. One such absolute right, he says, is the right to life "inherent by nature in every individual and it begins in contemplation of the law as soon as an infant is able to stir in the mother's womb."[21] May not, indeed, *must* not, the state protect that civil right?

Blackstone's *Commentaries* were first published in 1756. His and John Locke's natural law theories of the origin of absolute individual rights became the cornerstone for the legal thinkers who created our constitution.[22] If there was any book in the library of an American lawyer between 1760 and 1800 it was Blackstone's *Commentaries.* His discussion of the rights of persons begins with a discussion of the rights of unborn persons. Ought not reasonable minds to conclude, therefore, that at the time of the founding of our Republic, American lawyers, familiar with the teachings of Blackstone, agreed that each person's civil right to life commenced "in contemplation of the law" as soon as the infant was "able to stir in the mother's womb"?

In 1803, the law of England extended that protection to the time of conception with the passage of the Miscarriage of Women Act.[23] While there was some hesitation, gradually the American statutes also protected the life of the fetus from the moment of conception.[24] These statutes were clearly intended to protect the child's civil right to life.

Regardless of how one approaches the meaning of the status of the unquickened fetus from 1650 to 1803, where the statutes involved make no distinction between the quickened and the unquickened fetus, it is clear that the life revered under the statute is the fetus itself. All of the criminal abortion statutes in America ultimately prohibited abortion from conception, although the punishments sometimes varied with respect to abortion before "quickening."[25] The clear understanding of the purpose of these criminal statutes was that they were intended to protect the life of the unborn child.[26] They protected the child's civil right to life. Abortion when the mother's life was at stake was reluctantly allowed on an attenuated theory of self-defense (for the fetus could not very well be an aggressor) or, if you will, as an undesirable lesser of two evils, but always with the intent to save at least one life. Only lives could compete on this scale.

Even Professor Glanville Williams, an ardent advocate of legalized abortion, admitted that the historical reason for the control of abortion by the criminal law was that

the fetus is a human life to be protected by the criminal law from the moment when the ovum is fertilized.[27]

It is to repeat a truism to say that the existence of any of our civil rights depends first upon the existence and unfettered exercise of our civil right to life. To return again to the case which found the death penalty unconstitutional:

Death is truly an awesome punishment. The calculated killing of a human being by the State involves, by its very nature, a denial of the executed person's humanity. The contrast with the plight of a person punished by imprisonment is evident. An individual in prison does not lose "the right to have rights." A prisoner retains, for example, the constitutional rights to the free exercise of religion, to be free of cruel and unusual punishments, and to treatment as a "person" for purposes of due process of law and the equal protection of the laws. A prisoner remains a member of the human family. Moreover he retains the right of access to the courts. His punishment is not irrevocable. Apart from the common charge, grounded upon the recognition of human fallibility, that the punishment of death must inevitably be inflicted upon innocent men, we know that death has been the lot of men whose convictions were unconstitutionally secured in view of later, retroactively applied holdings of this Court. The punishment itself may have been unconstitutionally inflicted, see *Witherspoon* v. *Illinois,* 391 U.S. 510 (1968), yet the finality of death precludes relief. An executed person has indeed "lost the right to have rights."

In comparison to all other punishments today, then, the deliberate extinguishment of human life by the State is uniquely degrading to human dignity.[28]

The question to be asked, then, is Why is the destruction of human life in the womb any less degrading? The convicted felon has a civil right to life—why not the unborn? With that, let us turn to an analysis of the Texas and Georgia abortion cases to see how this legal schizophrenia came into existence.

ROE V. WADE

The state of Texas prohibited abortions unless "procured or attempted by medical advice for the purpose of saving the life of the mother."[29] Abortion in the Texas statute was defined as: "By 'abortion' is meant that the *life* of the fetus or embryo shall be destroyed in the woman's womb or that a premature birth thereof be caused."[30]

While the case was pending before the United States Supreme Court, the highest court of criminal appeals in Texas had an opportunity to review the constitutionality of the statute.[31] The Texas court concluded:

Appellant contends that any pregnant woman seeking an abortion operates within a constitutionally protected zone of privacy and that the State of Texas has no compelling interest to justify intruding into this zone of privacy by prohibiting all abortions except those procured for the purpose of saving the life of the mother. Without determining whether or not seeking an abortion is operating within a constitutionally protected zone of privacy, we do hold that the State of Texas has a compelling interest to protect fetal life.

The difference between preventing conception and terminating a pregnancy when conception has already occurred should be apparent to all. Something, albeit sub-microscopic, exists which did not exist before and has at least the potential of human life which may or may not be realized. The State of Texas is committed to preserving the lives of its citizens so that no citizen "shall be deprived of life, ... except by the due course of the law of the land." Texas Constitution, Article 1, Section 19. Article 1191, V.A.P.C., is designed to protect fetal life, see *Mayberry* v. *State,* 271 S.W. 2d 635, and this justifies prohibiting termination of the life of the fetus or embryo except for the purpose of saving the life of the mother.[32]

Ordinarily such statements by the highest court of the state would be binding on the United States Supreme Court in determining the meaning and purpose behind the act.[33] Instead, the United States Supreme Court dismissed the state court's interpretation of its own state statute in a footnote, and held the Texas statute unconstitutional.

The United States Supreme Court determined that "the right of personal privacy includes the abortion decision,"[34] and that the word "person as used in the Fourteenth Amendment does not include the unborn."[35]

This means, the court said:

A state criminal abortion statute of the current Texas type, that excepts from criminality only a *life saving* procedure on behalf of the mother, without regard to pregnancy stage and without recognition of the other interests involved, is violative of the Due Process Clause of the Fourteenth Amendment.

(a) For the stage prior to approximately the end of the first trimester, the abortion decision and its effectuation must be left to the medical judgment of the pregnant woman's attending physician.

(b) For the stage subsequent to approximately the end of the first trimester, the State, in promoting its interest in the health of the mother, may, if it chooses, regulate the abortion procedure in ways that are reasonably related to maternal health.

(c) For the stage subsequent to viability the State, in promoting its interest in the potentiality of human life, may, if it chooses, regulate, and even proscribe, abortion except where it is necessary, in appropriate medical judgment, for the preservation of the life or health of the mother.[36]

During the third trimester, or after viability, a state may proscribe in order to protect *potential* life *unless* the abortion is necessary for the preservation of the woman's health or life. Anyone familiar with American or English abortion practices under American Law Institute type abortion statutes will realize immediately that the word "health" means abortion on request.[37] Lest there be any doubt about that, the court specifically said that these health concepts could be considered by the physician: "physical, emotional, psychological, familial, the woman's age, distressful life and future, the unwanted child, unwed motherhood," etc., etc.[38]

The opinion not only implies, but actually says, therefore, that the fetus may not be protected at all for the first six months, and only thereafter as a form of potential life unless any countervailing interest of the mother determines otherwise.

DOE V. BOLTON

The Georgia case[39] involved an American Law Institute type statute.[40] Georgia allowed abortions only when based upon the physician's "best clinical judgment that an abortion is necessary" *because:*

(1) A continuation of the pregnancy would endanger the life of the pregnant woman or would seriously and permanently injure her health; or

(2) The fetus would very likely be born with a grave, permanent and irremediable mental or physical defect; or

(3) The pregnancy resulted from forcible or statutory rape.

Following the reasoning in the Texas case, the United States Supreme Court held (1), (2) and (3) unconstitutional, but affirmed that portion of Georgia's criminal law which allows abortion only when necessary in the physician's best clinical judgment.

The court held unconstitutional the residency requirement, the requirement that the abortion be performed in a licensed hospital or clinic in the first trimester, the JCAH hospital requirement, the committee approval requirement and the two-doctor concurrence requirement.

It held permissible the limiting of abortions to M.D.s, the requirement of reducing the physician's use of his judgment to writing, the requirements concerning reporting for M.D.s, the section removing the civil cause of action for wrongful death, and the conscience clause. It also held permissible the continued existence of criminal penalties for illegal abortions, whatever those may be.

The court deferred ruling on that portion of the Georgia statute which allows a solicitor general or a relative to petition the courts to protect "the constitutional or other legal rights of the fetus." Presumably this is one of the issues now pending before the Court of Appeals in the Fifth Circuit, although in its footnote the high court says: "What we decide today obviously has implications for the issues raised in the defendants' appeal pending in the Fifth Circuit."[41]

A CRITIQUE OF THE CASES

Among the many reasons the court uses to reach its conclusion, these dominate:

(1) The Hippocratic Oath, although a long-accepted and revered statement of medical ethics, represented the "apex of the development of strict ethical concepts in medicine";[42] as such, it was nothing but a dogma of the Pythagorean School, not the expression of an absolute standard of medical conduct.

(2) The common law: It is now doubtful, the court says, that abortion was ever firmly established as a common law crime, even with respect to the destruction of a quick fetus.

(3) American Law: The court posits that at the time of the adoption of our constitution, and throughout a major portion of the nineteenth century, abortion was viewed with less disfavor than under most American statutes now in effect, and a woman enjoyed a substantially broader right to terminate a pregnancy than she does today.

(4) In the court's opinion, the few state courts that interpreted their abortion statutes in the late nineteenth and twentieth centuries focused on the protection of the woman's health "rather than in preserving the embryo and fetus."[43]

The court makes this medical judgment:

(5) Abortion in the first trimester is safer than carrying the pregnancy to term.

More ominous than these reasons, but undeveloped by the court and barely noticed in passing, were these:

In addition, population growth, pollution, poverty and racial overtones tend to complicate and not to simplify the problem.[44]

The holding, we feel, is consistent with the relative weights of the respective interests involved, with the lessons and example of medical and legal history, with the lenity of the common law, *and with the demands of the profound problems of the present day.*[45]
(emphasis added)

What could those profound problems be?

THE HIPPOCRATIC OATH

Although the Oath "is not mentioned in any of the principal briefs" submitted to the court, nonetheless Justice Blackmun thought that a discussion and devaluation of the Oath, which for centuries has stood as a bulwark against abortion, was necessary. He felt that it was so necessary that he apparently did independent research to make his point.[46] Why? What was there about the Hippocratic Oath that made its demise an almost absolute imperative for Justice Blackmun—such that he would independently exert judicial energy to research in order to belittle and destroy? What are the psychological imperatives that compel those who would destroy human life to make their position ethical?

Justice Blackmun brushed aside two thousand years of medical history to accept a working hypothesis of one deceased historian as gospel. His entire research as evidenced in his opinion relies on a theory put forth by L. Edelstein which concludes that the Hippocratic Oath was merely the dogma of a small Greek sect, "a Pythagorean manifesto and not the expression of an absolute standard of medical conduct."

What then? Apparently those thousands upon thousands who have taken this oath: *"I will give no deadly medicine to anyone if asked, nor suggest any such counsel; and in like manner I will not give to a woman a pessary to produce abortion"*[47] were only the tools (or fools) of the Pythagoreans. Do we assume, then, that with the court's pronouncement they are henceforth released from the oath?

Or could not the court have just as easily chosen the position of the other, and many, scholars who have said:

But the most fascinating recent comment on the Hippocratic Oath is one which originated with Margaret Mead, the great anthropologist. Her major insight was that the Hippocratic Oath marked one of the turning points in the history of man. She says, "For the first time in our tradition there was a complete separation between killing and curing. Throughout the primitive world the doctor and the sorcerer tended to be the same person. He with power to kill had power to cure, including specially the undoing of his own killing activities. He who had power to cure would necessarily also be able to kill.

"With the Greeks," says Margaret Mead, "the distinction was made clear. One profession, the followers of Asclepius, were to be dedicated completely to life under all circumstances, regardless of rank, age, or intellect—the life of a slave, the life of the Emperor, the life of a foreign man, the life of a defective child." Dr. Mead emphasizes the fact that "this is a priceless possession which we cannot afford to tarnish, but society always is attempting to make the physician into a killer—to kill the defective child at birth, to leave the sleeping pills beside the bed of the cancer patient," and she is convinced that "it is the duty of society to protect the physician from such requests."[48]

THE COMMON LAW*

Apparently relying on a single law review article,[49] the court in *Wade* concluded that it is "doubtful that abortion was ever firmly established as a common law crime even with respect to the destruction of a quick fetus."[50]

We have already discussed this at some length in chapter 6 of this book. Briefly to restate the case: (1) At least from Bracton's time (c. 1225 A.D.) onward, the common law sought ways to protect the unborn child from abortion from the moment his existence as a separate, live, biological human being could be scientifically demonstrated; (2) problems of proving that the unborn child had been alive when the abortional act was committed, and that the abortion had been the cause of the child's death, were, in the early law, considered insuperable barriers to prosecution; (3) thereafter quickening evolved in the law, not as a substantive judgment on when human life begins, but as an evidentiary device to prove that the abortional act had been an assault on a live human being; (4) outside the criminal law, the common law, unburdened of problems of proof, regarded the unborn child as in all respects a human being;[51] (5) abortion after quickening, though a crime, was not homicide at common law (unless the child were born alive and then died) only because of the difficulty of proving that the abortional act had been the cause of the child's death; (6) the liability of the abortionist to a murder conviction, if the aborted child were born alive and then died, establishes that the unborn child was in law a person prior to birth because the common law defined crime as "generally constituted only from concurrence of an evil-meaning mind with an evil-doing hand,"[52] and the rule of concurrence means necessarily that the intra-uterine victim of the abortional act was at the time of the act a human person, or else the result could not be called murder; (7) problems of proof aside, abortion at any stage of pregnancy was considered *malum in se,* a secular

* This excellent outline was supplied by Prof. Robert Byrn of Fordham University School of Law and by Larry Washburn and Thomas Ford, New York attorneys who have been active in the defense of the unborn.

crime against unborn human life, as evidenced by the application of the common law felony-murder rule to the death of the aborted woman (even prior to quickening)[53]—the theory being "that at common law the act of producing an abortion was always an assault for the double reason that a woman was not deemed able to assent to an unlawful act against herself, and for the further reason that *she was incapable of consenting to the murder of an unborn infant...*";[54] (8) the application of the felony-murder rule to abortion belies the court's statement in *Wade* that "abortion was viewed with less disfavor than under most American statutes currently in effect";[55] (9) in the face of the abortion-murder rule and the general medical disapproval of abortion, it cannot be assumed that "throughout the major portion of the nineteenth century prevailing legal abortion practices were far freer than they are today...";[56] and finally (10) the common law is totally consistent with the claims of the right to life of the unborn child.

The court erred in its analysis of the common law.

THE PURPOSE OF AMERICAN STATUTES

This point has also been discussed at some length in chapter 6 of this book. The court, while citing only one case for its all-sweeping proposition, concluded:

The few state courts called upon to interpret their laws in the late nineteenth and twentieth centuries did focus on the State's interest in protecting the woman's health rather than in preserving the embryo and fetus.[57]

This extraordinary statement completely ignores the overwhelming majority of state court decisions to the contrary. The nineteenth-century American anti-abortion legislation is a continuum of the efforts of the common law to protect the unborn child from abortion from the moment his existence as a separate, live, biological human being could be scientifically demonstrated.

We will not burden this critique with a recitation of the cases on this point. In summary, there are at least eleven cases rendered prior to the "reform" movement of the 1960's which explicitly state that the protection of the life of the unborn child was at least one of the purposes for the nineteenth-century anti-abortion statutes.[58] There are nine other decisions which clearly imply the same intent.[59] Pro-abortionists have been able to cite only four cases contra[60] and the Supreme Court only one.[61]

The important question to ponder at this time is this: Why would the court ignore this great body of law? That is the sort of thing one might expect of an adversary, not from judges.

THE "SAFETY" OF INDUCED ABORTION

The decision accepted as "established medical fact" the contention that in the first three months of pregnancy "mortality in abortion is less than mortality in normal childbirth." While this statement is strongly suspect, all other complications which may arise from this procedure when performed in the first twelve weeks of pregnancy were conveniently ignored by the court. It is as if such things as infection, hemorrhage, perforation of the uterus, sterility, prematurity, ectopic pregnancy and spontaneous abortion in subsequent pregnancies, transplacental hemorrhage and guilt (cf. chapter 4, The Medical Hazards of Legally Induced Abortion) did not fit into the court's definition of health. To them, if you are alive, you are healthy, but you are only unhealthy when you are dead. In addition, when abortion is performed in the second trimester of pregnancy and within the limits set down by the court, there can be little question that the mortality exceeds that of childbirth.[62]

The court based its claim of safety on six sources—all written by people who have been open advocates of abortion on demand. Two of its sources did not deal with the comparison of abortion mortality statistics to maternal mortality statistics.[63] One was an English report which claimed safety in early pregnancy while looking only at Eastern European mortality statistics and ignoring much higher mortality rates in Denmark, Sweden and England which appeared in the same paper.[64] Two others were studies that directly dealt with the comparison, but relied entirely on Eastern European mortality statistics.[65] And the last reference that the court used was Lawrence Lader's book, *Abortion*.[66] Lader is not a physician or a statistician, but a freelance journalist who, as Chairman of the Board of Directors of the National Association for the Repeal of Abortion Laws, has made abortion-on-demand his own private crusade. It seems *incredible* that the highest court in the land could come to the decision they did on the basis of information supplied by a man of Lader's credentials. On no less than eight different occasions Justice Blackmun used Lader's book as a source of his information.[67]

It is clear that the court relied on the mortality statistics from Eastern Europe (especially Hungary, Czechoslovakia and Yugoslavia). These statistics are of highly questionable authenticity. Sir Norman Jeffcoate, highly respected British gynecologist, has given reasons for believing these figures to be "politically adjusted." He says, "If one talks to gynecologists from Hungary and Czechoslovakia when they are in this country and free to tell the truth they present a different story, one which fits with all other professional experience. They admit that deaths occur . . . that significant illness follows in 3-15% of cases."[68]

In this book (cf. chapter 4, The Medical Hazards of Legally Induced Abortion), there is a complete and thorough discussion of the complexity of these Eastern European statistics. In addition, it is shown that in states where the reporting is thought to be more reliable (Denmark and Oregon) the abortion mortality in the first three months exceeds the maternal mortality rate.

When one looks at Eastern European mortality statistics, one cannot help seeing the conditions under which abortions are performed. In Hungary, out-patient abortions are outlawed and abortions are allowed only in the gynecologic wards of hospitals or maternity homes. In general, hospitalization for 2-3 days after the abortion is mandatory.[69] In Czechoslovakia, abortions are performed *only* in the gynecologic departments of hospitals and the average hospital stay is 3-5 days.[70] Regardless of whether one accepts the Eastern European mortality statistics or not, it is obvious that the conditions under which they are performed are totally different from those anticipated in the court's decision. The majority opinion, while accepting wholeheartedly the Eastern European statistics, has turned away from any similar controls in this country. The "compelling" state interest to protect the health of women which the court so euphemistically endorses melts to hypocrisy in light of *all* the evidence.

The court made it very difficult for anyone to believe that they *ever* had any real concern for the health of women. Contriving data from Eastern Europe for application in this country without any consideration of other complications makes it even more clear that the court had preconceived concepts in this issue for which they made a poor attempt to find medical justification.

Consider for a moment the impending violence which the court's decision delivers to us as a people. In Hungary the prematurity rate in 1954 (before legal abortion) was 7%. In 1968 (14 years after legalization) it had increased to 12%.[71] The prematurity rate in Hungary is now the highest recorded in Europe.[72] Prematurity is the leading cause of mental and motor retardation.[73] If this same trend is seen in this country, and there is little reason for us to expect anything less, an additional 170,000 babies will be born prematurely each year as the result of legal abortion.[74] Of these, 12,000–30,000 will be retarded.[75] This is just one example of many that could be cited, but it should be all that is necessary.

VIABILITY

In considering viability, Justice Blackmun wrote, "Viability is usually placed at about seven months (28 weeks) but may occur earlier, even at 24 weeks."[76] For this, he cites the fourteenth edition of Williams' *Obstetrics,* p. 493. But Williams' textbook says, "Interpretations of the word 'viability' have varied between fetal weights of 400 g. (about 20 weeks gestation) and 1,000 g. (about 28 weeks gestation)."[77] *There is no mention of a 24-week definition for viability in Williams' textbook and there is no mention of 20 weeks viability in the court's opinion.* Furthermore, studies have shown that "non-white infants experience a better survival at low birth weights than do white infants."[78] The court's ruling imposes data for white babies upon non-white babies, where it is not applicable.

What is perhaps even more significant, however, is a consideration of what the court's 24-28 week cut-off really means. In a study of 650,000 live births in New York City where gestational age was calculated from the initial date of the last menstrual period, the information in Table One was obtained.

TABLE ONE: Percent of Children Who Survived the Neonatal[79] Period When Born at a Given Gestational Age by Ethnic Background

WEEKS GESTATION	UNDER 20	20–25	26–27	28–29
White	20.7%	25.5%	45.0%	65.0%
Non-White	21.7%	34.8%	58.8%	75.3%

The obvious racial differences can easily be seen. But even more impressive is the equally obvious survivability of children born even as early as 20 weeks gestational age. These children are certainly "viable" according to the court's own definition, ("potentially able to live outside the mother's womb"), but in accord with the majority opinion they were ruled unworthy to exist.

Live births resulting from abortion in New York have, of course, been justly labeled a scandal. The public is unaware that of the 195,823 reported abortions performed in New York during July 1971 through June 1972 approximately 0.4% (821) were done by the hysterotomy method,[80] which is nothing but a caesarean operation. *This abortion method always results in a live birth.*[81] Usually the children are then merely allowed to die. Lest anyone thinks this is the exaggerated claim of the shrill voices of the Right to Lifers, we publish herewith a table of live births taken from a scientific study on the subject, and covering only a six-month period:[82]

TABLE TWO: Live Births After Saline Instillation, or Other (July 1–December 31, 1970)

	Date	Initial	Method	Weight	Gestation (weeks)	Lived
1	July 22	P	Saline	1 lb, 8 oz	22	2 hr
2	August 20	L	Hysterotomy	15 oz	22	30 min
3	August 21	B	Saline	2 lb, 14 oz	25	6 hr, 35 min
4	August 23	C	Saline	1 lb, 9 oz	24	2 hr
5	August 23	W	Saline	2 lb, 8 oz	28	Alive
6	August 23	L	Saline	3 lb, 1 oz	20	4 hr, 55 min
7	September 1	R	Ethodine	1 lb, 13 oz	18	5 min
8	September 4	M	Saline	3 lb	20	1 hr, 5 min
9	September 9	V (1 of twins)	Saline	1 lb, 13 oz	20	15 hr
10	September 17	A	Saline	2 lb, 1 oz	24	47 hr, 40 min
11	September 24	V	Catheter	1 lb	17	2 hr 20 min
12	September 30	L	Saline	3 lb, 5½ oz	30	53 hrs, 15 min
13	October 3	N	Saline	2 lb	26	7 hr, 15 min
14	October 8	W	Saline	8½ oz	16	5 min
15	October 9	S	Saline	1 lb, 10 oz	19	1 hr 35 min
16	October 11	G	Saline	1 lb, 7½ oz	21	5 min
17	October 17	D	Saline	2 lb, 3 oz	20	5 hr
18	October 18	G	Saline	1 lb, 4 oz	19	3 hr, 30 min
19	October 21	L	Saline	14 oz	19	1½ hr
20	October 26	S	Saline	3 lb, 6 oz	24	24 hr
21	November 9	G	Saline	1 lb 14 oz	26	17 hr
22	November 20	R	Saline	1 lb, 14 oz	18	6½ hr
23	November 23	F	Saline	1 lb	21	30 min
24	November 25	M	Saline	1 lb, 8¾ oz	21	1 hr, 30 min
25	December 2	S	Saline	1 lb	20	55 min
26	December 7	P	Saline	1 lb, 5½ oz	20	2 hr, 40 min
27	December 16	R	Saline	1 lb, 11½ oz	20	2½ hr

Even by Coke's definition an abortion which causes a live birth and subsequent death is murder.

Furthermore, the Fourteenth Amendment very clearly provides:

All persons *born or naturalized* in the United States and subject to the jurisdiction thereof, are citizens of the United States and of the State wherein they reside. (emphasis added)

In all live births due to induced as well as spontaneous abortions, regular birth certificates are issued, regardless of length of either gestation or survival.

In fact, U. S. Public Health Service guidelines specifically state:

IMPORTANT: *If a child breathes or shows any other evidence of life after complete birth, even though it be only momentary, the birth should be registered as a live birth and a death certificate also should be filed.* (emphasis by Public Health Service)[83]

The point, then, is that regardless of whether an unborn child is a person under the Fourteenth Amendment, the child is a *citizen* under that provision upon delivery. We thus have a serious situation when live births caused by induced abortions can result in a citizenship status, but with no protection in the law for the United States citizen.

WHEN DOES LIFE BEGIN?

The court wrote, "We need not resolve the difficult question of when life begins. When those trained in the respective disciplines of medicine, philosophy and theology are unable to arrive at any conclusion, the judiciary, at this point in man's knowledge, is not in a position to speculate as to the answer."[84] Yet the court said that the state of Texas may not, nor may any other state, adopt a "theory of life" which posits the beginning of life before six months.[84]

In September 1948, the World Medical Association (to which the United States is a founding member), "after a lengthy discussion of war crimes based on information from the United Nations War Crimes Commission,"[86] adopted the Declaration of Geneva which said, "I will maintain the utmost respect for human life, from the time of conception; even under threat, I will not use my medical knowledge contrary to the laws of humanity."[87] This was followed in October 1949 by the International Code of Medical Ethics, which stated, "A doctor must always bear in mind the importance of preserving human life from the time of conception until death."[88] At that time, Dr. Paul Cibrie, Chairman of the Committee which had drawn up the International Code, stated that the abortionists were in fact condemned in the Declaration of Geneva.[89] This was reaffirmed by the World Medical Association in 1970 with the Declaration of Oslo, "The first moral imposed upon the doctor is respect for human life as expressed in the clause of the Declaration of Geneva: 'I will maintain the utmost respect for human life from the time of conception.' "[90]

Furthermore, on November 20, 1959, the General Assembly of the United Nations *unanimously* adopted the Declaration of the Rights of the Child. The Preamble to the declaration stated that the child, by reason of his physical and mental immaturity, needs "special safeguards and care, including appropriate legal protection, before as well as after birth."[91] Governments were called upon to recognize the rights and freedoms set forth in the Declaration and to strive for their observance by legislative and other measures.

In addition, the avidly pro-abortion California Medical Association wrote in September 1970 that "human life begins at conception and is continuous, whether intra- or extra-uterine, until death."[92] Dr. Alan Guttmacher, pro-abortionist head of Planned Parenthood-World Population, has written that at the exact moment of conception a new baby is created and that "at the exact moment when a new life is initiated (fertilization), a great deal is determined which is forever irrevocable—its sex, coloring, body-build, blood group, and in large measure its mental capacity or emotional stability."[93]

It is obvious that the consensus exists. It seems equally obvious that the court chose to ignore the consensus. No less than six times Justice Blackmun referred to this life as "potential" human life, and on at least two occasions he referred to the conception of a new human as one "theory" of life. There is nothing theoretical about the beginning of human life, and the unborn is actual, not potential. The child does exist in spite of the court's medical ignorance, and the decision of the court did nothing to disprove that. What it did do, of course, was to perpetuate the ignorance which is so common today in this area.

Individual human life begins at conception (the union of the mother's egg with the father's sperm)[94] and is a progressive, ongoing continuum until natural death (unless, of course, an unnatural death interrupts this chain of life). This is a *fact* so well established that no intellectually honest physician in full command of modern medical knowledge would dare to deny it. There is no authority in medicine or biology who can be cited to refute this concept. It is *not* a "theory," as Justice Blackmun wished to so easily pass it off.

THE NATURE OF THE RIGHT OF PRIVACY AND THE COURT'S ILLOGICAL FORMULATION OF THE ISSUE IN ROE

In *Katz* v. *United States*,[95] a 1967 case cited by the court in support of its decision in *Roe,* the court, per Mr. Justice Stewart, clearly pointed out that there are areas of the right of privacy which are not of a constitutional nature. Accordingly:

[The Fourth] Amendment protects individual privacy against certain kinds of governmental intrusion, but its protections go farther, and often have nothing to do with privacy at all. Other provisions of the Constitution protect personal privacy from other forms of governmental invasion. But the protection of a person's general right to privacy, his right to be let alone by other people, is, like the protection of his property and of his very life, left largely to the law of the individual states.[96]

In a footnote in *Katz,* the court noted that "virtually every governmental action interferes with personal privacy to some degree. The question in each case is whether that interference violates a command of the U. S. Constitution."[97]

The United States Supreme Court in *Roe* does not appear to have altered its view since *Katz.* In *Roe* the court wrote that "the court has recognized that a right of personal privacy, or a guarantee of certain areas or zones of privacy, does exist under the Constitution."[98] The correlative to this proposition of the court is that there are also certain areas or zones of privacy which do not exist under the Constitution. Assuming the soundness of this interpretation, the court's above-quoted statement in *Roe* is consistent with *Katz,* at least to the extent that there are areas or zones of privacy which are not constitutionally protected. The issue, then, in *Roe* is not, as the court indicated, whether the "right of privacy, . . . is broad enough to encompass a woman's decision whether or not to terminate her pregnancy," but rather *whether the decision to or not to terminate a pregnancy is within that area or zone of privacy which exists or is protected under the Constitution.* This is because not all areas within the "general right of privacy" *(Katz)* are constitutionally protected. The Supreme Court's formulation of the right to privacy issue in *Roe* is therefore logically unsound.

The issue which the *Roe* court should have formulated and resolved is whether the abortion decision is within that limited area or zone of the right to privacy which is protected by the due process clause of the Fourteenth Amendment.

Perhaps owing to the court's illogical formulation of the issue, it did not attempt to apply the standards which were developed in its own cases to determine whether a human act, such as an abortion, is founded in the concept of liberty and therefore protected under the due process clause of the Fourteenth Amendment. Rather, the court simply and without analysis declared the abortion decision to be part of the right of privacy. Furthermore, the court simply assumed, without analysis, that this particular area or zone of privacy is protected by the Fourteenth Amendment. It is to be deeply regretted that the U. S. Supreme Court has based such a far-reaching decision on an elementary flaw in Socratic logic and has, as a consequence and without analysis or explanation, simply decreed that the concept of liberty in the due process clause includes a right to terminate a pregnancy.

In the next section, the standards developed by the court will be applied to the abortion question to determine if, under the court's own teachings, the abortion decision could possibly have been absorbed by the Fourteenth Amendment.

The Standards Set by Meyer v. Nebraska and Palko v. Connecticut

One of the main legal problems presented in *Roe* v. *Wade* is whether the concept of "liberty" in the "due process" clause of the Fourteenth Amendment includes a right to an abortion. Two of the cases cited by the court, *Meyer* v. *Nebraska*[99] and *Palko* v. *Connecticut*,[100] establish a very strict standard for determining whether a particular human activity has been absorbed by and is included in the liberty concept of the Fourteenth Amendment. According to the U. S. Supreme Court in *Palko,* "[i]f the Fourteenth Amendment has absorbed [a privilege or immunity] the process of absorption has had its source in the belief that neither liberty nor justice would exist if they were sacrificed."[101] With respect to the narrow "double jeopardy" issue which faced the court, the court asked: "Does it [the particular kind of double jeopardy involved] violate those fundamental principles of liberty and justice which lie at the base of all our civil and political institutions?"[102]

In *Meyer,* an equally strict standard was established. The court, generally holding that the idea of liberty in the Fourteenth Amendment includes the right to teach and to be taught in a foreign language, wrote:

While this court has not attempted to define with exactness the liberty thus guaranteed, the term has received much consideration, and some of the included things have been definitely stated. Without doubt, it denotes not merely freedom from bodily restraint, but also the right of the individual to contract, to engage in any of the common occupations of life, to acquire useful knowledge, to marry, establish a home and bring up children, to worship God according to the dictates of his own conscience, and generally *to enjoy those privileges long recognized at common law as essential to the orderly pursuit of happiness by free men.* (citations) The established doctrine is that this liberty may not be interfered with, under the guise of protecting the public interest, by legislative action which is arbitrary or without reasonable relation to some purpose within the competency of the State to effect. (emphasis added)[103]

The Supreme Court in *Loving* v. *Virginia*[104] appears to have followed this strict standard, in particular the standard set forth in *Palko,* when it stated, in its alternative justification for its decision, that the right to marry is a "basic civil right, fundamental to our very existence and survival." The *Loving* decision can be justified on the basis of the *Meyer* standard as well, since "marriage"—the civil right involved—was mentioned as an example of an activity which is "essential to the orderly pursuit of happiness by free men" *(Meyer),* or if "liberty and justice would [cease] to exist if this right were sacrificed" *(Palko),* or if a right to abortion "lie[s] at the base of all our civil and political institutions" *(Palko).*

Of great significance in this context is the Supreme Court's uncertainty whether abortions were criminal at common law. The court wrote: "whether abortion of a quick fetus was a felony at common law, or even a lesser crime, is still disputed." Later the court concluded, "... it now appear[s] doubtful that abortion was ever firmly established as a common law crime even with respect to the destruction of a quick fetus." However, the preamble to the first English abortion act in 1803 very clearly indicated that the statute was being passed by Parliament because "no adequate means [statute] have been hitherto provided for the prevention and punishment of such *offenses*" (emphasis added). The reasoning obviously applied to the difficulty of proving the crime of abortion under the then existing common law which assumed there was no provable life until quickening.[105]

Since, in *Roe,* the court concluded that it has *doubts* whether abortion was ever firmly established as a common law crime, it is most difficult to understand how the *Meyer* standard of "long recognized at common law as essential to the orderly pursuit of happiness of free men" can serve as precedential support for the *Roe* decision. *Expressed bluntly, the Meyer standard should have directed the court to the conclusion that the "abortion decision" has not been absorbed by the Fourteenth Amendment.* Moreover, one could not conclude that a human act which was perhaps a crime at common law and most assuredly a statutory crime in England and in most states in the United States is of such a nature that "neither liberty nor justice would exist if they were sacrificed" *(Palko)*, or "lie[s] at the base of all our civil and political institutions" *(Palko)*.

The court neither attempted to apply its own principles nor to give any explanation for its conclusion that the "right of privacy includes the abortion decision." This conclusion, unsupported in law and unexplained by any reasoning process, is blatant judicial legislation, and, aside from the tragedy of the decision itself, is to be regretted from the standpoint of fairness, intellectual honesty, logic and judicial craftsmanship. Viewed in this light, the primary "balance" placed on the scales of justice by the Supreme Court exists only as a result of pure judicial fiat.

REFERENCES

1. Leon R. Kass, "Making Babies: The New Biology and the Old Morality," in *The Public Interest*, No. 26 (Winter 1972), pp. 18–56.
2. *Roe* v. *Wade*, 314 F. Supp. 1217, Supreme Court No. 70–18. Hereafter all references to this case and the companion case of *Doe* v. *Bolton*, 319 F. Supp. 1048, Supreme Court No. 70–40 will be to the Slip Opinion.
3. See, e.g., William T. Vukowich, "The Dawning of the Brave New World—Legal, Ethical, and Social Issues of Eugenics," *Illinois Law Forum*, Vol. 1971, No. 2, pp. 189–231.
   See also *Roe* v. *Wade*, p. 1 and p. 50. At both places the court calls attention to some of the concepts that (*de hors* the record) influenced it.
4. See ch. 14 of this book.
5. The parallels between the Texas and Georgia cases and the infamous *Dred Scott* v. *Sandford*, 60 U.S. 393 (1857), are startling. Prof. John Noonan has pointed out these parallels in his article in the *National Catholic Reporter*, Feb. 16, 1973, p. 9: "*Roe* v. *Wade* and *Doe* v. *Bolton* have been compared to the classic blunder of American history, *Dred Scott* v. *Sandford*. Are they really of the same order of magnitude? The following parallels exist:
   (1) *Dred Scott* attempted to resolve forever a deep moral issue agitating the American people; so do *Wade* and *Bolton*.
   (2) The method chosen by the court was to invalidate long-standing legislation as unconstitutional and to try to make it impossible for an

American black ever to be accorded the protections and privileges of citizenship. *Wade* and *Bolton* invalidate long-standing legislation and try to make it impossible for a fetus ever to be accorded the protection and privileges of a person.

(3) Each case was decided by a 7–2 majority. In *Dred Scott* a dissenting judge, Curtis, suggested that the Constitution had been subordinated to 'the individual political opinions of members of this court.' In *Wade* and *Bolton,* a dissenting judge, White, said that the court had exercised 'raw judicial power.'

(4) *Dred Scott* implied that the Supreme Court could go further and permit slavery in states which had prohibited slavery. *Wade* and *Bolton* imply that the Supreme Court can go further and eliminate other state protections of life.

(5) *Dred Scott* failed miserably to settle the moral issue. It was overturned by constitutional amendment. Will *Wade* and *Bolton* resolve the morality of destroying fetal life? Will they be overturned by constitutional amendment?"

6. Slip Opinion, p. 47.
7. *Byrn* v. *New York City Hospitals,* 31 N.Y. 2d 194, 335 N.Y.S. 2d 390, 286 N.E. 2d 887 (1972).
8. Queens County Supreme Court Slip Opinion.
9. *Byrn* v. *New York City Hospitals,* 38 A.D. 2d 316, 324, 329 N.Y.S. 2d 729 (1972).
10. Op. cit., note 7.at p. 199.
11. *Byrn* v. *New York City Hospitals,* 31 N.Y. 2d 194, 286 N.E. 2d 887, 890.
12. *Sierra Club* v. *Morton,* 405 U.S. 727 (1927).
13. Justice Douglas' concurring opinion, pp. 1–12.
14. Daniel Callahan, *Abortion: Law, Choice and Morality* (New York: Macmillan, 1972), pp. 497–498.
15. Garrett Hardin, "Abortion or Compulsory Pregnancy?" *J. Marriage & Family,* Vol. 30, No. 2, May 1968.
16. *Gulf, Colorado and Santa Fe RR Co.* v. *Ellis,* 165 U. S. 150, 160 (1897).
17. *Ibid,* p. 160.
18. *Furman* v. *Georgia,* 408 U.S. 238, 33 L. Ed. 2d 346, 382 (1972).
19. *Ibid.,* 33 L. Ed 2d at p. 376.
20. Cyril Means, "The Law of New York Concerning Abortion," 14 N.Y.L.F. 411, 508 (1968).
21. 1 Blackstone, p. 124 (1769).
22. Daniel J. Boorstin, *The Americans: The Colonial Experience* (New York: Vintage Books, 1958), p. 202.
23. 43 Geo. 3, C.58.
24. Eugene Quay, "Justifiable Abortion: The Medical and Legal Foundations," *The Georgetown Law Journal,* Winter 1960, Spring 1961, Vol. 49, Nos. 2 & 3, pp. 447–519.
25. *Ibid.*

26. See ch. 6 of this book.
27. Glanville Williams, *The Sanctity of Life and the Criminal Law* (New York: Knopf, 1957), p. 149.
28. *Furman* v. *Georgia*, 408 U.S. 238, 33 L. Ed. 2d 346, 378 (1972).
29. Ch. 9, Title 15, Texas Penal Code, Sec. 1196.
30. *Ibid.*, Sec. 1191.
31. *Thompson* v. *State of Texas*,   Tex Crim. App.   S.W. 2d   (1971).
32. *Ibid.*, p.
33. In *Eisenstadt* v. *Baird*, 405 U.S. 438, 31 L. Ed. 2d 349, 355-356 (1972) the court said: "As interpreted by the State Supreme Judicial Court, these provisions make it a felony for anyone, other than a registered physician or pharmacist acting in accordance with the terms of §21A, to dispense any article with the intention that it be used for the prevention of conception. The statutory scheme distinguishes among three distinct classes of distributees—first, married persons may obtain contraceptives to prevent pregnancy, but only from doctors or druggists on prescription; second, single persons may not obtain contraceptives from anyone to prevent pregnancy; and, third, married or single persons may obtain contraceptives from anyone to prevent not pregnancy, but the spread of disease. *This construction of State Laws is, of course, binding on us.* E.G., *Groppi* v. *Wisconsin*, 400 U.S. 505, 507 (1971)." (emphasis added)
34. *Roe*, p. 39.
35. *Roe*, p. 43.
36. *Roe*, p. 49.
37. John M. Finnis, "Three Schemes of Regulation," in John T. Noonan, Jr., ed., *The Morality of Abortion* (Cambridge, Mass.: Harvard University Press, 1970), pp. 172-207.
38. *Roe*, p. 38; *Doe*, pp. 11, 12.
39. *Doe* v. *Bolton*, 319 F. Supp. 1048.
40. The American Law Institute Model Penal Code, Sec. 230.3.
41. *Doe*, p. 7, footnote 8.
42. *Roe*, p. 17.
43. *Roe*, p. 36.
44. *Roe*, p. 1.
45. *Roe*, p. 50.
46. Burger Opinion, *Roe* p. 1.
47. *Roe*, p. 16.
48. Maurice Levine, M.D., *Psychiatry and Ethics* (New York: Braziller, 1972), Part II, ch. 6, "Hippocratic Oath for Physicians." Personal communication from Margaret Mead (1961), p. 377.
49. *Roe*, p. 20, footnote 26.
50. *Roe*, p. 21.
51. "We are also of opinion that the distinction between a woman being

pregnant, and being quick with child is applicable mainly if not exclusively to criminal cases ... " *Hall* v. *Hancock,* 15 Pick. 255, 257 (Mass. 1834).

52. *Morisette* v. *U. S.,* 342 U.S. 246, 251-52 (1952).

53. See cases collected in *State* v. *Harris,* 90 Kan. 807, 136 Pac. 264 (1913).

54. *State* v. *Farnum,* 82 Ore. 211, 161 Pac. 417, 419 (1916).

55. *Roe,* p. 25.

56. *Roe,* p. 43.

57. *Roe,* p. 36.

58. *Trent* v. *State,* 15 Ala. App. 485, 73 So. 834 cert. den. 198 Alabama 695, 73 So. 1002 (1916); *Dougherty* v. *People,* 1 Colo. 514 (1872); *Nash* v. *Meyer,* 54 Idaho 283, 31 P 2d 273 (1934); *State* v. *Alcorn,* 7 Idaho 599, 64 Pac. 1014 (1901);*State* v. *Miller,* 90 Kan. 230, 133 Pac. 878 (1913); *State* v. *Watson,* 30 Kan. 281, 1 Pac. 770 (1883); *Joy* v. *Brown,* 173 Kan. 833, 252 P. 2d 889 (1933); *State* v. *Gedicke,* 43 N.J.L. 86 (1881); *State* v. *Siciliano,* 21 N.J. 249, 121 A 2d 490, 494 (1956); *State* v. *Tippie,* 89 Ohio St. 35, 105 N.E. 75 (1913); *Bowlan* v. *Lunsford,* 176 Okla. 115, 54 P 2d 666 (1936); *State* v. *Ausplund,* 86 Ore. 121, 167 Pac. 1019 (1917); *State* v. *Howard,* 32 Vt. 380 (1859); *Anderson* v. *Commonwealth,* 190 Va. 665, 58 S.E. 2d 72 (1950); *State* v. *Cox,* 197 Wash. 67, 84 P 2d 357 (1938).

59. *Abrams* v. *Forbee,* 3 Iowa 273 (1856); *State* v. *Moore,* 25 Iowa 128 (1866); *Smith* v. *State,* 33 Maine 48 (1851); *Worthington* v. *State,* 92 Md. 222, 48 Atl. 355 (1901); *People* v. *Sessions,* 58 Mich. 594, 26 N.W. 291 (1886); *Montgomery* v. *State,* 80 Ind. 338 (1881); *Edwards* v. *State,* 79 Neb. 251, 112 N.W. 611 (1907); *Bennet* v. *Hymers,* 101 N.H. 483, 147 A. 2d 108 (1958); *Mills* v. *Commonwealth,* 13 Pa. St. 630 (1850); *State* v. *Crook,* 16 Utah 212, 51 Pac. 1091 (1898).

60. *State* v. *Carey,* 76 Conn. 342, 56 Atl. 632 (1904); *State* v. *Murphy,* 27 N.J.L. 112 (1858); *State* v. *Jordan,* 227 N.C. 579, 42 S.E. 2d 674 (1947); *Foster* v. *State,* 182 Wisc. 298, 196 N.W. 233 (1933).

61. *State* v. *Murphy,* 27 N.J.L. 112 (1858).

62. Reported death rates with saline amnioinfusion and hysterotomy, the two most common methods of second trimester abortion, have been 30/100,000 and 300/100,000 respectively. Cf. C. Tietze, Joint Program for the Study of Abortion (JPSA): "Early Medical Complications of Legal Abortion, *Studies in Family Planning,* Vol. 3, June 1972. This particular study is probably biased in the direction of good medical care since the participating hospitals and clinics are better institutions than a cross-section of American hospitals and clinics would provide. The maternal mortality rate in the United States is about 20/100,000, cf. N. 65.

63. C. Tietze, "Therapeutic Abortion in the United States, 1963-68," *Studies in Family Planning,* #59, Nov. 1970. This was defendant's exhibit No. 17 in the *Hodgson* v. *State of Minnesota* trial, which was a test of the constitutionality of the Minnesota Abortion law.

    Abortion Mortality—New York City, *Morbidity and Mortality*

Weekly Report, June 12, 1971, U.S. Dept. of HEW, Public Health Service.

64. D. M. Potts, "Postconceptive Control of Fertility," *Intl. J. Gynaec. Obstet.,* 8: 957-70, Nov. 1970.

65. C. Tietze, "Mortality with Contraception and Induced Abortions," *Studies in Family Planning,* #45: 6-8, Sept. 8, 1969. This was Defendant's Exhibit No. 20 in the *Hodgson* v. *State of Minnesota* trial, which was a test of the constitutionality of Minnesota's abortion law.

    C. Tietze, and H. Lehfeldt, "Legal Abortion in Eastern Europe," *JAMA,* April 1, 1961, pp. 1149-54.

66. L. Lader, *Abortion* (Boston: Beacon Press, 1966).

67. *Roe,* pp. 15, 17(2), 20, 24, 34, 44, 45.

68. T. N. A. Jeffcoate, "Abortion," in Morals and Medicine, 1970, London, BBC.

69. A. Klinger, "Demographic Consequences of the Legalization of Induced Abortion in Eastern Europe," *Intl. J. Gynaec. Obstet.,* 8:680-691, Sept. 1970.

70. A. Kotasek, "Artificial Termination of Pregnancy in Czechoslovakia," *Intl. J. Gynaec. Obstet.,* 9:118-119, May 1971.

71. Klinger, op. cit., p. 691.

72. A. Czeizel, "Mortality and Morbidity of Legal Abortion," *Lancet,* July 24, 1971, pp. 209-210.

73. S. J. Schaeffer, *Diseases of the Newborn,* 2d ed. (Philadelphia: W. B. Saunders, 1966).

74. About 250,000 babies are born prematurely each year in the United States. This is about 7% of all babies born (cf. D. Cavanaugh and W. R. Talisman, eds., *Prematurity and the Obstetrician* [New York: Appleton-Century-Crofts, 1969], p. 1). If the prematurity rate increased to 12%, there would be 420,000 premature babies born each year.

75. The incidence of mental retardation in infants weighing over 2,500 g. is 3.5%; 1,500-2,500 g. is 7.4%; and 1,500 g. or less is 17.7%. Cf. N. 74.

76. *Roe,* p. 45.

77. L. W. Hellman and J. A. Pritchard in Williams' *Obstetrics,* 14th ed. (New York: Appleton-Century-Crofts, 1971), p. 493.

78. C. L. Erhardt, G. B. Joshi, F. G. Nelson, B. H. Kroll, and C. Weiner, "Influence of Weight and Gestation on Perinatal and Neonatal Mortality by Ethnic Group," *Am. J. Pub. Health,* 54:1841-55, 1964.

79. Adapted from Erhardt, et al., article cited in Note 78.

80. Bulletin on Abortion Program of the New York City Department of Health, September 1972.

81. A British gynecologist, R. F. R. Gardner, has pointed out that abdominal hysterotomy "has many advantages in that the view is good and bleeding can be readily controlled. However, the removal of a perfectly formed, heart beating, chest moving, limbs waving fetus is most repugnant and quite literally a nauseating procedure both for the surgeon and

the theatre nurse." See his book *Abortion: The Personal Dilemma* (Grand Rapids, Michigan: W. B. Eerdmanns Publishing Co., 1972), p. 216.

"*Use of Fetuses for Research:* In May, 1972, the Advisory Group on the Use of Fetuses and Fetal Material for Research made its report to Sir Keith Joseph, the Social Services Secretary of Great Britain. The Report deals with the use of fetal tissue for research, a situation which has developed in England since the adoption of the Abortion Act. The increase in abortions since the Act dramatically increased the amount of fetal tissue available for research. The Report said that 'for ethical, medical, and social reasons we recommend that, for human fetuses, evidence of a period of gestation of 20 weeks should be regarded as prima facie proof of viability at the present time.' The Group further recommended that there be no monetary exchanges for fetal tissue, that the parents have the right to decide how a fetus is to be disposed of, and that a record be kept of all research uses." Reporter on Human Reproduction and the Law, I-A-29.

82. Pakter, et al, *Clinical Ob. Gyn.,* Vol. 14 (1971) at p. 290.
83. U. S. Department of Health, Education and Welfare, Public Health Service, National Office of Vital Statistics, Public Health Service Publication No. 593, 1958.
84. *Roe,* p. 44.
85. *Roe,* p. 47.
86. *World Medical Assoc. Bulletin,* Vol. 1, p. 22, April 1949.
87. Ibid.
88. *World Medical Assoc. Bulletin,* Vol. 2, pp. 5-34, Jan. 1950.
89. Ibid.
90. Ibid.
91. *Everyman's United Nations,* a complete handbook of the activities and evolutions of the United Nations during its first twenty years 1945-1965, 8th ed. United Nations, N.Y., p. 360.
92. "A New Ethic for Medicine and Society," *California Medicine,* official Journal of the California Medical Association, 113:67-68, Sept. 1970.
93. A. F. Guttmacher, *Having a Baby,* Signet Books (New York: New American Library, 1950), p. 15.
94. See the following: B. M. Patten, *Human Embryology,* 3d ed. (New York: McGraw-Hill, 1968), pp. 41, 43; C. B. Arey, *Developmental Anatomy: A Textbook and Laboratory Manual of Embryology* (Philadelphia and London: W. B. Saunders, 1965), p. 55; J. Langmann, *Medical Embryology,* 2d ed. (Baltimore: Williams and Wilkins, 1969), p. 3; H. Gordon, "Genetical, Social, and Medical Aspects of Abortion," *South African Medical Journal,* July 20, 1968, pp. 721-730; L. B. Shettles, *Ovum Humanum* (New York: Hafner, 1960), p. 60; J. Davies, *Human Developmental Anatomy* (New York: Ronald Press, 1963), p. 3; G. D. Dodds, *The Essentials of Human Embryology,* 2d ed. (New York:

Wiley, 1964), p. 2; M. S. Gilbert, *Biography of the Unborn* (Baltimore: Williams and Wilkins, 1938), pp. 2, 5; J. C. Heisler, *A Textbook of Embryology for Students of Medicine,* 2d ed. (Philadelphia and London: W. B. Saunders, 1901), p. 38; I. N. Quimby, "Introduction to Medical Jurisprudence: Address Delivered by the Chairman of the Section on Medical Jurisprudence at the Thirty-eighth Annual Meeting of the AMA, June 10, 1887," *JAMA,* 9:161-66, August 6, 1887.

95. 389 U.S. 347, 88 S. Ct. 507 (1967).
96. 389 U.S. 347, 350.
97. 389 U.S. 347, 350.
98. *Roe,* p. 37.
99. 262 U.S. 390 (1923).
100. 302 U.S. 319 (1937).
101. 302 U.S. 319, 326.
102. 302 U.S. 319, 328.
103. 262 U.S. 390, 399.
104. 388 U.S. 1 (1967).
105. See ch. 6 of this book.